VOLUME II: THE WAY OF THE SEEDED EARTH

PART 2

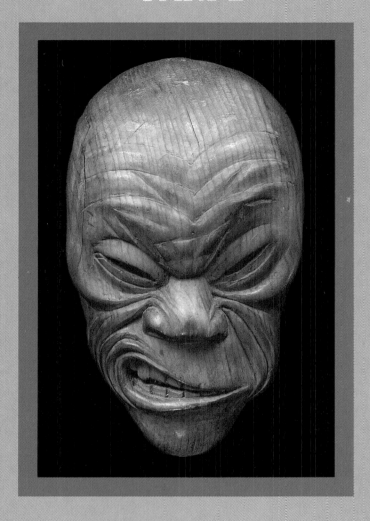

MYTHOLOGIES OF
THE PRIMITIVE PLANTERS:
THE NORTHERN AMERICAS

JOSEPH CAMPBELL

HISTORICAL ATLAS OF WORLD MYTHOLOGY

VOLUME II

THE WAY OF THE SEEDED EARTH

PART 2

MYTHOLOGIES OF THE PRIMITIVE PLANTERS: THE NORTHERN AMERICAS

PERENNIAL LIBRARY

HARPER & ROW, PUBLISHERS NEW YORK

GRAND RAPIDS, PHILADELPHIA, ST. LOUIS, SAN FRANCISCO
LONDON, SINGAPORE, SYDNEY, TOKYO

FRONTISPIECE

1. Yamunā Devī, goddess of the river Jumna. Elūrā, Kailāsanātha compound, A.D. 750–850. Standing among lotuses, supported by a great tortoise, the goddess of the river Jumna appears within the frame of a *makara torana*. The makaras (crocodilelike monsters symbolic of the sources of the flowing waters of life) are ridden by dwarf *yakshas* (earth spirits of fertility and wealth), while pouring into their open mouths from the mouths of two back-to-back makara heads above, streams of the waters of her life-supporting river shape the gateway *(torana)* of the deity's beneficent apparition.

TABLE OF CONTENTS

THE WAY OF THE SEEDED EARTH. MYTHOLOGIES OF THE PRIMITIVE PLANTERS: THE NORTHERN AMERICAS. Copyright © 1989 by The Joseph Campbell Trust. All rights reserved. Printed in the Netherlands. No part of this book may be used or reproduced in any manner whatsoever without written permission except in the case of brief quotations embodied in critical articles and reviews. For information address Harper & Row, Publishers, Inc., 10 East 53rd Street, New York, NY 10022. Published simultaneously in Canada by Fitzhenry & Whiteside Limited, Toronto.

Library of Congress Cataloging-in-Publication Data: Campbell, Joseph, 1904-1987
Historical atlas of world mythology. Includes bibliographical references and indexes. Contents: v.1. The way of the animal powers. pt.1. Mythologies of the primitive hunters and gatherers. pt.2. Mythologies of the great hunt—v.2. The way of the seeded earth. pt.2. Mythologies of the primitive planters: the Northern Americas. 1. Mythology. I. Title. BL311.C26 1988 291.1'3 87-40007
ISBN 0-06-055158-5 (v.2, pt.2)   89 90 91 92 93 10 9 8 7 6 5 4 3 2 1
ISBN 0-06-096351-4 (v.2, pt.2) (pbk.) 89 90 91 92 93 10 9 8 7 6 5 4 3 2 1

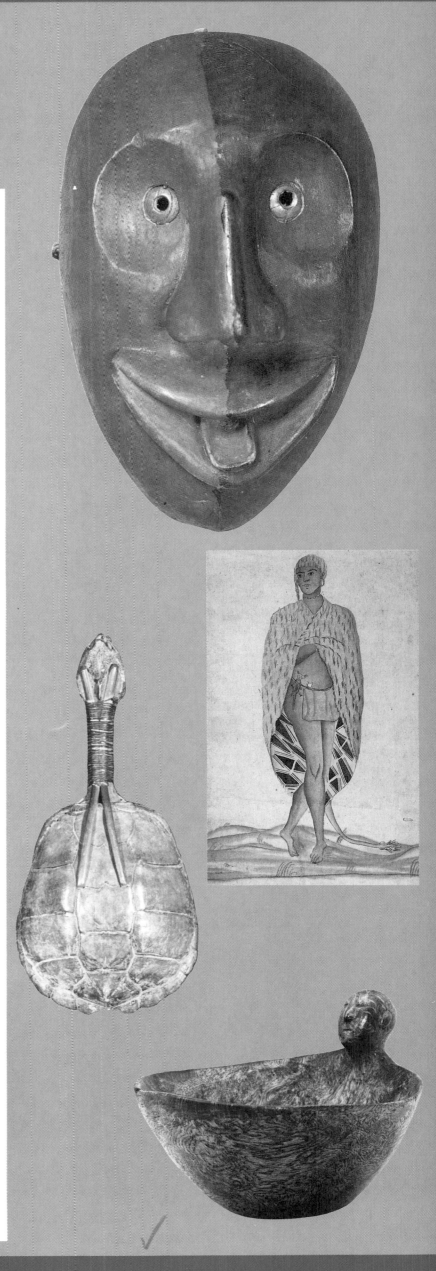

XX
291
Ca

10-10-97

AGRICULTURAL ORIGINS IN THE NEW WORLD

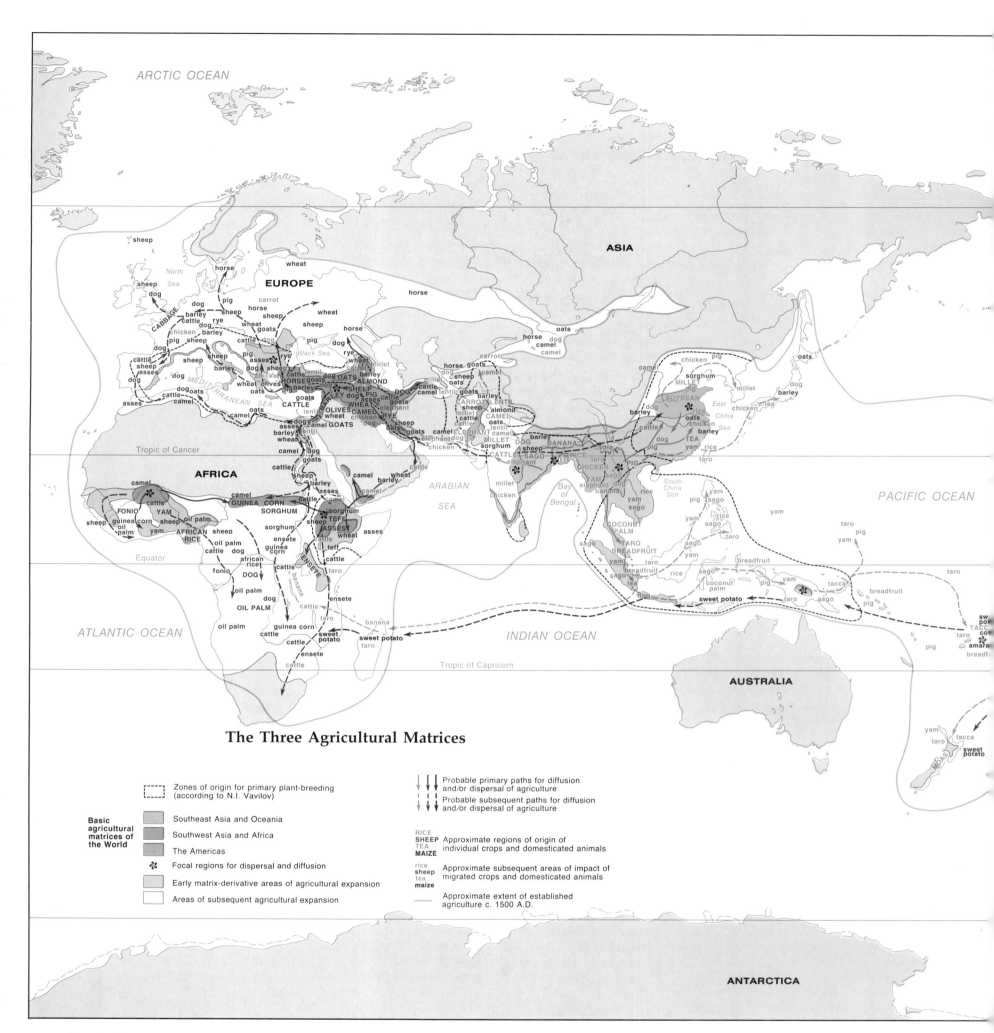

The Three Agricultural Matrices

Basic agricultural matrices of the World

Zones of origin for primary plant-breeding (according to N.I. Vavilov)

Southeast Asia and Oceania

Southwest Asia and Africa

The Americas

Focal regions for dispersal and diffusion

Early matrix-derivative areas of agricultural expansion

Areas of subsequent agricultural expansion

Probable primary paths for diffusion and/or dispersal of agriculture

Probable subsequent paths for diffusion and/or dispersal of agriculture

RICE
SHEEP
TEA
MAIZE
Approximate regions of origin of individual crops and domesticated animals

rice
sheep
tea
maize
Approximate subsequent areas of impact of migrated crops and domesticated animals

Approximate extent of established agriculture c. 1500 A.D.

Map 1. About 11,000 years ago (the exact date is a matter of some dispute), the attentions of our earliest hunting and gathering forebears turned from the transient mysteries of the Animal Powers to the regenerative potential of the Seeded Earth. As planting techniques improved and became more efficient, primitive agricultural communities began to flourish, and a new social order arose to supercede the old that centered around mobile bands of hunter-gatherers, and a new mythology was born. Three dominant agricultural centers arose, each cultivating its own particular plants and domesticating its distinctive animals. In a relatively short period of time, each of these core agricultural hearths expanded its sphere of influence over an ever-widening territory.

Two Agricultural Systems

ARCTIC OCEAN

Arctic Circle

Hudson Bay

NORTH AMERICA

ATLANTIC OCEAN

Tropic of Cancer

Gulf of Mexico

squash beans turkey

pumpkin

maize pumpkin

maize turkey

maize

BEANS
TURKEY
TOBACCO
DOG TOMATO
duck PUMPKIN
COTTON maize
SQUASH
AMARANTH beans
cotton
manioc

tobacco

Caribbean Sea

amaranth

TOBACCO
potato
maize
DUCK
SQUASH
ULLUCU MANIOC
CACAO SWEET POTATO
maize
COTTON
GUINEA PIG
DOG BEANS
amaranth
peanut QUINOA
LLAMA ullucu
MAIZE PEANUT
POTATO
llama
maize
beans
quinoa

Equator

taro
breadfruit
sweet potato

taro

sweet tacca
potato breadfruit
amaranth
taro
cotton

Tropic of Capricorn

manioc

SOUTH AMERICA

squash

duck

POTATO

Antarctic Circle

Two distinct agricultural systems are recognized in the world panorama of prehistoric cultures, and in the hemisphere of the Americas their geographical distributions are especially well defined. "Even now," states the geographer Carl O. Sauer, for more than forty years chairman of his department at the University of California at Berkeley, "a line drawn through the Florida Straits into the Gulf of Honduras and then winding southward through Central America to the Pacific Coast in Costa Rica approximates a separation between a northern and southern pattern of aboriginal farming. Between [the] West Indies and [the] United States mainland the separation is sharp, in Central America transitional. The Antillean farmers at the coming of the Europeans were Arawak and Carib, who had brought their ways from the southern *tierra firme* of the Caribbean. In Central America, the Caribbean side was occupied by natives of Chibchan affinities, living in the manner of their kinsmen in Colombia. The native stocks may long since have disappeared or have become blended into mestizo populations, but the plants and animals that are grown today and the habits of rural life still carry many qualities of ancient ways and days. This tropical culture is based strongly on the idea of vegetative reproduction."[1]

Agriculture by way of vegetative (asexual), as distinguished from sexual, seed reproduction, is described by Sauer as follows:

"Multiplication and selection is from clones. A piece of a plant is set into the ground to make a new plant. This may be by an offset or sprout from the parent, by dividing a root stock, by a stem cutting, or by a piece of underground stem or tuber. An individual plant is divided and multiplied indefinitely. The thing grown is [an] identical reconstitution of parent rather than variant progeny. Selection begins by choosing the individual plant to be divided in order to make a number of plants that are like the parent. Selection proceeds by observing and preserving desirable individual variation, as propagating an attractive chance root or bud sport, or by noting an accidental self-sown hybrid that is then divided for planting. In the long course of time, this continuous attention to the individual plant, and inattention to its sexual seeds, has given rise to an extraordinary lot of forms that are completely dependent on man for their existence. Seeds being of no interest, many such cultivated plants have lost the capacity to bear viable seeds, some as sterile polyploids, some in other ways. This culture operates by a very specific and sustained idea of reproduction; break the continuity of this operation and the plant may be lost."[2]

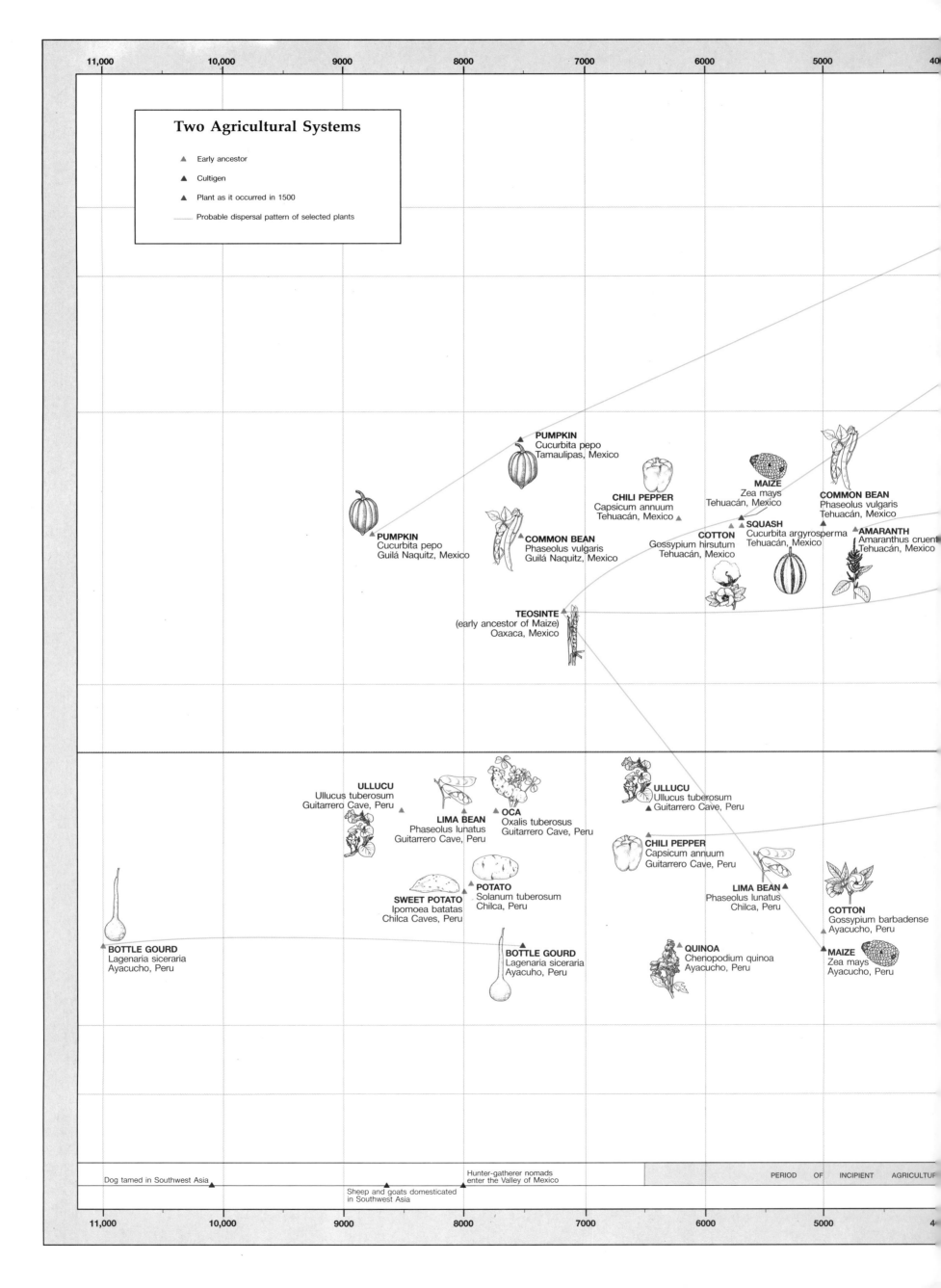

Two Agricultural Systems

▲ Early ancestor
▲ Cultigen
▲ Plant as it occurred in 1500
—— Probable dispersal pattern of selected plants

11,000   10,000   9000   8000   7000   6000   5000   40

PUMPKIN
Cucurbita pepo
Tamaulipas, Mexico

CHILI PEPPER
Capsicum annuum
Tehuacán, Mexico

MAIZE
Zea mays
Tehuacán, Mexico

COMMON BEAN
Phaseolus vulgaris
Tehuacán, Mexico

PUMPKIN
Cucurbita pepo
Guilá Naquitz, Mexico

COMMON BEAN
Phaseolus vulgaris
Guilá Naquitz, Mexico

COTTON
Gossypium hirsutum
Tehuacán, Mexico

SQUASH
Cucurbita argyrosperma
Tehuacán, Mexico

AMARANTH
Amaranthus cruen
Tehuacán, Mexico

TEOSINTE
(early ancestor of Maize)
Oaxaca, Mexico

ULLUCU
Ullucus tuberosum
Guitarrero Cave, Peru

OCA
Oxalis tuberosus
Guitarrero Cave, Peru

ULLUCU
Ullucus tuberosum
Guitarrero Cave, Peru

LIMA BEAN
Phaseolus lunatus
Guitarrero Cave, Peru

CHILI PEPPER
Capsicum annuum
Guitarrero Cave, Peru

POTATO
Solanum tuberosum
Chilca, Peru

SWEET POTATO
Ipomoea batatas
Chilca Caves, Peru

LIMA BEAN
Phaseolus lunatus
Chilca, Peru

COTTON
Gossypium barbadense
Ayacucho, Peru

BOTTLE GOURD
Lagenaria siceraria
Ayacucho, Peru

BOTTLE GOURD
Lagenaria siceraria
Ayacuho, Peru

QUINOA
Chenopodium quinoa
Ayacucho, Peru

MAIZE
Zea mays
Ayacucho, Peru

Dog tamed in Southwest Asia ▲

Sheep and goats domesticated
in Southwest Asia

Hunter-gatherer nomads
enter the Valley of Mexico

PERIOD   OF   INCIPIENT   AGRICULTUR

11,000   10,000   9000   8000   7000   6000   5000   4

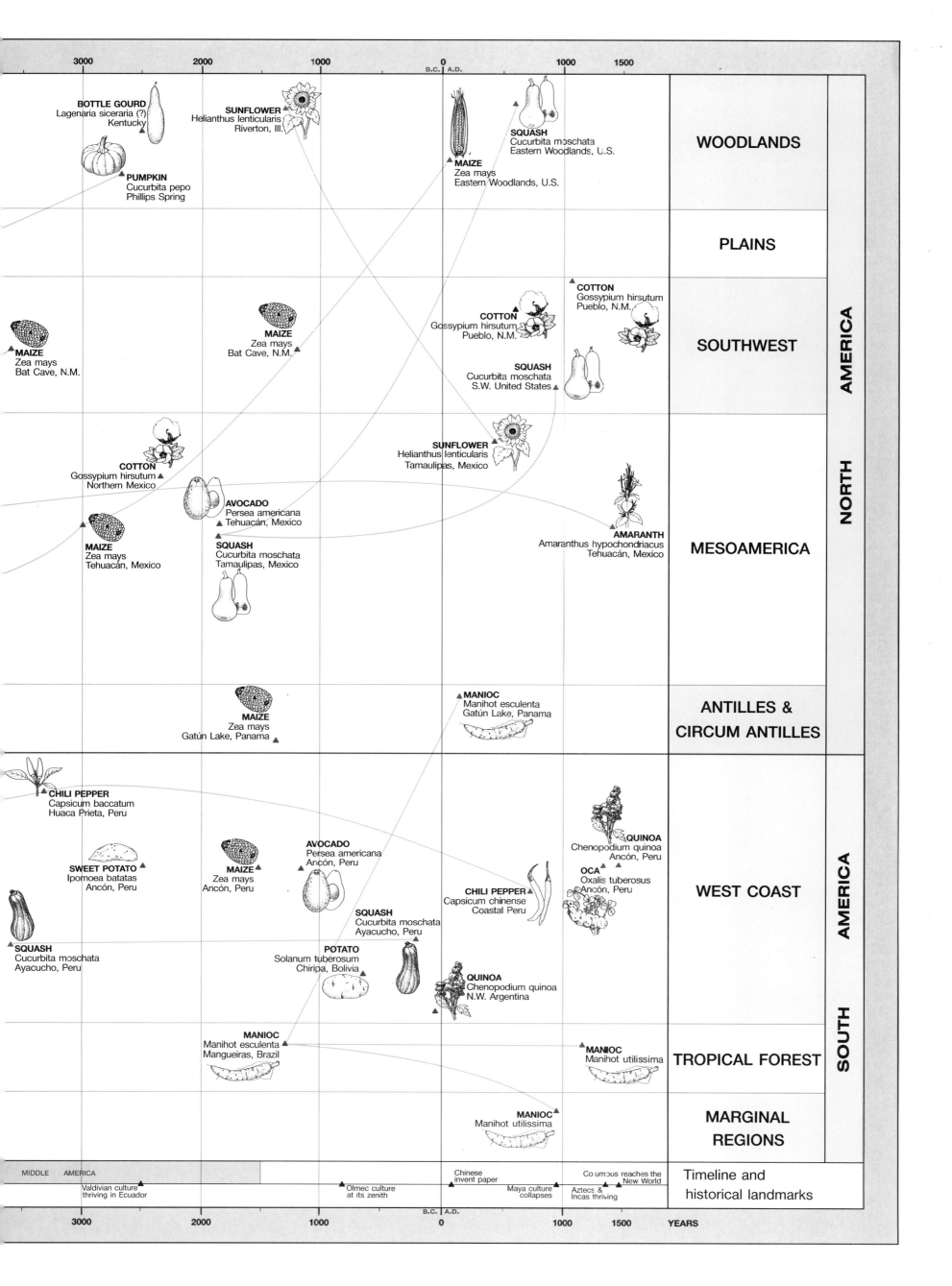

3000   2000   1000   0   1000   1500
B.C. | A.D.

BOTTLE GOURD
Lagenaria siceraria (?)
Kentucky

SUNFLOWER
Helianthus lenticularis
Riverton, Ill.

SQUASH
Cucurbita moschata
Eastern Woodlands, U.S.

PUMPKIN
Cucurbita pepo
Phillips Spring

MAIZE
Zea mays
Eastern Woodlands, U.S.

WOODLANDS

PLAINS

MAIZE
Zea mays
Bat Cave, N.M.

MAIZE
Zea mays
Bat Cave, N.M.

COTTON
Gossypium hirsutum
Pueblo, N.M.

COTTON
Gossypium hirsutum
Pueblo, N.M.

SQUASH
Cucurbita moschata
S.W. United States

SOUTHWEST

COTTON
Gossypium hirsutum
Northern Mexico

AVOCADO
Persea americana
Tehuacán, Mexico

SQUASH
Cucurbita moschata
Tamaulipas, Mexico

MAIZE
Zea mays
Tehuacán, Mexico

SUNFLOWER
Helianthus lenticularis
Tamaulipas, Mexico

AMARANTH
Amaranthus hypochondriacus
Tehuacán, Mexico

MESOAMERICA

AMERICA

NORTH

MAIZE
Zea mays
Gatún Lake, Panama

MANIOC
Manihot esculenta
Gatún Lake, Panama

**ANTILLES &
CIRCUM ANTILLES**

CHILI PEPPER
Capsicum baccatum
Huaca Prieta, Peru

SWEET POTATO
Ipomoea batatas
Ancón, Peru

MAIZE
Zea mays
Ancón, Peru

AVOCADO
Persea americana
Ancón, Peru

QUINOA
Chenopodium quinoa
Ancón, Peru

OCA
Oxalis tuberosus
Ancón, Peru

CHILI PEPPER
Capsicum chinense
Coastal Peru

SQUASH
Cucurbita moschata
Ayacucho, Peru

POTATO
Solanum tuberosum
Chiripa, Bolivia

QUINOA
Chenopodium quinoa
N.W. Argentina

SQUASH
Cucurbita moschata
Ayacucho, Peru

WEST COAST

AMERICA

SOUTH

MANIOC
Manihot esculenta
Mangueiras, Brazil

MANIOC
Manihot utilissima

TROPICAL FOREST

MANIOC
Manihot utilissima

**MARGINAL
REGIONS**

MIDDLE   AMERICA

Valdivian culture
thriving in Ecuador

Olmec culture
at its zenith

Chinese
invent paper

Maya culture
collapses

Columbus reaches the
New World

Aztecs &
Incas thriving

Timeline and
historical landmarks

3000   2000   1000   0   1000   1500   YEARS
B.C. | A.D.

Among the most important native plants of the tropical American agricultural system was, first of all, manioc (*Manihot utilissima*), or yuca. "It is widely grown," states Sauer, "in tropical forest lands on well-drained sites, but its home is not in the rain forest....There are very many races, largely unstudied; the wild parent is remote and uncertain. It is certainly an ancient cultigen....I should guess an origin in the Venezuela savannas....

"The bitter, or poisonous varieties of yuca have been distributed," Sauer continues, "in Atlantic drainage basins from Cuba to southern Brazil; they were unknown in Central America, most of Colombia, and in the Pacific Coast of South America. In the montaña at the eastern base of the Andes they are likely to be absent among the more archaic folk, and present among tribes that have moved up the Amazon from the east, especially those of Tupi and Carib affiliations. The manner of preparation follows a fairly standard pattern of grating, pressing, and washing to remove the hydrocyanic acid, followed by baking into the admirable and long-keeping flat bread, called *cazabi* (cassava). The sweet varieties appear to be grown wherever bitter manioc is, but their cultivation extends much farther, into extratropical latitudes and altitudes. Sweet manioc is mainly boiled or baked, without grating, and rarely is the staple food that the bitter forms commonly are."[3]

The sweet potato (*Ipomoea batatas*), in Sauer's view, is the next South American domesticate in importance and extent of distribution. "Along the Pacific the sweet potato was grown," he writes, "beyond the limits of yuca cultivation, both north and south. In interior South America Arawakan peoples seem to have favored its cultivation. Selection developed both sweet and starchy races, the latter giving the larger yields and hence perhaps of greater aboriginal use. The rapid and catastrophic collapse of Indian populations about the Caribbean by the Spanish conquest resulted in the loss of numerous varieties. Oviedo noted in 1526 that by that time some of the best kinds that he had known no longer existed. The Spaniards were not at all interested in the starchy kinds, but continued the cultivation of sweet races."[4]

Other cultigens on Sauer's list are the peach palm, or pejibae (*Bactris utilis*, syn. *Guilielma*), the fruits of which are boiled or baked and have a chestnut flavor; an aroid, *Xanthosoma* (*yautia* or *malanga*), which takes the place of taro and is still important in Puerto Rico, Haiti, and the northeastern South American mainland; the New World yam (*Dioscorea trifida*) and arrowroots (*Maranta arundinacea* and *Calathea allouia*); the racacha (*Arracacia xanthorrhiza*), which is parsniplike; coca, tobacco, and a number of barbascos (fish poisons), the most famous of which, *Tonchocarpus nicou*, is now a source of a commercial insecticide. "In northwestern South America the arborescent daturas, known in our gardens as angel's trumpets, furnished narcotic drinks," Sauer notes, "for initiation ceremonies which, according to dosage, bring visions, frenzy, stupor, or coma....Coca chewing and cultivation were pretty general through the south side of the Caribbean as well as in the Peruvian Andes. Tobacco may have been used first as a ceremonial drink, next in chewing and snuff, and

perhaps last, by smoking. The elder cultivated species is inferred to be *Nicotiana rustica*, which was grown from Chile to Quebec, and seems to have originated as a hybrid on the Peru-Ecuador border. The milder and to us more acceptable species, our commercial tobacco (*Nicotiana tabacum*), is also a hybrid of two wild species, formed apparently at the edge of the tropical forest in or near interior Bolivia. The tobaccos and cocas are grown from seed, but in carefully prepared seed beds from which they are planted out into fields. A similar transplanting practice has been noted in Southeastern Asia."[5]

The animals domesticated in association with this South American agricultural system were very few: in Peru, the llama and alpaca, primarily for their wool; the guinea pig and a low-slung dog fattened for food; the Muscovy duck—which, as Sauer remarks, "has nothing to do with Moscow or with musk. The name may have come from the Muisca Indians of central Colombia. It is a tropical tree-nesting bird that pretty well avoids human habitations. The domestic forms still extend from the Araucanian villages of Chile to the northern limits of high culture in lowland Mexico. They were known to the Spaniards as *patos caseros*, house ducks, which they still are, their swimming and flying habits almost lost."[6] And then, of course, there were those chickens (*hualpa*), after which the Inca Atahualpa seems to have been named.

The number of plants enumerated and discussed by Sauer in his article "Cultivated Plants of South and Central America" (in volume 6 of the *Handbook of South American Indians*), is enormous.[7] They include, besides the bottle gourd (which was in Precolumbian America a domesticate originating from Africa), the coconut (from Southeast Asia), the banana (also from Southeast Asia), an Old World cotton (known, apparently, already c. 5800 B.C. in Mexican Tehuacán), the peanut (an American domesticate known to China, c. 2100–1800 B.C., the pineapple (an American domesticate pictured, A.D. 79, in a mural at Pompeii), and maize (originating in the valley of Tehuacán, [c. 3000 B.C.] and apparently known before Columbus's time in Tibet, China, the Philippines, India, Persia, and Asia Minor)[8], a Chilean mango, quinoa, amaranth (known also in India and other Asian monsoon lands), the lupine, jackbean, kidney bean, scarlet runner bean, tepary bean, lima bean, various gourds and squashes, belladonna, mandragora and henbane, many kinds of potato, eggplant, Jerusalem cherry, melon pear, tomato, soursop, various peppers, avocado, capuli, cashew nuts, papaya, guava, cacao, and indigo (the main source of blue dyes).

Claude Lévi-Strauss, in the same sixth volume of the *Handbook of South American Indians*, in an article entitled "The Use of Wild Plants in Tropical South America," adds to this formidable catalogue another long list of wild plants utilized by the peoples of the South American jungle: manicoba (as a source of poison, or rubber, and of food), pine nuts, Brazil nuts, pindoba, numerous other nuts, the fruits of several palm tree genera, mushrooms, wild rice and roots of various kind, many plants furnishing poisons, and others recognized for medicinal use. "Few primitive

people," declares Lévi-Strauss, "have acquired as complete a knowledge of the physical and chemical properties of their botanical environment as the South American Indian. With the exception perhaps of the cinchona bark (*Cinchona* sp., several Rubiaceae, especially 'cascarilla' of the Spaniards, *Cinchona pubescens*), there is no species used in modern pharmacopoeia which was not familiar to the natives in pre-Columbian days."[9]

In contrast to the archaeologically documented chronicle of agricultural origins and dispersals that half a century of assiduous excavation has produced for the areas of seed culture represented in Map 15, the whole prehistory of vegetative planting in the South American culture field is in dispute. Not even a likely bottom dateline has been established. Nor has the place of origin of any one of the principal cultigens been demonstrated. What relationship (if any) tropical vegetative agriculture may have had to the development of seed planting in the northward temperate zones is moot, as is the tantalizing question of whether resemblances between the vegetative societies on either side of the Pacific represent diffusion or convergence. Sauer in *Agricultural Origins and Dispersals* rehearsed some of the South American ethnic traits that in his view were outstanding among the many resemblances to Indonesia.

"The natives were admirable boatmen and made dug-out canoes and pirogues of various and excellent designs. They were skilled net fishermen and used barbasco [fish poisons] cunningly. Some of them were adept at preparing arrow and dart poisons that caused sensible losses to the Spaniards. They colored food and painted themselves with the fruit of Bixa, whence, perhaps, the origin of the name red Indians. They made fermented drinks by chewing and used masticatories. The Spaniards found natives living in multifamily rectangular houses, many of them built on platforms set on posts (whence the name Venezuela) and not restricted to flood plains. Villages were surrounded by *palenques*, stockades through which the invaders had to hew their entry. The name cannibal is derived from the name Carib, and the Spaniards wrote gruesome accounts of the eating of human flesh, especially in western Colombia. Cannibalism is one of the less attractive traits that accompanies cognate planting cultures both in Southeast Asia and Africa.

"And, although the Spaniards were not aware of it, this was the first acquaintance of Europeans with an undisturbed matrilineal society. From Española to Colombia they met ruling queens and princesses. The Spaniards were titillated and shocked by what they considered licentiousness and worse, the unfamiliar mores of a society in which the males did not make the rules. The pattern of behavior was so different from their own, that, as civilized people, they unhesitatingly condemned it and proceeded to break it down. Out of these confident ignorances they built the myth of the Amazons [after which the river is named], in which there was some truth."[10]

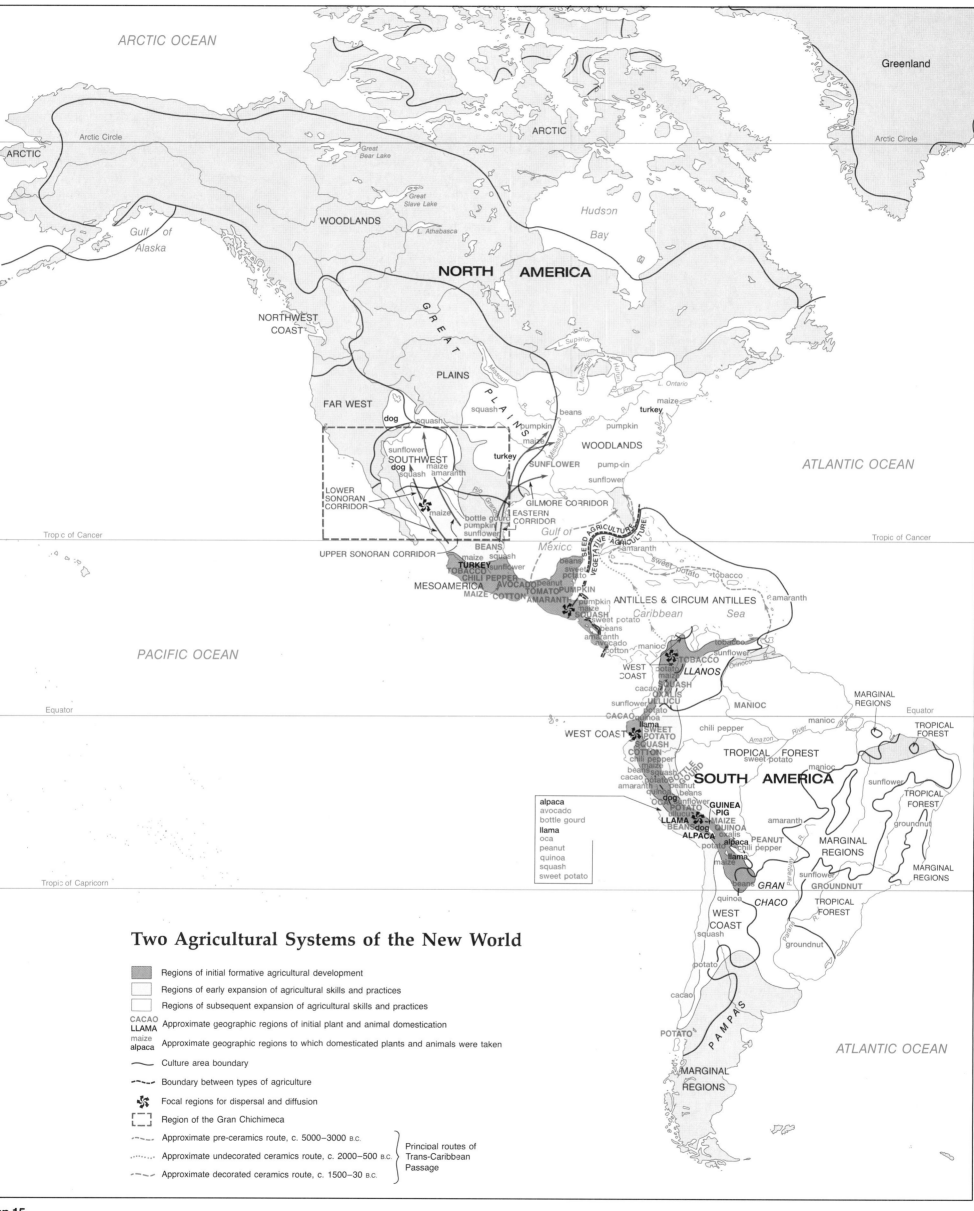

Two Agricultural Systems of the New World

Regions of initial formative agricultural development

Regions of early expansion of agricultural skills and practices

Regions of subsequent expansion of agricultural skills and practices

CACAO
LLAMA   Approximate geographic regions of initial plant and animal domestication

maize
alpaca   Approximate geographic regions to which domesticated plants and animals were taken

Culture area boundary

Boundary between types of agriculture

Focal regions for dispersal and diffusion

Region of the Gran Chichimeca

Approximate pre-ceramics route, c. 5000–3000 B.C. ⎫
Approximate undecorated ceramics route, c. 2000–500 B.C. ⎬ Principal routes of Trans-Caribbean Passage
Approximate decorated ceramics route, c. 1500–30 B.C. ⎭

Map 15.

121

From Nomadism to Seed Gardening

The first signs of an agricultural complex that was later to spread into North America already appear during what is known to American archaeology as the Period of Incipient Agriculture (c. 6500–1500 B.C.), when in Middle America the transition was made from Paleolithic hunting and foraging to a settled Neolithic style of village life and farming.[11]

The most important of the cultigens developed in Middle America during the course of these five thousand years was, of course, maize. The long search for clues to the time and place of its evolution led finally, in the early 1970s, to the high valley of Tehuacán in the Mexican state of Puebla, southwest of Mexico City. There, in a spectacular mountain setting, Richard S. MacNeish and his colleagues excavated a number of caves and rock shelters, from which they were able to reconstruct an unbroken stratigraphic sequence dating from some twenty thousand years ago to and through the Conquest.

Based principally on evidence from these excavations, as well as from similar undertakings in the Mexican state of Tamaulipas, the chronicle has been reconstructed of small bands of hunters settling down to village living as their dependency on plants increased.

One is to picture, in the beginning, small wandering companies of stone-age hunters (in scientific jargon, "nomadic microbands"), equipped with large flaked knives, pebble tools, and choppers—fifty to seventy per cent of whose subsistence was from hunting; the rest, from plant-gathering—leaving evidence among their vegetable remains of species that in later times would be domesticated: gourds and pumpkins, peppers, runner beans, agave, and apuntia (a kind of prickly pear).

Shortly after c. 6500 B.C. it appears that the inhabitants of the valley of Tehuacán were cultivating cotton, chili peppers, and a type of squash. As their dependency on domesticated plants increased, the community patterns of these hunting groups became adjusted to the rhythm of the seasons, two or three families annually settling down together (as "seasonal microbands") to take advantage of the earth's bounty when the plants ripened. Added to their equipment now were nets and baskets of a hard yarn string, twilled and plaited mats, and, for beauty's sake, shell beads.

Between 5000 and 3500 B.C., besides availing themselves of a local wild maize (with a cob less than an inch in length), these fledgling farmers were beginning to plant mutant forms showing signs of the husks characteristic of domestic corn. By this time, some seventy to eighty per cent of their subsistence was being derived from plants of their neighborhood, of which some five to eight per cent were now domesticated, including, besides both large and small varieties of pumpkin, chili peppers and various beans.

Among the earliest cultigens developed in North America, c. 4500 B.C., were squash and

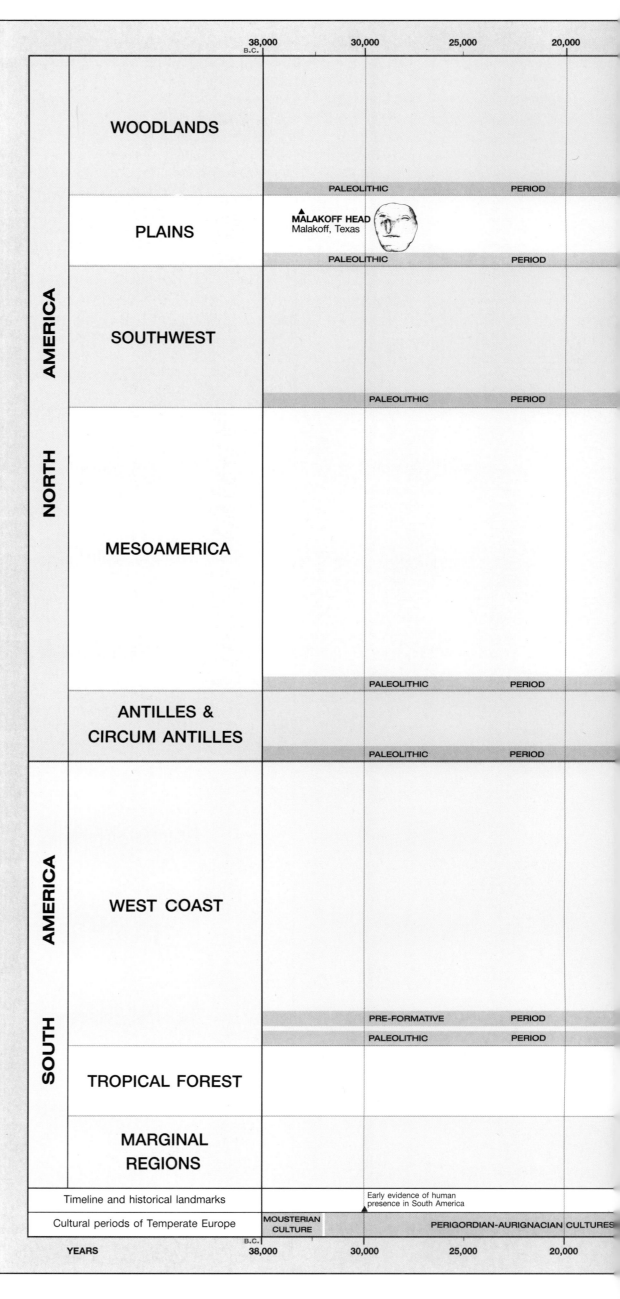

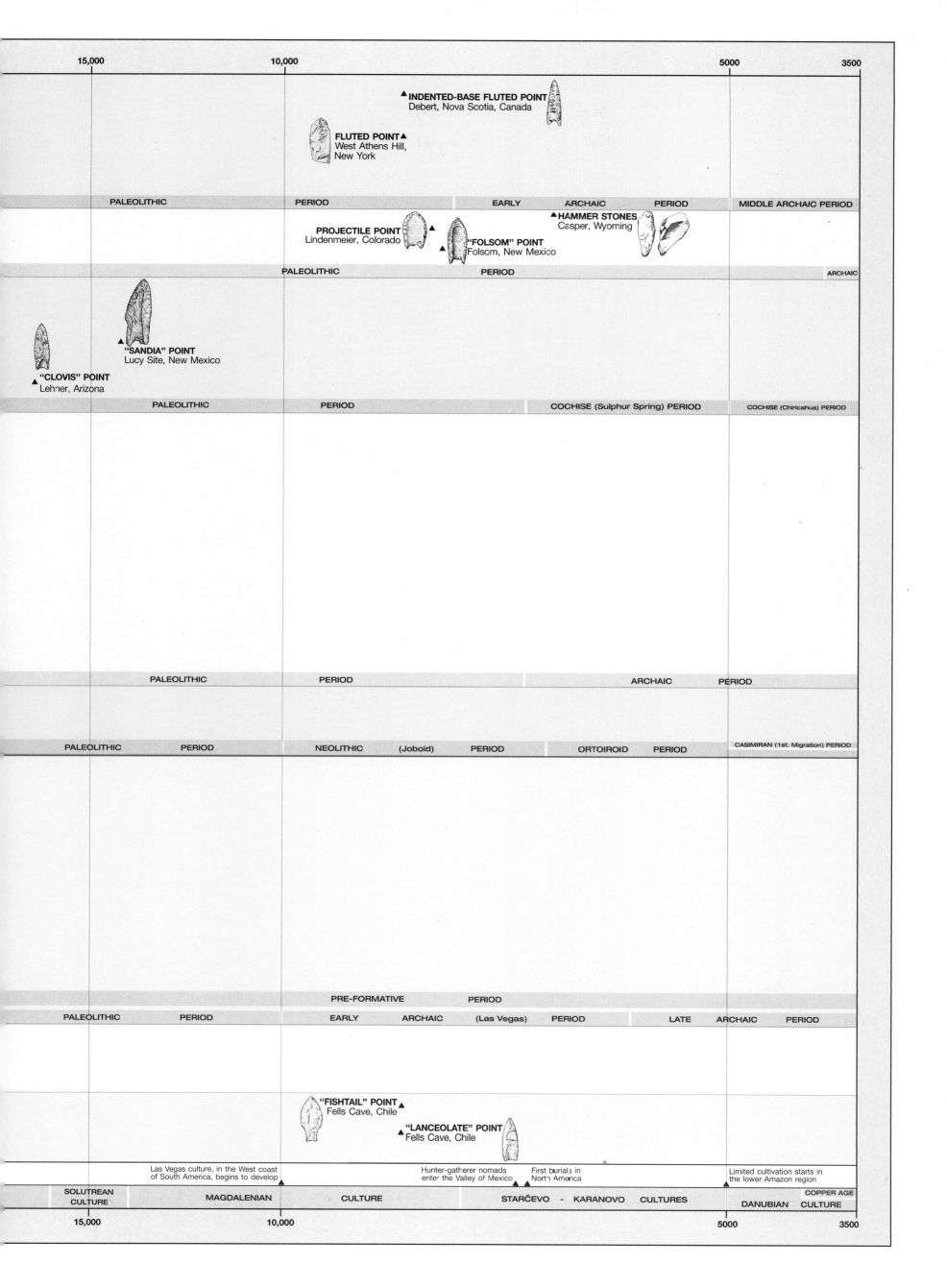

15,000   10,000   5000   3500

INDENTED-BASE FLUTED POINT
Debert, Nova Scotia, Canada

FLUTED POINT
West Athens Hill,
New York

PALEOLITHIC   PERIOD   EARLY   ARCHAIC   PERIOD   MIDDLE ARCHAIC PERIOD

HAMMER STONES
Casper, Wyoming

PROJECTILE POINT
Lindenmeier, Colorado

"FOLSOM" POINT
Folsom, New Mexico

PALEOLITHIC   PERIOD   ARCHAIC

"SANDIA" POINT
Lucy Site, New Mexico

"CLOVIS" POINT
Lehner, Arizona

PALEOLITHIC   PERIOD   COCHISE (Sulphur Spring) PERIOD   COCHISE (Chiricahua) PERIOD

PALEOLITHIC   PERIOD   ARCHAIC   PERIOD

PALEOLITHIC   PERIOD   NEOLITHIC   (Joboid)   PERIOD   ORTOIROID   PERIOD   CASIMIRAN (1st. Migration) PERIOD

PRE-FORMATIVE   PERIOD

PALEOLITHIC   PERIOD   EARLY   ARCHAIC   (Las Vegas)   PERIOD   LATE   ARCHAIC   PERIOD

"FISHTAIL" POINT
Fells Cave, Chile

"LANCEOLATE" POINT
Fells Cave, Chile

Las Vegas culture, in the West coast   Hunter-gatherer nomads   First burials in   Limited cultivation starts in
of South America, begins to develop   enter the Valley of Mexico   North America   the lower Amazon region

SOLUTREAN   COPPER AGE
CULTURE   MAGDALENIAN   CULTURE   STARČEVO - KARANOVO   CULTURES   DANUBIAN   CULTURE

15,000   10,000   5000   3500

gourds; and before 2500 B.C., cultivated bottle gourds, pepo gourds, and egg gourds were being grown by tribes in the Eastern Woodlands, as indicated by rind fragments identified at sites of that age and along the Little Tennessee River in Tennessee and the Green River in Kentucky.[12] It is supposed that the way of entry into the North American Woodland of these earliest Mesoamerican products would have been along the belt of prairie between the Edwards Plateau and the coastal plain of southeastern Texas—the so-called Gilmore Corridor, as proposed in 1935 by the ethnobotanist M. R. Gilmore (see Map 15).[13] The entrance to this corridor is the highland area of southwestern Tamaulipas and San Luis Potosí.

At Tehuacán, beans appear after 3500 B.C., along with a much-improved race of maize; thus, by 2500 B.C. the basic crops of maize, beans, and squash were in cultivation, and farming was providing some ten per cent of the food consumed, while hunting and gathering accounted for the rest.

In at least two of the cavern floors excavated in Puebla and Tamaulipas, at levels dated c. 3000–2200 B.C., remains were found of an early race of maize known as Early Nal Tel. The mystery of the time and place of origin of this fundamental American grain had long been a topic of debate when, during the course of the 1970s, the problem was solved with the recognition by Richard S. MacNeish of the mountain landscape around Tehuacán as the likely region and a period c. 5000–3000 B.C. as the likely date.[14] The question had been of especial interest because the cultigen is so far removed from any sort of known wild plant that its development must have required on the part of those who produced it, both a conscious intention, and a knowledge of how to cross-breed and hybridize. Plant domestication, that is to say, must have been by that time an already evolved practical art.

Pottery was being made in the Tehuacán valley by 2300 B.C., inspired, almost certainly, by an influence from the coast of Ecuador, where the earliest known pottery in the New World appeared c. 3000 B.C., bearing an astonishing resemblance to potteries of the same date from the island of Kyushu, Japan. Evidence of a passage of the knowledge of this art from Ecuador, not only northwestward into Mexico, but also northeastward to the Colombian Caribbean coast (at Porto Hormiga, c. 2875 B.C. ± 170 years), whence it passed by sea to the North American Southeast, is now too telling for easy dismissal.[15] The earliest pottery in North America, radio-carbon-dated to earlier than 2000 B.C., has been found in shell heaps on the Georgia coast near Savannah.[16] Another ceramic complex appears only shortly later in the St. Johns River area of northeastern Florida.[17] And from the region of Mobile Bay, Alabama, on the Gulf Coast, comes a dating of 1140 B.C. ± 200 years.[18]

These highly significant datings (all except the last, within the period of incipient agriculture), give evidence of a sea-way (uncharted) of south-to-north dissemination lying east of the four land-ways indicated on Map 15, stemming not from Middle America but from South America, and leading directly to the North American Southeast. In Alabama, Florida, and Georgia, the tribes learning the art of pottery

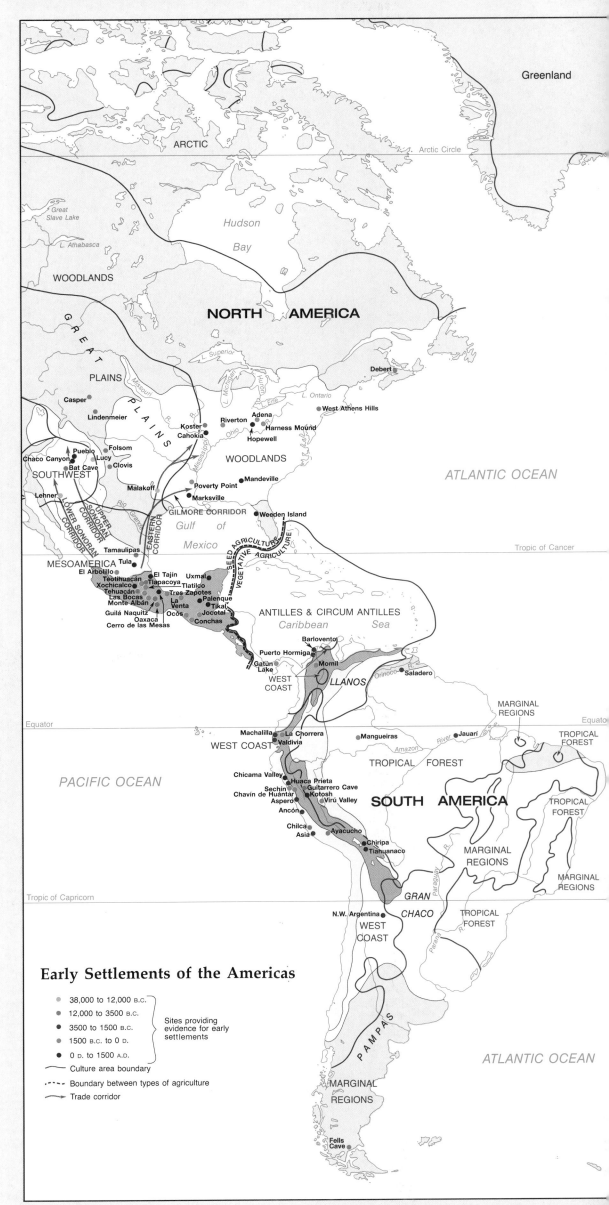

Early Settlements of the Americas

- ● 38,000 to 12,000 B.C.
- ● 12,000 to 3500 B.C.
- ● 3500 to 1500 B.C.
- ● 1500 B.C. to 0 D.
- ● 0 D. to 1500 A.D.

Sites providing evidence for early settlements

— Culture area boundary
----- Boundary between types of agriculture
→ Trade corridor

Map 16.

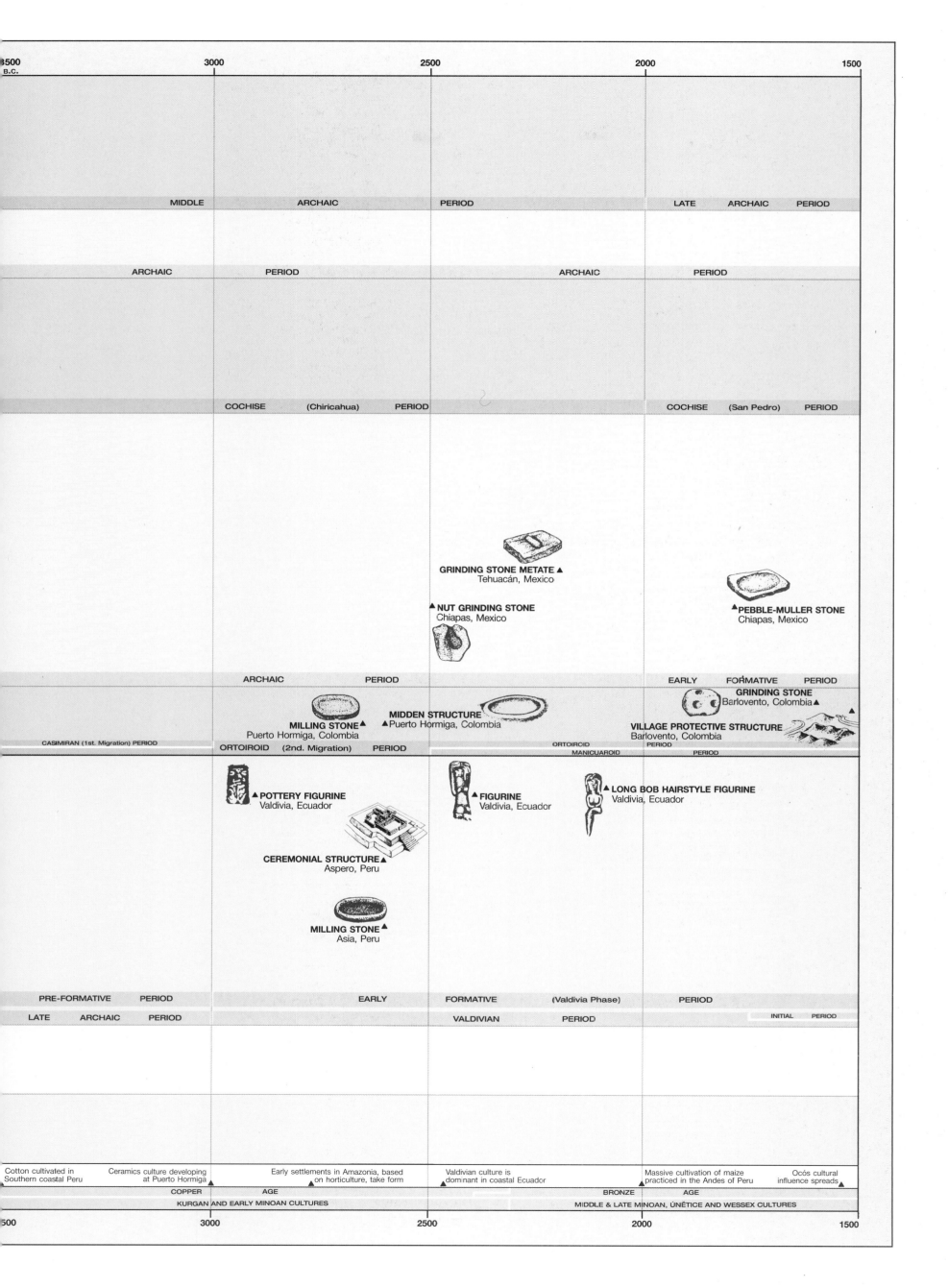

3500 B.C.	3000	2500	2000	1500

MIDDLE   ARCHAIC   PERIOD   LATE   ARCHAIC   PERIOD

ARCHAIC   PERIOD   ARCHAIC   PERIOD

COCHISE   (Chiricahua)   PERIOD   COCHISE   (San Pedro)   PERIOD

GRINDING STONE METATE ▲
Tehuacán, Mexico

▲ **NUT GRINDING STONE**
Chiapas, Mexico

▲**PEBBLE-MULLER STONE**
Chiapas, Mexico

ARCHAIC   PERIOD   EARLY   FORMATIVE   PERIOD

GRINDING STONE
Barlovento, Colombia▲

MILLING STONE▲
Puerto Hormiga, Colombia

MIDDEN STRUCTURE
▲Puerto Hormiga, Colombia

VILLAGE PROTECTIVE STRUCTURE
Barlovento, Colombia

▲

CASIMIRAN (1st. Migration) PERIOD   ORTOIROID   (2nd. Migration)   PERIOD   ORTOIROID   PERIOD
                                                                              MANICUAROID   PERIOD

POTTERY FIGURINE
Valdivia, Ecuador

▲ **FIGURINE**
Valdivia, Ecuador

▲**LONG BOB HAIRSTYLE FIGURINE**
Valdivia, Ecuador

CEREMONIAL STRUCTURE▲
Aspero, Peru

MILLING STONE▲
Asia, Peru

PRE-FORMATIVE   PERIOD   EARLY   FORMATIVE   (Valdivia Phase)   PERIOD

LATE   ARCHAIC   PERIOD   VALDIVIAN   PERIOD   INITIAL   PERIOD

Cotton cultivated in
Southern coastal Peru

Ceramics culture developing
at Puerto Hormiga ▲

Early settlements in Amazonia, based
▲ on horticulture, take form

Valdivian culture is
▲dominant in coastal Ecuador

Massive cultivation of maize
▲practiced in the Andes of Peru

Ocós cultural
influence spreads▲

COPPER   AGE   BRONZE   AGE

KURGAN AND EARLY MINOAN CULTURES   MIDDLE & LATE MINOAN, ÚNÉTICE AND WESSEX CULTURES

3500	3000	2500	2000	1500

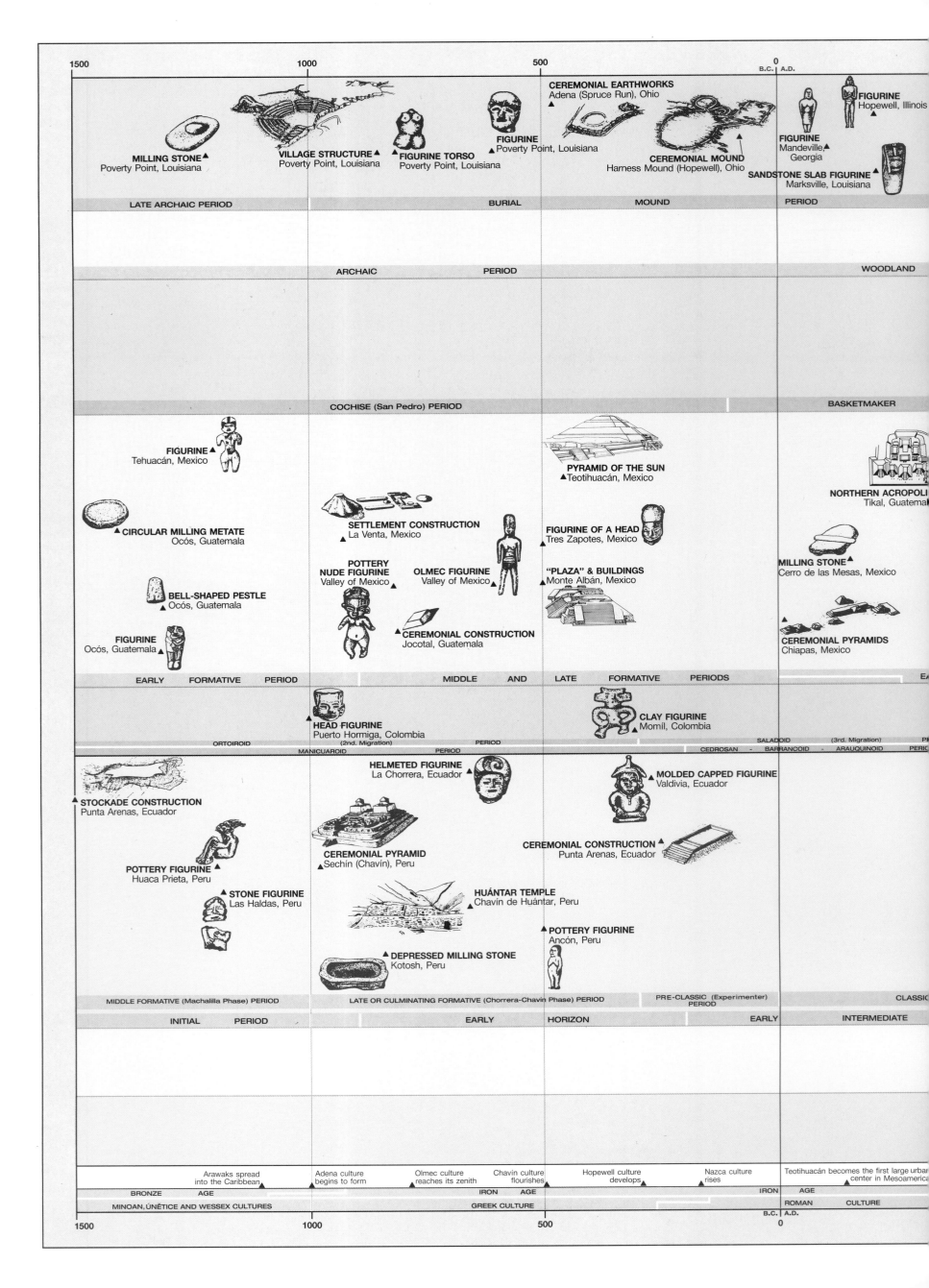

| 1500 | 1000 | 500 | 0 B.C. | A.D. |

MILLING STONE ▲
Poverty Point, Louisiana

VILLAGE STRUCTURE ▲
Poverty Point, Louisiana

▲ **FIGURINE TORSO**
Poverty Point, Louisiana

FIGURINE ▲
Poverty Point, Louisiana

CEREMONIAL EARTHWORKS
Adena (Spruce Run), Ohio
▲

CEREMONIAL MOUND
Harness Mound (Hopewell), Ohio

▲ **FIGURINE**
Hopewell, Illinois

FIGURINE ▲
Mandeville, ▲
Georgia

SANDSTONE SLAB FIGURINE ▲
Marksville, Louisiana

LATE ARCHAIC PERIOD · BURIAL · MOUND · PERIOD

ARCHAIC · PERIOD · WOODLAND

COCHISE (San Pedro) PERIOD · BASKETMAKER

FIGURINE ▲
Tehuacán, Mexico

CIRCULAR MILLING METATE
Ocós, Guatemala

SETTLEMENT CONSTRUCTION ▲
La Venta, Mexico

PYRAMID OF THE SUN
▲Teotihuacán, Mexico

FIGURINE OF A HEAD ▲
Tres Zapotes, Mexico

NORTHERN ACROPOLI
Tikal, Guatemal

BELL-SHAPED PESTLE
▲ Ocós, Guatemala

**POTTERY
NUDE FIGURINE**
Valley of Mexico ▲

OLMEC FIGURINE
Valley of Mexico ▲

"PLAZA" & BUILDINGS
▲Monte Albán, Mexico

MILLING STONE ▲
Cerro de las Mesas, Mexico

FIGURINE
Ocós, Guatemala ▲

▲ **CEREMONIAL CONSTRUCTION**
Jocotal, Guatemala

CEREMONIAL PYRAMIDS
Chiapas, Mexico

EARLY · FORMATIVE · PERIOD · MIDDLE · AND · LATE · FORMATIVE · PERIODS · EA

HEAD FIGURINE
Puerto Hormiga, Colombia
(2nd. Migration)

CLAY FIGURINE
▲ Momíl, Colombia

ORTOIROID · PERIOD · SALADOID · (3rd. Migration) · P
MANICUAROID · PERIOD · CEDROSAN - BARRANCOID - ARAUQUINOID · PERIO

HELMETED FIGURINE ▲
La Chorrera, Ecuador

MOLDED CAPPED FIGURINE ▲
Valdivia, Ecuador

▲ **STOCKADE CONSTRUCTION**
Punta Arenas, Ecuador

CEREMONIAL PYRAMID
▲Sechín (Chavín), Peru

CEREMONIAL CONSTRUCTION ▲
Punta Arenas, Ecuador

POTTERY FIGURINE ▲
Huaca Prieta, Peru

▲ **STONE FIGURINE**
Las Haldas, Peru

HUÁNTAR TEMPLE
▲Chavín de Huántar, Peru

▲ **POTTERY FIGURINE**
Ancón, Peru

▲ **DEPRESSED MILLING STONE**
Kotosh, Peru

MIDDLE FORMATIVE (Machalilla Phase) PERIOD · LATE OR CULMINATING FORMATIVE (Chorrera-Chavín Phase) PERIOD · PRE-CLASSIC (Experimenter) PERIOD · CLASSIC

INITIAL · PERIOD · EARLY · HORIZON · EARLY · INTERMEDIATE

Arawaks spread
into the Caribbean ▲

Adena culture
begins to form ▲

Olmec culture
reaches its zenith ▲

Chavin culture
flourishes ▲

Hopewell culture
develops ▲

Nazca culture
rises ▲

Teotihuacán becomes the first large urban
center in Mesoamerica ▲

BRONZE · AGE · IRON · AGE · IRON · AGE
MINOAN, ÚNĚTICE AND WESSEX CULTURES · GREEK CULTURE · ROMAN · CULTURE

B.C. | A.D.

| 1500 | 1000 | 500 | 0 |

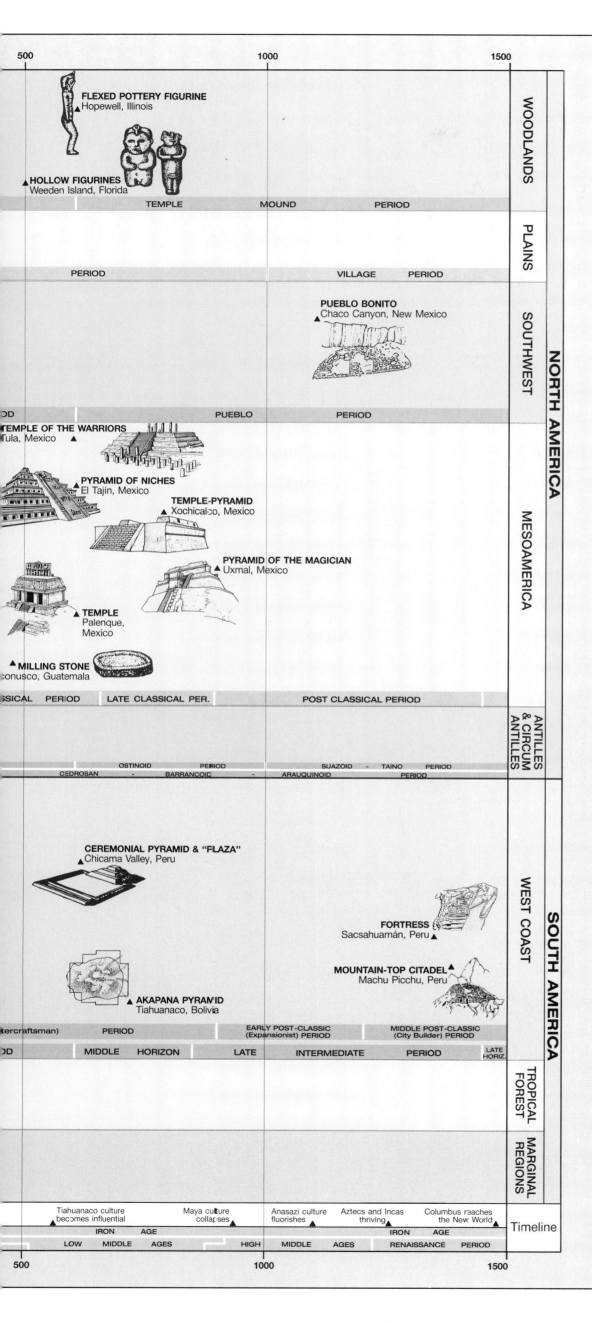

at that time, like those of Kentucky and Tennessee who were cultivating bottle gourds, were still basically fishers, hunters, and gatherers—though there is evidence that in Kentucky and Tennessee, besides the Mexican bottle gourds, native sumpweed and sunflower were also being cultivated, along with maygrass, lambsquarter, smartweed, and giant ragweed.[19] In the Tehuacán valley of Mexico, however, the tribes that were acquiring and fashioning pottery around 2300 B.C. had already begun to turn toward serious farming.

By 2200-1800 B.C. in Tamaulipas and Puebla, agriculture was furnishing as much as twenty per cent of the food, and in two of the excavated sites in Tamaulipas, scraps of wattle and daub have testified to the existence of permanent dwellings. (The "seasonal microbands," that is to say, were becoming "semisedentary macrobands.")

By c. 2000 B.C. permanent settlements of one hundred persons or so were appearing throughout Mesoamerica; between 1800 and 1500 B.C. small villages were beginning to appear, and by 1500 B.C. the stage was set for a style of settled village living justly comparable to what in the usual terminology of Old World archaeology is known as the Neolithic stage of civilization, and is termed the Formative Stage by American anthropologists.

The critical transition from nomadic hunting to that agriculturally grounded bondage to the seeded earth and round of the annual seasons out of which, in time, the phenomenon of an historic civilization might arise, had been accomplished.

What the mythologies and ceremonials of those prehistoric agricultural villages may have been we do not know. There are among the remains no signs that anyone has yet recognized anything of the kind. However, we do know that the knowledge of plant cultivation spread northward, and that among the myths and rites of those native North American tribes that received and then practiced the horticultural arts there are signs of a consistent mythological tradition associated especially with maize which must have been carried north together with the maize itself, and then adapted variously to the various local orders of mythology and life.

NORTH AMERICAN
AGRICULTURALIST
RITES AND MYTHS

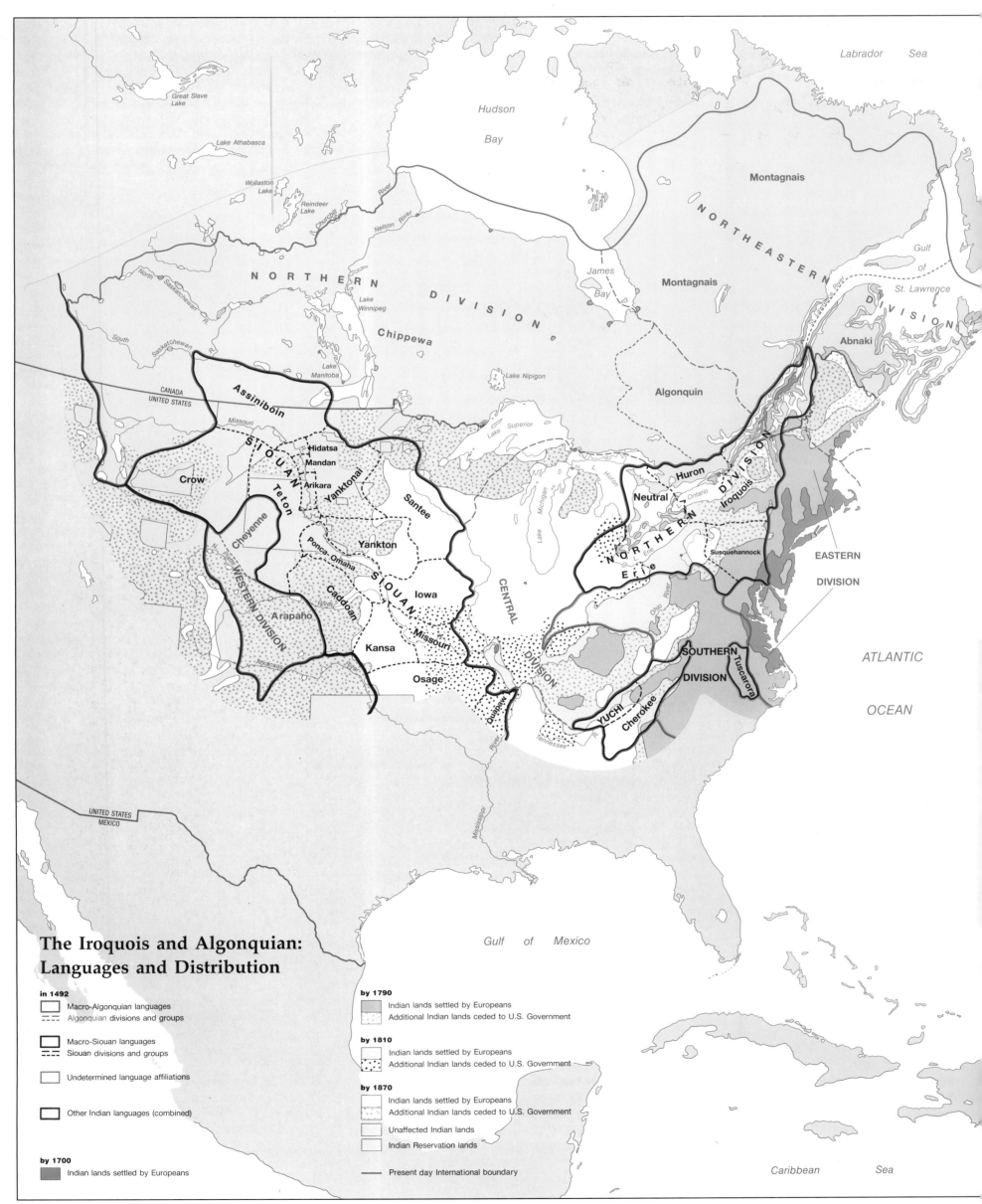

Great Slave
Lake

Lake Athabasca

Wollaston
Lake

Reindeer
Lake

Churchill
River

Nelson River

Hudson

Bay

Labrador   Sea

Montagnais

N O R T H E A S T E R N

Montagnais

James
Bay

Gulf
of
St. Lawrence

North Saskatchewan R.

N O R T H E R N   D I V I S I O N

South Saskatchewan R.

Lake
Winnipeg

Lake
Manitoba

Chippewa

Lake Nipigon

Algonquin

D I V I S I O N

Abnaki

CANADA
UNITED STATES

Assiniboin

Missouri River

Lake Superior

St. Lawrence River

S I O U A N

Hidatsa

Mandan

Crow

Arikara

Teton

Yanktonai

Santee

Lake Huron

Lake Michigan

Huron

Neutral

Erie

Lake Ontario

Iroquois

N O R T H E R N   D I V I S I O N

EASTERN
DIVISION

Cheyenne

N. Platte River

Ponca-Omaha

Yankton

S I O U A N

Susquehannock

WESTERN DIVISION

Caddoan

Iowa

C E N T R A L

Arapaho

Platte River

Missouri

Ohio River

SOUTHERN

Tuscarora

Kansa

Arkansas River

Osage

D I V I S I O N

ATLANTIC

OCEAN

Quapaw River

DIVISION

YUCHI

Cherokee

Tennessee R.

UNITED STATES
MEXICO

Mississippi River

Gulf   of   Mexico

The Iroquois and Algonquian:
Languages and Distribution

in 1492

☐ Macro-Algonquian languages

--- Algonquian divisions and groups

☐ Macro-Siouan languages

--- Siouan divisions and groups

☐ Undetermined language affiliations

☐ Other Indian languages (combined)

by 1700

☐ Indian lands settled by Europeans

by 1790

☐ Indian lands settled by Europeans

☐ Additional Indian lands ceded to U.S. Government

by 1810

☐ Indian lands settled by Europeans

☐ Additional Indian lands ceded to U.S. Government

by 1870

☐ Indian lands settled by Europeans

☐ Additional Indian lands ceded to U.S. Government

☐ Unaffected Indian lands

☐ Indian Reservation lands

—— Present day International boundary

Caribbean   Sea

Map 17.

The Iroquois

Of the Longhouse and the Wigwam

The Ojibwa legend of *The Origin of Maize* which Schoolcraft recorded around 1835 and Longfellow adapted in his *Song of Hiawatha* (1855), has already been recounted (I.2:207). So too has the Iroquoian *Corn-Mother* legend recorded by Jeremiah Curtin during his visit with the Seneca tribe in the 1880s (I.2:207–208). In both of these the essential idea is of a benign being from whose buried remains the original maize plant grew, which is such an idea as appears in legends of the origin of food plants, not only in the Americas, but also throughout Oceania and Southeast Asia.

and both shores of Lake Superior, extending west to as far as the Turtle Mountains of Manitoba and North Dakota. Only a few bands cultivated maize. Their native mythology, therefore, was of a northern, hunter-and-gatherer type with no knowledge of planting.

An essential requirement of every male adolescent as initiation to manhood among those tribes was that he should undertake a *vision quest*: a solitary fast of four days and nights in the wilderness, in meditation and prayer, with the expectation of the appearance in vision of some spiritual being who would become thereby the youth's guardian-familiar for life. The accent thus was on the individual's personal spiritual experience as the determinant both of his destiny and of his manner

and faint in his little hut, the boy fancied that he saw a handsome youth coming toward him from the sky, "richly and gaily dressed, having on a great many garments of green and yellow colors, but differing in their deeper and lighter shades. He had a plume of waving feathers on his head, and all his motions were graceful." This was a being who had been sent by "the Great Spirit who made all things," to be killed and buried, and from whose carefully tended grave there then presently appeared a "tall and graceful plant,

Dwelling communally in great, bark-covered longhouses (**226**), the Iroquois called themselves *Ho-de-no-sau-nee* ("People of the Longhouse"), thus proudly distinguishing themselves from their hunting-and-foraging neighbors (the "tree eaters"), who lived in single-family bark wigwams, such as this Penobscot encampment at Old Town, Maine (**227**).

How it became attached to the mythology of maize is a question which, as far as I know, has not been investigated.

The Ojibwa, or Chippewa, are a people of Algonquian linguistic stock who, in Schoolcraft's time, ranged as migratory hunters, fishers, and collectors of wild rice along the northern shore of Lake Huron

of service to his people, and in the Ojibwa maize legend, accordingly, we find the idea of the willing victim whose body was to become transformed into a source of nourishment for the tribe interpreted as an apparition invoked by a fasting youth during the days and nights of his vision quest. In the wilderness, alone, lying weak

with bright colored silken hair, surmounted with nodding plumes and stately leaves, and golden clusters on each side."[20]

The corn-mother legend of the Seneca, in contrast, was of a piece with, and indeed central to, the native mythological heritage of an agriculturally supported society. A people of Iroquoian speech, the

Seneca were the largest of the original Five Nations of the historic League of the Iroquois, or "People of the Longhouse" (*Ho-dé-no-sau-nee*). Until they made the fatal mistake, at the time of the American Revolution, of fighting for the British (thus calling down upon their villages the wrath, in 1779, of the victorious Colonials), the Seneca were the dominant power throughout western New York, between Seneca Lake and the Genesee River, and from Niagara south, along the Allegheny River into Pennsylvania.

As "People of the Longhouse," the Iroquois distinguished themselves proudly from the Algonquians, inhabiting wigwams, into whose territories they had penetrated, apparently from the south. There is an alternative hypothesis of their origin from the north, the vicinity of Montreal, on the northern banks of the St. Lawrence, where they are supposed to have lived in subjection to the Algonquian Adirondacks.[21] Everything about both their culture and their character points, however, to the south; whereas the Adirondacks, like the other Algonquians of that neighborhood (as recognized by Lewis H. Morgan's posthumous editor and publisher, Herbert M. Lloyd) were ignorant of agriculture and mere hunters and fishers of the wilderness. "Their very name," Lloyd notes, "means 'tree-eaters,' and was given to them by the Iroquois in contempt for their famine diet of buds and bark, to which, having no stores of corn, they were in winter sometimes reduced. Nor was the St. Lawrence valley, where the corn crop often failed, the place where a people would shift from fish to corn as a means of subsistence."[22]

In contrast, all "Five Nations" of the original League of the Iroquois—Seneca, Onondaga, Oneida, Cayuga, and Mohawk (as well as the Iroquoian Tuscarora, who, fleeing from North Carolina, were in 1715 admitted to the League as the "Sixth Nation")—dwelt as horticulturalists in palisaded towns of several hundred individuals. Nearby were their extensive clearings in which were cultivated the main domesticates of North American agriculture: maize, beans, and squash (all, of course, of Middle American origin), besides melons, watermelons, pumpkins, sunflowers, hemp, and tobacco. In the devastating, vengeful, punitive expedition against their villages executed by the triumphant Colonials in 1779, there were destroyed some 160,000 bushels of maize,

"with a vast quantity of vegetables of every kind," besides apple trees cut down, which were innumerable: in but one orchard 1500.[23]

The longhouse, too, was a feature of southern provenance. Covered with elm bark, having a door at each end, and looking much like an overturned great canoe, some 50 to over 100 feet long and housing perhaps ten to twenty matrilineally related families, the way of communal life which it signified was of such pride to the Iroquois (in contrast to the individual family huts of the neighboring hunting and fishing "tree eaters") that they likened their League itself to a longhouse. "To an Iroquois," states Lloyd, "the league was not *like* a Long House. It *was* a Long House, extending from the Hudson to the Genesee, in which around five fires the five tribes gathered. The Mohawk Wolf-clan kept the eastern door, the Seneca Wolves the western. At each fire the sachems like pillars upheld the roof, the chiefs were the braces that fortified the structure."[24] So that the name *Ho-dé-no-sau-nee*, "People of the Longhouse" was an intentional recognition and celebration of what the Iroquois regarded as the dignity and nobility of their culture, in contrast to that of the hunting and fishing foragers dwelling, native to the area, in bark wigwams.

The ceremonials of the Iroquois differed, likewise, fundamentally from those of the hunting, fishing, and gathering tribes, being based on a different order of concerns. It was distinguished, according to Lewis H. Morgan's account—recorded in the 1840s and published posthumously in his fundamental two volumes, *League of the Ho-dé-no-sau-nee, or Iroquois* (1901 and 1904)—by an annual round of six thanksgiving festivals.

"The first in the order of time," Morgan reports, "was the Maple festival. This was a return of thanks to the maple itself, for yielding its sweet waters. Next was the planting festival, designed, chiefly, as an invocation of the Great Spirit to bless the seed. Third came the Strawberry festival, instituted as a thanksgiving for the first fruits of the earth. The fourth was the Green Corn festival, designed as a thanksgiving acknowledgment for the ripening of the corns, beans, and squashes. Next was celebrated the Harvest festival, instituted as a general thanksgiving to 'Our Supporters' [the guardian Spirits principally of the Maize, the Bean, and the Squash, who were known to the Iroquois collectively as the "Three Sisters"], following the gathering of the harvest. Last in the enumeration is placed the New Year's festival, the great jubilee of the Iroquois [celebrated about the first of February], at which the white dog was sacrificed."[25]

Morgan is at some pains to interpret in terms appropriate to the outlook of the Iroquois the sense of this last, most "priminant act," as he calls it, of their seven-day-long festival in celebration of the renewal of the sun's light and life at the time of the winter solstice. One may detect in the observance a possible extension to eastern North America of the custom of dog-sacrifice that was reported, the first years of this century, of the Koryak of northeasternmost Siberia. Writing of the Koryak custom, Waldemar Jochelson remarked that, whereas among tribes of northwestern North America sacrifices of this kind were unknown, east of the Rocky Mountains dogs were sacrificed by both the Iroquois and the Sioux.[26] According to the seventeenth-century French Jesuit

228. Each longhouse was from 50 to over 100 feet long, was aligned west-to-east with a doorway at either end, and housed from 10 to 20 matrilineally-related families. This photograph of the reconstructed floor of one such longhouse (at Howlett Hill, New York) gives some indication of the immense size of the typical dwelling. The Iroquois considered their League itself to be the greatest longhouse, and accordingly, the Mohawk were the Keepers of the eastern door, while the Seneca kept the western (see Map 20).

missionaries, dogs were sacrificed, also, by Algonquian tribes; and as the Koryak sacrifices were elevated on poles (see I.2:**304**), so too were many of those observed by the Jesuits. "I was much grieved," we read in one French account of an Algonquian village in the Lakes region, 1676-77, "to see a great dog hanging at the top of a painted pole as a sacrifice to the sun."[27] And again, among the Wabash Illinois in 1712 or thereabouts: "There being a pestilence, they sacrificed as many as forty dogs which they carried on tops of poles, themselves singing, dancing, and cutting a thousand extravagant capers."[28] In the journals of General John Sullivan's punitive expedition of 1779, dog sacrifices are several times mentioned. In one instance: "In this town," we read, "a dog was hung up, with a string of wampum round his neck, on a tree, curiously decorated and trimmed. On inquiry I was informed," the report continues, "that it was a custom among the savages before they went to war to offer this as a sacrifice to Mars, the God of War, and praying that he might strengthen them. In return for these favours they promise to present him with the skin for a tobacco pouch."[29] Francis Parkman, in his valuable *The Jesuits in North America in the Seventeenth Century* (1867), states that by many tribes the *white* dog was sacrificed on an upright pole.[30]

There can be little doubt that the idea of the dog sacrifice entered North America from Siberia as a feature of that subarctic, hunting-and-gathering, snowshoe and bark-wigwam complex which is represented in Asia by the Paleo-Siberian Chukchi, Koryak, Yukaghir, and Kamchadals (see I.2:178–179), and in North America chiefly by Algonquian tribes.

In contrast, however, both the Iroquois and the Sioux, who are linguistically related (see Map 18), represent two extensions northward out of that well-developed, agriculturally based civilization known as the Mississippian, which from c. A.D. 800 to the time of the arrivals of the first European explorers had been centered principally in the lower Mississippi Valley, around the ceremonial capital of Cahokia (across the river from St. Louis), but substantially covering the whole mid-continent and southeast, from Oklahoma to Georgia and north through Illinois, Indiana, and Ohio (see I.2:211, Map 46, and 216–218). As vigorous carriers of elements of this planting-culture complex, the Iroquois had made their way north as an association of invincible warrior tribes, replenishing their inevitable losses of young braves by adopting into the tribe those captives whom they elected not to execute in the usual way of slow, ceremonial torture (see II.1:39–43). Thus their race had become mixed of their own and various alien strains, as had their culture of southern, agriculturally-based and

northern, hunting-and-gathering elements. Among the latter we may reckon (probably) the detail of the white-dog sacrifice in celebration of the winter solstice, when the nights would begin to grow shorter and the days longer.

Jochelson found among the Koryak that sacrifices, whether of dogs or of reindeer, were of three kinds: "preventive, to avert a possible calamity or malady; propitiatory, to remove a disaster which has already befallen; and for giving thanks, in gratitude for benefits received. Thus sacrifices are offered," he states, "not only at certain set times, but also on any and all occasions which may call for them. For instance, sacrifices are offered to secure a happy journey, that the hunt may prove successful, that a patient may be cured, that a storm may abate, that a famine may come to an end, or in gratitude for a happy consummation of a journey, for a recovery from disease, or for a successful hunt. …Almost all sacrifices are made by the family or the individual. Only the sacrifice offered to the guardian of the settlement may be considered as a sacrifice for the inhabitants of the entire village."[31]

"The Koryak," Jochelson states further, "offer bloody sacrifices mainly to the Supreme Deity, to the sun, the 'masters,' the spirits of killed animals, to sacred rocks, in some cases to figures [images] of Kalak [their house guardians], and to the kalau [evil spirits], to turn them away…. Soon after the winter solstice, the official elder of [the village of] Kuel offered a dog sacrifice to the Sun."[32]

Now with the exception of the last, all of these sacrifices are of the type that we have termed "transactional," in the sense of *do ut des*, "I give in order that thou mayest give," or *do ut facias*, "I give in order that thou shouldst do" (see II.1:72). Only in the sacrifice offered to the guardian of the settlement for the inhabitants of the entire village, or to the Sun, soon after the winter solstice, do we recognize anything of the spirit of the cycle of annual ceremonials that Morgan has described of the Iroquois. But these too, it might be argued, are transactional inasmuch as they are addressed to the favor of a supernatural power on whose goodwill the well-being of the community is supposed to hang. There is, however, a difference. For the goodwill of the Great Spirit—whose name here, according to Morgan, is *Hä-wen-né-yu*—is to be obtained, not by offering a dog, but by the cultivation of a sentiment of gratitude for the boons of life, which it is the function of the whole ceremonial cycle to foster, and of which the dog, then, is the token. Let us review the whole course of this "jubilee," as Morgan calls it, first as a typical and fine example of a communal, planting-culture ceremonial, and incidentally as a demonstration of what may be properly termed a religious, in contrast to a magical, sacrifice.

The Sacrifice of the White Dog

The name given to this festival literally signifies "The most excellent faith," or "The supreme belief."

In mid-winter, usually about the first of February, this religious celebration was held. It continued for seven successive days, revealing, in its various ceremonials, nearly every feature of their religious system. The prominent act which characterized this jubilee, and which, perhaps, indicated what they understood by "The most excellent faith," was the burning of the White Dog, on the fifth day of the festival. This animal sacrifice of the Iroquois has long been known, attracting at various times considerable attention. But the true principle involved in it appears not to have been rightly understood. In the sequel, it will be found to be a very simple and tangible idea, harmonizing fully with their system of faith and worship.

Several days before the time appointed for the jubilee, the people assembled for the confession of their sins. On this occasion they were more thorough in the work than at any other season, that they might enter upon the new year with a firm purpose of amendment. This council not unfrequently lasted three days, before all the people had performed this act of religious duty.

The observances of the new year were commenced on the day appointed, by two of the keepers of the faith, who visited every house in and about the Indian village, morning and evening. [These "keepers of the faith" (Ho-nun-dé-unt), were officers regularly appointed to officiate at festivals and take the general supervision of religious affairs.][33] They were disguised in bear skins or buffalo robes, which were secured around their heads with wreaths of corn-husks, and then gathered in loose folds about the body. Wreaths of corn-husks were also adjusted around their arms and ankles. They were robed in this manner, and painted by the matrons, who, like themselves, were keepers of the faith, and by them they were commissioned to go forth in this formidable attire, to announce the commencement of the jubilee. Taking corn-pounders in their hands, they went out in company, on the morning of the day, to perform their duty. Upon entering a house, they saluted the inmates in a formal manner, after which, one of them, striking upon the floor, to restore silence and secure attention, thus addressed them: —

"Listen, Listen, Listen: — The ceremonies which the Great Spirit has commanded us to perform, are about to commence. Prepare your houses. Clear away the rubbish. Drive out all evil animals. We wish nothing to hinder or obstruct the coming observances. We enjoin upon every one to obey our requirements. Should any of your friends be taken sick and die, we command you not to mourn for them, nor allow any of your friends to mourn. But lay the body aside, and enjoy the coming ceremonies with us. When they are over, we will mourn with you."

229. *White Dog Dream* (1985), 22" × 30", egg tempera and acrylic on handmade paper with ribbon work attached. The work of Seneca artist G. Peter Jemison, member of the Heron Clan, treats "...the stories and legends of the Iroquois people of which I am a part."[1]

After singing a short thanksgiving song, they passed out.

In the afternoon this visit was repeated in the same manner. After saluting the family as before, one of the keepers of the faith thus addressed them:

"My Nephews, my Nephews, my Nephews:—We now announce to you that the New Year's ceremonies have commenced, according to our ancient custom. You are, each of you, now required to go forth, and participate in their observance. This is the will of the Great Spirit. Your first duty will be to prepare your wooden blades (*Gä-ger-we-sä*) with which to stir up the ashes upon your neighbors' hearths. Then return to the Great Spirit your individual thanks for the return of this season, and for the enjoyment of this privilege."

Having sung another song, appropriate to the occasion, they departed finally, and when they had made the circuit of the village, the ceremonies of the first day were concluded.

On the first day, however, the White Dog was strangled. They selected a dog, free from physical blemish, and of a pure white, if such a one could be found. The white deer, white squirrel, and other chance animals of the albino kind, were regarded as consecrated to the Great Spirit. White was the Iroquois emblem of purity and of faith. In strangling the dog, they were careful neither to shed his blood nor break his bones. The dog was then spotted, in places, over his body and limbs, with red paint, and ornamented with feathers in various ways. Around his neck was hung a string of white wampum, the pledge of their sincerity. In modern times, the dog is ornamented with a profusion of many-colored ribbons, which are adjusted around his body and limbs. The ornaments placed upon the dog were the voluntary offerings of the pious; and

for each gift thus bestowed, the giver was taught to expect a blessing. When the dog had been thus decorated, it was suspended by the neck about eight feet from the ground, on the branching prong of a pole erected for that purpose. Here it hung, night and day, until the morning of the fifth day, when it was taken down to be burned. Oftentimes two dogs were burned, one for each four of the tribes. [The reference here is to the division of each nation (Seneca, Cayuga, etc.) into two phratries of four clans each. Morgan here uses the term "tribe" for "clan."][34] In which case, the people separated into two divisions, and after going through separate preparatory ceremonies, united around the same altar for the burning of the dogs, and the offering of the thanksgiving address to the Great Spirit.

On the second day all the people went forth and visited in turn the houses of their neighbors, either in the morning, at noon, or in the evening. They went in small parties apparelled in their best attire. It was customary, however, for the people to be preceded by the two keepers of the faith who made the recitations the day previous, as a matter of etiquette; the houses not being open to all, until these personages had made their call. At this time was performed the ceremony of stirring the ashes upon the hearth, which appears to have no particular idea attached to it, beyond that of a formal visitation. Putting aside the disguise of the day before, the keepers of the faith assumed the costumes of warriors, plumed and painted, in which attire they visited every family three times, in the morning, at noon, and in the evening. Taking in their hands wooden blades or shovels, they entered the lodge and saluted the family. One of them then stirred the ashes, and having taken up a quantity upon the blade of a shovel, and sprinkled them upon the hearth, he thus addressed the inmates as they were in the act of falling: "I thank the Great Spirit that he has spared your lives again to witness this New Year's celebration." Then repeating the process with another shovel full of ashes, he con-

tinued: "I thank the Great Spirit that he has spared my life, again to be an actor in this ceremony. And now I do this to please the Great Spirit." The two then united in a thanksgiving song prepared for the occasion, upon the conclusion of which they took their departure. Other parties of the people then came in successively, and each went through the same performances. In this manner every house was thrice visited on the second day, by the keepers of the faith in the first instance, and afterwards by the whole community.

The proceedings upon the third and fourth days were alike. Small dancing parties were organized, which visited from house to house, and danced at the domestic fireside. Each set selected a different dance, appointed their own leader, and furnished their own music. One party, for instance, took the Feather dance, another the Fish dance, another the Trotting dance, to give variety to the short entertainments which succeeded each other at every house. It was not uncommon, on such occasions, to see a party of juveniles, about a dozen in number, dressed in full costume, feathered and painted, dancing the War dance, from house to house, with all the zeal and enthusiasm which this dance was so eminently calculated to excite. In this manner every house was made a scene of gaiety and amusement, for none was so humble or so retired as to remain unvisited.

Another pastime incident to these days was the formation of a "thieving party," as it was called, a band of mischievous boys, disguised with false faces, paint and rags, to collect materials for a feast. This vagrant company strolled from house to house, accompanied by an old woman carrying a huge basket. If the family received them kindly, and made them presents, they handed the latter to the female carrier, and having given the family a dance in acknowledgement of the present, they retired without committing any depredations. But if no presents were made, or such as were insufficient, they purloined whatever articles they could most adroitly and easily conceal. If detected, they at once made restitution, but if not, it was considered a fair win. On the return of this party from their rounds, all the articles collected were deposited in a place open to public examination; where any one who had lost an article which he particularly prized, was allowed to redeem it, on paying an equivalent. But no one was permitted to reclaim, as the owner, any article successfully taken by this thieving party on its professional round. Upon the proceeds of this forced collection, a feast was eventually given, together with a dance in some private family.

Guessing dreams was another of the novel practices of the Iroquois, which distinguished these festive days. It is difficult to understand precisely how far the self-delusion under which the dreamer appeared to act was real. A person with a melancholy and dejected countenance entering a house, announced that he had a dream, and requested the inmates to guess it. He thus wandered from house to house, until he found a solution which suited him. This was either received as an interpretation of an actual dream, or suggested such a dream as the person was willing to adopt as his own. He at once avowed that his dream had been correctly guessed; and if the dream as interpreted, prescribed any future conduct, he fulfilled it to the letter at whatever sacrifice. The celebrated Cornplanter, *Gy-ant-wä-ka*, resigned his chiefship [about the year 1810] in consequence of a dream. In relation to dreams, the Iroquois had ever been prone to extravagant and supernatural beliefs. They often regarded a dream as a divine monition, and followed its injunctions to the utmost extremity. Their notions upon this subject recall to remembrance the conceit of Homer, that "dreams descend from Jove."

During the first four days the people were without a feast, from the fact that the observances themselves did not require the assembling of the people at the council-house. But entertainments were given in the evenings at private houses, where the night was devoted to the dance. Another amusement at this particular season was the Snow-snake game [slithering over the snow a "snake" of polished hickory, 5 to 7 feet long, to distances sometimes up to a quarter of a mile, and to heavy betting], which, like all Indian games, was wont to arouse considerable interest.

On the morning of the fifth day, soon after dawn, the White Dog was burned on an altar of wood erected by the keepers of the faith near the council-house. It is difficult, from outward observation, to draw forth the true intent with which the dog was burned. The obscurity with which the object was veiled has led to various conjectures. Among other things, it has been pronounced a sacrifice for sin. In the religious system of the Iroquois, there is no recognition of the doctrine of atonement for sin, or of the absolution or forgiveness of sins. Upon this whole subject, their system is silent. An act once done was registered beyond the power of change. The greatest advance upon this point of faith was the belief that good deeds cancelled the evil, thus placing heaven, through good works, within the reach of all. The notion that this was an expiation for sin is thus refuted by their system of theology itself. The other idea, that the sins of the people, by some mystic process, were transferred to the dog, and by him thus borne away, on the principle of the scapegoat of the Hebrews, is also without any foundation in truth. The burning of the dog had not the slightest connection with the sins of the people. On the contrary, the simple idea of the sacrifice was, to send up the spirit of the dog as a messenger to the Great Spirit, to announce their continued fidelity to his service, and also to convey to him their united thanks for the blessings of the year. The fidelity of the dog, the companion of the Indian, as a hunter, was emblematical of their fidelity. No messenger so trusty could be found to bear their petitions to the Master of life. The Iroquois believed that the Great Spirit made a covenant with their fathers to the effect, that when they should send up to him the spirit of a dog, of a spotless white, he would receive it as the pledge of their adherence to his worship, and his ears would thus be opened in a special manner to their petitions. To approach *Hä-wen-né-yu* in the most acceptable manner, and to gain attention to their thanksgiving acknowledgments and supplications in the way of his own appointing, was the end and object of burning the dog. They hung around his neck a string of white wampum, the pledge of their faith.

They believed that the spirit of the dog hovered around the body until it was committed to the flames, when it ascended into the presence of the Great Spirit, itself the acknowledged evidence of their fidelity, and bearing also to him the united thanks and supplications of the people. This sacrifice was the most solemn and impressive manner of drawing near to the Great Spirit known to the Iroquois. They used the spirit of the dog in precisely the same manner that they did the incense of tobacco, as an instrumentality through which to commune with their Maker. The sacrifice was their highest act of piety.

The burning of the dog was attended with many ceremonies. It was first taken down and laid out upon a bench in the council-house, while the fire of the altar was kindling. A speech was then made over it by one of the keepers of the faith, in which he spoke of the antiquity of this institution of their fathers, of its importance and solemnity, and finally enjoined upon them all to direct their thoughts to the Great Spirit, and unite with the keepers of the faith in these observances. He concluded with thanking the Great Spirit, that the lives of so many of them had been spared through another year. A chant or song, appropriate to the occasion, was then sung, the people joining in chorus. By the time this was over, the altar was blazing up on every side ready for the offering. A procession was then formed, the officiating keeper of the faith preceding, followed by four others bearing the dog upon a kind of bark litter, behind which came the people in Indian file. A loud exclamation, in the nature of a war-whoop, announced the starting of the procession. They moved on towards the altar, and having marched around it, the keepers of the faith halted, facing the rising sun. With some immaterial ceremonies, the dog was laid upon the burning altar, and as the flames surrounded the offering, the officiating keeper of the faith, by a species of ejaculation, upon a high key, thrice repeated, invoked the attention of the Great Spirit: "*Quä, quä, quä!* Hail, hail, hail...."

And there follows the delivery of a lengthy traditional prayer of thanks addressed to the informing spirit of the universe, which in the inflated theological prose of Morgan's translation produces such an effect of Protestant godliness that I cannot bring myself to reproduce it on these pages. Morgan names the prayer, the great thanksgiving address of the Iroquois. It was delivered, the year of his attendance at an annual ceremony held at Tonawanda, N.Y. (some ten miles north of Buffalo), by an old Seneca keeper of the faith, *Sose-há-wä*, whose role it had been for twenty-five years to speak it forth in precisely the same words, which were recorded about 1840 by his grandson, Ely S. Parker (*Hä-sa-no-an'-dä*).

And as the words poured forth, the old man repeatedly tossed leaves of tobacco onto the fire in which the dog was being burned, so that their incense should ascend throughout the address to the Lord on High.

"Hail, hail, hail!" *Sose-há-wä* called, and after imploring *Hä-wen-né-yu* to give ear to the ascending prayer of the people there assembled, the old spokesman of the once great Seneca nation [now a reduced tribe dwelling on a reservation a few miles from Niagara Falls], first, briefly prayed for protection from loss of the ancient faith and its ceremonies which in the past had been maintained by the tribe's warriors and mothers; after which, with great formality, he proceeded to a detailed enumeration of the blessings for which the Iroquois gave thanks. These were, first, that the sacred ceremonies had been maintained to the present hour, and that the lives of so many had been preserved to participate in the exercises of this occasion. Thanks then were given for and to "our mother, the earth," who had so plentifully yielded her fruits—to which a grateful prayer was added that in the season coming her fullness should not be withheld. Thanksgiving was expressed for the rivers and streams that run their courses upon the bosom of the earth; for the herbs and plants of the earth that preserve health and cure disease; for "Our Supporters," those "Three Sisters," spirits of the maize, the beans, and the squash, who had been the chief sustainers of life; for the bushes and the trees that provide fruits; and for winds, which, moving, banish disease. A prayer next was addressed to "our grandfather, the Thunderer," *Hé-no*, who provides happiness and comfort in wisely ordering rains to descend, giving water and causing plants to grow; thanks, further, for the moon and stars, which give light when the sun has set; and for the sun itself, who with a beneficent eye surveys the earth, regulating its seasons. "May we be given the wisdom," *Sose-há-wä* prayed, "which guides in the path of truth, that the sun may never hide its face from us in shame." And then, finally, thanks were given to the *Ho-no-che-nó-keh*, those invisible spiritual powers that have been provided for man's happiness and well being, and at last, "to thee, O *Hä-wen-né-yu*, in whom are embodied all things! Be kind to us, as thou hast been to our fathers in times long gone by. Harken to our words as they ascend, and may they be pleasing to thee, our Creator, Preserver, and Ruler of all things both visible and invisible. *Na-hó!*"

Following this address the people, leaving the partly consumed offering [of the dog], returned to the council-house, where the Feather dance was performed. With this the religious exercises of the day were concluded. Other dances, however, followed, for the entertainment of the people, and the day and evening were given up to this amusement. Last of all came the feast, with which the proceedings of the day were terminated.

On the morning of the sixth day, the people again assembled at the place of council. This day was observed in about the same manner as one of their ordinary religious days, at which the Thanksgiving dance was introduced.

The seventh and last day was commenced with the *Ah-dó-weh*—a thanksgiving council, opened by an introductory speech by one of the keepers of the faith, after which followed a succession of short speeches made by different persons, returning thanks to a great variety of objects, each concluding with an appropriate song, the words and music of which were of his own composing.

Ely S. Parker (1828-1895), who provided Morgan with the transcription of his grandfather *Sose-há-wä's* thanksgiving oration on this occasion, was a full-blood Seneca of the Wolf clan, a grand-nephew of that eloquent Red Jacket who, together with the Mohawk leader, Joseph Brant, had been largely responsible for bringing the Mohawk, Cayuga, Seneca, and Onondaga tribes onto the British side of the Revolution. (The Oneida and Tuscarora fought for the Colonials.) Serving under Ulysses S. Grant in the Civil War, Parker himself rose to the rank of Brigadier-General United States Army, and becoming General Grant's chief secretary (partly because of the elegance of his handwriting), it was he who actually penned, from Grant's dictation, the document of the articles of Robert E. Lee's surrender. Moreover, he was present at the meeting of Grant and Lee at Appomattox Court House on April 9, 1865, and it was to him, then, as Grant's secretary, that Robert E. Lee's acceptance was delivered.

Lewis Henry Morgan (1818-1881), by profession an attorney, became interested in the Senecas, first, as their advocate in an ugly legal dispute with something that called itself the Ogden Land Company which in 1838 all but succeeded (with approval of the U.S. Senate) in buying the shattered tribe out of its Tonawanda reservation at $1.67 an acre, one-tenth of what the land at that time was worth. As a young man already scientifically interested in aboriginal cultures, Morgan then became dedicated to a career, not only of study of the Iroquois, but also of championing the

230. Mohawk Chief Joseph Brant (*Thayendanegea*), oil painting, c. 24″ × 18″, by Wilhelm von Berczy (1744–1813). During the American revolution, the Great League was divided and destroyed by Brant's insistence on an Iroquois-British allegiance. To fuel the colonists' patriotic fervor, the popular press both vilified Brant and greatly magnified his bloody exploits.

231. Ulysses S. Grant and Robert E. Lee meet in the parlor of Wilmer McLean's home at Appomattox Court House, Virginia, to end the American Civil War. Oil painting by Louis Didier Guillaume (1816–1892). Behind Grant stands his chief secretary, a full-blood Seneca of the Wolf Clan, Ely S. Parker, to whom Lee delivered the Confederacy's acceptance of surrender.

Acts of kindness, personal achievements, political events, in a word, all the affairs of public and private life were open on this occasion to the indulgence of the grateful affections. Oftentimes one or two hours were consumed, before the people had all expressed their thanks to each other for personal favors, to the works of nature for their constant ministration to their wants, and to the Great Spirit and the ''Invisible Aids'' (the *Ho-no-che-nó-keh*) for their protecting care''.[35]

After this the Peach-stone game was introduced [a betting game of six peach stones tossed in a bowl], with the termination of which the New Year's jubilee ended.[36]

* * *

Red Man generally against white exploitation and defamation.

In 1847 Morgan was adopted into the Hawk clan of the Seneca tribe as *Sose-há-wä's* "son," receiving the name *Tä-yä-dä-o-wuh-kuh*, "one lying across," which is to say, as a bridge or bond between the white man and the Indians. In 1851 his *League of the Iroquois* appeared and was recognized as "the first scientific account of an Indian tribe ever given to the world."[37] His description there of the Iroquoian kinship system was, in fact, the first notice ever published of what is now known to ethnology as a classificatory system of relationships, wherein terms analogous to "father," "mother," "daughter," and "son" denote relationships, not of blood, but of clan and generation.

Upon learning that the Sioux and Ojibwa also denoted kinship in this way, Morgan next became inspired to some twenty years of worldwide researches, which yielded in 1871 a large quarto volume entitled *Systems of Consanguinity and Affinity of the Human Family*, published by the Smithsonian Institution, in which evidence was presented of the same system, not only throughout North and South America, but also as having once prevailed in India, Persia, Greece and Rome, as well as among the Celts, Germans, Slavs, Hebrews, and Arabs. Extrapolating still further from these findings, he next published, in 1877, a work, *Ancient Society, or Researches in the Lines of Human Progress from Savagery through Barbarism to Civilization*, in which a vast hypothesis of cultural evolution was proposed that has been generally rejected by critical scholars, but appealed to Friedrich Engels and Karl Marx and thus became, ironically, a Marxist scripture.

In evaluating and interpreting his account of the Seneca ceremonials that both he and Parker observed and recorded in the early 1840s, there are to be borne in mind three obvious considerations. The first, of course, is of the completely shattered, secondarily reconstructed condition of the society under observation 60-odd years after the devastating punitive job of 1779. A people that hardly more than a generation before had been supreme from the Hudson River to the Genessee and from Niagara to Pennsylvania, had just now barely escaped expulsion from a Government reservation of 7,547 acres, north of Buffalo. Consideration number two must be of Morgan's earnest wish to demonstrate to a cruelly disdainful American public the eligibility of the Indian for civilized respect. And thirdly, there is the consideration of Morgan's own Christianity, his explicit belief in biblical revelation as the supreme exposition of divinity, which so prejudiced his understanding that wherever he detected what he took to be a sign of incipient

monotheism he seized upon this, in all honesty, as evidence of the approximation of Indian worship to the highest truth.

"By the standard of Christian judgment," he states, for example, at the close of his account of his adoptive father *Sose-há-wä's* address to the Great Spirit, "it must be confessed that the Faith and Worship of the Iroquois make up a system which, in its approaches to the truth, rises infinitely above the theological schemes of all other races, both ancient and modern, which originated independently of revelation. Having a firm hold upon the great truths of natural religion, they established a ceremonious but simple worship. Unlike the bloody ritual of the Aztecs, its influence upon the mind, and upon the social life of the Indian, was mild, humanizing and gentle. The fruits of their religious sentiments, among themselves, were peace, brotherly kindness, charity, hospitality, integrity, truth and friendship; and towards the Great Spirit, reverence, thankfulness and faith. More wise than the Greeks and Romans in this particular, they concentrated all divinity into one Supreme Being; more confiding in the people than the priestly class of Egypt, their religious teachers brought down the knowledge of the 'Unutterable One' to the minds of all. Eminently pure and spiritual, and internally consistent with each other, the beliefs and the religious ceremonies of the Iroquois are worthy of a respectful consideration. A people of the wilderness, shut out from revelation, with no tablet on which to write the history of passing generations, save the heart of man, yet possessed of the knowledge of one Supreme Being, and striving, with all the ardor of devotion, to commune with him in the language of thankfulness and supplication, is, to say the least, a most extraordinary spectacle; not less sublime in itself than the spectacle of the persecuted Puritan, on the confines of the same wilderness, worshipping that God in the fullness of light and knowledge, whom the Indian, however limited and imperfect his conceptions, in the Great Spirit most distinctly discerned."[38]

*　　*　　*

To appreciate the difference between the rites and spirit of a people, broken, shamed, and put together again in the disposition of a Puritan decorum, and that of their earlier estate, one has only to look back two centuries, to an account in the *Jesuit Relation of 1655-56*,[39] of what Fathers Dablon and Chaumonot experienced at Onondaga of the "trick or treat" and "dream guessing" games of this same Iroquois Jubilee described by Morgan. Wrote the Catholic Fathers:

They not only believe in their dreams, but they have a special festival for the Demon of Dreams. This festival might be called the Festival of Fools, or the Carnival of Wicked Christians; for in it the Devil does as it were the same things that are done in the carnival and at the same season. They name this festival Honnonouaroia. The elders go to proclaim it through the streets of the town. We witnessed the ceremony on the 22nd of February of this year 1656. As soon as this festival was announced by these public cries, nothing was to be seen but men, women and children running like madmen through the streets and through the cabins, but in quite a different fashion from European masqueraders. Most of them are nearly naked and seem not to feel the cold, which is almost unbearable to those who are best covered. It is true that some give no other sign of their madness than to run half naked through all the cabins; but others are mischievous; some carry water or something worse and throw it upon those they meet; others take firebrands, coals and ashes and scatter them about without caring on whom they fall. Others break the kettles and dishes and all the houseware that they find in their course. Some go armed with swords, bayonets, knives, hatchets, or cudgels, and pretend to strike with those every one they meet, and all this continues until their dream is guessed and fulfilled; as to which there are two things quite remarkable.

The first is that it sometimes happens that one is not clever enough to divine their thoughts, for they do not state them clearly, but by enigmas, by phrases of hidden meaning, by signs and sometimes by gestures alone; so that good Oedipuses are not always found. Nevertheless they will not leave the spot until their thought is divined, and if one delays too long, if one does not wish to divine it, or if one cannot, they threaten to burn up everything; which comes to pass only too often as we came near experiencing to our cost.

One of these idiots darted into our cabin and insisted that we should guess his dream and fulfill it. Now we had declared at the outset that we would not obey these imaginings, yet he persisted for a long time to shout and storm and rave, but in our absence, for we withdrew to a cabin outside the village to avoid these disturbances. One of our hosts, tired of these shouts, came to him to learn what he wanted. The maniac answered, "I kill a Frenchman, that is my dream which must be fulfilled at any cost." Our host threw him a French coat, as if it had been taken from a dead man, and at the same time began himself to rage, saying that he wished to avenge the death of the Frenchman, that his destruction should be followed by that of the whole village, which he was going to reduce to ashes, beginning with his own cabin. Thereupon he drove out his relatives and friends and housepeople and all the crowd which had gathered to see the issue of this disturbance. Thus left alone, he shut the doors and set the whole place on fire. At the moment when everybody expected to see the whole house in flames, Father Chaumonot came up, returning from an errand of charity. He saw an awful smoke pouring from his bark house and being told what it was he burst in the door, threw himself into the midst of the fire and smoke, threw out the firebrands, put out the fire, and gently prevailed upon his host to leave, contrary to the expectation of all the populace, who never resist the fury of the Demon on Dreams.

The man continued in his fury. He ran through the streets and cabins, shouting loudly that he was going to set everything on fire to avenge the death of the Frenchman. They brought him a dog to be the victim of his wrath and of the Demon of his passion. "That is not enough," he said, "to wipe out the shame and the affront which has been done to me in wishing to kill a Frenchman lodging in my house." A second dog was brought to him, and he was appeased at once and returned him as quietly as if nothing had happened.

Please observe, in this connection, that as in their wars one who has taken a prisoner often takes only his plunder and not his life, in the same way he who had dreamed of killing someone often contents himself with his clothes without attacking his person. That is the reason that the Frenchman's coat was given to the dreamer.

Let us continue.

Our host wished to play his part as well as the others. He dressed himself like a Satyr, covering himself with corn husks from head to foot. He made two women array themselves like real Megaras, their hair flying, their faces black as coal, their bodies covered with two wolfskins, each woman carrying a club or a great stake. The Satyr seeing them well equipped marched through our cabin singing and howling at the top of his voice. Then climbing on the roof, he performed a thousand antics, shouting as if everything had gone to destruction, which done, he descended, marched gravely all around the town, the two Megaras leading on and smashing everything they met with their stakes. If it is true that every man has a grain of folly—since *Stultorum infinitus est numerus*—it must be confessed that these people have more than half an ounce apiece. But there is more to come.

Scarce had our Satyr and our Megaras disappeared from view when a woman rushed into our cabin. She was armed with an arquebus which she had obtained by her dream [a portable but heavy matchlock gun invented in the 15th century, fired from a support to which it was attached by a fixed hook]. She shouted, howled, sang, saying that she was going off to the war with the Eries, that she would fight them and bring back prisoners, with a thousand imprecations and a thousand maledictions if the thing did not come to pass as she had dreamed. A warrior followed this amazon. He carried his bow and arrows in his hand and a dagger. He dances, he sings, he shouts, he threatens: then suddenly he rushes at a woman who had come in to see this comedy; he levels the dagger at her throat, takes her by the hair, contents himself with cutting off a few locks, and then withdraws to give place to a Diviner who had dreamed that he could find everything that was hidden. He was ridiculously dressed and held in his hand a sort of caduceus [wand of Hermes] which he used to point out the place where a thing was hidden. Nevertheless his companion who carried a pot filled with some liquor or other had to fill his mouth with it and blow it over the head and over the face, over the hands and over the caduceus of the Diviner, who then

232. Cayuga miniature dream-guessing mask used during the Iroquois Midwinter Festival (see pp. 134–135, 137–138). Grand River Reservation, Ontario, Canada.

never failed to find the article in question. That is all I can tell.

A woman came next with a mat which she spread out and arranged as if she wished to catch some fish. This meant that we must give her some because she had dreamed it.

Another simply laid a mattock on the ground. They divined that she wanted a field or a piece of ground. That was just what she had in mind, and she was satisfied with five furrows for planting Indian corn.

After that they put before us a little grotesque puppet. We declined it and it was placed before other persons, and after they had mumbled some words they carried it off without further ceremony.

One of the chiefs of the town appeared in wretched attire. He was all covered with ashes, and because no one guessed his dream, which called for two human hearts, he caused the ceremony to be prolonged by a day, and con-

tinued his mad actions during all the time. He entered our cabin, where there are several fireplaces, stopped at the first, threw ashes and coals into the air, and at the second and third fires did the same, but did nothing to ours, out of respect.

Some came fully armed and as if they were in combat with the enemy, posturing, shouting and scuffling like two armies in battle.

Others march in bands, and perform dances with contortions of the body like men possessed. In short, one would never be done who undertook to relate everything they do during the three days and three nights that this madness lasts, with such a racket that one cannot find a moment of quiet. Yet this did not prevent us from conducting the regular prayers in our chapel, nor God from making evident his love for these poor people by some miraculous cures granted by virtue of holy baptism, of which we will not speak here. Let us finish the account we have begun of the obedience which they give to their imaginings.

It would be a cruelty and sort of murder not to give a man what his dream called for, for the refusal might cause his death. Therefore they may see themselves stripped of their all without any hope of recompense. For whatever they give is never returned to them, unless they dream it themselves, or pretend to dream it. In general they are too scrupulous to make such a pretence, which would, as they suppose, cause all sorts of misfortunes. Yet those are found who disregard their scruples and enrich themselves by a clever fiction.

The Satyr, of whom we have spoken, seeing that a great deal was taken from his cabin on our account because great and small dreamed of the French and we would not listen to them, while he because he liked us satisfied them, yet at length wishing to repay himself, put on the attire we have described, and counterfeited not only the Satyr, but also the phantom which he pretended had appeared to him by night and commanded him to get together forty beaver skins. This he did in this way. He set himself to shout through the streets that he was no more a man but had become a brute beast. Thereupon the elders held a council for the restoration of one of their chiefs to his natural form. This was accomplished as soon as he had received what he desired and pretended to have dreamed of.

A poor woman was not so fortunate in her dreams. She ran about day and night and got only an illness. They tried to cure her with the ordinary remedies of the country, which are emetics of certain roots steeped in water, but they made her drink so much that she died immediately, her stomach bursting to give passage to two kettles of water which they had made her take.

A young man of our cabin got off with being well powdered. He dreamed that he was buried in ashes. When he woke he wished his dream to come true, so he invited ten of his friends to a feast to fulfill his dream. They acquitted themselves excellently of this commission, covering him with ashes from head to foot and stuffing them into his nose and into his ears and everywhere. We were disgusted with such a ridiculous ceremony, but everyone else regarded it in silent admiration as a grand mystery. Do not these poor people deserve compassion?

Sun God and Great Spirit

"A people in the wilderness, shut out from revelation…yet possessed of the knowledge of the one Supreme Being," states Morgan above "…not less sublime in itself than the spectacle of the persecuted Puritan, on the confines of the same wilderness, worshipping that God in the fullness of light and knowledge, whom the Indian, however limited and imperfect his conceptions, in the Great Spirit most distinctly discerned."[40]

There is, however, a large question at issue here, which is, namely, of the interpretation, translation, and appropriate appreciation by an occidental believer of any religious term or concept whatsoever from without the pale of the biblical revelation. The question has nothing to do with anything of "Truth," or of whose conceptions might be imperfect; but simply with semantics; recognition of the intended reference—whether in this usage or in that—of the word "god."

What the Puritan meant by the monosyllable (always with a capital G) is sufficiently shown in Morgan's paragraph. The reference, namely, is to that "one Supreme Being" who was perfectly made known, first to the Jews, then also to Christians, in Revelation; which is to say, in the Bible. And the key concept of that revelation is succinctly and unambiguously stated in II Kings 5:15: "I know that there is no God in all the earth but in Israel." Divinity, according to this view, is not to be recognized in any gentile piece of earth, in the rivers and streams that run their courses upon the earth's bosom, the herbs that preserve health and cure disease, in thunder that sends rain, in the moon, the stars, or the sun. These may be said to make known the power and the glory of their Creator, but they are not in themselves "divine." For the announcement of this revelation divinity was withdrawn from the earth and concentrated in that "one Supreme Being" who is either eternally somewhere else ("Our Father, who art in heaven": Matthew 6:9), or historically only in Israel (II Kings 5:15), and on second thought, now also in the Church (Matthew 16:18–19). Only in such early-rejected texts as the Gnostic "Gospel according to Thomas" do we find anything like that ubiquitism of divinity which is of the essence of the so-called natural or animistic religions: as, for example, in Jesus' saying, there reported: "Cleave a piece of wood, I am there; lift up the stone and you will find Me there" (Logion 78) or "the Kingdom of the Father is spread upon the earth and men do not see it" (Logion 114).[41] The animists saw it, recognized, revered, and sought to live by and with it everywhere, and that—in short—was, and is, the virtue and whole sense of their thinking.

When translating such a religious text as that of Sosé-ha-wä's thanksgiving address to the Great Spirit, therefore, it makes a great deal of difference whether its words of gratitude be rendered as addressed *to* the earth or to the Great Spirit *for* the earth; *to* the maize or to the Great Spirit *for* the maize. In Morgan's rendition (which I have not directly quoted) the reading is *for:* which accords with his subsequent statement that the Iroquois "concentrated all divinity into one Supreme Being." But did they? Or rather, perhaps: Had they before the Jesuits arrived in the seventeenth century to instruct them in the sense of Revelation? We recall the ease with which the Jesuit Father Superior delivered his Gospel, not only to a young Iroquois brave about to be tortured to death, but also to his listening Huron captors! (See II.1:42) In short: Did the Iroquois think of the power that they are said to have addressed as *Hä-wen-né-yu* primarily as a person "out there," who made all these things, or primarily as a presence or power immanent within all, and thus made known through and within each?

"The beautiful and elevating conception of the Great Spirit watching over his red children from the heavens, and pleased with their good deeds, their prayers, and their sacrifices," wrote Herbert M. Lloyd, "has been known to the Indians only since the Gospel of Christ was preached to them. 'The primitive Indians,' says W. P. Clark, in his valuable book, *The Indian Sign Language,*[42] 'were limited pantheists—they did not believe that the universe taken as a whole was God; but that everything in the world had its spiritual essence made manifest in the forces and laws of nature.' Hence the regard of the Indian for the totem of his clan held much more of reverence than the feeling of a present-day Briton or American for the lion or the eagle. Not only was the clan totem reverenced, but each individual had his personal totem—[in Algonquin *manitou*, in Iroquois *aki*]. In youth after certain exercises and fastings he waited for a dream, and whatever he dreamed of became his manitou on which his fortune depended,—the Master of his Life, the Jesuits translated it. With one it might be a muskrat, with another a knife; and whatever the totemic object, it accompanied the Indian on his journeys and especially on the warpath. If the manitou were an animal, the skin, or the plumage of a bird, was taken as containing the spirit of the animal. It would seem that when the Senecas [during the Revolution] attacked [General Nicholas] Herkimer at Oriskany [a few miles northwest of Utica, N.Y.] they left in their camp their baggage containing many of these totemic objects. The capture of this baggage by Gansevoort was an even greater calamity than their defeat by Herkimer, and after that day they had no heart in the campaign. In all religions we have accounts of divine revelations in dreams and visions, but to

233. Iroquois Chiefs "read" a wampum belt (pictured fully below. Classically-inspired engraving from Joseph Lafitau's *Moeurs des Sauvages Amériquains* (1724).

the Indian every dream was a divine message, and to the Senecas especially none was too absurd to be obeyed.

"In addition to this limited pantheism the Iroquois recognized several personal deities. Ataentsic was the oldest of their deities, and dwelt with her grandson Jouskeha in a bark cabin in the land of souls. She has been connected with the Moon and he with the Sun. Areskoui, the God of War, is more evidently a Sun God. Most of the worship now given to the Great Spirit belongs historically to Areskoui. Tarengawagon was much reverenced, for he was the sender of dreams, and Hiawatha was an actual hero raised after his death to a place in the Iroquois Pantheon....

"Very far was all this from the pure theism which has been poetically ascribed, in the alleged belief in the Great Spirit.

"There was however one deity worshipped throughout North America, the all-seeing one, the dweller in Heaven, the giver of many blessings, the Sun. To him were paid prayer and sacrifice and thanks for such good gifts as food, sunshine, and victory over the enemy. When the missionaries told of the God of the white man and his attributes, the account seemed credible to the Indian, who accepted much of it as further history of his Sun God; and the sacrifices, thanksgivings, and offerings were still offered to the Great Spirit as in earlier days to the Sun. Though the preaching of Christianity made but slight direct impression upon the observances and actions of most of the Red Men, it did greatly affect their myths and beliefs, thus preparing the way for an ethical religion....Finally, what may be called the third period of Iroquis religion was inaugurated by the reforms of Handsome Lake [c. 1735–1815], who, preserving the old forms, associated them with the worship of a single supreme God and the doing of righteousness."[43]

Now, the sense of the terms "righteousness" and "ethical religion," which are of such common occurrence in the writings of occidental theologians, has, of course, nothing to do with the sense of any of the recorded historical acts, either of the one Supreme Being himself (as chronicled throughout the Old Testament) or of any of the historical peoples who have ever been motivated by his revelation (as, for example, the ethics of the Christian conquest and appropriation of the properties of native America). The terms "ethical" and "righteous" here refer, rather, to a mythological order derived historically from the Levant and first systematized in Zoroastrianism (see II.1:87), wherein temporal judgments, namely of "good" and "evil," are pictured as eternal, with a Supreme Being on the good side and an almost equally supreme Antagonist on the evil. The Roman Catholic version of this confusion was carried to northeastern

234. Lead medallion with serpent and cross, Onondaga, 1″ × ⅔″, c. 1682–1700.

North America in the seventeenth century by the Jesuits, and in the "New Religion" of which Handsome Lake was the inspired prophet, the imagery of the two Powers and their respective realms of heaven and hell was applied effectively to recall the Iroquois, following the disaster of 1779, from the vices introduced with civilization to the earlier way of virtue of their fathers.

"You know our practice," said a distinguished Onondaga chief, Canassatego, quoted by Morgan. "If a white man in travelling through our country, enters one of our cabins, we all treat him as I do you. We dry him if he is wet, we warm him if he is cold, and give him meat and drink that he may allay his hunger and thirst, and we spread soft furs for him to rest and sleep on. We demand nothing in return. But if I go into a white man's house at Albany, and ask for victuals and drink, they say, 'Where is your money?' And if I have none, they say, *'Get out, you Indian Dog.'*"[44] "They carried the principle of 'living in common' to its full extent," states Morgan. "Whatever was taken in the chase, or raised in the fields, or gathered in its natural state by any member of the united families, enured to the benefit of all, for their stores of every description were common.....A neighbor, or a stranger, calling from house to house, through an Indian village, would be thus entertained at every dwelling he entered;...and a relation was entitled to a home among any of his kindred, while he was disposed to claim it."[45]

The "ethical" religion introduced by Handsome Lake following the devastating punitive campaign of 1779 owed nothing, consequently, to the so-called ethics of the whites. His practical ethics were of Native America, though enforced now by a mythology of heaven and hell.

The Revelation to Handsome Lake

Handsome Lake (*Gä-ne-o-di-yo*) was the first of a series of Native American prophets who arose throughout the nineteenth century, desperately standing for the spiritual legacy of their vanishing race against both the civilization and the savagery of their economically motivated despoilers. A Seneca sachem of the highest class, he was born about 1735 in the Indian village of *Gä-no-waú-ges*, near present-day Avon, New York; half-brother by the same white father, but different Indian mothers, of the somewhat questionable war and political leader known as Cornplanter (*Gy-ant-wä-ka*), who during the Revolution fought for the British and subsequently participated in the negotiation of three treaties (1784, 1789, and 1794), ceding to the United States Government large tracts of Seneca land. Cornplanter (c. 1732–1836), known also as John O'Bail, was in 1810 displaced as leader of his people by the more aggressive Red Jacket, whereupon he retired on a U.S. pension to an estate awarded him by the Commonwealth of Pennsylvania, while his younger half-brother, Handsome Lake—who seems to have been of a brooding, indifferent temperament until inspired to his spiritual mission by a healing vision that had come to him during a very serious illness, about 1800—gave himself entirely to the preaching from village to village of his gospel.

According to his own report, as recounted by Lewis H. Morgan:

Having lain ill for a long period, he had surrendered all hope of recovery, and resigned himself to death, when in the hourly expectation of departure, three spiritual beings, in the forms of men sent by the Great Spirit, appeared before him. [In later visions they became four.] Each bore in his hand a shrub, bearing different kinds of berries, which, having been given him to eat, he was, by their miraculous power, immediately restored to health. After revealing to him the will of the Great Spirit upon a great variety of subjects, and particularly in relation to the prevailing intemperance [of his people, who were being destroyed by alcohol], having commissioned him to promulgate these doctrines among the Iroquois, they permitted him to visit under their guidance the realm of the Evil-minded, and to behold with his mortal eyes the punishments inflicted upon the wicked, that he might warn his brethren of their impending destiny. Like Ulysses and Aeneas, he was also favored with a glance at Elysium, and the felicities of the heavenly residence of the virtuous. With his mind thus stored with divine precepts and with his zeal enkindled by the dignity of his mission, *Gä-ne-o-dí-yo* at once commenced his labors.[46]

The sense of his teaching was of a desperate need for an immediate moral reform, a casting off the mantle of dissolute behavior adopted from the whites and a return, as far as still possible, to the orderly way of the People of the Longhouse before the shattering of their society. As recapitulated by *Sose-há-wä* in a discourse delivered at a mourning council of the Iroquois held at Tonawanda in October 1848, the first and most necessary appeal was to abstinence from intoxicants:

The Great Spirit looked down from heaven upon the sufferings and the wanderings of his red children. He saw that they had greatly decreased and degenerated. He saw the ravages of the fire-water. He therefore raised up for them a sacred instructor, who having lived and traveled among them for sixteen years,

235. Portrait of Seneca prophet Handsome Lake, from the print "The Trial of Red Jacket."

236. Red Jacket, in an 1828 portrait by C. B. King, wearing the medallion given him by George Washington.

237. Cornplanter, Handsome Lake's half-brother and Seneca chief, from a 1796 portrait by F. Bartoli.

was called from his labors to enjoy eternal felicity with the Great Spirit in heaven.[47]

Orderly marriage is enjoined, with care for the health and morals of the children, who, in turn, are to love, revere, and obey their parents; also called for are tenderness to orphans; reverence for the land, which is not a merchandise to be sold, but a heritage for generations; and festivals of thanksgiving for the bounty of the earth, to be celebrated seasonally, as of old — for all things are gifts of the one Great Spirit, who alone must be upheld as the giver.

Love each other [declared *Sose-há-wä*] for you are all brothers and sisters of the same great family. The Great Spirit enjoins upon all, to observe hospitality and kindness, especially to the needy and the helpless; for this is pleasing to him. If a stranger wanders about your abode, speak to him with kind words; be hospitable to him, welcome him to your home, and forget not always to mention the Great Spirit. In the morning, give thanks to the Great Spirit for the return of day and the light of the sun; at night renew your thanks to him, that his ruling power has preserved you from harm during the day, and that night has again come, in which you may rest your wearied bodies.[48]

The Messenger said further to Handsome Lake—tell your people, and particularly the keepers of the faith, to be strong-minded, and adhere to the true faith. We fear the Evil-

minded will go among them with temptations. He may introduce the *fiddle*. He may bring *cards* and leave them among you. The use of these are great sins. Let the people be on their guard, and the keepers of the faith be watchful and vigilant, that these evils may not find their way among the people....

It was the original intention of our Maker, that all our feasts of thanksgiving should be seasoned with the flesh of wild animals. But we are surrounded by the pale-faces, and in a short time the woods will be all removed. Then there will be no more game for the Indian to use in his feasts. The four Messengers said, in consequence of this, that we might use the flesh of domestic animals. This will not be wrong. The pale-faces are pressing you upon every side. You must therefore live as they do. How far you can do so without sin, I will now tell you. You may grow cattle, and build yourself warm and comfortable dwelling houses. This is not sin; and it is all that you can safely adopt of the customs of the pale-faces. You cannot live as they do. Thus they said.

Listen further to what the Great Spirit has been pleased to communicate to us: — He has made us as a race, separate and distinct from the pale-face. It is a great sin to intermarry, and intermingle the blood of the two races. Let none be guilty of this transgression.[49]

So much for the moral injunctions, which for all the Christianized talk of sin, the Evil-minded, and (instead of the Sun) the Great Spirit, were of virtues that had been formerly intrinsic to the culture;

whereas the vices, such as drink, playing cards, and the fiddle were of the way of life of the whites! The native gambling peach-stone game was not forbidden by Handsome Lake but even enjoined as a constituent of ceremonies of the fourth day of the annual Thanksgiving jubilee. For as Herbert Lloyd points out in his commentary to Morgan's chapter; the association of the Iroquois gambling games with their religious life was so close that when the French Jesuits became aware of it, they deliberately introduced European counterparts to break the religious connection.[50] Handsome Lake's intention was just the opposite; namely, to reclaim gam-

ing and gambling (to which many of the North American tribes were incurably addicted) from the secular, merely economic domain of personal achievement, realigning them with socially supportive, religiously associated ceremonials.

An especially interesting, even astonishing, aspect of the Handsome Lake revelation is to be seen in the likeness of this prophet's visions, not only to certain Zoroastrian and Christian visionary visits to hell and heaven, but also, in the following detailed account of the forked way of the soul's passage to the afterworld, to the forked way described in a cluster of Greek Orphic tablets from perhaps the fourth century B.C.[51]

At one time [declared *Sose-há-wä*] the four Messengers said to Handsome Lake, Lest the people should disbelieve you, and not repent and forsake their evil ways, we will now disclose to you the House of Torment, the dwelling-place of the Evil-minded. Handsome Lake was particular in describing to us all that he witnessed; and the course which departed spirits were accustomed to take on leaving the earth. There was a road which led upwards. At a certain point it branched; one branch led straight forward to the Home of the Great Spirit, and the other turned aside to the House of Torment. At the place where the roads separated were stationed two keepers, one representing the Good, and the other the Evil

238. *Handsome Lake Preaching His Code at the Tonawanda Longhouse*, 1936 watercolor, 15″ × 20″, by Ernest Smith.

Spirit. When a person reached the fork, if wicked, by a motion from the Evil keeper, he turned instinctively upon the road which led to the abode of the Evil-minded. But if virtuous and good, the other keeper directed him upon the straight road. The latter was not much travelled; while the former was so frequently trodden, that no grass could grow in the pathway. It sometimes happened that the keepers had great difficulty in deciding which path the person should take, when the good and bad actions of the individual were nearly balanced. Those sent to the House of Torment sometimes remain one day (which is there one of our years), some for a longer period. After they have atoned for their sins, they pass to heaven. But when they have committed either of the great sins (witchcraft, murder, and infanticide), they never pass to heaven, but are tormented forever.

Having been conducted to this place, Handsome Lake saw a large and dark-colored mansion covered with soot, and beside it stood a lesser one. One of the four then held out his rod, and the top of the house moved up, until they could look down upon all that was within. He saw many rooms. The first object which met his eye was a haggard-looking man; his sunken eyes cast upon the ground, and his form half consumed by the torments he had undergone. This man was a drunkard. The Evil-minded then appeared, and called him by name. As the man obeyed his call, he dipped from a cauldron a quantity of red-hot liquid, and commanded him to drink it, as it was an article he loved. The man did as he was directed, and immediately from his mouth issued a stream of blaze. He cried in vain for help. The Tormenter then requested him to sing and make himself merry, as was his wont while on earth, after drinking the fire-water. Let drunkards take warning from this.

Others were then summoned. There came before him two persons, who appeared to be husband and wife. He told them to exercise the privilege they were so fond of when on earth. They immediately commenced a quarrel of words. They raged at each other with such violence, that their tongues and eyes ran out so far they could neither see nor speak. This, said they, is the punishment of quarrelsome and disputing husbands and wives. Let such take warning, and live together in peace and harmony.

Next he called up a woman who had been a witch. First he plunged her into a cauldron of boiling liquid. In her cries of distress, she begged the Evil-minded to give her some cooler place. He then immersed her in one containing liquid at the point of freezing. Her cries then were that she was too cold. This woman, said the four Messengers, shall always be tormented in this manner.

He proceeded to mention the punishment which awaits all those who cruelly ill-treat their wives. The Evil-minded next called up a man who had been accustomed to beat his wife. Having led him up to a red-hot statue of a female, he directed him to do that which he was fond of while on earth. He obeyed, and struck the figure. The sparks flew in every direction, and by the contact his arm was consumed. Such is the punishment, they said, awaiting those who ill-treat their wives. From this take seasonable warning.

He looked again and saw a woman, whose arms and hands were nothing but bone. She had sold fire-water to the Indians, and the flesh was eaten from her hands and arms. This, they said, was the fate of rum-sellers.

Again he looked, and in one apartment he saw and recognized his former friend, *Ho-ne-yä-wus,* "Farmer's Brother." He was engaged in removing a heap of sand, grain by grain; and although he labored continually, yet the heap of sand was not diminished. This was the punishment of those who sold land.

Adjacent to the house of torment was a field of corn filled with weeds. He saw women in the act of cutting them down; but as fast as this was done, they grew up again. This, they said, was the punishment of lazy women....

Further warnings were announced, against thieving, inhospitality, neglect of the old, and excessive displays of mourning for the dead, after which the prophet Handsome Lake was conducted to heaven.

The four Messengers at another time declared to Handsome Lake that they would show him the "Destroyer of Villages" (*Ha-no-dä-gä-ne-ars:* George Washington), of whom we have so frequently heard. Upon the road leading to heaven he could see a light, far away in the distance, moving to and fro. Its brightness far exceeded the brilliancy of the noonday sun. They told him the journey was as follows: First, they came to a cold spring, which was a resting place. From this point they proceeded into pleasant fairy grounds, which spread away in every direction. Soon they reached heaven. The light was dazzling. Berries of every description grew in vast abundance. Their size and quality were such that a single berry was more than sufficient to appease the appetite. A sweet fragrance perfumed the air. Fruits of every kind met the eye. The inmates of this celestial abode spent their time in amusement and repose. No evil could enter there. None in heaven ever transgresses again. Families were reunited, and dwelt together in harmony. They possessed a bodily form, the senses, and the remembrances of the earthly life. But no white man ever entered heaven. Thus they said.

He looked, and saw an enclosure upon a plain, just without the entrance of heaven. Within it was a fort. Here he saw the "Destroyer of Villages," walking to and fro within the enclosure. His countenance indicated a great and good man. They said to Handsome Lake: The man you see is the only pale-face who ever left the earth. He was kind to you, when on the settlement of the great difficulty between the Americans and the Great Crown (*Go-wek-go-wä:* the British), you were abandoned to the mercy of your enemies. The Crown told the great American, that as for his [the Crown's] allies, the Indians, he might kill them if he liked. The great American judged that this would be cruel and unjust. He believed they were made by the Great Spirit, and were entitled to the enjoyment of life. He was kind to you, and extended over you his protection. For this reason, he has been allowed to leave the earth. But he is never permitted to go into the presence of the Great Spirit. Although alone, he is happy. All faithful Indians pass him by as they go to heaven. They see him, and recognize him, but pass on in silence. No word ever passes his lips.

Friends and Relatives: — It was by the influence of this great man, that we were spared as a people, and yet live. Had he not granted us this protection, where would we have been? Perished, all perished.

The four Messengers further said to Handsome Lake, they were fearful that, unless the people repented and obeyed his commands, the patience and forbearance of their Creator would be exhausted; that he would grow angry, and cause their increase to cease.

Our Creator made light and darkness. He made the sun to heat, and shine over the world. He made the moon, also, to shine by night, and to cool the world, if the sun made it too hot by day. The keeper of the clouds, by direction of the Great Spirit, will then cease to act. The keeper of the springs and running brooks will cease to rule them for the good of man. The sun will cease to fulfill his office. Total darkness will then cover the earth. A great smoke will rise, and spread over the face of the earth. Then will come out of it all the monsters, and poisonous animals created by the Evil-minded; and they, with the wicked upon the earth, will perish together.

But before this dreadful time shall come, the Great Spirit will take home to himself all the good and faithful. They will lay themselves down to sleep, and from this sleep of death, they will rise, and go home to their Creator. Thus the four Messengers said.

I now have done. I thus close, that you may remember and understand the fate which awaits the earth, and the unfaithful and unbelieving. Our Creator looks down upon us. The four Beings from above see us. They witness with pleasure this assemblage, and rejoice at the object for which it is gathered. It is now forty-eight years since we first began to listen to the renewed will of our Creator. I have been unable, during the time allotted to me, to rehearse all the sayings of *Gä-ne-o-dí-yo.* I regret very much that you cannot hear them all.

Counsellors, Warriors, Women and Children: — I have done. I thank you for your attendance, and for your kind and patient attention. May the Great Spirit, who rules all things, watch over and protect you from every harm and danger, while you travel the journey of life. May the Great Spirit bless you all, and bestow upon you life, health, peace and prosperity; and may you, in turn, appreciate the great goodness. *Na-hó.*[52]

The Woman Who Fell from the Sky

In the regions above there dwelt manlike beings who knew not what it is to see one weep, or what it is to see one die. Sorrow and death were unknown to them. And the lodges belonging to their matrilineal families were large and very long.

Now within one of these there were dwelling, at that time, a little brother and sister who, as they say, were "down-fended." [Confined, that is to say, to a place of strict seclusion sprinkled carefully about with cat-tail down, any disarrangement of which would betray an intrusive visit. Any child whose birth had been especially uncanny—as born with a caul or to some other sign of extraordinary *orenda*—was to be kept in this way until puberty, apart from all contact except of a chosen guardian. The custom was of old, and remained in observance among the Iroquois, apparently, almost to the present century.[53]]

The lodges of that region all faced the rising sun, extending toward its setting. And of the inhabitants it was the custom, after eating their morning meal, to go forth to their several duties. The abode of the down-fended sister was an added room on the south side of the lodge; that of her down-fended brother, an added room on the north side. And every morning, when all had gone forth, the sister habitually took advantage of the opportunity to come through her doorway, cross the large room and enter, on the opposite side, the down-fended abode of her brother. There, habitually, she dressed his hair, and when she had finished, it was her custom to cross back to her own abiding place. And it was in this manner that she daily devoted her attention to her brother, dressing and arranging his hair.

After a time it came to pass that she to whom this young female person belonged perceived that, indeed, it would seem that she was in delicate health; indeed, that one might think that she was about to give birth to a child. So that, after a time, they questioned her, inquiring: "To whom, of the male-beings dwelling within the precincts of this village, art thou about to deliver a child?" But she answered not a word. And so also, time and again, they questioned her repeatedly, but in response to their queries, she nothing replied.

Then arrived the day of her confinement, and she gave birth there to a child, a girl, yet persisted in the refusal to reveal its father.

Now during the days preceding that birth, the male-being responsible occasionally overheard his kinsfolk in conversation remark that his sister was about to bear a child; whereupon he began to spend his time in meditation on the circumstance, and presently became ill. Moreover, when the moment of his death arrived, his mother sat beside the bed, gazing at him in his illness. She knew not what this might be. She had never before seen anyone ill. For in truth, no one in that region where these manlike beings resided ever had died. And when his breathing, then, had nearly ended, he spoke to his mother, saying to her: "Very soon, now, I shall die." To which the mother responded: "What is this, thou sayest? What thing is about to occur?" And he answered: "My breathing will cease; my flesh become cold; the joints of my bones will stiffen. When my breathing stops, thou must close my eyes with thy hands. And thou wilt weep then moved to do so. All those, furthermore, who may be at that time in the lodge with their eyes fixed upon me as I die: they too, I say, will be in the same way moved. You will all weep, and your minds then will know grief."

His mother understood nothing of what was said, notwithstanding his explanation. Yet now he told her something more.

"When I am dead," he said, "you will make a burial case. You will use your best skill, and dress and adorn my body. You will then place my body in the burial case, close it up, and in the added room inside the lodge, well prepare a place for it, high up, toward the rising sun."

And so, in truth, when his breathing ceased, his mother, with her two hands, closed his eyes. And as soon as this was done, she wept, as did those others, also, who were looking on. Affected in the same way, they all wept, notwithstanding that never before had they ever known anyone either to die or to weep. And indeed, they made for him then a burial case, and there, within the lodge, in the added room, high up, prepared with care a place whereupon they set the burial case.

And the girl-child that had been born lived in the very best of health, and besides, grew rapidly in size. Moreover, she had now reached the size and age when she could run hither and thither, playing about. She now could talk, furthermore. And then suddenly those within the lodge were surprised that that girl-child began to weep, for never had it happened before to any of those there with children that these had had the custom of weeping. Her mother patted her, trying to divert her mind, doing many things to this purpose.

239. *Our Earth, Our Mother*, 1936 oil painting, 24" × 18", by famed Seneca artist Ernest Smith (Geo yaih, "From the Middle of the Sky"), who from 1935–41 produced over 240 paintings based on subjects from Iroquois mythology.

Others, also, sought to comfort her. Yet none of their efforts succeeded, until, finally, the girl-child's mother suggested: "We might try to pacify her by showing her the burial case up there, on high, in which the body rests of the man-being who died."

So then they carried the girl-child up there and uncovered the burial case. She looked upon the dead man-being and immediately stopped weeping. After a long while, they brought her down; for she no longer wept. And besides, her mind was again at ease.

So it stood for a very long while. But then again she began to weep. And her mother, this time, as soon as possible, brought her up to where the dead man-being lay, whereupon her weeping immediately ceased, and it was long before they brought her down therefrom. And now again she went tranquilly about from place to place, joyfully at play.

So now they made a ladder and set it up in such a way that whenever she wished to see the dead man-being, she might climb to him by herself. And indeed, whenever now she desired to see him, she went up to him alone.

In that way matters rested while she developed to maturity. Whenever she wished to see the person who had died, she habitually climbed up to him. Moreover, it often happened that when she would be up there sitting, where the burial case lay, those dwelling in the lodge would overhear her conversing, as though responding to something said; and besides, at times she would laugh.

So when the time of her maturity arrived and this girl-child had grown up, she again came down, as was her custom, from the place where the dead man-being lay, and said: "Mother, my father...." And when she had said, "my father," it was known for certain who her father was. "....father," she said, "has said to me: 'it is time for thee to marry. Far away,' he said, 'toward the sunrise he lives; it is he who is chief there of the people dwelling in that place; and he it is, in that place, who will be married to thee.' Moreover, my father said to me, further: 'Thou art to tell thy mother to fill for thee one burden basket with bread of sodden corn, putting forth her best skill in preparing it, mixing berries with that bread which thou art to carry on thy back, by a forehead strap, while going to where he to whom thou art now to be married dwells.'"

Then it was that her mother made a bread of maize softened by boiling, and she mixed with the corn bread berries. And when it was ready she placed the bread in a burden basket, which it filled to the very brim. And it was then, at that time, that the young woman-being said: "I think I shall go and report of this to my father." And she climbed again up to the place where the dead man-being lay.

Then those who were in the lodge heard her saying: "Father, my mother has finished the bread." But that he made any reply to this, no one heard. And in that manner it was that she continued there conversing with her dead father. Sometimes she would say: "So be it, I will." At other times she would laugh. Then, after a while, she came down and said: "My father said to me, 'Tomorrow, very early in the morning, thou shalt start.'"

So when the next day came and they had finished eating their morning meal, the young woman-being, at that moment, said: "Now I believe I shall start; but I believe I shall also tell my father." And she went again to where the ladder stood and, climbing to the place where lay the burial case of the dead man-being, she said: "Father, I am starting now on my journey." So that, thus again, from what she herself said, it was learned that he was, indeed, her father.

And it was at that time that he told her all that would befall her on the journey to her destination, as well as what would occur when she arrived. And when she had again come down, her mother lifted up for her the burden basket full of corn bread, settling it on the back of the young woman-being, to be borne by the forehead strap. Whereupon that young woman-being went forth from the lodge and started on her journey. The path extended toward the sunrise; and thither did she wend her way.

But it was surprising to her, how little the sun had moved, when she arrived at the place where her father had said there would be a river to be crossed by a floating log. Usually wayfarers passed the night there, it being just one day's journey away. And so, concluding that she must have lost her way, having taken a wrong path, she retraced her steps. And again, the sun had hardly moved when she reached her starting place. "I do not know," she said, "but I seem to have lost my way. I must again question my father." And again she climbed to the place where her father lay in the burial case, and those who were at that time in the lodge overheard her say: "Father, I have returned, thinking that perhaps I lost my way, since I arrived so quickly at the place thou didst describe to me, where I should have remained the night. The sun had hardly risen before I came to a river to be crossed by a floating log. And it was from there that I have returned."

He made answer, but she alone heard what he said. Those others who were in the lodge at that time heard nothing of his speech. It is said, however, that he replied, saying: "In fact, thou didst not lose thy way." It is also said that he asked: "What kind of log is there used for the crossing?" And she replied (or so it is said): "Maple is the kind of log that is there used for the crossing. It is supported on either side of the stream by young sapling clumps of basswood, respectively, and ironwood." He answered (as they say): "that indeed appears to be correct; in fact, thou didst not lose the way." At that time, therefore, she again came down and resumed her journey.

And again, it seems, the sun had moved but very little before she again reached the place from which she had formerly turned back. So she now kept on and crossed the river. And having gone but a short length further on her way, she heard a man-being in the shrubbery say, "Ahem!" She paid to him no attention, of course, but continued on her way; for her father had already told her what was to happen to her on this journey. In this manner then, she hastened, as she went on to her destination. Again, at times, some other man-being would say from the shrubbery, "Ahem!" when she would only quicken as much as possible her pace, continuing on her journey.

And when she had about reached the point where she would be leaving the forest, she was surprised to see a man-being coming toward her on the path; and he, while coming, still at a distance, began to talk. "Stop for a moment," he said. "Thou art weary. Take a rest." But acting as though she had not heard, she kept on, and he, giving up since she would not even pause, only mocked her, saying: "And art thou not then ashamed that the man thou comest to seek is so old?" Nevertheless, she trudged on, neither changing her course, nor hesitating. Her father had revealed to her everything that would happen as she held to the course of her journey, and that was the reason she never even hesitated or paused.

So, after a while she reached a grassy clearing, a clearing that was very large. And in the center of it lay a village. And in the center of the village stood the lodge of its people's chief. Directly thither, to that place she went, and when she arrived at the place where stood the lodge, she kept right on and entered. In the center of the lodge there burned the fire. And on either side of the fire there was a raised bed of mats, on one of which reclined the chief. She went on to him, set beside him her burden basket of corn bread, and said: "We two now marry." To which he replied: "Do thou then sit the other side of the fire." And so it came to pass that those two had between them the fire. And they uttered together not a word more, even until it became dark.

Then, when the time came, after dark, when people habitually retire to sleep, he made up his mat bed, after finishing which he made up her mat bed at the foot of his own; then said: "Thou art to lie there." Whereupon she there lay down, and he, too, lay down. They did not lie together, only placed their feet together, sole to sole.

*   *   *

And when morning dawned those two arose and now he himself kindled the fire. And when he had finished making the fire he passed into another room, out of which he returned bearing a string of ears of white corn. "Thou hast work to do," he now said to her. "It is customary for that one to work who dwells among the people of her spouse. Thou hast mush to make of hulled corn." So she thereupon shelled the corn and he himself went to bring water. He also brought a pot, very large, into which he poured the water. And this he hung, then, over the fire.

And when she had finished shelling the corn, she hulled it, parboiling the corn in the water. And when it was parboiled, she poured the grains into a mortar. She next took up the pestle from where it stood and pounded the corn to meal. But she brought the pestle down only once, and the meal was finished.

The chief marveled; for he had never seen meal made in so short a time.

When she had finished the meal, the water in the pot which he had hung over the fire was already boiling, and she, of course, was thereupon about to pour into it the meal; but he said: "Take off thy clothes." So she undressed. And when she had done that, she poured the meal into the water, then stirred it, using for the purpose a pot stick, while the man himself lay alongside on the mat bed, eyes fixed upon her as she labored. And, of course, since the mush continually spattered, flakes of it continually fell upon different places, all over her naked body. But she went on as though she did not feel this. By the time the mush was sufficiently cooked, her whole naked body was bespattered. And himself then, at that time, removed from the fire the great pot, and moreover, then turning, opened a door not far away, and called: "My slaves, you two, come here!" Whereupon there emerged two animals. They were large dogs; and he said to them: "Lick now from all over her naked body the mush that has fallen upon her." At which command, his slaves, two individuals in number, and besides of equal size, went over to the place where she was standing. And of course, they licked her naked body many times in many places. Moreover, it is said that their two tongues were so sharp that it was exactly as if a fiery rod were being drawn along her naked flesh. It is said that wherever those two licked the blood came forth. And so it is said that when those two had finished their work, she stood bathed in blood. And he thereupon said to her: "Do thou now dress thyself again." She did so. And he called (it is said) to his two slaves: "Here, come! You two, my slaves! The food is ready that was made for you." So then those two beasts ate. And when they had finished eating, he said to them: "Now go back, you two, into the other room." They went back, and he shut the door. Then (as they tell) he said to her: "It is true, is it not, thy desire that thou and I should marry? So now, thou and I do marry."

And it was thus that everything which had come to pass since her arrival in that place had been already known to her, as foretold by her father. For that reason she had been able with fortitude to suffer without flinching the burns of the spattering mush of her cooking. Had she flinched when the hot flakes fell upon her, the chief would have said to her: "I do not believe it is true that thy wish is that thou and I should marry." Besides, she had borne with fortitude the pain of the time when the two large dogs had licked the mush from her body. Had she flinched to the point of refusing to endure the ordeal, it is certain that he would have said to her: "It is of course not true that thou desirest that thou and I should marry." And when his two beasts had finished eating and been dismissed, he showed her (it is said) just where his food was kept, and when she had prepared it and completed the preparation, those two then ate their morning meal.

It is said that she passed there three nights, and that they two did not once lie together. Only this was done, as is reported, namely, that when they two lay down to sleep they placed their feet together with their heads in opposed directions. Then he, it is said, on the third morning told her: "Thou shalt now return to the place whence thou didst come to me. A burden basket of dried venison shalt thou carry on thy back by the forehead strap. I mean to give to thy people some meat. Moreover, the whole village of those with whom thou formerly didst dwell is to share equally, when thou dost arrive, in division of the meat."

He then climbed up, they say, and threw down quarters of meat which had been dried. And they say that before he descended there was a high pile in the lodge. He thereupon packed the meat into her basket until it was full and then, they say, took up the basket and shook it to pack the meat close. It settled down so much, they say, that it looked as though in the basket there were very little. So now, again, he began to pack the basket. And again it was

filled. And again he shook it, to make the meat settle. And again it settled, occupying in the basket little space. Thus he used all the meat thrown down, and still the basket was not full. So three times more he climbed, they say, and three times more threw down quarters. And each time, they say, the lodge with that meat was nearly filled. And not until then was that burden basket fully packed.

So then, it is told, when the basket was filled he said to her: "When thou dost arrive, thou and the inhabitants of that place shall assemble, and the meat shall be then equally portioned. Moreover, thou art to tell them all to remove, when evening darkness falls, the thatched roofs of their lodges. And all the maize that will then fall as hail into their lodges, they must store. For indeed and verily, it will hail kernels this very night, when thou dost arrive. And so now, therefore, by means of the forehead strap thou shalt bear upon thy back this burden basket of dried meat." He thereupon took up for her the basket, saying: "Take care to adjust properly the burden strap in its place. For no matter how tired thou mayest become, to readjust the strap will be impossible until thou wilt have arrived. At that time thou wilt let the burden down."

So therefore, when she had finished her preparations, she adjusted the burden strap to cross her forehead at the fittest place. And she said to him: "I believe I now am ready and have fixed properly this strap."

So he took his hands from holding up for her the basket, and she started on her homeward journey. The basket that she carried was at first not heavy at all. But it began to be a little heavy when she had gone perhaps half the way. And as she then continued on her journey, it became gradually heavier until, finally, the instant she entered the lodge, the burden strap became detached, the basket dropped to the ground and all the dried meat, tumbling out of it, filled the lodge. For had she not, truly, transported on her back a load? And had he not, in his lodge, pulled down quarters of venison four times when packing that basket, as he was making up the burden?

It was now, therefore, that she told them to remove the roofs of their lodges before night fell. "He has sent you meat, so now, my kinsmen," she told them, "gather up the meat here scattered in this lodge." And indeed, her people were then gathering up the dried meat, to carry it off. And she told them, further: "Before going to sleep, remove the thatched roofs of your lodges. My spouse sends word that during the time of your sleep he will bestow on you a quantity of white grain. During the time of your sleep, it will rain kernels of white maize." And indeed, when darkness fell, it would shower maize that entire night, so that when day dawned they would possess white maize in abundance. They removed, therefore, the thatched roofs of the many lodges, and all retired to sleep. And indeed, when they woke, there lay in the lodges an abundance of white maize. The grains were up to their knees. Because so long as they slept, it had showered maize. And the reason for his giving to this people of this bounty was, that he had married one of their members.

After a suitable interval of time, she started back to the village and lodge of her spouse. And truly, the journey was again accomplished in the time it had taken, the first trip.

And when she then arrived, she of course, at that time, related to him all that had happened to her on the journey, both to and from home. For of course the two now abode together, since of course they two were now married.

Then, after a certain time, he said: "I am ill."

And his people then marveled at what had been said; for they knew not what it was for one to be ill. And so, therefore, at that time, when they surmised what might (with regard to him) have occurred, they of course severally studied the matter and, as is customary, made suggestions to the one who was ill as to what might be done. Yet it would seem (as may be imagined) that his illness was not thereby abated, and that, although many individuals made suggestions, no recovery was effected. And so thus it stood.

And they continued to strive to understand his case. And having failed in the cure, they further questioned him therefore, inquiring: "What then, perhaps, can we do that from being thus ill thou mayest be healed?"

And he replied, saying: "I am now thinking that perhaps I might recover from my illness if you should uproot the tree that stands outside my door; and that if there, beside the hole from which the tree will have been uprooted, I might lay me down."

So his people thereupon uprooted the tree. It was a tree of the dogwood kind, which had been ever adorned with blossoms giving light to the people thereabout dwelling: white blossoms shedding light. And to the people dwelling thereabout that tree had been as the sun. Therefore, when the tree had been uprooted, the one who was ill said to his spouse: "Do thou now spread for me something beside the hole where formerly stood the tree."

Whereupon, she in fact there spread for him something, and there he laid himself on what she had spread for him. And when he there lay, he said to his spouse: "Do thou now sit beside me." And she did, in fact, then place herself beside his body, where he lay. When he said to her: "Do thou now let thy legs hang into the abyss." For where the tree had been uprooted, such a hole was left as extended through and opened to the world below. And indeed, it came then to pass as there he lay that his suffering was mitigated. All his people were assembled about. Moreover, as he lay there ill, their eyes were fixed upon him, marveling at this thing which had befallen him. For those dwelling in that place had known nothing of what it is for one to be ill.

And so, having recovered, thus, seemingly, from his illness, he rolled over, turning upon his side, and resting on his elbows, looked down into the hole. After a while, he said to his spouse: "Do thou, too, look into this opening, thither, and see what things are occurring down there, yonder." Whereupon she bent forward her body toward the opening and peered down. At which moment, he placed against the nape of her neck his fingers and pushed her, and she fell into the hole.

Then he arose to a standing posture and said to his people: "Replace, now, the tree that was uprooted. There it lies." And immediately they reset the tree, so that it stood just as it had stood before.

* * *

But as to this woman-being: she of course fell into the hole and kept on falling through its darkness, and after a while passed through its length. And when she had passed quite through onto this other world, she of course looked in all directions and saw on all sides about her that everything was blue, and that there was nothing else to be seen. She of course knew nothing of what would perhaps happen to her, since she did not cease from falling. Yet after a time, as she looked she discerned something, though she knew not what it was she saw. In fact, she was now looking upon a great expanse, indeed, of water, albeit herself not knowing what it might be.

And so this is what she saw.

On the surface of the water, floating about hither and thither, like veritable canoes, were all sorts and forms of waterfowl. And it was thereupon Loon who first noticed her. He cried out suddenly, saying: "There is a man-being, a female, coming up from the water depths." Then the Bittern spoke: "She is not, in fact, coming up from below; she is, in fact," he said, "falling from above." Whereupon they gathered in council to decide what they should do to provide for her safety, and determined, finally, to invite the Great Turtle to serve. Whereupon Loon said to him: "Do thou float thy great body above the place in the water-depths of thine abode." And immediately they sent up to her a flight of numerous ducks of various kinds, which in a very compact body elevated themselves to meet her on high. And on their backs, thereupon, her body did indeed alight. So then slowly they descended, bearing on their backs her body. And the Great Turtle having satisfactorily caused his carapace to float, right there, upon his back, they placed her. Then Loon called: "Now come, all ye who are deep divers. Try which is able so to dive as to fetch up earth." And one by one, thereupon, they severally dived. And it was then Beaver who made first the attempt and dove. The time was long and there was only silence. It was very long indeed before his back reappeared. But he had come up dead, his breath having failed. They thereupon examined his paws, but he had brought up no earth. The Otter said: "Well, then let it now be my turn. Let me make the attempt." Whereupon he dove. An even longer time elapsed before he came to the surface, and he, too, in his turn, came up dead. Then they examined, also, his paws. Nor had he, it is said, brought up any earth. So then it was Muskrat who declared: "I, too, will make the desperate attempt." And forthwith he dove into the water. Still longer was the time that he, in turn, remained submerged. After a very long while, he came floating to the surface, coming up dead, having lost his breath. Whereupon, again, they looked inside his paws. And they found mud. There was mud in his paws, and his mouth was full of mud, as well.

So then it was that they made use of that mud, coating with mud the edge of the cara-pace of the Great Turtle. And other muskrats then dove, in turns, into the water to fetch more, all floating to the surface, dead. It was in such a way that they worked until they had made a circuit of the carapace of the Great Turtle, placing upon it mud until the two terms of the work came together and Loon said: "There is now enough. This will suffice." Whereupon the muskrats ceased their diving to bring up mud.

*   *   *

240. Iroquois (Ontario) turtle shell rattle, with the turtle's head and neck used for the handle, c. 1900.

And so that man-being rested on the cara-pace of the Great Turtle, and after a lapse of sufficient time she went to sleep. Then after a time, she awoke. The carapace of the Great Turtle was now covered with mud completely. Moreover, the earth whereupon she sat had become in size enlarged. At that time, she looked about and saw that willows along the edge of the water had grown to be bushes. Then too, when she again awoke, the carcass lay there of a deer, recently killed, and besides, there burned there a small fire, and there lay there, also, a sharp stone. So she now, of course, dressed and quartered the deer carcass and roasted thereof some pieces, of which she ate her fill. And when she had finished her repast, she again looked about her.

For the earth, assuredly, had now greatly increased in size. For indeed, it had rapidly grown. Moreover, another thing she saw; namely, growing shrubs of the rose willow along the edge of the water. And moreover, not long after, she saw take up its course a little rivulet. In that way, in their turn things came to pass. The earth rapidly was increasing in size. She then looked and saw all kinds of herbs and grasses spring from the earth and grow, as she watched, toward maturity.

So when, then, the time had come for her to be delivered, she gave birth to a female, a girl child. And those two, of course, mother and daughter, remained there together. It was quite astonishing how rapidly the girl-child grew.

So then, when she had attained her growth, she of course was a maiden. They two were alone; no other man-being moved about there, anywhere. And of course when she had then grown up and was a maiden, her mother of course had the habit of admonishing her child,

habitually saying: "Thou wilt let me know what manner of person it is who will approach thee and say repeatedly: 'I desire that thou and I should marry.' Do not thou give ear to this, but say repeatedly: 'Not until first I ask my mother.'"

And so it was that matters progressed. First one came along, then another, each severally asking her to become his wife, and she repeatedly replied: "Not until I first ask my mother." Moreover, when she would tell her mother what manner of person had asked, her mother would answer, saying repeatedly: "No, he is not the one."

But after a spell of time the maiden said: "One who has a deep fringe along his legs and arms paid me a visit." And the elder woman said: "That is the one. I think that would be the proper one for you to marry."

So the maiden returned to the place where the young man stood and said: "She says we should marry." To which the young man answered, saying: "When it is dark, I shall return." And so, when the appointed time arrived he indeed came back; and then it was that he paid court to her. But, I think, they two (he and she, the maid) did not lie together. When she lay down, so that she might sleep, he laid one of his arrows beside her body, and thereupon departed. On returning, he took up his arrow and again departed, bearing it away with him. And he never came back again.

Presently, the elder woman became aware that the maiden was increasing in size, caused by the fact that she was pregnant. And so, when the day of the delivery had come, the daughter brought forth twins, two infant males. During the time that she had been in travail, however, she had heard the two talking inside her body. One of them had said: "This is the place through which we two should emerge. It is much the shorter way; for, look thou! There are many transparent places." The other had replied, however: "Not at all! By going that way, undoubtedly, we should kill her. Howbeit, let us get out this other way, which is that which anyone becoming a human being will [in the future] use for exit. Let us turn around and in the downward direction, the two of us then go." So then, the first who had spoken confirmed what the latter had proposed, and said: "so shall it continue to be."

However, he now argued another proposition. When the second had said: "Do thou take the lead," he replied: "Not at all; do thou go ahead." And so then it was that in this manner the two contended. And he who said "Right in this very place let us two go straight out; for certainly this way is as near as that," gained his point. The other agreed, finally, that he should himself take the lead. Whereupon, he turned himself about and at once was born. Whereupon his grandmother received him, took him up and took care of him, then laid him aside. At which time, she returned her attention to her daughter; for now, indeed, was she suffering another travail. But this other emerged from another place. He came out of her armpit. And so, to him, he killed his mother. Then his grandmother took him up and attended to his needs. And when this charge was accomplished, she laid him alongside the one that had first come out; after which she devoted her attention to her child who was dead.

Turning, then, to the place where she had laid the two male infants, the grandmother asked: "Which of you two destroyed my child?" One of the two answered, saying: "Truly, I believe, it was he." This one, who answered, was an especially marvelously strange person as to his form. His flesh was nothing but flint. Along the top of his head there was a sharp comb of flint. And it had been on this account, in fact, that he had come out by way of the armpit. But the flesh of the other was in all respects like that of any man-being. He responded, saying: "It was, in fact, he himself who killed her." The other replied: "Not at all; not at all." And again he declared: "It was he who killed her." And in this manner the two debated.

But the one who was, in fact, guilty of killing her held firm to his denial and finally won his point. Whereupon, the grandmother took up the body of the one whose flesh was actually that of a veritable man-being and with all her might flung him far into the bushes. And the other, whose flesh was flint, was taken up by her and cherished. And it was also wonderful how much she loved him.

But then, in turn, she again laid her hands on the fleshly body of her own girl-child, who now, verily, was no longer alive. She cut off her head and said: "Thou art now dead; nevertheless, shalt continue to have a function to perform." And she took up the fleshly body and hung it on a tree that stood hard by her lodge, and said: "Thou shalt continue to give light to this here present earth." And the severed head she hung in another place and said: "Thou, too, shalt continue to serve a function. Less power shalt thou have, and yet give light." In that manner, then, she completed her preparations for supplying herself with light; having now, assuredly, made fast for herself the sun and likewise the moon. She laid on them the duty of furnishing her, of themselves, with light. And indeed, verily, it was the head of her girl-child who was dead that she had used to make the moon, whereas the body she had made into the sun. They were to remain fixed in place, and not to move from this place to that. Furthermore, she restricted them to herself and to her favored grandson, saying: "We two, and we two alone, shall be ever illuminated by this light. No one else shall use it, only we two, ourselves."

And when she had now, indeed, accomplished all of this task, she was surprised by a moving of the grasses about the area into which she had cast the other of her grandsons. He was alive. He had not died. She had thought when she had cast him far away that he would of course die. Nevertheless, he had not died. He walked about there among the bushes. After a while, however, he had come thence toward his grandmother's lodge. And she now ordered him away, saying: "Get thee off, far yonder. I have no desire to look on thee. For it was thou, assuredly, didst kill my girl-child. Get thee, therefore, far off, yonder." And truly, he then turned away. However, he remained moving about in a place not far from that in which her lodge stood. Furthermore, that male-child was in good health and his growth was rapid.

241. *Creation Battle* (1980) acrylic, 2'5¾" × 2', by Mohawk artist John Fadden (Kahionhes), b. 1938, member of the Turtle Clan.

Presently, he made for himself a bow and also an arrow. And of course he now went about from place to place, shooting. He went about, indeed, a great deal from place to place; for the earth now of course was of considerable size. The earth indeed, verily, was continuing to grow in size. But he would return, at times, to the neighborhood of the lodge. And the younger boy, his brother, looked and saw that he had a bow; also, an arrow. Then he spoke to his grandmother, saying: "Thou shouldst make for me a bow; also an arrow; so that I, too, may have such things." So she thereupon made for him a bow; also an arrow; and then, therefore, they both had bows and arrows. And so now, verily, they two wandered about, shooting.

* * *

So then he whose body was like that of a man-being went in his shooting along a lake shore, even at the water's edge. And there stood there a stand of bushes, whereon there rested a flock of birds. He shot at them, they flew over the lake, and the arrow fell into the water. Whereupon he went thither, to the water's edge, and cast himself into the lake.

He thought to recover his arrow. But when he had dived into the water, he did not feel that he was in water. He had fallen supine on ground. There was no water there. He got up and was surprised to see that a lodge stood there. He was at its doorway. Looking into the lodge, he saw therein a man. The man sitting in the lodge called: "Come in!" So he entered. And he who was sitting there said: "Thou hast arrived. It was I, in fact, invited thee. And here, now, is the reason. It is because of the kind of language I continually hear thy grandmother using against thee. She declares she does not love thee; for she believes that what Flint is continually telling her is true. He is of course telling her that it was thou didst kill the mother of you both. What he is thus continually telling her is untrue, yet your grandmother believes absolutely what he tells her. And so that is the reason I wanted thee to come hither. The fact is, she discriminates, loving him, but not thee. Here then, I have made for thee a bow; also an arrow. Take them."

242. Paddle used for stirring corn, unfinished wood, 21″ high, 1918, western New York State.

Thereupon, therefore, he accepted them. They were in appearance marvelously fine. He said: "As thou goest about shooting, thou art to make use of these. Hadst thou asked thy grandmother to make thee a bow somewhat better than the one thou madest for thyself, she would, in her way, not have given ear, but, in her way, have refused and ordered thee off. She would, in her way, have said: 'Get thee away from here. I have no desire to look on thee. For it was thou, assuredly, didst kill my girl child.' For this, customarily, is her kind of discourse.—But now, furthermore, something else! Here are two ears of maize. These thou must take with thee. One of the ears is not yet ripe; it is still in its milky state. The other is mature. Thou art to take them with thee. And as to the one that is mature, it is for seed corn." Thereupon, when he had then finished explaining, he said: "Here they are, then." Whereupon he took them. And it was at that time, as well, that he spoke to him, saying: "And now, as to one other matter: I am thy father."

Thus it was declared by him whose lodge there stood and who, indeed, is the Great Turtle. And the young man thereupon departed.

*   *   *

So when he had returned, traveling, to his own place, he would habitually run along the lake shore, saying: "Let this earth keep on growing. The name that I am called is Maple Sapling." And in truth, as far as he would thus customarily run, the earth would increase anew in size and maple saplings produce themselves. It was his custom to do this in this way. And no matter which way along the lake-shore he ran, as far as he would run, just so far would this come to pass: new earth would form of itself with maple saplings growing into trees. And as he ran along he would be saying: "Let the earth increase in size!" and again: "As Maple Sapling, I shall be known." Thus it was, and by this means, that the earth became enlarged to the size it now has when we look at the size of this world.

So then, it was also at that time that he formed variously the bodies of the animals. He would pick up a handful of earth and toss it into the air. Customarily, as many as the handfulls thrown, just so many hundreds of living things flew away in all directions. Customarily then, he would say: "This shall be your condition. When you go from place to place, you shall fly in flocks." And so, a duty would devolve upon such a species; for instance that it should habitually make nests.

And now, of course, the different animals were severally asked to volunteer to help man. Whichever species gave ear to this plea would reply: "I (I think) will volunteer." Whereupon, that species would be asked: "Well then, let us see how thou wilt act when protecting thy offspring." When the Bear volunteered, he behaved so rudely that it was very marvelously terrifying. The ugly manner in which he would act would (I should think) kill people. So that when he showed how he would protect his offspring, they said: "Not at all (we think) shouldst thou volunteer." Whereupon, of course others also offered themselves, who, however, were unacceptable because of their terrible ways of defending their offspring. One after another, they volunteered. Then, presently, the Pigeon said: "It is time now, I think, for me to volunteer." Whereupon they answered: "How then wilt thou behave in protecting thy offspring? Let us see!" Hither and thither the Pigeon flew, uttering cries as it went. Then sometimes it would alight on the bough of a tree, and in a short time again fly, winging from place to place, uttering cries. So they said: "Now, this will be suitable." And they had lying by them a dish containing bear's oil, into which they immersed the Pigeon, saying: "So fat shall thy offspring customarily be." For which reason it is that the pigeon's young are as fat usually as a bear.

But now, Flint, during all this time, was watching what Sapling was up to. And he began to imitate him by also shaping animals. The work, however, was too difficult for him to perform correctly. He failed to fashion properly any of the bodies, as they should have been. He formed, for example, what he thought to be the body of a bird, and when he had finished, let it go. It flew. Indeed, it was able to fly, but it flew without any objective point. It had not become a bird, but had the body of what we know as a bat.

When Sapling, on the other hand, had completed in their order the bodies of the marvelously various kinds of animals, they all began to wander over the face of this present earth. But as Sapling himself then was traveling about, he began to notice and marvel, after a while, that he could not discover anywhere any of the animals he had formed. Everywhere over the face of the earth he traveled, seeking for them. And he thought, forsooth: "This matter is astonishing. Where, perhaps, can they have gone: all the animals whose bodies I made?"

So then, as he went from place to place, while searching for his animals, he was suddenly startled. A leaf nearby made a noise, and, looking at it, he was surprised to see a mouse peering up there among the leaves. The kind of mouse that he saw is called Deer-mouse and he was of course about to shoot it, when the mouse spoke to him, saying: "don't kill me! I will tell thee where all those things have gone that thou art seeking: the animals." So he decided not to kill it, and then spoke to it, asking: "Where then have they gone?" Whereupon the Deer-mouse said: "There is in that direction a range of great mountains of rock. There in the rocks they abide. They have been shut up. If, when thou arrivest there thou wilt look about, thou wilt see a large stone placed over the cavern for the purpose of closing it up. It is Flint himself and his grandmother, who together have done this. It is they who have imprisoned all the animals."

Sapling, therefore, went that way, and found that it was true. A great stone lay over the place where there was an opening into the rock, and by which it was closed. So he removed the stone and called: "Come forth. Surely, when I gave you life, I did not intend you to be imprisoned here. I meant you to roam from place to place over this whole earth which I have caused to become enlarged." And thereupon, they indeed came forth. There was a rumbling sound as their feet came pounding as they kept on coming forth. And Flint's grandmother, at that time, asked: "What can now be happening? There is a rumbling sound." She was talking to her grandson, but before he could reply she again spoke, saying: "It is true! Sapling has found them, where thou and I imprisoned them. So let us two go immediately to where we shut them in."

They went out and ran thither without delay. And when they arrived, it was even so: Sapling stood there, having opened the rock cavern, and a line of animals ever so long was running out. The two rushed forward and, taking up the stone again, again closed in those that had not yet come out, and those are animals, great in size, that are still in there.

Sapling kept saying: "Don't again shut them away!" But Flint and his grandmother went right on, even piling on more stones. So that the sorts of animals we know are only those that at that time had got out.

*   *   *

So then it came to pass that Sapling, as he traveled about from place to place, was going along the shore of the lake when he saw Flint [whose name, *Tawískaro*, means also "Ice-coated"] making for himself a bridge of stone [or ice] across the lake. It already extended far out on the water. And so Sapling went right up to him and when he arrived, said: "Flint, what is this thou art up to?" He answered: "I am fashioning a pathway for myself." And then pointing in the direction toward which he was building his bridge, he added: "Over there is a land inhabited by mighty beasts of fierce dispositions, and as soon as I shall have completed this work, they will be able to come over. Along this road they will continually come across the lake to eat the flesh of the human beings then living on this earth." And Sapling said to him: "Thou shouldst give up in this work. The intentions of thy mind are not good." But he answered: "I will not give up; for it is good that these great animals should come over to eat the human beings that will be living here." And of course he continued to build his bridge. Whereupon Sapling left him, and returned to dry land.

Now, growing along the shore of the sea there were shrubs, and sitting on a branch of one of these, Sapling saw a bluebird. And he said, then, to the bluebird: "Thou shalt now kill a cricket, remove one hind leg of it, and with this in thy mouth, fly to the place where Flint is laboring. Hard by that place, thou shalt alight and cry out." The Bluebird answered, "Very well!" and forthwith looked about for a cricket, which, presently, he found and killed, and pulling off one of its hind legs, taking this in its mouth, flew, winging to the place where Flint was at work on his bridge. The Bluebird alighted hard by and shouted: "Kwe, kwe, kwe, kwe, kwe!" Whereupon Flint raised his head and looked and saw there sitting a bird. From what he saw he thought the bird was holding a man-being's thigh in its mouth, and that its mouth was covered with blood. Immediately, Flint sprang up and fled. And as fast as he ran the bridge behind him disappeared.

Just as (comments the recorder of this legend) "so fast as winter recedes, so rapidly the ice on rivers and lakes disappears."[54] "The bluebird (he remarks again)...is among the first of the migratory birds to return in the spring, which is a token that the spring of the year has come, and that the power of the Winter power is broken."[55] "This incident shows definitely that Flint, or rather Ice-coated or Crystal, is the Winter power. There has been a substitution of rock for ice, just as there has been in the name of this important nature force."[56]

*   *   *

Now then, verily, Sapling's father had given him sweet maize, which now he roasted; and a great sweet odor was diffused. When Flint's grandmother got wind of it, she said: "What thing is this that Sapling is now roasting for himself?" And she spoke to Flint. "Let us go, we two, to where he has built his fire, and discover what this thing is." So now of course the two stood up and ran, arriving at the place where Sapling had kindled his fire, and they saw that it was true, that he was roasting for himself an ear of maize. The juice of it was

issuing in streams among the kernels and along the rows of kernels, so fat was that ear of maize. And the grandmother asked: "Where didst thou get this?" "My father gave it to me," he replied. She answered: "And dost thou even intend that the man-beings who will dwell here on this earth should live as pleasantly as this?" Whereupon she took up a handful of ashes, cast them on the ear of maize there roasting, and at once the fat of the maize stopped pouring from the roasting ear. Sapling rebuked his grandmother sharply for this act, took up the ear and wiped off the ashes. Then he again set it to roast. But it now was possible for it to exude only a small amount of fatness, as today when ears are roasted. So little fatness shows, it is barely visible.

Another day and the grandmother was shelling some of the maize that Sapling had planted. She then poured it into a mortar and taking up the pestle, with it pounded the grain. She worked hard at her pounding and said: "Truly, thou wouldst have mankind exceedingly well provided. They should rather, however, be much wearied in getting their bread to eat. And so this now is the way they shall customarily have to use the mortar and pestle." Whereupon Sapling rebuked her, saying: "That which thou hast done is not good."

*   *   *

Sapling, traveling, was astonished to find it becoming dark. He then mused: "Why, indeed, this would appear to be a marvelous occurrence: this thing now taking place." He returned home and, arriving there, found that the sun was nowhere to be seen. Nor could he find either his brother Flint or his grandmother. Searching about, he then perceived a glow of light that was like dawn and understood that the sun was in that place. And so now he set about seeking servants who would help him to recover it.

Spider volunteered; so also, Beaver; and Hare; and so also, Otter. And then, together, they made themselves a canoe. When they had done this, they all got in and, of course, began to paddle, directing the bow toward the place where the dawn was showing. And there lay the sun, on the top of a tree. So then Sapling said: "Thou, Beaver, do thou cut down that tree; and thou, Spider, shalt climb it, and at the top of the tree fasten the cord. Thou shalt then descend, hanging by thy cord, until thou reachest the ground." And to Hare he said: "As soon as the tree falls thou must seize the sun. Adept as thou art at running through the underbrush, no matter how difficult the ground, if now, at this time, thou art pursued from place to place, thou art able to escape by stealth. And thou, Otter," he said, "shalt care for the canoe. If it be that we all get aboard, thou shalt turn back the canoe at once."

All this then came to pass. Beaver of course bit out pieces from the tree. Spider, for his part, climbed to the top and, having reached it, fastened there his cord. Then letting himself down, he again alighted on the ground. And so then, when there was little left to be cut and the prospect was encouraging that it

243. *Corn-Pounding Scene*, watercolor and graphite on board, 14" × 20", by Onondaga artist Tom Dorsey (Two Arrows), member of the Wolf Clan.

should be possible to fell the tree, Spider pulled on the cord. The tree toppled over. Hare rushed forward and seized the sun; for, indeed, both Flint and his grandmother now came running. And it was then that Hare took flight, bearing the sun away. They of course pursued him right and left, he fleetly scurrying through the shrubbery, but then, after a spell, coursing straight for the canoe. Because the others, indeed, his friends, were already aboard. He came at a bound, jumped in, and therewith, Otter instantly pushed the canoe off, and they all began again to paddle.

So then, as they were paddling back, Otter, it is said, kept talking. They told him to keep quiet, but he kept right on until someone struck him with a paddle a blow on the mouth, and that is why the otter's mouth now looks as though it had somehow been broken. The lower jaw is shorter than the upper. You can see where someone's paddle struck him.

And so, when they were safely home, Sapling said: "It must not go on this way: that one person alone should have charge over the sun." And he flung the sun up to the center of the sky, with the command: "Up there in the heavens shalt thou henceforth remain, and besides, keep moving along." He then pointed to the west. "The place it goes down into the deep," he said, "shall be known as the place of the sunset, the down-going and immersion. Then, verily, darkness will overtake this earth. And the place where the sun comes up, people shall know as the place of thy looking forth, and they will say: 'Now the sun-being has appeared.' For at that time, thou shalt ascend from the depth. And in this way thou shalt have a service to perform, ever giving light to this earth." Then Sapling declared further: "Whenever thou art mentioned, they will speak of you as 'The Great Warrior, who gives us light.'"

And then too, of course, that other luminary, the Moon, which had been his mother's head and which his grandmother had also placed on the top of a standing tree, this too he tossed up to the sky, saying: "The power of thy light at night shall be less great." And he added: "They will see thee at times as full, but every night thereafter thy size shall diminish until it disappears. Then again, every night thou shalt increase in size from a small beginning, growing nightly until the time arrives when thy growth shall have been completed. And so that, now, is to be thy manner of existence." Moreover he said: "Whenever thou art mentioned by the people who are to dwell here on earth, they will speak of thee as 'Our Grandmother, luminary of the night.'"

Then Sapling formed the body of a man of the race of mankind; also that of such a woman.—His younger brother, Flint, was watching.—And when Sapling had caused those two to live, he placed them side by side, and then started off on a journey, to inspect the current condition of those things which he had fashioned for this earth. Presently returning to see what the man and woman were doing, he found them doing nothing at all but sleeping. He just looked at them and went away. But then again returning, he found that their condition was unchanged. They were still, just sleeping. And so it continued to be, every time he returned to them. All they did was sleep. So then he took from each a rib [there may well be a biblical influence here,

though with a new and interesting application], and substituting one rib for the other, he implanted each in the other body. And then, of course, he watched them, wondering what perhaps might now occur.

It was not long before the woman woke. She sat up and at once she touched the breast of the man lying at her side, just where her rib had been placed, and of course that tickled him. He woke. And then of course it started: that occasion which most concerns man-beings in their living, and for which, in their kind, their bodies are provided, that matter for which purpose he is a male human being and she a female human being.

Then Flint, too, fashioned a human being, but he was unable to match what Sapling had done, as the form of his poorly made creature showed. He addressed his brother: "See!" he said. "I too can make a human being." But when Sapling looked at what had been achieved, he recognized that what had been formed were not human beings at all. They had human faces, but the bodies of monsters. Sapling said to him: "This, exactly, is the reason I told thee not to try to imitate my accomplishments." Flint responded: "Thou shalt nevertheless see that I, after all, can do as well as thyself; for my power is no less than thine." And with that, the two separated. Sapling resumed his traveling from place to place, over the surface of the earth, to review the works of his creation, and in time was again strolling along the shore of the sea, when he beheld Flint there moving about. At the water's edge lay the body of a man-being as white as foam [or as snow: this man was Winter]. Sapling approached his brother and said: "What is this that thou art doing?" Flint replied: "I have formed the body of a male man-being. This person's body, lying here, is better looking, surely, than the one that thou hast made. I told thee that I have as much power as thou hast: yes, that my power is greater than thine. Thou canst see! This body is as white as the one that thou didst form." Sapling answered: "What thou sayest would surely seem to be true. So then, if so it be, let me see him make some movements and get up. Let me see him stand and walk." Whereupon Flint said: "Come now! Arise!" But the one lying there did not move. Then Flint of course did everything he could to cause his creature to live and to arise. He tried everything possible, but to no avail. He had no effect; his creature did not come to life. Then Sapling said: "Is it not just as I have been saying? Thou art not able to do as I do." But he added: "What purpose, however, would be served by leaving his body here lying without life? Is he to lie here, this way, forever?" Flint replied: "Well then, do thou cause him to rise." And Sapling, consenting, went over to where the creature lay, bent down and breathed into his nostrils, when the form at once began to breathe and was alive. Sapling said to him: "Do thou arise and move about on this earth." The body of a woman had also been made there, and Sapling, at that time, caused them both to live.

*   *   *

Flint, in those days, went about undoing many of the works that Sapling had accomplished. The rivers in their different courses

were altered, for example; for Sapling, in forming them, had provided them with two currents running in contrary courses, in such a way that objects might be floated in opposite directions. That is to say, there was down the middle of each river a division, with the water of each side flowing the opposite way to the other. Because Sapling had intended mankind should not have, as a usual thing, any difficult task while traveling. If a person, for any reason, should wish to go down a river, it would be no problem for him simply to place himself on a canoe and then, of course, ride the current; and should he then have to return, he would, of course, paddle over to the other side and, just as soon as he passed the division of the stream, his canoe would turn back and he would again be descending the current. That is what Sapling intended: that mankind should have it easy this way, while traveling on his rivers. But Flint spoiled this. It was Flint, furthermore, who made all these immense, uplifted mountains; also, all these jagged cliffs. He did all this so that the people who would be living here should have reason for trouble and anxiety as they traveled.

Sapling and Flint, at that time, were dwelling together in one lodge, each occupying the opposite side of the fire to the other. And it was while they were thus dwelling there that Flint kept questioning Sapling as to what object he most feared, what object would most quickly kill him. To which Sapling answered: "A certain weed that grows in swamps; a kind of sedge called 'it cuts a person.' I think, now that I think of it, that that weed would cut through me." Flint asked: "Is there nothing else you fear?" Sapling answered: "I often think the spike of a cat-tail flag might kill me, if anyone should strike me with it." (Those are the two things Sapling's father had told him to say, when he had been in his father's lodge.) Then Sapling asked: "And what thing is it thou dost fear?" Flint said: "Yellow flint; also the horns of a deer. I suppose, when I do think of it, that I should perhaps die at once if struck with either of these."

So after that, wherever Sapling traveled, if he saw a stone of the yellow chert kind, he would pick it up and set it on some high place; or if he saw a deer's horn, he would pick that up and place it, also, on a high place. Now it was so, that in their lodge the floor on one side of the fire was higher than the other. Sapling occupied the higher side and Flint the lower. Then it happened that when Sapling was increasing the fire by feeding it with hickory bark, it became so hot that the legs of Flint began to chip and flakeoff. He said: "Thou hast made the fire too hot. Do thou not feed it any more bark." Sapling, however, threw another piece into the fire and the heat of course increased. And so now the fire was indeed extremely hot, and Flint's whole body began flaking off in chert chips. He became very angry as Sapling kept putting bark into the flames, and besides, his side of the lodge being so low, he had very little space in which to find shelter. He writhed in the heat and became, at last, so angry that he left the lodge and running into a marsh, tore up stalks of the sedge called 'it-cuts-a-person,' with which he then came running back to the lodge and cried, "Sapling, I now kill thee," striking blows with stalks that he carried.

So then those two began to fight, Flint striking the other with his stalks. Then he realized that Sapling was not being cut by his blows, and again darting out, he this time went to get spikes of the cat-tail flag. Returning, he rushed at Sapling, once again dealing him blows. And again the blows failed to injure. Turning, he fled with Sapling in pursuit, and now, in every direction over the entire earth that pair of brothers ran. Wherever Sapling saw on a high place a yellow flint-stone or a deer horn, he seized it and struck at Flint. Chert chips would fly when he hit him. And he kept on striking as they went running. Every time he saw a horn or yellow chert stone, he grabbed it and struck at Flint. Thus, finally, he killed him.

And to this day, there is a range of mighty mountains here extending toward the west across the whole earth. There, so it is said, the body of Flint lies extended. There he fell, when killed. And as we look about, considering the condition of the earth as it is today, it is evident that its surface is uneven, some places high, with ranges even of mountains, while others are for their part low. That was brought about, of course, by those two as they raced from place to place, fighting as they ran. That is the reason why the surface of the earth is uneven.

*   *   *

Continuing in his custom of traveling about, Sapling one day met a male man-being and said to him: "What is it thou dost do as thou goest about?" The other answered: "I come inspecting the earth, to see whether it is just as I put it forth." Sapling replied: "Well, this truly, indeed, is an amazing enterprise of thine, since it was I who completed this earth." The other responded: "Not at all; for it was I myself accomplished this." "Well then," said Sapling, "if that be so, let it be made quite plain that it was thou that didst complete this earth. At our two backs, in the distance, there is a range of high mountains of sheer rock, in appearance like a wall. Let thee now bring them nigh to thy body. Should it be that perhaps thou art able to do this, then surely it will be shown that thou didst indeed complete this earth. Do thou, therefore, only speak, ordering that mountain range to come hither." And he added: "So now, then, go ahead!" The other answered: "I doubt not, it will come to pass." And he called out: "Come thou, yon mountain range, move thyself higher! Come stand by my body!" But the mountain range remained where it was; the mountains were unchanged. Nothing moved. Sapling said: "So there! That is exactly what I have been saying. Thou hast not established this earth." The other replied: "Well then, let it become evident, if true, that thou art the one. Come, do thou move that wall of rock hither." And Sapling said: "Thus, indeed, will I do." Whereupon he called out to the range: "Come, move thyself this way." And verily, it moved. It approached, and at his back, close to his body, came to a standstill. The rock wall even lightly grazed his shoulder blades. Then Sapling said: "Now turn thyself around and look to see where the mountains be."

So the other thereupon turned around and his nose struck the rock and became awry.

Then he spoke and said: "Truly, indeed, thou it is who hast completed and established the earth here present. It was not I at all who did this. If, then, if thou wilt consent to it that I may live, I shall then ever continue to aid thee. I shall protect at all times thy people who are to dwell here on this earth."

And Sapling, replying said: "Truly, it shall be thus. 'Mask' shall mankind ever call thee; also 'Grandfather.'"

Another day, and Sapling was again traveling about, to inspect anew those things that he had accomplished on this earth, when he saw another male man-being. He addressed him, saying: "What art thou doing on thy way?" The other answered: "It seemed necessary for me to see thee." Sapling replied: "that is evidently true." Said the other: "I desire that thou shouldst permit me still to live. If thou wilt consent to what I say, I shall give to thee assistance. I shall watch over their bodies and give life and support, and moreover, shall continue to defend the mankind that thou wilt cause to dwell on this earth that thou hast completed." Replying, Sapling said: "Let me see what sort of power is thine." Whereupon the male man-being, whose name is *Thunder* (*hi'no*), started on a run and ascended into the clouds, when, verily, rumblings were heard. It thundered in the clouds and lightnings were emitted, and moreover many flashes broke forth, so rapidly they seemed to be one. After which the man-being came down again to where Sapling stood, and said: "So now, thou hast seen what sort of power I have." And Sapling, replying, said: "It is indeed true that thou art able to do as thou didst tell. Wilt thou be able also to cast down water on this earth, when the summertimes come?" He answered: "I can do that." Sapling said: "So then let me see how that will be." And the other replied: "Very well!" He went up again into the clouds and again it thundered, and besides, the lightning flashed and the clouds became thick and black. Then it happened: from the sea it came over the dry land, raining as it came. It was marvelous as it approached. And then of course the rain passed. And then again he returned to the place where Sapling was moving about. Whereupon Sapling spoke to him and said: "What thou art able to do is satisfactory. So let it be, as thou just now didst request. It will be thy duty continually to travel about: for thou thyself requested this. Do not ever fail in this duty. Thou must be ever vigilant. If at some time there should come dangers to the lives of men, because of great serpents moving from place to place in the depths of this earth, or in the sea; if it should come to pass that at some time these great serpents might desire to seize people moving from place to place: thou must then kill such serpents, and when thou wilt have killed them, they will be that on which thou shalt feed. Other animals also, equal in *otkon orenda* (malific magic power) to these, shall become, like them, thy fare. Thou wilt ever have these to watch, as thy adversaries. And now, of course, that is settled. Such is the office thou hast assumed. Mankind will name thee 'Our Grandfather-whose-voice-is-customarily-sounded-in-divers-places' (*Raksot'hǎ'ne'Rawěñnota'tie'se'*)." Then, indeed, they two parted.

There the legend ends.[57]

Commentary on The Woman Who Fell from the Sky

Symbolic themes of the planting-culture stage appear immediately at the opening of this truly magnificent legend with its introduction into the eviternal mythic sphere of an act unleashing the transformative force of the principle of time. Such an unprecedented and irrevocable thing done, terminating an originally timeless Mythological Age antecedent to the earthy, is characteristic of origin myths generally, whether in the Old World or in the New. Among hunters, whose origin tales transpire normally in a setting already of this earth in its unformed original state (whereupon a World Shaper appears who arranges everything, whether by intention or by chance, exactly as it is today), the irrevocable act terminating the Mythological Age consists usually in the breaking of some divinely ordered, unexplained tabu; whereupon the offended god, in anger, sends death into the world, heaven separates from the earth, and day and night begin to alternate in a way that has continued to the present. (See I.1:108–110, African Pygmy tales, and I.1:123–125, tales of the Andamanese).

The biblical example of the broken-tabu motif terminal of the Mythological Age, represented in Genesis 3, is of a specifically African type that has been recognized, both in a Pygmy tale recorded in the Congo by Father Paul Schebesta to his own expressed amazement (see I.1:109–110), and in the Bassari legend collected by Frobenius in Togo (see I.1:14). Of especial interest is the Pygmy version which so startled Father Schebesta, since the plucking and eating of the fruit of the forbidden tree is there ascribed to the urging of a pregnant woman persuading her spouse. The act, witnessed and reported to the Creator by his female companion, the Moon, so enraged him that he cursed the human race to die.

The very great and essential difference between hunter and the planter versions of the mythological act derives from the fact that, whereas in the former the transformation (viewed as a catastrophe) follows from an act of disobedience, either intentional or accidental, violating the expressed will of a personified Power superordinated to the field within which he operates, in the planter myths there is no such superior authority anywhere to be recognized or offended. There is only something more like a generally prevailing state of mind, a field of consciousness and of being, or, to use an oriental term, a kind of Buddha-realm, where personifi-

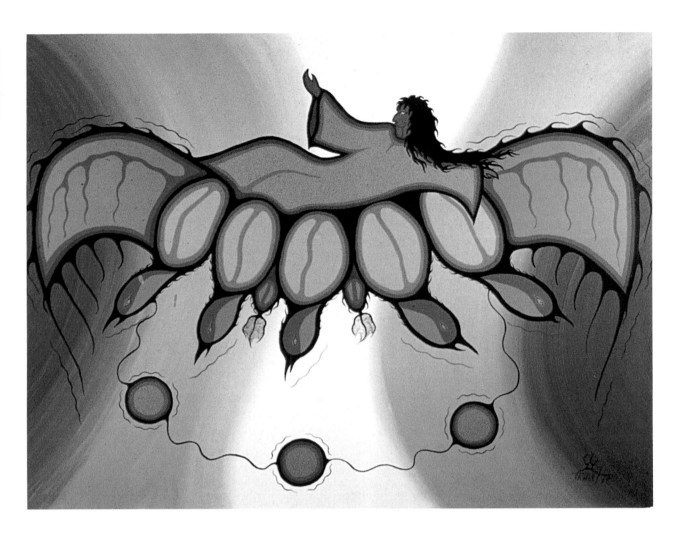

244. *Sky Woman* (1977), acrylic painting by David General, b. 1950. General's wide experimentation with styles of Native American art have made him one of the more powerful and original Iroquois artists of today.

cations of its manner of consciousness and being reside, untouched by time and unknowing, therefore, of the pangs either or loss or of desire.

Accordingly, the critical event is an act introducing the immediate experience of either a death or of a birth; whereupon the whole plane of consciousness and being in the realm undergoes a transformation—indeed, a continuous sequence of compelled and compelling transformations, unprecedented yet predictable, like those of a plant unfolding from its seed. The experience of Being has turned into that of Becoming. Impounded energies and ideas which formerly had been static now play through ephemeral appearances. This is the order of imagery represented in Bastian's "elementary ideas," in C.G. Jung's "archetypes of the collective unconscious," and implied in all legendary narrative. And so the wonderful story begins of the destiny and creative career of the woman who fell from the sky.

Her initial adventures, occurring on the archetypal plane, established there the model of a life course in Quest, Accomplishment, and Fulfillment. No part of the adventure is consciously intended. Her "down-fended" mother had set it first in motion by following an instinctive urge to be with her "down-fended" brother. In that sky world those two had been exceptional, hence set apart from the commonality of "those who know not what it is to see one weep, or what it is to see one die."

It is significant that the movement was initiated, not by the brother, but by the sister. One is given to think of the oriental concept of the *śakti* as female: the wife or beloved, whether of a human being or of a god, as incorporating the motivating sense and energy of his life; or on the cosmic, universal scale, *māyā-śakti-devī*, the Great Goddess (*devī*), who is at once the motivating enerergy (*śakti*) and the formative appearance (*māyā*) of phenomenality. There is an apt statement recorded by Leo Frobenius, of an Abyssinian woman explaining why she and her friends ignored the advice and instruction of their husbands.

"A woman's life," she said, "is very different from a man's. God has ordered it so. A man is the same from the time of his circumcision to the time of his withering. He is the same before he has sought out a woman for the first time, and afterwards. But the day when a woman enjoys her first love cuts her in two. She becomes another woman on that day. The man is the same after his first love as he was before. The woman is from the day of her first love another. That continues so all through life. The man spends a night with a woman and goes away. His life and body are always the same. The woman conceives. As a mother she is another person than the woman without child. She carries the print of the night nine months long in her body. Something grows. Something grows into her life that never again departs from it. She is a mother. She is and remains a mother even though her child die, though all her children die. For at one time she carried the child under her

heart. And it does not go out of her heart ever again. Not even when it is dead. And this the man does not know; he knows nothing. He does not know the difference before love and after love, before motherhood and after motherhood. He can know nothing. Only a woman can know that and speak of that. That is why we won't be told what to do by our husbands. A woman can only do one thing. She can respect herself. She can keep herself decent. She must always be as her nature is. She must always be maiden and always be mother. Before every love she is a maiden, after every love she is a mother. In this you can see whether she is a good woman or not."[58]

The little stone carving of the *Venus of Laussel*, also known as the *Woman with the Horn* (I.1:**66, 109**), which is from a Late Paleolithic rock shelter in southwestern France (Dordogne), is situated but a few miles from the great painted Temple Cave, Lascaux, and is of the same Mousterian age, c. 20,000–18,000 B.C. Held elevated in the pregnant woman's right hand is a bison horn upon which are engraved thirteen parallel strokes. Her face is turned as though regarding this, while her left hand rests on her belly. As remarked by Alexander Marshack in his volume *The Roots of Civilization* : "The count of thirteen is the number of crescent 'horns' that may make up an observational lunar year; it is also the number of days from the birth of the first crescent to just before the days of the mature full moon."[59]

Marshack's important book is a documented report of his examination with a microscope of the enigmatic spirals and rows of nicks and notches found occasionally on Paleolithic artifacts—plaques, staves, and so on, of horn, bone, or mammoth ivory—which, as he discovered, had been made generally by differing instruments, presumably at different times, and as though signifying day counts. He interpreted them, accordingly, as "time factored," constituting in this sense the earliest known evidence anywhere of human temporal reckoning. The numberings and arrangements suggest reckonings, furthermore, of lunar phases, as possibly by women keeping tally of their periods. The eloquent posture of the *Venus of Laussel* speaks convincingly for this argument, while a second rock carving in the same style from the same rock shelter (I.1:**110**) provides the only known scene from the Paleolithic ages of human sexual union. The female is here in a position above the male, as in Egyptian representations of the sky-goddess Nut above the earth-god Qeb, her spouse—which of course would be the position, also, of the woman who fell from the sky in relation to the earth-upholder, her cosmic daughter's spouse, the Great Turtle.

It is observed (in Volume I) that in the period of the Late Paleolithic animal art of the great painted caves (Lascaux, Altamira, and the rest), there was flourishing in association especially with dwelling sites and certain exceptional rock sanctuaries (that of Laussel, for example) an altogether different art of sculptured stone, of bas-reliefs and figures in the round (see I.1:**108–129**, especially **109–113**), where the interest was not in animals and the magic of the hunt, but in the human female nude. The contrast of the two contemporary styles, both in form and in content, is outstanding. Leo Frobenius recognized and identified in them (I.1:40–41, 82, and I.2:129) two distinct traditions: one, native to the animal plains of the European "Great Hunt," of engraving and painting on flat stone surfaces, reducing three- into two-dimensional forms, analytical and illusory; and the other, imported from regions to the south, of *a second kind of culture*, from Africa (the continent of Frobenius' specialization), where wood and wood carving in the round have been ever the material and preferred technique of art, producing three-dimensional, self-standing forms, which then in Paleolithic Europe would have become models for such an art of carving in the round in stone.

No matter what their separate prehistories may have been, however, in Late Paleolithic Europe the animal art of the painted Temple Caves remained for millennia exclusively associated with male technology, magic, observation and spiritual training for the requirements of the contemporary hunt, which is to say, the spiritually demanding and physically very dangerous art of compassionate killing (see I.1: 90–91, and captions to **160/161** and **165**), while the esthetically contrasting series of stone-sculptured female figurines remained no less exclusively dedicated to the province of the intimate mysteries and transformative physical effect of the act of procreation.

During the immediately subsequent Meso- and Neolithic periods of incipient plant and animal domestication, the formerly dominant animal art of the painted caves disappeared and the entire field was overtaken by a galaxy of female figurines, now fashioned not only of stone, but also of fired clay. Marija Gimbutas, in her fundamental, ground-breaking work, *The Goddesses and Gods of Old Europe 7000-3500 B.C.*,[60] has published a unique display of no less than 450 of these unequivocal testimonials to a period of civilization when the Great Goddess (Sanskrit, *devī*) was the dominant, even sole divinity seriously regarded by the populations of those innumerable little agricultural settlements that had arisen where once had ranged the reindeer and the woolly mammoth.

"As a supreme Creator who creates from her own substance she is the primary goddess of the Old European pantheon," Gimbutas states of the envisioned Maya-Shakti-Devi of these symbolic figurines. "Her accentuated pubic triangle may have been linked with the concept of 'The Great Mother Womb,' or the 'lap of the subterranean queen,' but she was not," Gimbutas holds, "entirely feminine. She was androgynous in the Neolithic period, having a phallus-shaped neck; divine bisexuality stresses her absolute power....As supreme Creator who creates from her own substance she is the primary goddess of the Old European pantheon."[61]

But she seems also to have been, it must be added, whether by parallel development, diffusion, convergence, or, as some might hold, supernatural revelation, the primary goddess, one way or another, of every primary horticultural mythology.

In Arnhem Land, northern Australia, where (as noticed in I.2:140–142 and Map 33) an agriculturally-based mythology originating from Southeast Asia had been at some remote time introduced, she appears as the "Old Woman," an All-Mother who in the form of the Rainbow Serpent arrived with children already inside her—people who made more people. Likewise, even in the Andamans, where (see I.1:118–121) evidence has been found of similar influence, the same already-pregnant All-Mother appeared, "in the Beginning," in the form of "a big joint of bamboo of a kind that does not grow in the Andamans," which came floating in from the sea and split, whereupon "there came forth from it, like a bird from its egg, an infant, the First Man, whose name was Jutpu, 'Alone.'"

In our present, Mohawk version of the Iroquois legend of the woman who fell from the sky, it is told that she arrived on earth already pregnant, bearing within her a girl-child who was to become, not only the mother of the twin World Shapers, but also the source and very substance of the moon and the sun, as well as of maize. So that what we have here is a North American example of what appears to have been a well-nigh universally recognized early planting-culture mythology, wherein, by analogy with the seeded earth, the creative and motivating force (*śakti*) of the world illusion (*māyā*) was envisioned, and in fact experienced, as female (*devī*).

245. *Chée-ah-ká-tchée, wife of Nót-to-way* (an Iroquois living among the Ojibwa), in an 1835-36 portrait by George Catlin (see p. 218), who was at the time traveling the Great Lakes' southern shores.

As Frobenius' Abyssinian informant remarked: "The woman conceives.... Something grows. Something grows into her life that never again departs from it." The eloquent posture of the *Venus of Laussel*, hand on belly while regarding the increasing crescent, tells of the recognition already in the Paleolithic period of an affinity of some kind, identifying the most inward female experience with the transformative mystery of time. And to quote again Oswald Spengler (see II.1:8): "this is not cause and effect, danger and willed response, but a single process of nature that is taking place around, with, and within.... The individual is not free to look out for itself, to will for itself, or to choose."[62]

By contrast, mythologies of the Happy Hunting Ground are generally of actions voluntarily undertaken by individuals, usually male, whether mortal or divine, animal or human, within a vast, enduring room wherein whatever transformations occur are of cause and effect, an act and a result, either as intended or as failed. A World Shaper fashions a figure of clay, breathes life into it, and it moves. Neither has it been physically conceived, nor is it of the god's own substance. The mythologies are thus (again to quote from Spengler's insight) of "little worlds for themselves within another, larger world.... free and independent in the face of the universe";[63] or, as represented in the opening of our Mohawk legend: "knowing not what it is to see one weep, or what it is to see one die."

The brother and sister set apart, "down-fended," as uncanny, because born to some sign of extraordinary orenda, have in their birth to solitude touched in experience a deeper sense of the impulse to life than that made visible to those whose minds are turned only outward. Mythologically and historically, the brother-sister, or father-daughter, incest motif has been associated with ideas of supernatural endowment. Ramses II's most favored and celebrated wife was his daughter; and the great Egyptian god Osiris' wife was Isis, his twin sister, who conceived of him, Horus, the Savior.

And so likewise of the daughter born of this sacred union, her instinctive urge to seek out, discover, and communicate with her dead father became the determinant of a lifetime. And the pattern of her destiny, set forth for his daughter by that father whose death had been the temporal complement of her own conception and birth, was exactly that which, in *The Hero with a Thousand Faces*, I have outlined as the fundamental "Monomyth" (James Joyce's term) known to all the peoples of the earth, wherein the individual quest for and achievement of a personal experience is metaphorically formulated.[64] The pattern is a magnification of the sequence universally represented in all "rites of passage" (Arnold van Gennep's term),[65] *separation—initiation—return*.

Briefly: The mythological hero (or heroine, as here), setting forth from his (or her) accustomed dwelling place, proceeds to a "threshold of adventure" (in this tale, the river to be crossed), beyond which lies the unknown. A region is then traversed of mysterious tests and presences and associated tests (the forest of adventure), through which the voyager comes safely only by virtue of spiritual aid (here, the instructions by a dead father). At the destined place of fulfillment (the lodge of the mysterious chief) further tests of increasing severity are endured (the splattering hot mush, sharp tongues of the two dogs), until fulfillment can be symbolically confirmed (in this case, in a mystic marriage with the master of the axial Tree): whereafter, the monomythical requirement of a "Return," gift-bringing, from the achieved adventure is in this extraordinarily sophisticated revelatory legend represented by way of *two* culminating passages. The first is of the woman's return to her native sky-village bearing a marvelously filled basket of meat and the message of a miraculous rain of maize that was to fall that night; while the second is of her subsequent descent as an avatar from the Sky World to this earth, bearing in her womb the gift of a race of human beings, heavenly endowed, to join in mutual regard the supportive animal population already present.

Interpretation of the outstanding symbolic features of this heavenly marriage-journey and its outcome can be attempted

246. Iroquois woman with papoose (compare Fig. 245). Typically idiosyncratic drawing from Lafitau's *Moeurs des Sauvages Amériquains* (see Fig. 233).

only by way of a comparative method of clarification, since there has been (as far as I know, at least) no account from a traditional Iroquoian source ever published to which one might turn for support. The essential features of the legend are all fairly standard over a great part of the world, however, as "elementary ideas," and so, it should be possible, unless there are hidden some very unusual local implications, to come reasonably close to a sufficiently accurate reading.

The opening move, for example, of the woman herself setting off with her basket of corn-bread to offer herself in marriage, not only echoes the initial episode of the "down-fended" sister entering her "down-fended" brother's room, but also reflects what appears to have been a recognized custom in that matrilineal society. The Jesuit Fathers in their reports to Rome occasionally remarked the prominence of women in tribal councils. There have been accounts, also, of colonial women captives, who, when given the opportunity to return to their Christian homes, refused. The force of the mother-goddess principle, which we have recognized in the mythology, could be recognized, also, apparently, in the local manners of life.

The woman sets off toward the sunrise, which in American Indian tales generally is the way to be followed by anyone setting out for the House of the Sun. We may therefore suppose that the mysterious one whom she is destined to marry will be in some way a personification of the sun. His dwelling is discovered at the place of the axial Tree, and this would seem to confirm that supposition. Moreover, when he later loads the basket that is to be carried by his wife to her people, he fills and shakes it down four times. Four is the number of the quarters of space. In the Indian calumet ceremony, the lighted pipe is addressed first to each of the world-quarters, then held elevated, stem upward, so that the sun may take the first puff. And so there again we have the four of space and in the middle the place of the sun, the axial center, place of the axial Tree: T.S. Eliot's "still point of the turning world.... Where past and future are gathered."[66] The same "elementary idea" is to be seen in the Bo-tree of the Buddha's illumination; the Norse Yggdrasil upon which Othin hung for nine days, himself a sacrifice to himself;[67] Holy Rood, Christ's Tree of Salvation; and the Christmas Tree in the Christian home.

The wedding-ordeal of the self-offering wife—in the House of the Sun, at the site of the World Tree—by which she both gained and revealed her own truth, consisted first in the trial of a splattering over her whole naked body of boiling hot corn mush. By her endurance of this without flinching, she was confirmed and established in her character as Corn Mother, from whose body (or, as modified in this version of the legend, from the buried body of whose daughter) the gift of maize was to be given to mankind. (Compare I.2:207, and Longfellow's *Song of Hiawatha*, Chapter 5, "Hiawatha's Fasting," the Algonquian, Ojibwa legend of the origin of maize from the buried body of an incarnate corn-spirit, in that instance, male.)

The second trial was of the two great dogs with rasping tongues, licking from all over her naked body the corn mush. Marija Gimbutas, writing of the Old European, Neolithic Great Goddess whose body was the universe of her creation, states that in her character as Moon Goddess, her intimate animal double and associate was the dog. "Dog, the howler by night, was the goddess' principal animal," she writes; "....Ferocious-looking dogs with three-clawed paws, fur bristling and tails raised, flying through cosmic space, appear painted in black or chocolate brown on Late Cucuteni ochre-red vases, notably on large pear-shaped *pithoi* and on binocular pots....Dogs are portrayed on either side of a tree, perhaps a life-tree, the symbol of all life, wild and cultivated....In the Balkan countries it is believed that eclipses of the sun and moon are caused by dog-headed monsters."[68] There have been reports of the Indians of the Plains mercilessly beating their dogs on the occasion of an eclipse, to move the animals' celestial counterpart to release the occluded light. The associations suggest, I would say, by simple analogy, that the legendary Sun Chief dwelling at the place of the Cosmic Tree must have been keeping those two large dogs in expectation of the arrival, one day, of his female counterpart, the Moon-Virgin, who was then to be tested for her true character as at once corn mother and moon virgin by the painful trial of feeding from her entire body those two symbolic beasts.

We are told that as a wedding rite the couple lay together, foot to foot, for three nights. As four is a number associated with the quarters of space and with the sun, by which space is illuminated, so three is the number associated with the passing of time—past, present, and future—and with the phases of the moon, by which temporality is measured and marked; the periods, also, of the female and of birth (nine moons, or 3 × 3). The pictured moon-dogs recognized by Gimbutas had, accordingly, "three-clawed paws."

The heavenly marriage of the sun and moon is a classic theme of mythology. Observationally, it is associated with the fifteenth night of a lunation, when the full moon, rising, confronts the blaze of a setting sun from the opposite horizon. We have already remarked the allusion to this theme in Durer's woodcut of the Crucifixion (II.1:**97**). It is a feature, also, of Tibetan tankas representing Bodhisattvas. For the myth of the marriage of the sun and moon connotes a realization of the identity in transcendence of the two planes of consciousness, of eternity (the solar light) and of time (the fluctuant light of the moon). Both in Christ, as at once True God and True Man, and in the Bodhisattva as that one who, while in knowledge of the peace of Nirvana yet remains to participate fully in the sorrows of this temporal world, that same, cardinal experience and idea at the heart of all mystically informed religion is personified.

And so it was, also, in this truly marvellous Native American mythological statement, that at the place of the axial Tree, where rest and movement, endurance and change, eternity and time come together, the world-transformative mythological event takes place, which is, first, of a mystical marriage of the sun and moon, eternity and time, and then, the living descent of the moon-messenger into this temporal field, bringing knowledge of the play of eternity through all time and the festival of an everlasting resurrection of life out of death, as the moon, periodically casting its shadow, is ever reborn.

But did the Mohawk know what these symbols mean? Do Roman Catholics know what these symbols mean—why Good Friday and Easter, for example, fall on the first weekend after the first full moon following the spring equinox?

These are treasures out of the whole human past; utterances of the human soul to the mind, addressed in a vocabulary of vision, and there have always, fortunately, been seers having inner ears to hear, inner eyes to see, and hearts to preserve and pass on the messages of these archetypal metaphorical forms.

The basket, quadruple-loaded of venison, carried by the woman back to her village from the mystery-house at the foot of the axial Tree, is in its way an example of the archetypal mythological Inexhaustible Vessel, which in Oriental folklore appears in the begging bowl of the Buddha. In European folklore it is perhaps earliest represented in the cauldron of the Irish sea-god Manannan MacLir, from which, in his palace in the Land Below Waves, he ladles ale without cease to his guests. In medieval romance such a vessel appears as the Grail, in which sense, it is likened to the chalice of Christ's holy blood (compare the chalice in Durer's woodcut, II.1:**97**). An important feature of the Mohawk episode is the increasing weight of the loaded basket as the woman trudges with it homeward, until at the very threshold of the council lodge the head-strap breaks and it falls to the ground, spilling open. One is reminded of the medieval legend of the giant St. Christopher, who had devoted his life to bearing travelers across a river. A small child one

247. Woman with burden basket, detail from *Louisiana Women Walking along a Bayou*, 1847 oil painting by Alfred Boisseau (1823–1901).

day asked to be carried and was lifted piggyback, but in the course of the crossing grew heavier until in mid-stream the weight was so great that, staggering, the giant had all he could do to reach the farther shore, where he learned that the weight had been of the universe and of Him who had made it; whereafter, the good giant's name was called Christopher, "Christ-bearing." The bounty that spilled from the basket was of venison, gift of the universal Hunter, the Sun, while the rain of maize which that night fell was of the proven goddess Moon, herself.

The ominous scene at the opening of the floor of the sky where the luminous Tree had been standing is surely one of the most heavily charged with latent import in the oral literatures of the world. The portentous illness of the chief repeats the motif already familiar from the opening of the legend, of the father of a child that is about to be born falling ill, and about to die. In the context of celestial eviternity the occurrence either of a birth or of a death would constitute a traumatizing shock, shifting radically the plane of consciousness from a timeless unknowing "of what it is to see one weep, or what it is to see one die," through an experience of irrevocable change, to knowledge of the compulsion of time. Such a trauma, indeed, is the connoted sense of the biblical eating of the fruit of the Tree, in immediate consequence of which the now sexually aware, leaf-clad "First Parents" are ejected from the Garden and condemned (as though by an angry god) to the knowledge of death as well. The comparatively innocent Paleolithic motif of the "one forbidden thing" and broken tabu, which had been earlier known to the goat-and-sheep herding, nomadic Israelites, had in Canaan become significantly sophisticated through an assimilation of local planting-culture motifs from the conquered agriculturalists identified in Genesis 4 with the character of Cain. The reciprocity of birth and death as the complementary terms of an experience of the mystery of time, marking, respectively, the Alpha and Omega of the breakthrough of Life out of Eternity, is the fundamental, innovative, "elementary idea" of mythologies of the seeded earth. And the encapsulating symbolic image condensing in one eloquent sign the whole load of connoted mythic implications (like the keystone element of a dream, "the point at which it ascends into the unknown," which, as Freud declares, is inexhaustible of its meanings[69]), is the mythologem discussed above (see II.1:34–72) of The Sacrifice.

The mystic marriage of the Moon and Sun on the eviternal plane is symbolic of a recognition in temporal phenomena of an aspect of eternity—as in Blake's aphorism in *The Marriage of Heaven and Hell*, "Eternity is in love with the productions of Time." However, as the light of the sun reflected in the moon is there subject to a process of repetitive waning and waxing, it cannot be contained in eviternity, which is of endurance everlasting, like the light of the sun, which is a constant. The marriage-moment had been that of the moon at its full, on its fifteenth night (equivalent allegorically to a maiden in her fifteenth year), which when rising had rested for a magical moment directly confronting a setting sun on the opposite horizon. The two were then of equal size and radiance. From that instant onward, however, there has been a waning of the lunar sphere, a darkness overclosing the light, until by the end of its cycle darkness prevails and the moon has disappeared into night.

The scene of the pulling up of the Tree and deliberate shoving of the Moon-bride down through the opening in the floor of the sky, replacement of the Tree, and recovery then of the chief, tells of a recognized separation of heaven and earth, which is to say, a drop in the level of consciousness, from that of the heavenly rapture of experienced non-duality (the marriage of Moon and Sun), to an unilluminated earthly mode of prosaic common sense, where facts are facts, ideas are

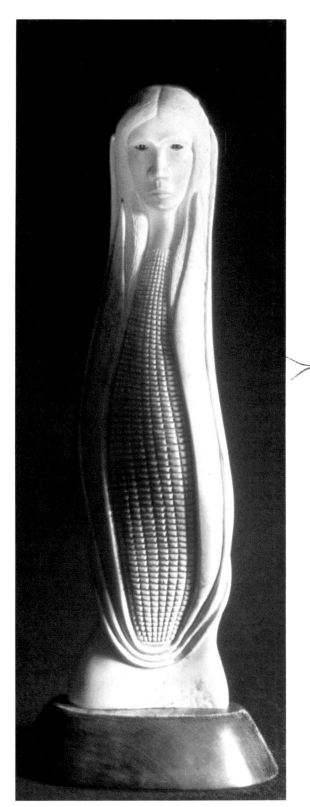

248. *Corn Spirit* (1983), 1'1½", moose-antler sculpture by Mohawk artist Stanley R. Hill, member of the Turtle Clan.

ideas, and you and I are not as one, but two. The woman's fall is at once a death (to the sky) and a birth (to this earth), and is represented by way of a truly astonishing sequence of Neoplatonic and Tantric motifs—which may be by coincidence, but even so would represent a problem.

The fall is, first, through a length of darkness, which then opens "in all directions" to an expanse of blue and of light, whereupon below her she sees water and below this, as we later learn, is earth.

In Tantric thought the mystery of creation is represented as the emanation of a "sound" or "vibration" (*nāda*) out of an inconceivable precondition, through a sequence of five elements of increasing tangibility: Space (here, a length of darkness), Air (an expanse to the four directions), Fire (light, giving visibility), Water (of perceptible forms) and Earth (of tangibility). Antecedent to the coming of light, the forms of Space and Air are invisible. The initial plane of visibility is in Water, wherein, as in a mirror, forms invisible of Space and Air appear reflected but inverted. Loon it was, therefore, the deep diver, who first perceived the descending form. Bittern it was who recognized that the advent was from above, through the air. The bittern is a marsh bird, very like a small heron. Bittern feathers bear a camouflage pattern, streaked in variegated brown and buff, enabling them to escape detection by standing upright with bill pointed upward, imitating the reeds and grasses of their habitat. It will have been while standing thus with eyes and bill fixed to the air above, that Bittern was first to recognize the reality of the situation.

The pretty episode, then, of the flight of ducks ascending to ease the woman's fall; the earth divers in willing sacrifice of their lives preparing hastily a place upon which to receive her; Great Turtle becoming, also willingly, the supporting ground of a new earth, upon which the "man-being," as a new arrival from the sphere of Air, would rest—for a while as in dream, while the new earth took form around her—represents a point of view with respect to the relationship of man to nature, and of the creatures of nature to man, that is in striking contrast to that defined in Genesis 3:14-19, where man is cursed, woman is cursed, the serpent is cursed, and the earth is cursed to "bring forth thorns and thistles." There are to be difficulties indeed, as the woman herself in her later years provides along with her grandson Flint. But the basic and sustaining sense of the relationship to mankind of the natural world and its creatures in this Native American origin myth, is of compassion, harmony, and cooperation.

* * *

From this point forward the legend is carried by way of an adaptation of one of the most widely dispersed of all Native American heroic tales, that namely of First Woman and her sons, the Primal Twins. These are the same contending brothers who appear in Tierra del Fuego, at the southernmost extremity of South America, in tales told by the Yamana (or Yahgan) as accounts of the adventures of their wandering, ancestral Yoálox family, composed of a mother, three sisters, and two brothers, to whom they attribute every detail of an extremely simple, locally adapted, hunting-and-fishing technology and order of life. (See I.2:259–262). Most, if not all, of the preserved North American examples are also set in a hunting environment, rehearsing deeds of the contending sons of a solitary deer hunter and his wife. Versions of the tale must have been known in both Americas for centuries, possibly millennia, before the rise of agriculture and development of anything as sophisticated as the Mississippian Civilization (c. A.D. 700–1200; see I.2:Map 46; also below, Map 23), which I am assuming was the interaction sphere out of which the maize-beans-and-squash planting-mythology derived, of which the Iroquois legend of the woman who fell from the sky is our outstanding Northeastern Woodland example. The aboriginal hero-folktale from archaic hunting times has been here adapted and reworked to the burden of a new order and degree of spiritual and metaphysical insights.

As represented in the elegant Mohawk interpretation of the legend, the Moonbride, already pregnant, fallen from the eviternal sky world, gave birth on the hastily fashioned island Earth, not to the legendary twins themselves, but to a daughter who would be their mother. The idyllic scene, then, of this madonna with her newborn babe, alone in the midst of an unfolding living landscape, opens the first chapter of this gentile revelation of the earthly condition of mankind following an ancestral Fall by the Tree. The infant rapidly grew, and when she arrived at a liable age was warned to defer all proposals by answering that she first had to ask her mother.

But who, one might reasonably wonder, might the maiden's possible suitors be, when she and her mother were the only two people on earth? The question has been reasonably asked, also, with regard to the possible ancestry of the wives of Adam and Eve's three sons, Cain, Abel, and then Seth. In contrast, the answer in the present case lies at hand: for was not the earth already populated with all those compassionate birds and beasts that had facilitated the mother's landing? "One has paid me a visit," the maiden said, "who has a deep fringe along his legs and arms." "That is the one," said the mother. And thus it was the Earth-Supporter, Great Turtle himself in the form of a young man, who laid an arrow by the Maiden's side and became in that sufficient way the father of her contending sons.

In all versions of the folktale it is standard that in giving birth the mother either should die or have been killed. In most cases she is brutally slain, either by her husband, her father-in-law, a stranger, or an ogre; her belly then slit open and the unborn twins flung, one into a corner of the lodge, and the other outside, into a lake or spring. There is a classic example of this initial episode from the buffalo-hunting, Siouan, Crow tribe of the upper Missouri and its tributaries, where the names of the two boys are, appropriately, Thrown-behind-the-Curtain and Thrown-into-a-Spring. The setting is the solitary tepee of a hunter and his pregnant wife.

The hunter was away one day hunting deer when a wicked woman, named Red Woman, entered the lodge and killed his wife, cut her open and, discovering twins, tossed one behind the tepee curtain and the other outside, into a spring. Then she stood the woman up, supporting her with a pole stuck into the ground, and burned her upper lip to make her appear to be smiling. When the husband, returning fatigued from the weight of the deer that he had killed and carried, saw his wife there standing as though laughing at him, he said angrily, "I'm hungry and tired, why do you stand there just laughing at me?" and he pushed her. She fell back, her stomach opened, and he realized she was dead. Then he knew that it was Red Woman who had killed her.

One night when he was sitting alone at supper he heard a voice call to him, "Father, give me some of your supper." Looking about and seeing no one, he went on eating; but when again the voice called, he replied, "Whoever you are, you may join me. It's not much. I am poor and alone."

From behind the curtain a young boy appeared who declared that this name was "Thrown-behind-the-Curtain." Every day after that, when his father would be away hunting, the boy would play about the lodge and in the neighboring woods.

"Father," he said one day, "make me two bows and some arrows for both." "Why two?" The man asked, and the boy replied, "I want to change about."

The father made the bows, but suspecting that his son had some other reason, next day when he had left the lodge he circled back and hid in a place from which to watch. And what he saw were two boys of about the same age at play, shooting arrows.

That evening the father asked, "Is there not another boy of about your own age around here?" "Yes," replied his son, "he lives in the spring." "You should bring him home," said the man, "to live with us." "I can't," said the boy; "he has sharp teeth, like an otter. But if you will make me a rawhide suit to wear, I'll try."

The father made such a suit and next morning said to his son, "I'll stay in the lodge and you tell your friend I'm away, hunting deer."

Going out clothed in the rawhide suit, Thrown-behind-the-Curtain called, "Come on out! Let's play arrows." But the other replied, "I smell something." "No you don't," said his playmate; "my father has gone to hunt deer."

Persuaded, Thrown-into-a-Spring came out, and when Thrown-behind-the-Curtain disputed a point in their play and Thrown-into-a-Spring stooped over to see how close his arrow had come, he was grabbed from behind with his arms pinned. Fiercely struggling, he tried to bite, but his teeth could not penetrate the rawhide suit. From the tepee the father came rushing to help, and from the spring the water came rushing to help Thrown-into-a-Spring. But the wild boy was dragged to a high place to which the water could not reach, and there, when the father burned incense under his nose, he became human.[70]

It is exceptional, in our Iroquois tale, that the son thrown away should have been the gentler one, Sapling and not Flint. This, however, accords with the negative

249. Stanley Hill's *Squash Spirit*, (1984), 7½" moose-antler sculpture. Hill stresses his links with his people's past by working only in traditional bone and antler.

transformation of the woman who fell from the sky, when, on becoming a grandmother, she found that her daughter had been killed in giving birth. Her metamorphosis, then, into a selfish witch carried into its final phase that series of inevitable transformations wrought by the principle of Time which throughout her lifetime had been illustrated in her body's and mind's irrevocable changes: first, on the eviternal plane, from growing child to fully matured bride; then, as bearing the seed of life (and therewith death), separating from the eviternal state to full participation in the processes of Time; giving birth, but smitten, then, by the appearance of death, hardening into a selfish hoarder of the goods of her own creation.

Her act in beheading her dead daughter and hanging the head and body, as moon and sun, on the tree beside her lodge— thereby reflecting on the earthly plane the axial Tree which had stood, and indeed still stands, above, by the lodge of her solar spouse—was a creative act reflective in its little way of the universal mythological theme of the world and its produce originating from the body of some primal being. In a fragmentary folktale version of the remembered Iroquois legend collected by Jeremiah Curtin in 1883 from a member of the Seneca tribe,[71] the

250. *Tree of the Middle Place*, painting from *Codex Borgia*, Mexico, c. A.D. 1500. Rising from the body of an earth goddess recumbent on the spines of the caiman of the abyss, the Tree, encircled by the World Sea, is surmounted by a quetzal bird of bright plumage. Two streams of blood pour into the goddess, and from her body rise two ears of maize, one yellow, the other red. The gods in attendance are Quetzalcoatl, the Feathered Serpent, god of the breath of life (of whom the quetzal bird is an attribute), and Macuil-xochitl, known also as 5 Flowers, lord of the dance and music, and of play.

Personifying the fertile earth, this goddess of life out of death is normally identified by a skull or skeletal jaw, which may be represented either as her head or as a kind of crown. She is known as the Maize Stalk Drinking Blood, also as 9 Grass. She is the mother of the gods and is in legend associated with a place called Skull (that is, Place of the Skull; see II.1:69, 97). In Mesoamerican art generally, skulls, skeletal jaws, and skeletonization appear as symbols not simply of death, but of generation and fertility out of death.

daughter, anticipating death, informed her mother, before bearing her twins, of what was about to occur.

"I am going to die," she said. "You must bury and cover me well. From my breasts will grow two stalks, on each of which an ear will appear. When ripe, give one to each of the boys that I am about to bear."

Here it is the origin of maize that is named as the gift of the mother's body, whereas in the Mexican account of the goddess Tlalteutli torn apart by the two great gods, Quetzalcoatl, the Plumed Serpent, and Tezcatlipoca, the Smoking Mirror (see II.1:37), it is the universe that is composed of her body and limbs. Likewise in the image of the Tree of the Middle Place (II.1:69), which is certainly a counterpart of the Tree of the Iroquois legend, it is from the body of a prostrate goddess that the axial Tree, symbolic of the universe, appears.

In all of these metaphorical images the Primal Sacrifice is represented as of a goddess, not of a god: and this holds in principle, as well, for the medieval, thirteenth century, cult in veneration of the Virgin (see II.1:70), to which we owe the glory of the art of the French cathedrals, where it was not indeed to a goddess, supernatural and distant, but to a living human embodiment of the quality of motherhood to whom the mind turned in gratitude and expectation for the gift of what in theological terminology is known as "God's" Mercy.

The most ancient Old World example of the mythologem of the dismembered goddess appears in a famous Babylonian text from c. 1750 B.C., telling of the cosmic goddess Tiamat, who was slain by her grandson, the sun-god Marduk, and of whose dismembered body the universe then was made.[72] The idea turns up again in the medieval Icelandic Eddas, in the figure of the torpid androgynous giant Ymir, of whose dismembered hulk the gods created the world.

> *Out of Ymir's flesh was fashioned the*
> *   earth,*
> *And the mountains were made of his*
> *   bones;*
> *The sky from the frost-cold giant's*
> *   skull,*
> *And the ocean out of his blood.*[73]

In India the motif is interpreted as a metaphysical metaphor connoting that Being of beings, *brahmātman*, that is "One as he is Person there, and many as he is in his children here," at whose departure we die;[74] our Immortal Self and Inner Controller, "other than whom there is no seer, hearer, thinker, or knower";[75] the Solar Self of all that is in motion or at rest;[76] that of which it is said that our powers "are merely the names of *its* aspects";[77] or again, the Self, from whom all action stems;[78] the Self that is omniscient.[79]

It is worth noting that in the Iroquois version of the image of the primal goddess transformed into the universe, it is not a male who performs the operation (like Babylonian Marduk, or, in the case of the ripped-apart Mexican nymph, Quetzalcoatl and Tezcatlipoca), but another female, her mother. Possibly of relevance here is the previously-noted observation by Marija Gimbutas in *The Goddesses and Gods of Old Europe: 7000-3500 B.C.*, that the principal, or perhaps indeed sole divinity of the earliest European planting-culture settlements (amply illustrated in her volume) was a goddess whose living body itself was conceived of as the universe. Her dismemberment and transformation by the very much later Babylonian Marduk will then have been an altogether uncalled-for act of violence, symptomatic of a catastrophic patriarchal assumption of authority in that formerly peaceful part of the world. The Iroquois legend shows no sign of any such overturning of an original mythic base. The image, rather, is of the one goddess in dual form, simultaneously as mother and as daughter, voluntary giving of her body, with the mother representing the process, and the daughter the substance, or primal matter, to be transformed.

That the woman who fell from the sky should then have allowed herself to be deceived by Flint accords with her own radical transformation of character at this time; for she is now a figure of the past, not of the present, and, as such, representative of all that is fixed and unchanging. Her retaining of the light of the Tree to herself and later impounding of the animals casts her in the archetypal mythological role of the Creator as Hoarder—of which, of course, the outstanding representative among the creator-gods of the world is Yahweh of the Old Testament, who, when everything had slipped from his control following the occasion of the adventure of the Tree, turned paranoid and destructive, hoarding Paradise and its Tree to himself, cursing in every cell the life that he had just created, and taking umbrage at the pretension even of a seven-story ziggurat, as though about to scale and break into his heaven.

The character of the deceiver, Flint, is of all in the legend the most complex and compactly compounded of associations. As an antithetical creator, he is a counterpart of the Persian Angra Mainyu, the Deceiver, Lord of Darkness, who as negative counterplayer to the Lord of Truth and Light, Ahura Mazda, cannot truly create, but only imitate and undo, pouring darkness, evil and imperfection into a universe already made, of light, harmony and perfection. This is the character who in Christian thought has become the Devil; and it may well be that the Iroquois, on learning of this figure from the seventeenth-century Jesuits, recognized the identification.

The name Flint itself, in explicit contrast to Sapling, announces a mythological theme of considerable importance. The mystery and enduring silence of the stone carries into the field of Time the suggestion of eternity. Sacred stones, megalithic monuments (tombstones, Stonehenge and the rest, for example), give notice of a recognition in stone of what Mircea Eliade has termed a "hierophany" (Greek, *hieros*, powerful, supernatural, holy, sacred; + *phainein*, to reveal, to show, to make known). In the plant, and more especially the tree, is a hierophany of opposite kind, of process and transformation in the flow of Time. Adolf Jensen has published a relevant fragment of myth from West Ceram (Indonesia), where it appears that "in the Beginning" there was some question as to whether mankind should be of the nature of a stone or of a tree.

At that time it was not yet certain what the character of mankind should finally be, and a banana tree and stone were in heated argument on the subject. Said the stone: "I want the people to look like me and to be as strong as I am. They should have only one side, the right, with but one arm, one leg, and one ear. Moreover, they should not die." To which the banana tree responded: "Not at all! The people should be like me. They should have two arms, two legs, two eyes, two ears and, like me, bring children into the world." The argument continued with the two ever more vehemently abusing each other until the stone, in a rage, flung itself at the banana tree and cut it down.

Next day, however, there were standing in the place of the tree its children, and the eldest son, who was of all the strongest, took up and resumed the argument. Again the stone, finally in a rage, flung itself at the banana tree and felled it. But again, on the following day, there were young banana trees there standing, and the eldest son, who was again the strongest, picked up the argument and continued. And so it went on and on, with an eldest son of the banana lineage ever there to maintain the banana trees' part, until one of them, growing at the edge of a steep cliff, said to the stone: "We are going to have to continue this thing until one of us wins." Whereupon the stone flung itself at the tree, but missed and passed over the cliff.

Then all the banana trees cried out in delight: "We have won! You can no longer fly at us." And the stone called back: "Very well then! The people shall be as you say. But like you, they shall also die."[80]

As by the maize-cultivating Iroquois, so also by the root and sago cultivating head-hunters of Indonesia, it was the complementarity of death and birth in the reproductive continuity of life through successive generations (as represented in the plant world) that was recognized in both ritual and myth as matter of the highest social concern, in contrast to the Paleolithic ideal of the Australian shaman, for example, who thought to become as indestructible as stone by acquiring a body filled with quartz crystals (see I.2:170). Such a body was the body of Flint. An extension of the idea may be recognized, as well, in the "diamond body" of the oriental yogi or monk, which is but an envisioned concretization of the metaphysical metaphor of the immortal, omniscient Self, with which, through breath control (*prāṇayama*) and the rest, he is to achieve identification and become thus released from the conditions of death and rebirth, restored to that original state which is no state but sheer transcendence, beyond all categories, whether of experience or of thought. The technical term is *kaivalya*, complete and perfect "isolation." "This universe," we read in the words of such a one, "is but a state of consciousness. In reality it is nothing. Those self-existing beings who cognize both existence and non-existence never cease to be."[81]

What I think I see, therefore, in the Iro-quois handling of the character of Flint is a rejection on the part of the "People of the Longhouse" of every kind of shamanic pretension to achieved invulnerability and, in contrast, the acceptance in affirmation of the mutuality of death and birth in the way of life in relation to a community. There is a curious cluster of negatively inflected oriental yogic motifs attached to the character of Flint, which I cannot believe can have come together either by chance or by convergence (for the term "convergence," see II.1:18–19). The Buddha was born from his mother's side; Flint, from his mother's armpit. Flint killed his mother by choosing this unnatural way to enter the world; the Buddha's mother died within ten days of his birth from her right side—or rather, according to a second-century A.D. Mahāyāna version of the event, was assumed to heaven alive, like the Mother of Jesus Christ.[82] An essential metaphor of Buddhism, as also of Jainism—which is a very much older doctrine of the way to release (*moksha*) from the sorrowful round of deaths and births (*samsára*)—is of a spiritual crossing of the torrential tide of Time to a "Yonder Shore" beyond knowledge of what it is to

251. *Stone Giant Emerging* (1978), 1'4" steatite sculpture by Cayuga artist Joe Jacobs, b. 1934, member of the Bear Clan.

see one weep or what it is to see one die. Buddhism is known, therefore, as the "vehicle" or "ferryboat" (*yāna*) to the Yonder Shore (*hīna-yāna*, "Little Ferryboat," for monks and nuns alone; *mahā-yāna*, "Big Ferryboat," for laymen as well), while in Jainism the succession of those great "Victors" (*jina*) recognized as founders of the doctrine—the last of whom, Mahavira (d. c. 529 B.C.) was an older contemporary of the Buddha—are called the "ford makers," *tīrthaṅkaras*, for opening a passage to the Yonder Shore, for others to follow.

And is it not, then, remarkable that the only original deed attributed in the legend to Flint was that of constructing a stone bridge across a lake to its yonder shore? The aim, however, of Flint's construction was not to open a way for man to gain release from death, but on the contrary, a way for deadly monsters from the invisible farther shore to come across and wipe out mankind. In Native American folklore the north is generally associated with danger, demons and disease. The most terrifying and dangerous monsters of Iroquois mythology were Stone Giants, or Ice Giants, from the north. The mythological Tirthankaras of the earliest eons of Jaina mythology are described, meanwhile, as immense giants, altogether negative to the goods and values of life anywhere in the universe, whether on earth, in the heavens, or in the purgatorial hells, who, by standing for centuries perfectly erect, motionless as monoliths, in the yogic posture called "dismissing the body" (*kāyotsarga*), had so completely disengaged their reincarnating life-monads (*jīvas*) from every impulse to engagement in the field of matter, which is of action (*karma*), that, light as bubbles, purified of material weight, they in spirit ascended to a summit of the universe beyond even highest heaven, where now in luminous omniscience they forever reside.[83]

I cannot but suspect that in this Iroquois legend of the anti-creator's unnatural birth, his body of stone, killing of his mother, and building of a bridge to an invisible yonder shore, what we have is a North American extension of a constellation of Central Asian "elementary ideas" associated with shamanic powers which in the period of the Indus Valley Civilization (c. 2300–1750 B.C.)—when figures in yoga posture first appear in works of art—was applied to the symbolization of yogic spiritual states and disciplines; whereas in the infinitely earlier, primary planting cultures which had appeared and developed, apparently independently, in three parts of the world from c. 10,000 B.C., these same metaphorical forms had already been unfavorably interpreted and rejected, as pertaining to a philosophy and practice of individualistic violence which, while appropriate to nomadic hunting tribes, in the comparatively complex conditions of agricultural village life was

finally intolerable. In Volume 1 there is reviewed an Apache myth describing the refutation and domestication of the conjuring shamans of the first ages by a sober class of priestly deputies of the life-giving mother Earth (see I.2:241–243). The issue, as there described, was between the claims of the spiritual leaders of the earlier, nomadic, hunting-and-gathering days—each with his own powers and familiars—and the priestly guardians of the socially authorized ceremonials of an agriculturally grounded commonality. This was the moment, in short, of the spiritual transition of mankind from the paideumatic force of the animal powers to that of the way of the seeded earth.

* * *

Flint's name, *Tawískaro*, we are told, means also "Ice-coated"; which explains how his building of a stone bridge could have been read as allegorical of the freezing over of the Great Lake. The monsters from the North would then, in fact, have been ice-giants turning everything alive into the condition of stonelike blocks of ice. For winters in upper New York State can be very cold winters indeed, dropping temperatures to some twenty to forty degrees below zero fahrenheit. The apparition, then, of the first bluebird of spring is a long-awaited, welcome sight.

What has happened here has been that in this last portion of the legend the timeless hunting themes of the contending-brother cycle have to such an extent taken over, that the woman who fell from the sky, now metamorphosed into her negative mode as Hoarder and Inhibitor, has been relieved even of her cardinal function as giver of maize (to which on her wedding night she had been consecrated), with the part now assigned, incongruously, to a character from the pre-planting Paleolithic ages of the animal messengers. So that, when Sapling one day was roasting the maize which his father had given him, and his grandmother, attracted by the odor, saw the sweet juice issuing from the kernels and along the rows of kernels, she cast ashes over the ear and at once the fat stopped pouring—and so it has been ever since, the ears exuding only a small amount of such fatness. "Dost thou intend," she asked, "that the man-beings who will dwell here on this earth should live as pleasantly as this?"

Another day, and when pounding maize herself, instead of finishing with one stroke, as in the sky world she had finished such work, she now made a tedious job of it, so that people, as she told Sapling, "should be much wearied in getting their bread to eat." Compare the words of Genesis 3:19: "In the sweat of your face you shall eat bread." Or the words, in Tierra

del Fuego, of the Younger Yoálox brother: "It will be very much better for people to have to make some effort and work."

Those were the two final acts in this, her own legend, of the woman who fell from the sky. From the period of her marriage, when her shelling and boiling and pounding of maize had been accomplished with such ease and skill, to this final term of her season of transformations through the course of irreversible Time, she had indeed matured in wisdom, in the way described to Frobenius by his Abyssinian female informant: from maidenhood through motherhood—like a new moon waxing to the full. But then continuing on the irreversible course, having given of her light and become dark, she has been turned into a nasty witch, resentful, hateful, and mean.

This moment, in comparative perspective, concludes the legend's representation of the elementary idea of the "Separation of Heaven and Earth," which had been first announced in the woman's fall from the sky: as though, between that moment of descent from the eviternal sphere and this, of the disappearance or departure of the heavenly ancestress, the interval of a kind of "Dream Time" had obtained (to use the Native Australian term: see I.2:135–142), when "the Lord God" (to use now the biblical vocabulary) "walked in the garden in the cool of the day."[84]

The interval has been described as the Mythological Age proper: of the Ancestors, the Fathers, or, as in this legend, the Mothers; the "Initiators" in both senses of the word (as "Originators" of the world order, and as "Instructors" in knowledge of the same), who were here in the Beginning, when all things were transparent to the archetypal ground over which phenomenality plays. The immediately following age, of the Sons and Daughters—the Ancestors having now disappeared—is then to be made in the mode, rather, of a Heroic Age: of Quest, Conflict and Transformation.

In such a context the contending mythological brothers of the old hunting tale have acquired the qualities of opposed seasonal gods, with Flint, the congealing breath of winter, converting everything to a stonelike state, and Sapling, the restorative warmth and spirit of Spring (see Botticelli's Primavera, II.1:**2**), releasing the world again to life. Wherever he goes things spontaneously increase, the earth expands and maple saplings grow into trees.

Sapling's fundamental adventure is that of going to and meeting with his father, which in world mythology is an archetypal adventure required of any youth seeking knowledge of his destiny. One thinks, for example, of Telemachus, in the Odyssey, summoned by Athene to leave his mother's house and search for his father

Odysseus. Or one may recall the Gospel episode recounted in Luke 2:41-51, of the boy Jesus, at the age of twelve, separated from his parents in Jerusalem and discovered, after three days, conversing in the Temple with the doctors of the Law. When asked why he had abandoned his earthly parents in this way, he replied (depending on which translation one reads): "Did you not know that I must be in my Father's house?" or "must be busy with my Father's affairs?"

American Indian mythologies abound in examples of the Father Quest; also, of the Father's testing of his son or sons. In the present case there is in addition the contrast of Flint's attachment to his dangerous grandmother, which has removed him from the regenerative influence of the unknown sire of his life.

The pattern of Sapling's going to his father's lodge is the same, essentially, as was that, in the sky world, of his grandmother's going to the lodge of her predestined spouse at the foot of the axial Tree; namely, (1) a *separation* (passing from a known into an unknown realm); (2) *initiation* (by the predestined spouse, or as here, by the father), and (3) a *return* to the world, bearing beneficial gifts.

In Sapling's story the first stage of the adventure is dramatically abridged. He shoots an arrow at a bird and it misses, falling into a lake (water-threshold: in the grandmother's experience, this was the river to be crossed). Diving to recover his arrow, Sapling lands, not in water, but flat on the ground, having passed right through to the bottom of the lake, where, lo! directly before him is the house of his unknown father.

The role of the arrow here is interesting. When the daughter of the woman who fell from the sky reported to her mother that she had been paid a visit by one with a deep fringe along his legs and arms and the mother responded, "That is the one," a young man that evening laid an arrow at her side. One of the two sons so conceived by the virgin mother is now led by the flight of an arrow to the lodge of his hidden father, who not only has been awaiting his arrival, but has prepared for him the gift of a bow and arrow. "As thou goest about shooting," Sapling is told, "thou art to make use of these." Warned against his grandmother and brother, he is presented next with two ears of maize and then learns that the one to whose underwater dwelling his arrow has led him is the Earth-supporter, his father.

*   *   *

Following the disappearance from her legend, therefore, of the woman who fell from the sky, the narrative is carried by way of a miscellany of standard episodes from the repertory of her grandsons, the contending twins of the old hunting-age heroic tales of the Beginning, when the earth was acquiring shape. Sapling, following his visit with the Earth-supporter, Great Turtle, his father, has been traveling about, causing the earth to increase and creating animals—anachronistically, however, since the animals were already here when his grandmother descended from on high. (Composite legends of this kind are never edited for consistency. Compare carefully, for example, the very different creation stories of Genesis 1 and 2; the first dating from c. fourth century B.C., the second, c. tenth to eighth.)

In council, the animals have agreed willingly to give all the help they can to mankind, and in the episode of the "Hiding and Recovery of the Light," Beaver, Spider, Hare and Otter have heroically assisted. As already noted, this adventure of a squad of animal helpers, each with a special skill, is a world favorite of animal tales. Their cutting down, in this legend, of the axial solar and lunar Tree marks the end of the important symbolic series, first, of the self-luminous Tree in the sky beside the sun-god's mystery lodge; next, the earthly tree by the moonwife's abode, which, when the body and head of her sacrificed daughter were hung upon it, became a simulated counterpart on earth of the axial Tree above: limited in its light, however, to the interests only of its maker. Finally, by tossing into the sky from this tree—for the illumination of the world—the body and head of his sacrificed mother, Sapling in this remarkable scene definitively terminates what may properly be called the "Saturnian" age of his grandmother; and by naming the sun, the Great Warrior, and the moon, Our Grandmother, he restores, by reflection, the symbolic sense of the marriage of the Sun and Moon at the place of the celestial Tree.

A biblical influence has been suggested for the motif in the scene of Sapling's creation of man and woman, of his implanting one rib of the male in the body of the female and one rib of the female in the body of the male. The suggestion is striking. However, no less important is the psychological sophistication of the rib-motif as here interpreted. For the woman is not drawn as a rib from the body of the male, as a projected anima-image (in James Joyce's appropriate phrase, "the cutlet-sized consort"),[85] but the male and female are created equal. Moreover, in the sequence of their responses to the interesting situation, it is the female who first wakes and touches the male just where her rib is implanted. And so again, as in the opening scene of the "down-fended" sister and brother above, it is the female who is the initiator of the action. Biblical inspiration has been suggested, also, for the scene of Sapling's breathing life into the inert clod that Flint has fashioned in imitation. The mythological motif of a god's breath (or blood) as life-giving to his creatures is a normal feature, however, in American tales of creation.

The final killing-contest of the two contending brothers bears all the marks of a shamanic challenge-combat. An affinity can be recognized in the scene from the Icelandic Poetic Edda of Baldr, standing up to a challenge, slain by a mere twig of mistletoe hurled by his enemy Hoth.[86] And that a mighty mountain range should be pointed out as the remaining body of the overcome giant Flint is an explicit example of the venerable hunting-age theme of a mythologized landscape bearing traces of the great happenings of the Mythological Age (see I.1:125, I.2:135, and **237**).

The concluding two episodes of the legend are again of a shamanic challenge type, ending, however, not in the killing, but in domestication of the challengers. The Iroquois False Face Societies, of which one version of the origin legend is supplied, were village organizations of spiritually endowed, local visionaries, dedicated to the corporal act of mercy of visiting, masked, in full membership, and attempting thereby to cure, the sick (by a kind of shock effect, as well as by magically suggestive, shamanistic means: see I.2:208, where a Seneca version is given of the Mask Society origin legend).

Sapling's consummate ease, finally, in the second of his last two adventures, in domesticating and assigning socially useful tasks to a thunder-god who has come to him already impressed by his power, bears testimony to the majesty of his spiritual position. For again, the climatology of New York State has here to be taken into account. Washington Irving's story of Rip Van Winkle asleep among the rolling thunder storms of the Catskills says something of the prominence in that part of the Hudson valley of these manifestations of a supernatural presence. Altogether, among deities, wherever thunder and great lightning storms prevail, there is none to surpass the awesome psychological effects of this bestower of the indispensable gift of rain. It was Giambattista Vico's thought that mankind's earliest notion of a threatening, yet fostering, almighty power in the heavens was first inspired by the terrifying voice of thunder.

Relevant, further, to the presentation of Sapling's position in this final episode of his legend is his designation of great serpents moving about in the depths of this earth or in the sea as the proper enemies to be watched for and killed by a socially useful thunder-god. The archetypal theme of the instinctive enmity of the bird (thunderbird or sunbird) and the serpent—one soaring high in the heaven vault, the other in bondage to this earth—has been through millennia a theme of metaphorical import in myth (see I.1:50–51). In India the combat between the great, fair-feathered solar bird, Garuḍa, and the Nāgas, members of the multitudinous serpent race, is accounted for by a legend of their descent as contending relatives from the two wives—respectively, Vinatā, the Heaven Vault and Kardü, Mother Earth—of the Old Turtle Man, Kaśyapa. The legend is of unmeasured age, derived from a context long antedating the Indo-European, Vedic-Aryan body of mythological traditions in which it has been incorporated and preserved. The locus classicus of the legend is a late Vedic, mytho-historical dramatic ballad, mixed of prose and verse, of undetermined date, called *Suparnādhyāya*, "About the Fair-feathered One," where the story is told of old Kaśyapa, his two competing wives and their progeny, about as follows:

The two wives, Mother Earth and Overarching Heaven, having conceived of the Old Turtle Man, gave birth (not inappropriately) to a certain number of eggs. Kadrü, the Earth, laid a multitude, out of which came snakes of every kind in countless number. Vinatā, Heaven, however, laid only three, and for a long time nothing whatsoever appeared from any one of them. Jealous of her prolific rival and curious to know what she had herself produced, Vinata imprudently broke open one of her three and, since the heavenly being inside was still unformed, out gushed lightning—*zutt!*—and disappeared in the sky.

Cautioned by this experience, Vinatā controlled her impatience for a while, but presently could support the strain no longer and broke open her second egg. A luminous youth was there, but incomplete, who could not walk [according to one of the Hindu theories of embryology, an organism develops from the head to the feet, and so this heavenly youth's feet had not yet been formed]. He could stand, but not walk. He would never stride across the heavens, but only rise, stand briefly, and vanish from view. His name was Aruṇa, "The Reddish One." [He is a male embodiment of the dawn and evidently, therefore, of pre-Aryan lineage, since in Vedic mythology, as in Greek, the personification of Dawn is female: Ushas/Aurora.]

Undone entirely by this second misadventure, Vinatā allowed her third egg to mature until, after five hundred years it burst of itself and out soared the golden-feathered sun-bird, Garuḍa, only member of the family fully formed. What he found was that, as the consequence of a curse that Aruṇa had put upon his unfortunate mother, she had incurred the ugly fate of becoming a slave both to Kadrü and to her numerous brood of snakes. Garuḍa immediately rescued her in a glorious conquest of his cousins, and in continuation of his mother's hatred, which he inherited, he has been pursuing snakes to this day and will do so forever.[87]

Whatever the explanation may be, it is evident that Great Turtle, in one context or another, has long been recognized over a considerable part of the Northern Hemisphere as metaphorical in some way of a life caught between the two worlds, below and above. From China there is the curious symbolic image known as the Somber

Warrior (*hsüan-wu*), of a turtle in the sexual embrace of a serpent. The turtle here is female, *yin*, associated with the Northern Quarter, and with winter. Examples of this figuration appear in Chinese art from the period of the Later Han Dynasty, A.D. 23–220. However, already from the royal tombs that are now being excavated at the ancient Shang capital at An-yang, now dated as from c. 1300–1100 B.C., among the many thousands of inscribed oracle bones and shell fragments that have been found, no less than 160,000 pieces of turtle shell have been identified, suggesting, as Professor Kwang-chih Chang points out in his volume, *Shang Civilization*, a total of approximately 16,000 turtles carried to the capital either by officials of the Yin court or by people with close ties to the Yin king, to be questioned by necromantic means concerning the well-being of the monarch.[88] The antiquity of the idea of the turtle in his microcosmic housing as a carrier of the burden of time is definitively established in these findings.

But the evidence from India is of an even greater antiquity, since the Vedic-Aryan invasions were about contemporary with the establishment of the Shang capital at An-yang, while the sorry tale of Kaśyapa and his wives is of an earlier period than the Vedic-Aryan invaders.

From the standpoint of a comparative mythologist and historian, late twentieth century A.D., in consideration of this really vast outspread through both space and time of what is apparently a single constellation of elementary ideas, the first observation will certainly be of a remarkable consistency of thematic concerns throughout: essentially conflicts, whether of heavenly and earthly values, eviternal and temporal; or, within the temporal field, creative and obstructive forces. These are themes of ethical and psychological import, grounded, I would think, in what C.G. Jung has termed the "archetypes of the collective unconscious." They are of the essence of the human condition and, though under differing circumstances variously interpreted, are not culturally determined, little vary from one period or culture to the next, and endure as the ground of all the colorfully inflected narratives and figurations of both the oral and the literate traditions of mankind.

The second observation will be of the propriety of the metaphorical images by which these archetypal forms or elementary ideas have been mythologically connoted; these images being of two orders: (1) *ecumenical*, of such universally experienced phenomena as the sun and moon, stars, earth, light and dark, trees, rocks, and the flight of birds; but then also, (2) *provincial*, of such local creatures and possibilities of experience as turtles, freezing cold, or prodigious thunder. In literate traditions, symbolic images may be car-

ried into periods and regions where they would be otherwise unknown, lions into medieval England, for example. In primary oral traditions, on the other hand, the images are almost without exception of local experience, imported tales becoming appropriately recast in terms of the local scene. One of the interesting aspects of the constellation of myths and tales around Great Turtle and his progeny is in the consistency of its imagery, whether in India, in a pre-Vedic dramatic ballad (c. 2000 B.C.) of Kaśyapa and his contending children, Garuḍa and the Nāgas, or in New York State (nineteenth century A.D.), in a remembered Iroquois legend of a Great Turtle's son assigning to a flashing thunder-god the task of securing mankind against serpents; Great Turtle himself, in this story, being the Earth-supporter, bearing on his back the island Earth, as in India the god Vishnu in the form of his incarnation as a turtle (*kūrmāvatāra*) supports on his back the universe.

The final question, then, must be of the possible place and time of origin of this remarkably consistent cycle of symbolic tales; and the most likely answer, it seems to me, must be about the same as that already suggested (see page 160) for the combination of motifs that in India became associated (c. 2300–1750 B.C.) with the imagery of yoga, and which in the Iroquois legend of the contending twins is attached to the birth story of the unnatural giant Flint. In a Late Paleolithic grave discovered at Mal'ta, near Lake Baikal in Siberia, at the eastern end of that range of distribution of Paleolithic goddess figurines at the western term of which is the Venus of Laussel, no less than twenty female statuettes of mammoth ivory were found, as well as six flying birds and one swimming, suggesting geese and ducks, all of mammoth ivory, and a roughly rectangular ivory medallion, showing on one side a stippled spiral of seven turns with S-forms enclosing it and on the other side, three cobra-like wavy serpents. The probable dating of this site, which is within two hundred miles of the northern border of Mongolia, is c. 16,000 to 13,000 B.C.; that of the Venus of Laussel, c. 20,000 to 18,000 B.C. Flowing north from the Baikal region are the Yenisei and Lena rivers, which every one of the hunting bands passing from Asia by way of Beringland into America (see I.1:Maps 7, 11, 12, and 14) will have either to have followed or at least to have crossed. A more likely distribution center for a Late Paleolithic to Early Neolithic mythology would be difficult to imagine.

252. Iroquois False Face Mask of painted wood with eyes of beaten metal, human hair, and sharks snaggle tooth, c. 13″ high, late nineteenth century.

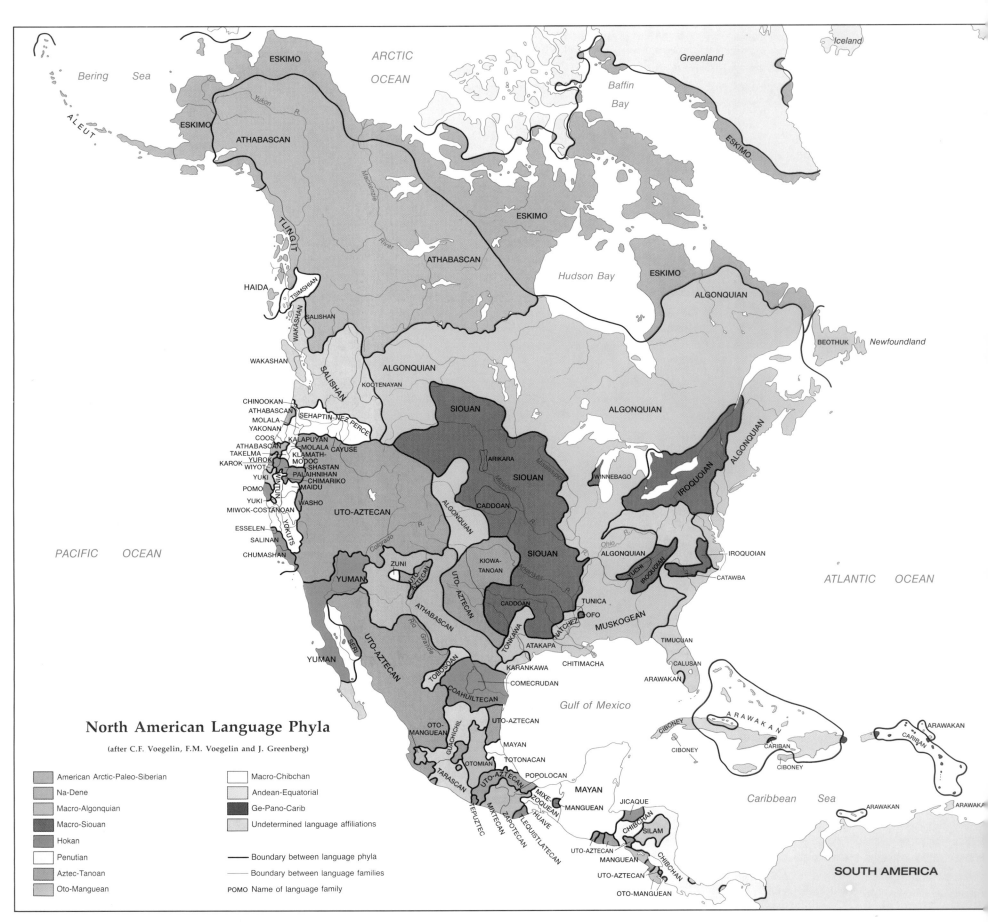

North American Language Phyla

(after C.F. Voegelin, F.M. Voegelin and J. Greenberg)

American Arctic-Paleo-Siberian
Na-Dene
Macro-Algonquian
Macro-Siouan
Hokan
Penutian
Aztec-Tanoan
Oto-Manguean
Macro-Chibchan
Andean-Equatorial
Ge-Pano-Carib
Undetermined language affiliations
Boundary between language phyla
Boundary between language families
POMO   Name of language family

Map 18.

164

The Algonquians

Historical Introduction

From Labrador to the Carolinas, and from the Atlantic to the Rockies, tribes of the Algonquian linguistic family had been flourishing for millennia when, in the sixteenth and seventeenth centuries, the French, Dutch and English began settling the Atlantic coast (Map 17). People of no other single linguistic stock had ever occupied in North America such a vast, geographically diversified domain. Culturally, the tribes differed enormously. Whereas in Virginia, for example, Pocahontas and her father, Chief Powhatan, were Algonquians of the high, "Mississippian" stage of the Native American civilization (see I.2:210–211, 200–221), the meaning of the name Nascapi, of an Algonquian hunting, fishing and foraging tribe of northern Labrador, is "crude, uncivilized people." At one extreme, the simplest fishers, hunters and gatherers, at the other, elegantly civilized, town-dwelling agriculturalists, the Algonquians were the first Americans north of the Gulf of Mexico to be confronted by Europeans and dispossessed by them (no matter what their cultural standings may have been) of both their homeland and their gods.

The prehistoric source of this widely dispersed linguistic family has not (as far as I know) been established. Cultural affinities are evident, however, when the wigwam and snowshoe culture of the northeastern-most Siberians (I.2:131–133, Map 31, and 178–179) is viewed in relation to the culture of any of the Algonquian Canadian tribes (see Map 17). As recognized by Waldemar Jochelson in his fundamental study of the northeast Siberian Koryak: "Nothing points so plainly to a very ancient connection between the Koryak and Indian mythologies as the similarity of the elements of which they are composed; for while some of the religious customs and ceremonies may have been borrowed in recent times, the myths reflect, for a very long time and very tenaciously, the state of mind of the people of the remotest periods.... We find in the Koryak myths elements of the Raven cycle of the Tlingit, Haida, and Tsimshian; those of the cycle of tales about Mink of the Kwakiutl and

neighboring tribes; of myths about wandering culture-heroes, totem-ancestors; and of tales about animals current among tribes of British Columbia; also myths of the Athapascan of the interior, and the Algonquin and Iroquois east of the Rocky Mountains."[89]

The appellation Algonquin, or Algonkin (which is possibly from the Micmac, *algomeaking*, "at the place of spearing fish and eels"),[90] was the name originally of a single hunting and fishing tribe formerly dwelling on the Ottawa River, which was early applied by the French, however, to any of the linguistically related tribes of New France, in extended sense the form of the word now favored is Algonquian, or Algonkian. Classified geographically the Algonquians fall into five great divisions:

1. *the Northern Division,* sub-classified as of two groups dwelling chiefly in Canada, north of the Great Lakes and St. Lawrence, (a) *the Algonkin group,* comprising the Nipissing, Temiscaming, Abittibi, and Algonkin proper; and (b) *the Chippewa group,* made up of the Ojibwa (or Chippewa proper), Cree, Ottawa, and Missisauga;

2. *the Northeastern Division* (occupying the Canadian Maritime Provinces, eastern Quebec and Maine), sub-classified also as of two groups (a) *the Montagnais group,* comprising the Montagnais and Nascapi, Mistassin, Bersiamite and Papinachois; and (b) *the Abnaki group,* of the Micmac, Malecite, Passamaquoddy, Sokoki, Arisaruntacook, Norridgewock and Penobscot;

3. *the Eastern Division* (originally along the Atlantic coast, from New England to North Carolina, of whom no more than the echoes of their names remain): the Pennacook, Massachuset, Wampanoag, Narragasset, Nipmuc, Montauk, Mohegan, Wappinger, Delaware, Shawnee, Nantocoke, Conoy, the Pamlico and (Pocahontas' tribe) the Powhatan;

4. *the Central Division* (comprising groups formerly of Wisconsin, Illinois, Michigan, Indiana and Ohio): the Menominee and the Sauk group (including Sauk, Fox and Kickapoo), the Masconten, Potawatomi, Illinois branch of the Miami group (Cahokia, Peoria, Kaskaskia, Tamaroa and Michigamea), as well as, finally, the Miami branch of the Miami group (the Piankashaw, Miami proper, and Wea);

5. *the Western Division:* five formerly powerful tribes who once ranged along the eastern slopes of the Rockies: the Arapaho, Cheyenne, and three members of the Black-

foot Confederacy, the Kainah, Siksika, and Piegan.[91]

Comparative linguistic studies conducted by Mary R. Haas in the 1950s revealed a significant number of precise phonetic correspondences between the Algonquian languages and those of an extensive "Gulf" group (formerly in the southeastern United States), which in the 1920s had been assigned (by Edward Sapir) to the Hokan-Siouan linguistic phylum. These were the natives originally of Mississippi and Alabama, Georgia and Northwest Florida: the Muskogeans (Choctaw and Chickasaw, Alabama and Kosati, Muskogee [or Creek] and Seminole, Mikasuki and Hitchiti); as well as of Louisiana: the Natchez, Atakapa, Chitimacha and Tunica; and of eastern Texas: the Tonkawa.[92]

Recognized today as being of a single *Macro-Algonquian* phylum, this immense constellation of linguistically related tribes must at one time have dominated without significant opposition practically all of North America east of the Rockies; and that they occupied also, for a time at least, some part of the Pacific coast is suggested by the presence in northern California of two salmon-fishing Macro-Algonquian tribes, the Wiyot (on the lower Mad River, Humboldt Bay, and lower Eel River), and Yurok (to the north, on the lower Klamath River and adjacent coast).

The remoteness in immemorial time of the prehistoric migrations out of Asia, through Alaska, into North America, of those Paleolithic hunting tribes whose widely dispersed, culturally differentiated, remotest descendants are now recognized as being of this single Macro-Algonquian heritage, may be judged from the fact that both Alaska and the Canadian Northwest have become occupied, since that distant time, by two later waves of Asian Immigrants (Map 18), namely the Na-Dene, or Athabascans, and the Eskimo-Aleut. A roughly-estimated dating for the inception (in regions around the Bering Sea) of this last, or Eskimo tradition, and for its subsequent passage along the Arctic circle to Labrador and Greenland, has been suggested as having been probably from c. 2000–1000 B.C.[93]—by which time the Algonquians will have already been long established, apparently unchallenged, in their North American home.

Two simultaneous incursions from the south, commencing possibly c. A.D. 1000, by tribes of another language phylum, the

Macro-Siouan (Map 18) inaugurated a violent history of tribal displacements, annihilations and recombinations, which in the sixteenth and seventeenth centuries became disastrously exacerbated with the arrivals along the Atlantic coast of the French and English rivals for supremacy over the continent. The Dutch were soon *hors de combat*. In Florida and to the south the Spanish (with the Pope's [i.e. God's] blessing) were already in control. Pressing inland, therefore, from their respective Atlantic beachheads, the contending French and English became engaged in North America (as they were already engaged in India) in the opening military campaigns of what was to become, through the next three centuries, an ever augmenting succession of worldwide wars for economic and political domination of the planet. In their ubiquitous campaigns, moreover, the two were about equally apt in engaging to their purposes the natives of whatever piece of property they might at the time have been intending to appropriate to themselves. And so it came to pass that in northeastern North America, both the Algonquian tribes and the Macro-Siouan became, in their native conflicts, pawns on the board of a European game, the aim and end of which was to be the subjugation and extinction of themselves.

The Macro-Siouan tribes advancing up the Mississippi and Missouri valleys (Map 18) were of two distinct sub-groups: (1) *the Siouan proper* (the Winnebago, who ultimately settled in what is now Wisconsin; Hidatsa and Mandan, in North Dakota; Crow, in eastern Montana; Dakota (Sioux), on the northern plains; Omaha, Kansa, Ponca, Osage and Quapaw, on the central plains; and on the Gulf Coast (today extinct), the Ofo, Tutelo, and Biloxi; then (2) *the Caddoan tribes*: Arikara in the Dakotas; Pawnee, on the Kansas plains; Caddo, in Arkansas; and the Wichita, in Oklahoma and Texas.

Simultaneously advancing up the eastern coast were tribes of the *Macro-Siouan/Iroquoian* linguistic phylum: the Cherokee, who settled in the southern Appalachians; Tuscarora, in what is now North Carolina; Seneca, Cayuga, Onandaga, Oneida and Mohawk in New York State; and in southeastern Ontario, the Wyandot and Huron. Two additional branches of the same linguistic phylum were at the time represented in the (now extinct) Catawba of the Carolinas and Yuchi (now all but extinct, with a recent count of about a hundred) of the southern Appalachians.

The original Apalachee, after whom the Appalachian mountain system was named, were a Muskogean (Macro-Algonquian) tribe once dominant in northwestern Florida from the region around Apalachicola Bay to present-day Pensacola. They were agriculturalists, prosperous and industrious, as well as noted for their fighting qualities, with their principal towns in the areas of present day Tallahassee and St. Marks. Although visited in 1528, and again in 1539, by the military expeditions of Narvaez and De Soto, they successfully resisted subjugation by the Spaniards until about 1600, when they were Christianized and disarmed. By 1655 there were Franciscan missions in eight of their considerable towns, serving a pacified Christian population of some 6000 to 8000. Industrious still and again prospering, with many substantial villages throughout their extensive territory the Apalachee for a hundred years survived as one of the earliest and most successful native Christian communities in the New World.

Around 1700, however, they began to be seriously harried by the repeated raids of their pagan Algonquian relatives to the north, who were being incited to these massacres by the Protestant Christian governors of the English colony of Carolina; until finally, in the year 1703, a formidable expedition under Governor Moore of the colony, constituted of a thousand or more assembled Indians from various tribes and a dozen or so of English officers, invaded and ravaged the whole Apalachee countryside, demolishing towns and missions, together with their fields and orange groves. The Spanish garrison commander was killed; one of the friars was burned at the stake; more than two hundred Apalachee fighting youths were slain and fourteen hundred or more of men, women and children were carried off and sold into slavery. A second expedition completed the operation a year later, when the remnants of the destroyed people took refuge, either among friendly neighboring tribes, or with the Catholic French at Mobile—whence, in 1763, following the cession of Florida to England, these crossed the Mississippi into French Louisiana and there preserved their identity until as late, at least, as 1804, when there were fourteen Apalachee families still living on Bayou Rapide.[94]

The fate of the Algonquians to the north was to be in the end about the same as that of the annihilated Apalachee of the south. For added there to the violence of the predatory Europeans from without, was that of the Iroquois from within. Spengler's succinct definition of a European nation as a "folk in form for war," defines the character, as well of the Macro-Siouan, as of the Indo-European, warrior tribes. So that the combined effects, from the seventeenth century onward, of the two, equally heartless, simultaneous onslaughts was of one definitive calamity after another. Cyrus Thomas and James Mooney, in a 1907 publication of the Bureau of American Ethnology, delineated in the following terms the main course of this appalling history.

"As the early settlements of the French, Dutch, and English were all within the territory of the eastern members of the [Algonquian] family, they were the first aborigines north of the Gulf of Mexico, to feel the blighting effect of contact with a superior race. As a rule, the relations of the French with the Algonquian tribes were friendly, the Foxes being the only tribe against whom they waged war. The English settlements were often engaged in border wars with their Algonquian neighbors, who, continually pressed farther toward the interior by the advancing white immigration, kept up for a time a futile struggle for the possession of their territory. The eastern tribes, from Maine to Carolina, were defeated and their tribal organization was broken up. Some withdrew to Canada, others crossed the mountains into the Ohio valley, while a few bands were located on reservations by the whites, only to dwindle and ultimately become extinct. Of many of the smaller tribes of New England, Virginia, and other eastern states there are no living representatives. Even the languages of some are known only by a few words mentioned by early historians, while some tribes are known only by name. The Abnaki and others who fled into Canada settled along the St. Lawrence under the protection of the French, whose active allies they became in all the subsequent wars with the English down to the fall of the French power in Canada [in 1763]. Those who crossed the Allegheny mountains into the Ohio valley, together with the Wyandot and the native Algonquian tribes of that region, formed themselves into a loose confederacy, allied first with the French and afterward [following the Revolution] with the English against the advancing settlements with the declared purpose of preserving the Ohio River as the Indian boundary.... In 1815 those who had taken part against the United States during the War of 1812 made peace with the Government; then began the series of treaties by which, within thirty years, most of the Indians of this region ceded their lands and removed west of the Mississippi.

"A factor which contributed greatly to the decline of the Algonquian ascendency was the power of the Iroquoian confederacy, which by the beginning of the seventeenth century had developed a power destined to make them the scourge of the other Indian population from the Atlantic to the Mississippi and from the Ottawa River in Canada to the Tennessee. After destroying the Huron and the Erie, they turned their power chiefly against the Algonquian tribes, and ere long Ohio and Indiana were nearly deserted, only a few villages of Miami remaining here and there in the northern portion. The region south and west they made a desert, clearing of native inhabitants the whole country within five hundred miles of their seats. The Algonquian tribes fled before them to the region of the upper lakes and the banks of the Mississippi, and only when the French had guaranteed them protection against their deadly foes did they venture to turn back toward the east."[95]

The Indian in the North American Conscience

The mystery of the origins of these aboriginal defenders of the continent now being claimed for civilization by a self-designated "superior" race excited the curiosity and imagination even of those engaged in programming their extermination. Of interest also were the enigmatic mounds in many parts of the country—the long-winding "Serpent Mound," for example, near Locust Grove, Ohio (See I.2: **354**). In a paper entitled, "The Complications of American Psychology" (1930), the psychiatrist Carl G. Jung remarks on his discovery in the symptomatology of North American patients evidence of a deeply suppressed fascination with an ambiguous image of the heroic American Indian. "Man," states Jung, "can be assimilated by a country. There is an x and a y in the air and in the soil of a country, which slowly permeate and assimilate him to the type of the aboriginal inhabitant, even to the point of slightly remodeling his physical features."[96] And he asks: "Is the American white man nothing but a simple white man, or is he in some way different from the European representative of the species? I believe," he suggests, "that there is a marked difference between them, within as well as without. European magazines have recently published pictures of well-known Americans in Indian headdress, and in the opposite column some Red Indians in European costume, with the question, Who are the Indians?"[97] "The external assimilation to the peculiarities of a country is a thing one could almost expect. There is nothing astonishing in it. But the external

similarity is feeble in comparison with the less visible but all the more intense influence on the mind. It is as though the mind were an infinitely more sensitive and suggestible medium than the body. It is probable that long before the body reacts the mind has already undergone considerable changes, changes that are not obvious to the individual himself or to his immediate circle, but only to an outsider."[98]

There is, furthermore, a subtle psychological appeal exerted upon the historically sophisticated, so-called "superior" mind by the apparent simplicity of an aboriginal society in accord with the order of nature. "The 'inferior' man," states Jung, "has a tremendous pull, because he fascinates the inferior layers of our psyche, which has lived through untold ages of similar conditions—*on revient toujours à ses premiers amours.*' He reminds us—not so much our conscious as our unconscious mind—not only of childhood but of our prehistory, which would take us back not more than about twelve hundred years so far as the Germanic races are concerned…. But the defences of the Germanic man reach only as far as consciousness reaches. Below the threshold of consciousness the contagion meets with little resistance."[99]

Interest in the tribal thought and languages of the American aborigines began,

253. Frank Cushing (1857-1900) in traditional Native American dress, from an 1880 photograph. An ethnologist for the Bureau of American Ethnography, Cushing was adopted by the Zuni and made a member of the Macaw Clan. He eventually became second chief of the tribe.

254. Peter Lindestrom's late seventeenth-century sketch of (in front) early trade between the Delawares and the Swedes, while tribal warfare rages behind.

of course, with the early missionaries: Dominicans and Franciscans in Spanish Florida and the Caribbean; Jesuits in French Canada and down the Mississippi to the Gulf. Accounts by these trained scholars of their experiences and findings are the earliest documents that we have, out of which to reconstruct an impression of the mental environment of the North American Eastern Woodland tribes. In Protestant New England and Virginia, on the other hand, there seems to have been little or no interest taken, either in missionizing, or in understanding and appreciating the mentality of the natives being scoured from the land. For in contrast to the colonial policies of the Latins—French, Spanish and Portuguese—whose aim was not to eradicate, but to convert and incorporate aborigines into an already multiracial, Roman Catholic world-community, the Anglo-Saxon ideal was, rather, to establish in occupied territories extensions of the English nation, if possible removing, and in any case retaining beyond the pale of English life, whatever population may have encumbered the valuable property when it was first claimed for the Crown.

Fundamentally distinguished from either of these colonial policies was that represented in the earliest full declaration of U.S. national policy toward the native tribes which in the Northwest Ordinance of 1787 was declared and defined in the following (today astonishing) terms:

"The utmost good faith shall always be observed toward the Indians, their lands and property shall never be taken from them without their consent; and in their property, rights, and liberty, they shall never be invaded or disturbed, unless in just and lawful wars authorized by congress; but laws founded in justice and humanity shall from time to time be made, for preventing wrongs being done to them, and for preserving peace and friendship with them."[100]

As one of the first declarations of the U.S. Congress under the constitution, this fundamental doctrine was embodied in the act of August 7, 1789. Moreover, an extended definition of the legal and political rights of the tribes was then explicitly developed in the early opinions of the Nation's fourth Chief Justice, John Marshall, notably in the case of *Worcester v. Georgia* as follows:

"The Indian nations had always been considered as distinct, independent, political communities, retaining their original natural rights, as the undisputed possessors of the land, from time immemorial.... The settled doctrine of the law of nations is, that a weaker power does not surrender its independence—its right to self-government—by associating with a stronger, and taking its protection. A weak state, in order to provide for its safety, may place itself under the protection of one more powerful, without stripping itself of the right of government and ceasing to be a state."[101]

Nor was there any suggestion in any of these originating statements by the founders of the Nation that missionaries were to be allowed to invade with impunity the privacy of the protected aboriginal tribes, divesting them of immemorial beliefs, to impose by force or spiritual intimidation one or another of the current European varieties of Christianity. For these Fathers of our Nation were neither Catholic nor Protestant, but eighteenth-century Deists who rejected the doctrine of the "Fall" and with that, the necessity for "Redemption" as well as the idea of a special Judeo-Christian revelation. Man's nature, in the Deist view, is not corrupt; the idea of God is innate in man's mind from the beginning; so that by reason alone man has arrived, everywhere, at a recognition of God which is sufficient. The beliefs immemorial of the primal mind of "noble savagery," uncorrupted by historically conditioned sociological modifications, may be regarded in their own right, therefore, as revelations of a body of natural religious knowledge that is in every person inborn and may, through the use of reason, be recovered.

255. Henry Rowe Schoolcraft (1793–1864).

256. Ojibwa Midewiwin Scroll (detail), birchbark, 3′9″ × 10½″, late nineteenth century.

The Midewiwin (Grand Medicine Lodge) created such scrolls as mnemotic records of the complex sequences of songs and prayers used in their various religious rituals. Each figure impressed into the birchbark represents a given moment in a particular sacred ceremony.

Although Woodland Indian artists were capable of rendering the human figure more representationally (see Figs. 274, 275, 280), the naive depiction used in this scroll is typical of the archaic graphic style associated with Ojibwa sacred art. The figures with horns represent individuals that possess special supernatural powers (see I.2:**269-272**).

Schoolcraft's Surprising Discovery of a Native American Oral Literature

That the vanishing Native American race possessed an oral literature of myth, legend, anecdote and humorous fiction of its own, was in 1839 made known to the Neo-American community by the young college dropout and frontiersman, Henry Rowe Schoolcraft (1793–1864), who in 1822 had assumed the position of Indian Agent at a remote trading and military outpost, Sault Ste. Marie, at the outlet of Lake Superior, where he had married the granddaughter, Jane Johnston, of an Ojibwa chief, Wabojeeg. George Catlin (1796–1872: see I.2:226–231), a young dropout lawyer turned painter, was at work, those same years, among the Plains tribes of the Upper Missouri (the "Wildest Tribes of Indians in North America," as he termed them), painting, sketching and writing his invaluable "Letters and Notes on Their Manners, Customs, and Conditions, 1832–1839."[102]

"My connection with the Johnston family," Schoolcraft states in his *Personal Memoirs of a Residence of Thirty Years* (1851), "has thrown open the whole arcana of the Indian's thoughts."[103] And in the "Preliminary Observations" to his "Indian Tales and Legends," (1839)—from which Longfellow drew *The Song of Hiawatha* (1855)—we read, as follows, of the circumstances of what, apparently to himself, as well as the most of his reading public, was an altogether unexpected revelation:

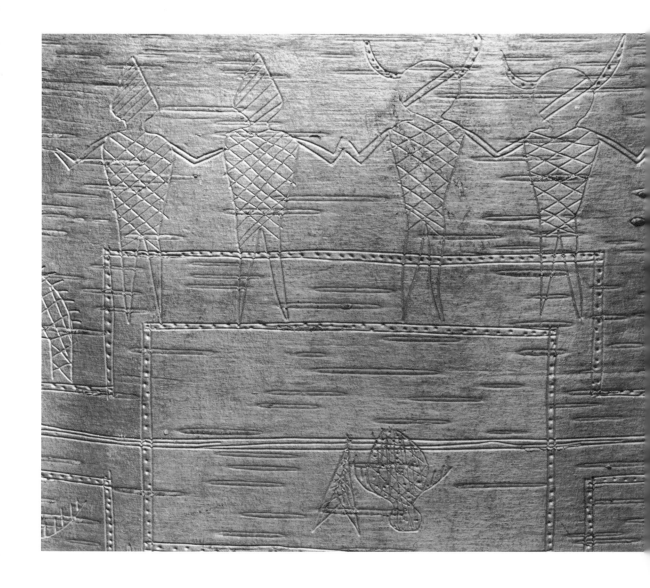

"My attention was first arrested by the fact of the existence of such tales among the Ojibwa nation inhabiting the region about Lake Superior in 1822. Two years previous, I had gone out in that quarter as one of the members of a corps of observation, on an expedition to the head waters of the Mississippi. The large area of territory which it was found this tribe occupied, together with their number and warlike character, induced the department of war to extend a military post to the Falls or *Sault* of St. Mary's, near the outlet of Lake Superior, in the year above named. I accompanied this force, and assumed, at the same time, an official relation to this tribe, as Agent of Indian affairs, which led me to inquire into their distinctive history, language, and characteristic traits. It was found that they possessed a story-telling faculty, and I wrote down from their narration a number of these fictitious tales, some of which were amusing merely, others were manifestly intended to convey mythological or allegorical information. The boundaries between truth and fiction are but freely defined among the aborigines of this Continent, and it was found in this instance, that the individuals of the tribes who related the tales were also the depositories of their historical traditions, such as they were; and these narrators wove the few and scattered incidents and landmarks of their history into the web and woof of their wildest tales. I immediately announced this interesting discovery in their moral character to a few friends and correspondents, who were alike interested in the matter; and a new zest was thus given to the inquiry, and the field of observation greatly extended. The result was the finding of similar tales among all the northwestern tribes whose traditions were investigated. They were also found among some of the tribes west of the Mississippi.... To find a trait which must hereafter be deemed characteristic of the mental habits of these tribes, so diffused, furnishes a strong motive for extending inquiries farther and wider. It may be asked whether the South American aborigines possessed, or still possess, this point of intellectual affinity with the tribes of the North. Did Manco Capac and Montezuma employ this means to strengthen political power, inspire courage, or console themselves under misfortune? Do the icebound and impoverished natives of the Arctic circle draw inspiration in their cruel vicissitudes from a similar intellectual source? What sound deductions can be drawn from a comparison of Eastern and Western fable, as thus developed? And, finally, is this propensity connected, in other of the American stock tribes, with a hieroglyphic system of notation...which will bear any useful comparison with the phonetic system of Egypt, the Runic of Iceland and Norway, or with any other mode of

257. Bark records collected (1903–05) from Leech Lake, Minnesota, by Ojibwa chief William Jones, that detail a healing-ceremony chant sung before water drawn from the lake is mixed with tobacco to make a salve.

perpetuating the knowledge of events or things known to the human race?

"A few remarks may be added respecting the character of the tales now submitted to inspection. And the first is, that they appear to be of a homogenous and vernacular origin. There are distinctive tribal traits, but the general features coincide. The ideas and incidents do not appear to be borrowed or unnatural. The situations and circumstances are such as are common to the people. The language and phraseology are of the most simple kind. Few adjectives are used, and few comparisons resorted to. The style of narration, the cast of invention, the theory of thinking, are eminently peculiar to a people who wander about in woods and plains, who encounter wild beasts, believe in demons, and are subject to the vicissitudes of the seasons. The tales refer themselves to a people who are polytheists; not believers in one God or Great Spirit, but of thousands of spirits; a people who live in fear, who wander in want, and who die in misery. The machinery of spirits and necromancy, one of the most ancient and previous errors of the human race, supplies the framework of these fictitious creations. Language to carry out the conceptions might seem to be wanting, but here the narrator finds a ready resource in the use of metaphor, the doctrine of metamorphosis, and the personification of inanimate objects; for the latter of which, the grammar of the language has a peculiar adaption. Deficiencies of the vocabulary are thus supplied, life and action are imparted to the whole material creation, and every purpose of description is answered. The belief of the narrators and listeners in every wild and improbable thing told, helps wonderfully, in the original, in joining the sequence of parts together. Nothing is too capacious for Indian belief. Almost every declaration is a prophecy, and every tale a creed. He believes that the whole visible and invisible creation is animated with various orders of malignant or benign spirits, who preside over the daily affairs and over the final destinies of men. He believes that these spirits must be conciliated by sacrifices, and a series of fasts and feasts either follow or precede these rites, that by the one they may be rendered acceptable, and by the other, his gratitude may be shown. This constitues the groundwork of Algic [i.e., of Algonquian] religion; but superstition has ingrafted upon the original stock, till the growth is a upas [an immense, poisonous tree] of giant size, bearing the bitter fruits of demonology, witchcraft, and necromancy. To make the matter worse, these tribes believe that animals of the lowest, as well as highest class in the chain of creation, are alike endowed with reasoning powers and faculties. And as a natural conclusion, they endow birds, and bears, and all other animals with souls, which, they believe, will be encountered in other shapes in another state of existence. So far the advantages of actual belief come in aid of their fictitious creations, and this is the true cause why so much importance is attached to the flight and appearance of particular birds, who, being privileged to ascend in the air, are supposed by them to be conversant with the wishes, or to act in obedience to the mandates of the spirits; and the circumstance of this belief deserves to be borne in mind in the perusal of their tales, as it will be found that the words put into the mouths of the actors express the actual opinions of the natives on life, death, and immortality, topics which have hitherto been impenetrably veiled.[104]

Schoolcraft's surprise in his discovery in North America of an oral tradition of native lore is itself surprising, since there had been already for three hundred years a general, indeed even detailed, knowledge of such matters current in the colonies, not only of Spain, to the south, but also of France, to the immediate north and west. One thinks of the accounts of native belief and ceremonial sent annually to Rome in the *Jesuit Relations;* also, of the expositions of Aztec and related Mesoamerican mythologies represented in such works, for example, as the sixteenth-century *Historia de las cosas de Nueva España,* by the missionary historian, Bernadino de Sahagún (c. 1490–1590). Indeed, Columbus himself on his second voyage (1493–94) assigned to a certain Catalonian friar, Ramón Pané, the charge of living with the Indians, learning their language, and reporting on their beliefs, which, in fact, he did.

That for three hundred years within the English pale there should have been no interest whatsoever shown in the religions of the native tribes says something, surely, for the combination of demonophobia and sheer snobbism in the Puritan witch-burning fix of the mind. One thinks of the Salem witch trials (May–October, 1692). One thinks, also, of Samuel Johnson's retort to a remark of his biographer, Boswell, "Don't cant to me about savages!"

258. Georgia Militia under General Floyd attacking the Creek Indians at Autosee, November 29, 1813. Heeding the message of Tecumseh, the great Shawnee leader, about half the Creeks (the Red Sticks) determined to make a stand against the encroaching whites. They were crushed by Gen. Andrew Jackson, who soon afterwards forced all the Creeks (including his erstwhile allies, the White Sticks) to cede their ancestral lands to the U.S. government.

The establishment of the Republic, however, brought into authority (though for no more than half a century, 1781–1828) that exceptional company of eighteenth-century humanists by whom the civilized ideal was proclaimed of an American nation established in justice, protective and respectful of the humanity and legal rights of the continent's nations of native race. Thomas Jefferson (1743–1826), James Madison (1751–1836), and John C. Calhoun (1782–1850), recognizing the importance of ethnological information for the conduct of such a protectorate, initiated a vast government program of scientific expeditions and research, underwritten by federal funds, to report, not only on the geography of the as yet unsettled regions to the west, but also on the inhabiting tribes, their languages, religious beliefs, rituals and ceremonies. And it was in connection with one of these research teams that Schoolcraft, in 1820, in the capacity of geologist, had been appointed by Calhoun (at that time U.S. Secretary of War) to an explorative expedition, to be conducted by Governor Lewis Cass of the Michigan Territory, to mark the headwaters of the Mississippi. In 1842, Albert Gallatin (1761–1848)—who in August 1814, as U.S. Secretary of Treasury, had negotiated at Ghent the end of the War with Great Britain of 1812, and from 1832 to 1839 had been President of the National Bank—having been for years an interested student of the Indian tribes, founded for the continuation of such studies the American Ethnological Society of New York.

Thus from the first year of the century a formidable, Government supported, scientific program of research into the character and conditions of the North American Indian tribes had been established and was in full career, when, on the political front, in 1828, the Indian-fighter Andrew Jackson—who on March 27, 1814, at the so-called "Battle" of Horseshoe Bend (on the Tallapoosa River, at Tohopeka, Alabama) had with cannon obliterated the last, fugitive remnant of the Creek nation—became seventh President of the United States.

Two contrary Government programs have, since that date, been deliberately pursued. The first, inspired by the humanistic ideals of the authors of our nation and best represented in the magnificent annual publications of the Bureau of American Ethnology has issued in the constitution, finally, of a publicly invisible literary memorial to a vanished civilization stowed for scholars on library shelves; while the second, continuing the impulse of what has been termed Jacksonian Democracy, achieved on the historical plane (commencing, 1838–1839, with the obscene episode of the Cherokee "Trail of Tears") that popular polishing off of a continent which the poet and novelist, Helen Hunt Jackson, has memorialized in her presently forgotten volume, *A Century of Dishonor.*[105]

Tales of the Northeast Woodland

The Folktale, in Contradistinction to Myth

From the standpoint of a historian of literature and myth, Schoolcraft's recording and publishing at the opening of the nineteenth century of a collection of Native American folktales may be viewed as a New World counterpart of the work being done in Germany at that time by the Brothers Grimm, whose enormously successful *Kinder- und Hausmärchen* (Vol. 1, 1812, Vol. 2, 1815) had awakened both the scientific and the literary circles of Europe to an interest in the exact recording and critical interpretation of the folk traditions of mankind. Elias Lonnrot's reconstruction of the Finnish *Kalevala* (1835) was an expression of this movement. Longfellow happened to be in Heidelberg the year of that publication, and on returning, the next, to his professorship at Harvard, he was ready and alert to recognize in Schoolcraft's *Algic Researches* (1839) material for a comparable American folkloric epic. *The Song of Hiawatha*, the moment it appeared in 1855 (composed in the same trochaic tetrameter as Lonnrot's versified folk narrative: see I.2:150-151), evoked such a sentimental outburst of popular appreciation for the vanishing romance of American Indian life and lore, that, throughout the catastrophic final decades of their banishment from the Continent, an ephemeral literary afterglow of Indian spiritual presences hovered wraithlike over the repeated scenes, from state to state, along the progress westward, of genocidal massacre. Psychoanalytically, the phenomenon may be interpreted as the compensatory reflex of a desperately suppressed recognition of unutterable racial and national guilt, such as must be locked to this day in the defensively cauterized unconscious of many an educated American (see Jung's surprising discovery noted above). Helen Hunt Jackson's romantic Indian novel, *Ramona* (1884), exposed to notice, for a moment, the plight of the brutalized race and even aroused a brief stir of ineffectual sentiment for improvement of the inhuman conditions described.

Meanwhile, in Europe, the Grimm Brothers had supposed that the *Märchen* they were collecting might be late fragments, broken away and reworked, of an Old Germanic mythology. Jacob (1785–1863), the elder of the two, was a leading philologist of the century. His description (known as Grimm's Law) of the regular shifts of consonants of the Indo-European family of languages in the course of their development out of a hypothetical parent base (for example: Sanskrit *pitr*, Latin *pater*, English *father*, German *vater*; Sanskrit *dva*, Latin *duo*, English *two*, German *zwei*, as announced in his ground-breaking publication, *Deutsche Grammatik* [1819–37]), testified to a continuity of tradition through no less than four millennia. The homologous mythological pantheons represented in Vedic-Aryan, Persian, Greek, Roman, Celtic and Germanic religious texts reinforced this linguistic evidence for a predictable consistency in the evolution of oral traditions. Accordingly, it was supposed that the nineteenth-century folktales that the brothers and their friends were collecting in Kassel and Marburg should be epigonic of a mythology dating back, at least, to the Old High German sixth century or so. Likewise, the Finnish tales collected by Lonnrot should point to an ancient Finnish mythology, and the materials collected by Schoolcraft, accordingly, to an otherwise forgotten, primal Algonquian tradition.

259. Woodland Indian hunting a moose. Engraving from Charles Godfrey Leland's classic compilation of. and commentary on, Native American lore: *The Algonquin Legends of New England*, first published in 1898.

Unfortunately for the clarity and simplicity of this view, however, there appeared in 1859 a translation of the *Panchatantra*, a Hindu book of fables published by the sanskritist Theodor Benfey, who in his introduction demonstrated that a number of the Indian stories had in the Middle Ages reappeared as European folktales. The way of development of an oral tradition, that is to say, was not exactly as the Grimm Brothers had assumed. The Indian collection had been originally recorded and arranged, probably in Kashmir, about 200 B.C., as an entertaining *niti-sastra*—"textbook" (*sastra*) on the "wisdom of life" (*niti*), or the "art of getting along." In the sixth century A.D. a Persian translation appeared which in the eighth was translated into Arabic; and the Arabic then, about the middle of the thirteenth, into Spanish and Hebrew. Around 1270, a certain John of Capua turned the Hebrew into Latin, and from here the book passed not only into both German and Italian, but also from the Italian into English— not a few of the fables, meanwhile, having already become popular, here and there, in Europe and thoroughly assimilated to the local scenes and manners of life.

"Out of the literary works," wrote Benfey, "the tales went to the people, and from the people they returned, transformed, to literary collections, then back they went to the people again, etc., and it was princi-

pally through this cooperative action that they achieved national and individual spirit—that quality of national validity and individual unity which contributes to not a few of them their high poetical worth."[106]

The two hundred tales of the Grimm collection, reviewed in the light of this discovery and demonstration, have been classified by scholars of the Finnish school, both according to type, by Antti Aarne, and according to the recognized historic periods of their invention or adoption by Friedrich von der Leyen.[107]

The folktales gathered by the Grimm Brothers and their friends from willing storytellers of the farms and villages, spinning rooms and beer halls, of nineteenth-century Hessen can have had little indeed to do with the mythologies that in the period before Caesar's invasion of northern Europe had supplied the spiritual inspiration and life-structuring ritual forms of the inhabiting Germanic tribes.

The folktale rides a very much shallower and more fluent sea than the myth. Its function is entertainment; that of the myth, the structuring of human life, either to accord with an intuited order of nature, or—as in the biblical religions, where nature is "fallen," the living earth is "dust" (Gen. 3:19), to a certain historical people a special supernatural revelation is supposed to have been awarded—to accord, in despite of nature, with the interests and ideals of a singular society. In either case, whether inspired of nature or dictated by some historical purpose, mythologies are inherently culture-bound, whereas the entertaining features of a well-told tale break easily away from whatever social applications they originally served, to float off and recombine with the features of other traditional inventions in the nightsea of the human imagination.

Folktale collections are to be classified and understood, therefore, as of two distinct categories. There are those, on the one hand, of tales received from the lips of the locally recognized storytellers of an originating people, like the Bushman accounts of the comical misadventures of their insect-divinity, Mantis, published by Lorna Marshall directly from accredited aboriginal narrators (see I.1:91–93, 98–101). Such tales, though related for amusement, may be understood as embedded still in the matrix of an antecedent mythology. Whereas, in contrast, there are such twice-told tales as those of the Grimm collection, which have been carried down through centuries, reworked, transformed, and attuned to later audiences; or as those of the following Algonquian selections, which have been without exception recovered from informants already of Christian faith, and as far removed as their interviewers from immediate knowledge and experience of the primal mythological ambient of native belief.

Foreword to the Algonquian Tales

The earliest recorded of the following selection of Algonquian tales is the last of the series: the Ottawa Chief Pontiac's visionary narrative entitled "Paradise Opened to the Indians," which is an obvious reflex of Dante's visionary ascent on Easter Saturday, 1300, of the Mountain of Purgatory. Chief Pontiac's version of such a visit to God's throne dates from an episode of the French and Indian Wars (1754–1763) when in 1760 a British force, under a certain Major Robert Rogers, on its way to occupy in the Great Lakes area a chain of surrendered French forts had required safe passage through the territory of Pontiac's Ottawa tribe. The unit was allowed to pass unmolested on condition that Chief Pontiac and his people should be treated with the same consideration and respect they had hitherto enjoyed from the French. It soon appeared, however, that the British presence was to be of a different kind. The Indians found themselves no longer welcome in the forts and within months an overwhelming tide of settlers began clearing and farming the Indians' ancestral lands. Whereupon Pontiac organized (in what has been called a conspiracy) practically every Indian tribe from Lake Superior to the lower Mississippi, to resist and throw back the encroaching tide, and in 1763, following the fall of French Quebec and concession by the French to Great Britain of their whole claim to what, for over a century and a half, they had though of as New France (Treaty of Paris, February 18, 1763), the Indians took over alone in the futile last stand known as Pontiac's War (1763–1764) the impossible task of defending themselves, their families and their way of life, against the might of an increasing empire that for the next 184 years would be expanding to military and economic control of the planet—until, after one world war too many, the Empire in 1947 would collapse.

As appears in Chief Pontiac's report of God's message to the American Indian—as delivered to the visionary at the conclusion of his Dantean ascent to the summit of a mountain as smooth as glass, in a "place of unequaled beauty"—the war which the Native American tribes were by God himself commanded to wage, together with the French, against those enemies of God who had arrived to take possession of their homeland, was to be, in fact, a holy war, in the name of the Master of Life Himself. For, as an instructed Roman Catholic, Chief Pontiac was interpreting the global conflict into which he and his people had been drawn from the point of view of the Counter–Reformation. Of the French, God tells the visionary: "I love them, they know me, they pray to me; I supply their wants, and give them what they bring to you. Not

so with those," God declares, however, "who are come to trouble your possessions. Drive them away; wage war against them. I love them not. They know me not. They are my enemies, they are your brothers' enemies. Send them back to the lands I have made for them."

260. Engraved portrait of Ottawa Chief Pontiac, from G. Bird Brinell's *Indians of Today* (1900).

Chief Pontiac's vision was composed, that is to say, as a deliberate summons to the chiefs of the neighboring tribes to unite and take heart *in the name of God* to repel this intruding swarm—which suggests, surely, that there must have been among them other leaders who were also, in some sense, Roman Catholics. The appeal is not to Native American powers conceived as in contest with an alien force, but to a European, thirteenth-century idea of God and his program for mankind in contest with a seventeenth-century notion of the same. The manuscript is in French, composed either, as Schoolcraft supposed, by a professional record keeper, or, as Francis Parkman conjectured in his *History of the Conspiracy of Pontiac* (1851), by a French priest.[108] As messengers of the Master of Life, French Jesuits had been accepted in the region for no less than two hundred years and, as noticed already in our discussion of tales of the Iroquois, whereas the highest Native American mythological entity was universally a personification of the light, power, and authority of the sun, the more abstract concept of a "Great Spirit"—or as here rendered, "Master of Life"—is a reflection of missionary influence. So that already in Chief Pontiac's time, the mythological thinking of the Great Lakes tribes had been significantly transformed by assimilated medieval European ideas.

In the period, a century later, of Schoolcraft's uncovering of what he supposed was the "whole arcana of the Indian's thoughts," the ancestral age, out of which

his tales derived, when some of them might have borne to the ritual order of tribal life a significant relationship, was not only remote and forgotten, but not even thought of as relevant to an appreciation of the original, contextual function of the stories told. The Ojibwa mother of Schoolcraft's wife was herself already a Christian. John Johnston, the father, was a white trader of influence in the frontier post of Sault Ste. Marie. The four daughters have been described as "gentle, secluded, and very Christian." One of them, Charlotte McMurray, was the wife of a Protestant minister. And not only these young women of ladylike, nineteenth-century sensibility, but also most of the other suppliers of Schoolcraft's "Indian Legends," were to such an extent removed from the life and times and manner of thought of the originators of their tales, that in many instances episodes and details thought to be in bad taste were toned down or omitted from the telling, or as Schoolcraft himself, who was a deeply religious man, acknowledged, had to be "cut short off."

Half a century later, and the informants of Silas T. Rand, Frank G. Speck, Charles G. Leland and Elsie Clews Parsons, collecting crumbs of a sometime feast from the memories of impoverished old people dwelling here and there in remoter parts of the Canadian Maritimes and New England, were not only old-time Christians, but classifiable as Indians chiefly because of an unforgotten strain of Montagnais or Nascapi, Micmac or Passamaquoddy in their mixed pedigrees, which had served to set them a little apart. Their region had been colonial to Europe for no less than three hundred years.

There is for example, the Micmac tale of "Making the Princess Laugh," which is an outright European (most likely Irish) tale of magic. There is the anecdote of "How Godchild [i.e., the infant Jesus] Made the Moon and Sun." And there is the inverted Passamaquoddy history of "How Glooscap Went to England and France...." Old Norse motifs have been recognized in the legend (also Passamaquoddy) of "How Glooscap Came to this Country...." Other Old Norse suggestions appear in the Passamaquoddy tales of "How Glooscap Bound the Great Wind Bird..." and of "How Glooscap is Making Arrows...." The Micmac tale of "The Bird Whose Wings Made the Wind," is but a variant of the possibly Nordic "Wind Bird" theme.

The reader is thus made aware throughout of the mixed heritage of this selection of recent Algonquian tales. There is not one of them that can be properly classified and understood as representing a mythology. They are exactly folktales, disengaged from whatever mythological background may ever have sustained the formative rites of any of the vanished cultures out of which they severally originated.

And yet, here and there among them,

traits do appear of a probably native Algonquian mythology of some kind: not distinctly, by any means, nor consistently. But with a watchful inner eye, one may detect and tentatively reconstruct what may indeed have been significant mythic features at one stage of another in the millennial prehistoric development of this once great and extensive, now functionally extinct, oral tradition.

Schoolcraft's powerful Ottawa tale of "The Undying Head," for example, carries into the contemporary period a charge of primeval magic that may date from as early as 200,000 B.C., of the Bear cult and the Head cult of the Riss-Wurm Interglacial age (see I.1:51–58). Also announced here is the immemorial theme of the primal horror of menstrual blood.

The Nascapi animal tale of "How Summer Was Brought North...."—which in a variant reappears in the Ojibwa tale of "Ojeeg Annung...."—is of a folktale type of literally world-wide distribution, as recognized in Stith Thompson's *Motif-Index of Folk-Literature* under Heading B 296, "Animals go a-journeying."[109]

At the end of our two Algonquian versions of the adventure, the leader of the expedition is transformed into a constellation, which adds to the tale a second well-known motif or theme: *Ascent to stars* (Thompson A 761: "People or animals ascend to the sky and become stars"). In the Paleolithic painted caves of southern France and northern Spain, c. 17,000–12,000 B.C. (I.1:58–66 and 73–79, especially Figures 91/92 and 136), there is an evident suggestion of this theme in the great chambers of both Altamira and Lascaux, where animals of the Paleolithic hunt appear depicted on the ceilings. Likewise, in the rock paintings of the South African Bushmen (I.1:90–99 and Figures 176–178), visions of flying antelope-men among heavenly scenes, animals and trooping files of the dead are unmistakable representations of this theme. The best known example from Greek mythology is of the origin of the Pleiades, who, as seven sisters fleeing from the giant hunter Orion, rise into the heavens with him and his dog in close pursuit, where they are all transformed, and today are to be seen, respectively, as the Pleiades, the constellation Orion, and Sirius, the Dog Star. (Compare below the Algonquian legend of "The Celestial Sisters.")

In one form or another, ascents to become stars are a frequent occurrence in North American tales. Stith Thompson lists numerous examples under headings, A 773, *Origin of the Pleiades*, and R 321, *Escape to the stars*.[110] In Volume I examples have been given, first, from the Eskimo of Smith Sound (in northernmost Greenland), who declare that "when men die, they ascend to the sky and become brightly shining things up there" (I.2:185); and in Tierra del Fuego, at the other extreme of the inhabited earth, among both the guanaco-hunting Selk'nam and the fishing and sea-hunting Yamana. The former declare, not only that it was Kenos, their legendary World Shaper, who in the Beginning "lifted the heaven vault to its present place, where he himself stands now as a star," but also that their Ancestors, "following Kenos to the sky, became stars or clouds" (I.2:255). The Yamana, meanwhile, having it, that the original shaman of their Time of the Beginning, Kwanyip, "painted himself red and ascended with his whole family to the sky, where he now can be seen with his relatives all around him" (I.2:257); furthermore, that there was an original Sun-Man who, when threatened with death by a company of raging women, "fled to the sky, to become a star which has since faded and disappeared" (I.1:259); and again, that when their ancestral Yoálax family grew old, they "rose to the sky and are seen today as stars" (I.2:262).

Another motif known especially to animal tales from many parts of the world apears in this same tale of "Animals a-journeying" when the comedian of the company, Otter, caught by the enemy and threatened with death by drowning, screams "Oh no! Not that!" and is tossed into his own element, to swim away with a laugh. One recalls Joel Chandler Harris's Uncle Remus story (1880) of Brer Rabbit tossed into his briar patch. The motif has been classified by Thompson as K 581, *Animal "punished" by being placed in favorite environment*, and by Antti Aarne as Folktale Type 1310, with the following variations: (1) Drowning the Crayfish (or Eel, Crab, or Turtle, etc.); (2) Briar-patch Punishment for Rabbit; (3) Burying the Mole; and (4) Throwing the Bird from a Cliff.[111]

Of tales more specifically Algonquian, bearing signs of a distinctive mythological heritage, those of the Trickster Hero named Tseqabec by the Montagnais, Glooscap by the Micmac and Passamaquoddy, and by the Menomini and Ojibwa, Manabozho, are the most consistent. Such a Trickster is itself, of course, a mythic, as well as folkloric, figure of world-wide distribution. Moreover, all of the adventures attributed to the Algonquian hero finally are of classic themes, catalogued in Thompson's *Index* chiefly under headings A 500–599.[112]

However, there are certain recurrent themes and persistent patterns of relationship that prevail throughout these Algonquian tales, selections of essential motifs, which make for an overall world picture that is distinctively North American. Paul Radin has written of the legend of *The Twins* as "The Basic Myth of the North American Indians." "The constituent elements of this myth, the plot, themes and motifs, are found distributed fairly unchanged over an area extending," he states, "from Canada to southern South America and from the Pacific to the Atlantic Ocean. Because of this wide distribution and because of the importance and significance attached to it everywhere, I feel it is not an exaggeration to designate it as the basic myth of aboriginal America."[113]

In the Iroquois myth of "The Woman Who Fell from the Sky," the theme of the Contending Twins is fundamental, whereas in the following Algonquian series it is of little notice, and when it does appear (as in the Micmac tale "Glooscap and his Brother, Malsum the Wolf"), it is rather as an incident, than as an essential structuring feature of a world-origin myth and associated hero-legend. The Iroquois Contending Twins are the grandsons of an original "Woman Who Fell from the Sky," the body of whose daughter—conceived above, before the fall, who died giving birth to the second of her sons—became in death transformed into maize. There is nothing of this in our Algonquian selections, where the mythic associations are rather with a loose complex of animal tales than with a symbolically structured agricultural origin legend.

The source of the North American agricultural tradition was, of course, Mexico, whence not only maize but also a related ritual order and maize-goddess mythology derived, which spread in well marked stages (I.2:210-211) across the greater part of Woodland North America south of the Great Lakes and St. Lawrence. These stages have been defined and described as Burial Mound Stage II (c. 300 B.C.–A.D. 700: Adena and Hopewellian cultures, see I.2: Maps 44 and 45) and Temple Mound Stages I and II (A.D. c. 700–1200 and 1200–1700: Mississippian diffusion, see I.2: Map 46). It is significant that *all* of the Algonquian tales of the following selection are from areas north of the northernmost of these burial and temple sites and may be supposed to represent, therefore, a mythic field into which motifs from the maize-mother mythologies of the south will have entered only as adjunctive features. The attribution of an opposed twin brother to an earlier, single Trickster Hero and World Shaper was an innovation, apparently, of this kind, representing a marginal influence from planting cultures to the south upon a Paleolithic, hunting-and-gathering order of life and thought prevailing still in the North. Schoolcraft reported of his own findings in this all but lost, archaic zone of the Native American mythological heritage, as follows:

"Their most intelligent priests tell us that their forefathers worshipped the sun; this luminary was regarded by them, as one of their medas told me, as the symbol of divine intelligence, and the figure of it is drawn in their system of picture writing to denote the Great Spirit. This symbol very often occurs in their pictures of the medicine dance, and the wabeno dance, and other sacred forms of their rude inscriptions.

"They believe, at least to some extent, in

a duality of souls, one of which is fleshly, or corporeal, the other, incorporeal or mental. The fleshly soul goes immediately at death, to the land of spirits, or future bliss. The mental soul abides with the body, and hovers around the place of sepulcher. A future state is regarded by them as a state of rewards, and not of punishments. They expect to inhabit a paradise, filled with pleasures for the eye, and the ear, and the taste. A strong and universal belief in divine mercies absorbs every other attribute of the Great Spirit, except his power and ubiquity; and they believe, so far as we can gather it, that this mercy will be shown to all. There is not, in general, a very discriminating sense of moral distinctions and responsibilities, and the faint out-shadowing, which we sometimes hear among them, of a deep and somber stream to be crossed by the adventurous soul, in its way to the land of bliss, does not exercise such a practical influence over their lives as to interfere with the belief of universal acceptance after death. So firm is this belief that their proper and most revered term for the Great Spirit is *Gezha Monedo,* that is to say, Merciful Spirit. *Gitchy Monedo,* which is also employed, is often an equivocal phrase. The term *Wazheaud,* or Maker, is used to designate the Creator, when speaking of this animated works. The compound phrase, *Waosemigoyan,* or Universal Father, is also heard.

"The great spirit of evil, called *Mudje Monedo,* and *Matche Monito,* is regarded as a created, and not a pre-existing being. Subordinate spirits of evil are denoted by using the derogative form of the word, in *sh,* by which *Moneto* is rendered *Monetosh.* The exceeding flexibility of the language is well calculated to enable them to express distinction of this nature.

"The tribe has a general tradition of a deluge, in which the earth was covered with water, reaching above the highest hills or mountains, but not above a tree which grew on the latter, by climbing which a man was saved. This man was the demigod of their fictions, who is called Manabozho, by whose means the waters were stayed and the earth recreated. He employed for this purpose various animals who were sent to dive down for some of the primordial earth, of which a little was, at length, brought up by the beaver, and this formed the germ or nucleus of the new, or rather rescued planet. What particular allegories are hid under this story is not certain; but it is known that this and other tribes are much in the habit of employing allegories and symbols, under which, we may suspect, they have concealed parts of their historical traditions and beliefs. This deluge of the Algonquin tribes was produced, as their legends tell, by the agency of the chief of the evil spirits, symbolized by a great serpent who is placed, throughout the tale, in an antagonistical position to

261. Iroquois (Seneca) Cornhusk Mask of the Husk Face Society ("Bushyheads"), worn by members when they appear at the Midwinter Festival (see I.2:**341**).

the demi-god, Manabozho. This Manabozho is the same, it is thought, as the *Abou* and the *Michabou,* or the Great Hare of older writers....

"One of the most curious opinions of this people is their belief in the mysterious and sacred character of fire. They obtain sacred fire, for all national and ecclesiastical purposes, from the flint. Their national pipes are lighted with this fire. It is symbolical of purity. Their notions of the boundary between life and death, which is also symbolically the limit of the material verge between this and a future state, are revealed in connection with the exhibition of flames of fire. They also make sacrifices by fire of some part of the first fruits of the chase. These traits are to be viewed, perhaps, in relation to their ancient worship of the sun, above noticed, of which the traditions and beliefs are still generally preserved. The existence among them of the numerous classes of *jossakeeds,* or mutterers (the word is from the utterance of sounds low on the earth), is a trait that will remind the reader of a similar class of men, in early ages, in the eastern hemisphere. These persons constitute, indeed, the Magi of our western forests. In the exhibition of their

art, and in the peculiar notions they promulgate on the subject of sacred fire, and the doctrine of transmigration, they would seem to have their affiliation of descent rather with the disciples of Zoroaster and the fruitful Persian stock, than with the less mentally refined Mongolian hordes."[114]

The essential principle or concept underlying the whole manner of thought, experience, and imagination here set forth is denoted in the Algonquian term *manitou,* or as here inflected, Monedo or Monito. The reference is to a supernormal energy or force, thought of as empowering, not only such a mythic being as Gitchy Monedo, but also, in reduced degree, every earthly being, place, thing, or aspect of the environment that may strike the mind as revelatory of a transcendent dimension of reality. Mircea Eliade's term for such an experience of a disclosure is *hierophany* (from *hieros,* "powerful, supernatural, holy, sacred," plus *phainein,* "to show, reveal, or make known"). For in contrast to the biblical teaching of the earth and its creatures as "dust" (Gen. 3:19), from the point of view of any of the other mythologies of mankind, the earth, the sky, and all their creatures are alive; and in certain moments, under certain circumstances, the informing spiritual ground and consciousness of this universal life may with augmented force become evident. In Eliade's words, "hierophanies have the peculiarity of seeking to reveal the sacred in its totality, even if the human beings in whose consciousness the sacred 'shows itself' fasten upon only one aspect or one small part of it. In the most elementary hierophany *everything is declared.* The manifestation of the sacred in a stone or tree is neither less mysterious nor less noble than its manifestation as a 'god.' The process of sacralizing reality is the same; the *forms* taken by the process in man's religious consciousness differ."[115]

God, gods, and the apparitions of vision are without exception personifications of differing quanta (so to say) of this mystical realization, which is known, not only as *manitou* in Algonquian tongues, but in the Iroquoian as *orenda,* Dakotan as *wakanda,* and in Melanesia as *mana.* In relation to the African Bushman experience in trance dancing of an overpowering surge of vision-awakening energy it is known as *ntum* (I.1:94–96); also, in the Congolese Pygmy understanding of their term, *megbe* (I.1:107), and in Andamanese *ot-kimil* (I.1:120). Such enrapturing experiences are of the essence of the classic shamanic visionary initiation (I.2:156–179), as well as of the consequent spiritual influence of a shamanic presence on a society. Indeed, a mythology might well be defined as a constellation of such shamanic hierophanies, translated by means of ritual into a structuring model for life.

Among the Algonquians, before the arrival of the Christian missions, the preeminent hierophany of the *mysterium tremendum et fascinans* known as *manitou* was the sun, as the visible sign of the source of all life and light, or as Schoolcraft was authoritatively told, "the symbol of divine intelligence." But not only the Algonquians; all of the North American tribes revered the sun. Even into South America the sun retains its supreme position, though qualified occasionally by a challenge of the moon. Personified in the mythologies, both the sun and moon are generally male, and where the Hero myth is of Twins, the second born may be fathered by the moon—as for example in the Navaho legend of "Where the Two Came to Their Father" (see I.2:244–248)—but here, the brothers are not in opposition, but cooperate in a single task.

In planting-culture mythologies a principle of polarity is symbolically recognized and resolved. In the Iroquois tales of the Contending Twins, for example, where the names of the two are Sapling and Flint, the opposition suggested is of plant and stone, the becoming and the become, future and past, life and death. One may recognize, also, a suggestion here of the contrast between the Neolithic, planting and nurturing, and the Paleolithic, hunting and butchering, orders of life.

The archaic, Paleolithic type of Trickster and Transformer, who arrives without a brother, alone, with no sense either of limitation or of complementarity, is in North American mythology generally an incarnation of solar power, sheer and uncontrolled. And yet, unknown to himself, he is subject here to the conditions of space and time—which he did not create. And he may appear, consequently, either as invincible, or as a fool, depending on whether it be tangible monsters he is facing, as a god, or the laws of the limitations of temporal life. In the Montagnais tale "Tseqabec Snares the Sun..." this ambiguity of the god become man, who has failed to take into account the complementarities and limitations of existence in this world, is brought out, in typical folktale fashion, through an astonishingly simple device.

For Tseqabec, unknown to himself, is an incarnation of the sun, consubstantial with it, though apparently apart. Having fashioned a snare and set it in the East, he has trapped the rising orb and the result is night everlasting—which he had not anticipated. There is only the moon to light the world, which is not enough; and so all the animals are at pains to release the blazing sphere, but in vain, until....

But no! That would be to give the story away.

So let us now turn to the tales themselves. But first, there is one more story to be especially noticed, the Ojibwa tale, "Aggodahgauda and His Daughter..." of which there is an important counterpart in the origin legend of the Blackfoot association known as All Comrades, whose function it was to regulate the tribal rites through which the animals slain each year were returned to life (see I.2:234, "The Buffalo's Wife"). Both tales are of Thompson's classification, B 611.4 *Bull paramour* (compare the Greek, of Europa and the Bull). But whereas the Blackfoot version has been turned (like the Greek) into a pseudo-historical narrative, accounting for the origin of a social institution (as, in the Classical example, the Cretan Minoan civilization), the Ojibwa piece, collected by Schoolcraft from his friends, has acquired a fresh life and form of its own, as an entertaining fantasy of unnatural love.

And so, to the entertainment:

262. *Fire Dance,* 1971 opaque watercolor, 25" × 25", by Navaho artist Robert Chee, born in 1937, whose acclaimed career was cut short by his death in 1971.

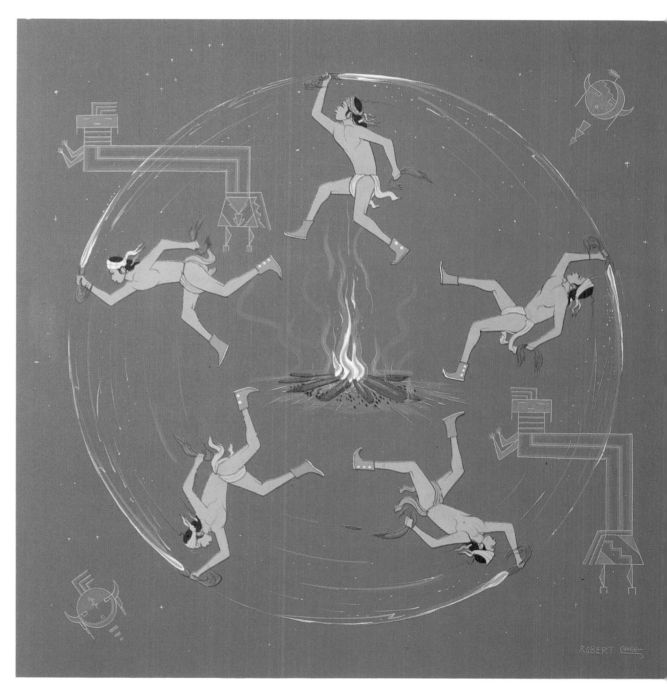

TALES OF THE MONTAGNAIS AND NASKAPI

These are two nomadic, hunting, fishing, and gathering tribes, speaking almost identical dialects and differing chiefly in their adaptations to very different environments: the Montagnais, of eastern Quebec, inhabiting the vast forested area north of the Gulf of St. Lawrence, and the Nascapi (whose Algonkian name means, "crude, uncivilized people"), disputing with the Eskimo the bleak grassland and tundra plateau of glaciated Labrador.[116]

"There exists at present," states Frank G. Speck, in comment on the tales of his publication (1925) from which the following selections have been drawn, "no collection of myths and folktales from the widely scattered bands of the Montagnais. Their territories lie in a zone about eight hundred miles long and two hundred miles wide between the Gulf of St. Lawrence and the mountains forming the Height of Land of the southern Labrador peninsula. Although they were visited and described by the Jesuits early in the seventeenth century, no systematic attention has since been given to their beliefs and traditions. As a beginning toward an exposition of the life and beliefs of this little-known but important group of the Algonkian family, the following sets of tales have been selected from material, some of it in text, taken from the lips of these Indians during the last fifteen years.

"Being spread over so wide an area, the various divisions of the Montagnais vary somewhat in dialect and in customs. Their folklore has not yet been collected from all parts of their habitat in sufficient quantity to justify us in speaking definitely of its character as a whole. But so far as we can judge from the material in hand, there is a noticeable stability in incident and concept throughout the area. It would seem that the mythology of the Laurentian tribes from James Bay to the Atlantic is of the same general character.

"The relationship of Montagnais folklore to mythologies outside this area is fairly evident. Some of the human tales suggest Eskimo influence, and this is not too improbable, since the Montagnais of the seventeenth century broke out into the domains of the Eskimo and fairly extirpated them from the Gulf and southern Labrador coast. On the whole, however, the resemblance of these tales to those of the Algonkian Cree and Ojibwa is their most striking characteristic. Practically every incident related among the Montag-

263. Montagnais camp on Grand Lake, Labrador. Photograph taken in July of 1891. Note the bark canoes drawn up on the rocky beach, the traditional bark and cloth lodgings, and the strips of wood being dried in preparation for the making of more canoes.

nais, from one end of their territory to the other, can be found, for instance, among the Ojibwa somewhere in the now numerous published collections from this group of tribes.

"The western extension of the Laurentian culture is along the St. Maurice River, which separates from the Montagnais the people known as Têtes de Boule, who speak a dialect more closely related to the Ojibwa. In the province of folklore this frontier marks the eastward limit, in this northern area, of certain well-known and widely distributed tales which are notably absent among the Montagnais and the Nascapi. I have frequently asked narrators for the Earth Diver story, but have never found that it was known to any one in the Montagnais territory. Nor is it found among the Wabanaki. No sign of the tale has been discovered in northern New England or in eastern Canada, except for the one reference in the Jesuit Relations (le Jeune, *Jesuit Relations*, 5:155), the authenticity of which may be doubted....

"The same frontier also marks the eastern limit (in this northern territory) of social customs which play an important part to the westward, such as the mother-in-law taboo [that a man may not meet and/or talk with his mother-in-law], the *mide'win* or shaman's medicine society, and the dice-and-bowl game; in the field of material culture, of the cradle-board, twill-woven rush mats, basswood or cedar-bark baskets, porcupine quill-work, the square-headed snowshoe, and other characteristic objects.

"Nevertheless, in folklore this western limit (in this northern area) marks a lesser differentiation than the southern frontier along the St. Lawrence. While comparisons are perhaps premature, it would seem safe to say that the character of folklore differs more between the Montagnais and the Wabanaki directly south of the St. Lawrence, than between the Montagnais and the Cree. Thee is a noticeably low proportion of cognates found among the peoples on the opposite side of the St. Lawrence, though an increase of material from the Montagnais may later cause us to reverse this estimate. The cleavage along the course of the St. Lawrence holds good, not only in regard to folklore, but in the degree of differentiation of dialects and of physical type. On the other hand, it is noticeably absent in material culture."[117]

264. Montagnais birchbark box, c. 9" × 10" × 16", nineteenth century, Quebec. The design, suggestive of Hopewellian ornaments (see I.2:210–216), was made by outlining birchbark templates with the tip of a knife and then selectively peeling away sections of the outer bark.

People of another (earlier) world were living in a village. They knew that a new world was going to be formed.

One day a number of them started to quarrel. One of the number was North Star. The others fell upon him, meaning to kill him, but he fled and soared into the sky. All started after, but when they saw they could not get him: "Well," they said, "let him be! He is North Star. He will be of use to the people of the world that is to come, as a guide by night to their travels."[118]

How Summer Was Brought North; or The Origin of the Constellation Ursa Major

A long time ago there was a child who had lots of lice. His people left him. Others came and took him, to bring him up. They killed the lice, all but two, one male, one female, which they left on him. "As long as man lives," they said, "picking lice will be a pastime."

The child was always crying, even when they gave him things to play with. They made a bow for him, but just the same, he kept crying. "What can we do?" they said. "He never stops."

The child then said to them: "Not till I have summer birds at which to shoot with my arrows will I stop crying." And when they heard that, the people said, "We are ready. We'll go and get what he wants."

So they started off to get Summer.

"Let's leave Otter behind," one suggested. "He laughs too much. He'll just spoil it for us."

"What is that, you are saying about me?" Otter asked.

"You," they said, "stay here. You can't come. When we're dividing up the bear grease, you'd be taking more than your share."

"No," said he. "I, too, pity the boy. You can keep your bear grease. I'm going along."

They got started, and when they had come to Beaver's house and were in there apportioning the grease, Otter, half-way through, started laughing. They jumped on him and began tickling him till he couldn't speak, for so much laughing. He slipped out from under and gave up what he had taken of the grease; then they returned to the camp from which they started.

When they got there, the child was still crying. "Oh well!" they said; "we'll try again. But this time, we'll *not* take Otter along."

"No! No! I'm coming," he declared. "You're not going to visit Beaver's house without me."

"All right," they said. But when they arrived at Beaver's place, they warned Otter to stay outside. "We'll bring out your share of the grease," they said; and the rest of them went in.

Inside, when they had all taken their places and Beaver was apportioning the grease, "There is one of us," they told him, "who did not come in this time." He gave a portion to each, and when all had eaten, they presented to Beaver tobacco and came out, bringing to Otter his share.

"Mine must have been bigger than that," he said. "You people have eaten my portion." But he took and ate what they gave him. And as soon as he was done, the party set off for where Summer was kept.

There was a very big, long wigwam. "Wonder where the Summer is kept. Someone better go in and find out," they said.

One of them was a bird. "You go," they said to the bird.

"No!" said he. "When I fly, my wings make too much noise. Someone else should go."

"No," they said. "Let's see; let's try. Fly close to our heads."

He flew close to their heads. They could hardly hear his wings. "You're the one," they said. "Now go."

The bird flew off and alighted on the wigwam. He peeked in through a hole in the door and could see where the Summer was kept. Those inside could feel that there was someone looking at them.

"There is someone looking at us," they said. "The way he acts, he must be a stranger."

"From what direction is he looking?" they asked, and an old man said, "From the daylight direction." Then they saw him: two small eyes. "There he is," they cried, "the one who is looking!" And eager to see, they ran out of the wigwam, but saw nothing. "It is nothing," they said. "Nothing at all, only our imagination."

But then, far out in the water they saw a muskrat swimming around. "A stranger seems to be coming our way. Let us invite him to come in," they said. And they called to him.

"You! Out there swimming! Who are you?"

"I'm Muskrat," he replied; "always swimming around alone."

"Haven't you any friends?" they called.

"No," said he; "always alone."

"Then come ashore!" they shouted. He approached the shore. "Come ashore!"

"I never come onto shore except over rocks."

"If you'll come we'll give you grease to eat."

"Throw some of it over here," he said. So they threw to him some of their grease.

"I don't find in it any taste," he said. "I made a mistake. I mixed water in my mouth. Throw me some more. This time make it big."

They threw to him some more of their grease. "If you'll come ashore, you'll get a bigger share. Is it good?" they asked when he had eaten. "If it's good, then come ashore."

"It's good," he answered; "but too rich for me." And he turned to swim away. "Don't tell anybody you've seen us," they called.

"No, no!" said he. But then he spoke to himself. "I'll be telling it all pretty soon," he said as he dove. And they saw him no more.

Muskrat returned to his friends. The bird was there who had seen where the Summer was kept. Said the bird: "Along the length of the big wigwam, where the ridge pole points at noon, just there is where the Summer is kept."

"And every morning," added Muskrat, "they paddle over to the narrows, where moose go across."

"Well then, tonight," they told him, "you go gnaw their paddles and bite the bottoms of their canoes. And as soon as it is morning, swim over toward the narrows where the moose generally cross, pushing before you the root of a big tree."

Accordingly, Muskrat swam next morning with the tree before him, looking like the antlers of a moose who might be swimming toward the narrows. They saw the branches, looking like antlers, and one of them called, "Over there! Over there goes swimming a moose!"

They ran and jumped into their canoes. Only Sucker and Sturgeon stayed back. They were the guardians of the Summer. And when all the others were out over the water, the People of the North rushed suddenly in from hiding and, seizing Sucker and Sturgeon, pasted over their mouths a thick sturgeon-glue (from a vessel that was standing near), to keep them from crying out. That done, they hurried into the great wigwam, took hold of Summer and ran off with it.

Sucker and Sturgeon were at first unable to yell. But then one of them picked up an arrow, punched it into his mouth and called: "Our Summer! They've taken it away from us! Come back! Paddle back!"

The people tried to paddle hard, but their paddles broke where Muskrat had gnawed them. Others sank to the bottom, where he had bitten through their canoes. After a while, though, some arrived. "What's that you two were saying?" they asked.

"They've taken our Summer away."

"Well then, we've got to catch them," they said, and all started in pursuit.

Soon they were catching up. "They are gaining on us," those fleeing said. "Who will engage and delay them?"

"You!" they told Otter. "Run off and get under a stump."

Otter ran and got under a stump. And when the pursuers arrived, "Why, hello!" they said. "Here is one of them in this hole here! Catch hold of him!" And they seized him.

"How shall we get rid of him?"

"Let's throw him into the fire," said one.

"When the flames fly out," Otter warned, "You'll all catch fire and die."

"Let's beat him to death," said another.

"The blood from my wounds will slay you."

"Let's drown him," somebody suggested; as though in terror, screaming, Otter cried out, "Oh no! Not that!"

They grabbed and flung him into the lake, where, after a time he reappeared, far out. "This is where I live," he called back. "For me to die here is impossible," he laughed.

They started off again in pursuit, and as they gained, those fleeing with the Summer asked, "Who next will engage and delay them?"

"How about you?" they said to Fisher Cat.

"What can *I* do?" the Fisher asked.

"Run up a tree," they told him.

Fisher ran up a tree, and when the pursuers arrived, "Where is he?" they said. "He must be up this tree." They looked up and shot an arrow at him. But he was circling so fast around the trunk, they only ripped off part of his tail.

"Where is our expert bowman?" they called.

"He has not yet arrived," came the answer.

Then he appeared. "It's your turn," they said. Twice the bowman shot, and twice he missed Fisher, who kept circling around the trunk of the tree. Once again he shot. "I got you this time," he called.

But Fisher, with the arrow still stuck in him, flew up and away into the sky. They watched, and up there, high above, he remained. He is the constellation, Great Bear. "We couldn't kill him," they said. "He'll be a sign for mankind in the future." And again they started in pursuit.

But now there was everywhere about them the singing to be heard of summer birds, and there they saw the child no longer crying, shooting at the birds with his arrows.

Then everybody went off in different directions.[119]

The Little People

Many tales are told by the Montagnais of a race of dwarfs known as the "Little People," who are about knee-high to men and live in the deep forest, underground or in thickets. They possess the peculiar quality of sudden magical disappearance. When seen by men they disappear from vision the instant they dart behind any object. Hunters claim to have heard them rustling among leaves or in a pile of brush. Yet they are friendly to man and their appearances are taken as omens of warning.

To them also is attributed a fondness for stealing human children, whom they carry to distant places and abandon. There is living today—[about 1920, the date of the recording this telling]—at Lake Mistassini [Quebec], a young man slow of wit whose name is Pileated Woodpecker. He was found wandering in the woods along the shores of the lake, at a point where signs of the dwarfs have occasionally been seen. He was unable to speak at the time and seemed not to know where he had come from, or who his people were. The Mistassini tribe, who adopted him, surmise that he had been stolen from some far distant district and left by the dwarfs when they tired of him, to be rescued and cared for by the Indians.[120]

The Narrow-Faced Spirits

There is a tribe of spirits called "Narrow Face," who have the size and form of human beings. Their faces are almost as narrow as a knife. They dwell in remote parts of the country, but have been occasionally seen by the Montagnais. When encountered it is usually toward dark, and as though ashamed of their faces, they immediately hang their heads.

Several in a canoe once were seen by a party of Montagnais, and the moment they noticed the Indians, they turned and drove their birchbark canoe directly into a ledge of rock and disappeared. Once inside, they threw their paddles out to the Indians and could be heard in there laughing loudly.[121]

The Hunter Who Married the Caribou

"Caribou Man," Atekwabeo, was the youngest of four brothers. They were hunting, following a herd of caribou near which they camped one night in an open shelter, where Atekwabeo dreamed that a female caribou came from the herd to him and, speaking, called him to live with the caribou as her husband.

Next morning he left camp alone, proceeding to the place indicated in his dream. And there he saw a caribou doe that appeared to be waiting for him. He approached her, and when he reached her side, she led him to where three other caribou stood watching, evidently as scouts. These then led him away and he joined the herd, living thereafter with the caribou.

From place to place he now wanders with them, eating moss as the caribou do, sometimes riding on the back of a big buck. His clothing being of caribou skin, when more is needed, he is allowed to kill for this purpose one or two of the herd. On freezing Canadian-winter nights, several of the herd lie close, to keep him warm. His offspring are all caribou, like the rest.

265. *Mik-um-wess*, an Alogonquian imp or sprite.

Thus, year after year, he has survived among the animals as one of them, occasionally seen by Indians, who on encountering his herd, refrain from killing. Several people have conversed with him, and what he is reported to have told is that what troubles the caribou most today is that hunters are now killing too many of them. When hunters encounter his herd, he allows them to kill no more than for the renewal of their clothing and for food.

As reported by those who have heard from him his story, he was twenty-one years old when he left his brothers' camp, which must have been some forty years ago [around 1880, according to the date of this retelling of his tale]. He belonged originally to the Seven Islands division of the Nascapi and was last seen by a party of Montagnais hunters seven years ago [perhaps around 1912], and the place of that encounter, they say, was near Lake Mitchikamau.

To the French Canadians he is known as *Le Roi des Caribou*. There is a river bearing his name, flowing into the *Ashwapmouchouan*. And in the forest somewhere, a small lake has been named in his memory.[122]

FOUR TALES OF THE TRICKSTER-HERO TSEQABEC

Tseqabec and the Cannibal Girls

Two handsome girls lived on a mountain. They were cannibals and especially relished the flesh of young men. They had a swing that swung out over a deep pit, and when they had induced into it a proposed victim, they would swing and whirl him so high that he would drop into the pit and be killed. The bottom of the pit was covered with the bones of young men who had been eaten by those girls. "Come! Come!" they would call to a passing youth. "Let us swing. It is great fun. You first! Then you can swing us. It's real fun. You will enjoy it. Come! Let's try!"

Tseqabec knew all about those girls, and since he wished to rid the world of cannibals, he climbed their mountain and there met them. "Come! Come!" they called. "Let's swing! It's

fun! You first! We'll swing you ever so high."

He climbed into their swing and they pushed: first easily, but then higher; and when they were ready to turn him clear over and drop him into their pit, he jumped free and came down beside them. "Great fun!" he cried. "That was really fun. Now it's your turn."

They could not refuse, but proposed that he should swing one of them at a time. "It would be too heavy if we both got in," they said.

"No indeed!" he replied. "I can easily swing you both. It will be much more fun that way."

So they mounted and he started. He swung them out and then all the way over, so that down they fell into the pit and were killed.

Now Tseqabec always talked contrary-wise. If asked if he were going away, he would reply, "No, I'm arriving." If he had killed some monster or cleared the wilderness of a dangerous tribe and was asked about it, his answer would be, "No, I haven't killed anybody."

So when he returned home, and was asked if he had killed them, he said, "No! They tried to kill me by whirling me out of a swing into a pit. But I jumped. Then I swung them, and they fell into their pit and died."[123]

Tseqabec Marries the Cannibal's Two Daughters

"Huge Man," Mictabeo, was a ferocious giant who ranged the country searching for people's tracks, then following them to their camps, where he would kill and eat them. He had a wife and two beautiful daughters. The wife was a cannibal, as evil as himself, but the daughters were by nature good. They, too, ate human flesh, but longed to be cured of such habits.

The parents employed their daughters to induce young men to their camp. There was a big rock in their wigwam, and they killed the young men by seizing their feet and dashing their heads on the rock. There was also an immense cauldron in there, into which the bodies were then flung to be boiled.

One day Tseqabec was heard by his sister singing to the strumming of his bowstring. The bow was braced against his foot and he was tapping the string with an arrow, changing toes by the pressure of his other hand on the string.

"Are you going to kill somebody?" she asked.

"No," he replied, "Only squirrels."

"You *are* going to kill somebody," she said.

"No! No!" he said. But he had actually decided to kill Mictabeo and his wife, Mictabeockweo. His idea was to take their two daughters away, thinking the parents might one day turn on the girls and eat them. So he said to his sister, "Give me my traveling packet of bear grease."

"What are you going to do with it?" she asked.

"Nothing, just give me the packet."

So she fetched the little bag of grease and away he went. For some time he traveled; and when he had come within sight of Mictabeo's camp, the two girls could be seen at work outside, scraping the hair from a caribou skin. They saw him arriving and started to laugh.

"What are you laughing at," called their mother from inside the wigwam.

"Nothing, mother, only a whiskey jack."

"It's more than a bird, to make you laugh like that. I think there must be a man coming."

"No, mother, it's just the bird," they said. "He looks so funny as he comes along, pecking this way and that at bits of meat." They said this to protect Tseqabec.

But the old woman then saw him: for he walked right into her wigwam. Immediately she seized him and was about to dash his head on the rock, when he calmly said, "If you do that, there'll be no grease in the soup. Throw me into the pot alive, and you'll then have all the grease you want."

So she threw him into the cauldron, where, when he had sunk beneath the surface, he opened the little bag and a thick covering of grease rose to the top. Grabbing a huge spoon, the old woman began eagerly skimming off the surface, where more and more kept coming up to her. But the water was becoming hotter, and Tseqabec began to feel, pretty soon, that he couldn't stand it much longer. So he called to her, "Come closer! You're not getting the grease over here!" So she moved in closer, and with the big spoon was just reaching over, when Tseqabec jumped up and out, overturning the scalding cauldron upon her, and she died.

Then he took home to his sister the two beautiful daughters and said to her, "Here are your sisters-in-law."[124]

Tseqabec Snares the Sun and Becomes Transformed into It

In ancient times there was an old man who had a wife and a son named Tseqabec, "Finished Man." They were the only people living, and Tseqabec was the first finished child.

The old man was the Master of the small animals and birds of the earth. They lived in the woods around him, and when he wanted anything from them, all he had to do was to call.

In those early days the sun was so hot that the birds and small animals were unable to live. They were dying, killed by the sun. So in great distress the old man decided to capture the sun and put an end to its work. At the edge of the world, where the sun comes up, he started to build a deadfall of logs, but when his son saw what he was doing, he said, "That won't work. If you want to capture the sun, it will have to be with something better than a wooden trap." So he said to his father, "I'll make you a snare." And that night Tseqabec made a loop snare of rawhide, which he arranged where the sun comes up, at the edge of the world.

Next morning, the sun coming up got caught in Tseqabec's snare and stopped short, so that when the animals woke it was still dark and they thought the end of the world had come. Different ones among them went to the place where the light should have appeared, and there they saw the sun caught in a snare. Several tried to approach, to cut the rawhide, but no use. First Rabbit tried; but his fur got burned. The birds were unable to get there at all, unable to fly in the dark. Then Field Mouse tried, who runs close to the ground; also Mole, who goes underground. But neither could get close.

When the old man's wife woke late in the day and saw that everything was still dark, she said to her husband, "What have you done now? You have captured the sun!"

"No I," said he. "I only tried. Tseqabec succeeded. That sun was burning up the world."

"Well," she said, "you've done a very bad thing. It's so dark we can't even see to keep

alive. This is no great thing at all that you have accomplished."

Tseqabec himself tried to get close enough to release the sun. He held in front of his face a piece of hide and tried to get near, but had to give up. And all this time, everything was quiet. The sun never even cried out. Only the moon was left to light the earth, and it was very hard for the old people. Only the owl and one or two of the other animals who had eyes large enough to see in the night could find their way in the dark woods.

Finally, the old man's wife picked up her hook and line and went off to the lake to fish. When she cast the line, Tseqabec was standing close by and the hook, flying back, striking one of his eyes, tore it out. So there he stood. And he had only one eye left. "You have been punished for snaring the sun," said his old mother, and when he had made his way home, he said to his father: "I've had my eye torn out, so now I can't see. Call your birds and take an eye from the owl and put it here, in place of mine. The owl has good big eyes and easily flies in the dark."

So the old man called the owl to him, plucked out one of his eyes and set it in the head of his son, who found that he now could see with the owl's eye better than ever with his own. He went off hunting in the forest and there, in the dark, was seeing very well. So when he returned, he told his father to call the owl again and give him the other of its eyes. Which the old man did. And Tseqabec then had two big round eyes, like an owl.

He next wanted to get married. So he traveled about, looking for a wife; and pretty soon he found somebody. But the first night, instead of lying down with her, he said to her, "Follow me!" and went off through the woods, hunting. All night he led her about in the dark, and since she was unable to see, she kept bumping into trees and falling down. So he took her to his father and said, "Get her an eye like mine, from an owl." The old man again called his birds together and from an owl took one of its eyes, which he placed in the woman's head; so that now, she too could see, and along with her spouse, she traveled about in the dark.

Pretty soon she bore him a son, whom they named "Little Tseqabec," Tseqabejis. When born, he had two big round eyes, like an owl.

He could see in the dark as well as any owl, and when he grew a little older, he said to Tseqabec, his father: "It was you who snared the sun, and that is why it is now so dark we have to have these big round eyes."

"Well, yes!" said Tseqabec.

"Well then," declared Little Tseqabec, "I'm going to set a snare for the moon."

He made a rawhide snare and set it where the moon comes up, and it was right on the path that his father followed when attending his traps. Tseqabec walked into it; so that, instead of the moon, it was he that was caught, snared by the legs, hanging in air, hollering for help.

Presently his son arrived. "So instead of the moon, it's you I've caught," he said. "You're now punished for snaring the sun. Well, you can hang there." And he walked away.

Tseqabec, they say, became the sun, and Tseqabejis continued to live with his mother.[125]

Tseqabec Departs But Promises to Return

Toward the end of his life Tseqabec disappeared. But he had promised to come back at the end of time to set an example. When he returns it will be necessary for every creature on earth to follow all of his commands. He will select and appoint certain persons to whom he will show himself, and these then will be the principal ones in the world. He will tell them what he wants done and they will do it. They will be the good people.

Tseqabec at that time will dispel evil, but in so doing, he will probably cause a war. No one now sees him. However his followers, those of his selection, may be even now going abroad in the world. Parents sometimes name their children after him. In Chicoutimi there is a hunter, Joseph Xavier, who has lately given Tseqabec's name to his son.

When he lived here, Tseqabec killed all the evil monsters in the world. Whenever he learned of the whereabouts of a monster, he went and killed him. But he always denied having done whatever he did. When his family would notice him preparing for a journey and ask what he was going to do, he would deceive them. His custom, when about to start on any of his trips, was to sit strumming on his bowstring —the lower end of the bow braced against his foot—producing a soft melody. When his sister then would ask if he was about to kill some monster, he would answer, "No! I'm just going to kill a few squirrels." For a little while he would sing, and then get up and go.

Tseqabec's sister was very good. She had a very tender heart and did not want him to kill any creature in the world, not even evil ones, like monsters. In fact, she was forever telling him not to keep going about, killing. Perhaps that is why he did not want her to know what he was going to do.

When he had completed his labors in this world, Tseqabec took with him his mother and wife and climbed to the top of the great mountain. A tall tree was standing there. He told them to go up the tree, and up they climbed. He followed, taking with him an arrow, the end of which he placed in his mouth. Then he blew, and the arrow, flying, left a trail along which he led his mother and wife to the realm where they now abide.[126]

266. Painted deerskin toque, Eastern Woodlands, n.d.

ABNAKI TALES: OF THE MICMAC, PASSAMAQUODDY, AND PENOBSCOT

The term Abnaki (also Wabanaki) refers to a confederacy of northeastern-woodland, Algonquian tribes organized to resist the Iroquois. Composed at first of the tribes in (present) New York State immediately northeast and east of the Mohawks, the association expanded through Vermont, New Hampshire and Maine, to New Brunswick, Nova Scotia and Prince Edward Island, where the Micmac—whose Algonquian speech greatly differs from that of their neighbors (which may indicate a later prehistoric arrival) and whose name means "allies"—constituted an associated confederacy of their own. Southward the Abnaki range expanded through eastern Pennsylvania into the country of the Delaware, who were being persistently harassed by far-reaching Iroquois war parties from the north striking briefly and returning to base.

The Micmac of New Brunswick, Nova Scotia and Prince Edward Island were the largest and most important of the tribes of Canada's eastern Maritime Provinces. The Passamaquoddy and Penobscot were of coastal Maine, the former on Passamaquoddy Bay, the St. Croix River and Schoodic Lake, and the latter claiming Penobscot Bay and the entire Penobscot river basin. All were seasonal hunting, fishing and gathering nomads, dwelling in winter in conical wigwams covered with skins or birchbark, hunting moose, caribou and small game, while in the summer occupying flimsy open-air shelters, gathering shellfish along shores, fishing and hunting seals.

Having been among the first to accept Jesuit teachings and to intermarry with the settlers of New France, these tribes, throughout the eighteenth century, were constant allies of the French, their whole great wilderness having been turned by contending European armies into a bloody battleground: French and British, from 1673 to 1759; but then, to the end of the War of 1812, British and American. Next to nothing is known of the native religious beliefs of these Algonquian tribes. Their fragmentary folktales cluster chiefly around an archetypical trickster-hero transformer (a counterpart of Tseqabec of the Montagnais) named Glooscap.[127]

Colloquies of the First Priest and the Indians

When the priest first came, most of the Indians were witches. Some were willing to be christened, some were unwilling. They asked the priest, "What is christening for?" — "If you are not christened, you are lost for good." — "Lost, in the woods?" — "No, in Hell." — "Where's Hell?" — "Black place, fire there burns the soul." — "How do you go there, by road?" — "No, your soul goes there." — "Where is my soul?" — "You might sicken and die. After you die, you might see your soul." — "How can a soul go out from the birchbark cover, bound tightly around the dead body?" — "You should dig a hole and put the dead in it." — "That would be even harder to get out of, couldn't go anywhere then." — "Yes, you could go to Heaven." — "Heaven? What is Heaven?" — "Nice music in Heaven, nice berries there." — "How go there?" — "If you do not fight, do not talk bad, you can go there. If you murder, steal, you will go to Hell, for your sin." — "Sin? What is sin?" They knew nothing.

Finally, very few refused to be christened, and afterwards, as the priest wanted, they come to confessing. But three men would not go to be christened, among the biggest witch of them all. He was very much against the priests. He said, "No Heaven. No Hell. When you die, you gone, can't speak." He was the worst fellow of all. He was about forty-five.

Old lady [his wife] coaxed him. "Better go, get christen, like the rest." At last he went. "What name do you like?" they asked him. "Best name, the Lord." — The priest said, "Nobody can have that name, only one Lord. What other name?" — "I'll be named, the Devil." — "You can't have that name." — "Well, I'll be named, Swallow." — "No, you can't have that name. That's a bird's name." — "I have proposed three names. You refuse them all. I am going home." — "No, you can't go." Then the friend he went hunting with said he would give him a name — Gabrio [Gabriel]. "All right," he agreed to that, "that's a nice Indian name."

He was a heavy witch, he had a bag of little bone animals. If he wanted anybody to be sick, he sent an animal to him. If he wanted you well, he sent an animal to you. They wanted to take away his bag, the whole outfit. "All right," he said. "Since I am going to be christened, you can take my outfit to the priest." The priest told some men, "Tie this bag with a rope, put hooks on it and great big stones. Put it in a canoe, go to the deepest water and sink the bag, so it never comes back to him." Two men did this, they sank the bag in deep water, deeper than their long poles. The man was lonesome after he lost his bag. He took his pipe and smoked. He thought, "Sometimes my bag did me good. When I asked him to send me moose down here, moose came." — The old woman said, "No, God Almighty did not want that." He took a big smoke. In the morning the bag was under his head, it had come back.

The old lady went to tell the priest. "That bag you fixed, he's got it under his head this morning." — "Well, well, well! very queer that bag came back. The Devil brought it back," said the priest. "Tell the man to bring it to me himself."

She told her husband. "What does he want it for? The bag is all right. It was christened, as well as myself. It won't hurt anybody any more." — "It will," said the old lady. Well, at last he carried the bag to the priest. The priest said, "Come, kiss this bible, promise to give up the bag for good." — "Didn't you christen it yesterday? I will take it to Heaven with me?" — "No. You must give up that bag for good." — "What will you give me for that?" — "Nothing, but I will send you to Heaven, if you're a good old man and don't hurt anybody. But that bag you've got to give up."

He took off his cap, got down on his knees. The priest closed the bible with a slam and said, "You're got to give up the bag for good." — "All right." — "Have you got the canoe ready?" — "Yes." — "Well, I am going along this time. Tie up the bag, fasten *three* stones to it this time." So in the deepest water they could find they sank um. Last end. That bag never came back to him.

Ever since that, folks have been christened, praying, paying Indian taxes.[128]

How God-Child Made the Moon and Sun

After God-child was born from Virgin Mary Christmas night, there was no light, only one star. God-child said, "Not enough light." He made the moon. Our Saviour thinks, "My children not satisfied yet." Then he put up the sun. That's the time the sun was made.[129]

267. Penobscot powderhorn, 12¾" long, domestic cattle horn, nineteenth century, Maine. Europeans introduced powderhorns (and firearms) to the Americas. Native artisans, taking note of the incised decorations on the colonists' prototypes, appropriated the form, but ornamented their creations with their own designs. Motifs similar to those on this powderhorn, also appear painted and incised on both bark and wood, and, among the Micmac at least, in bead-embroidery works.

An Indian family resided on the seashore. They had two sons, the elder of whom was married and had a family of small children. They lived principally by fishing, and their favorite food was eels.

Now it came to pass at a certain time that the weather was so stormy they could not fish. The wind blew fiercely night and day, and they were greatly reduced by hunger. Finally the old father told his boys to walk along the beach, and perhaps they would find a fish that had been floated ashore. So one of them started off, and when he reached a point where the wind blew so fiercely he could hardly stand against it, he saw the cause of all the trouble. At the end of the point there extended a series of rocks far out to sea, which at low tide were separated by shallow water, but at high tide were all nearly covered. On the farthest rock there stood a large bird, the Storm King, flapping his wings and, by the wind so raised, causing all the trouble. Planning to outwit him, the Indian called to the bird, addressing him as "my grandfather."

"Are you cold?" he called.

"No," answered the bird.

The Indian replied, "You *are* cold. Let me carry you to shore on my back."

"Do so," came the response.

So the man waded out to the distant rock, took the bird on his back, and from rock to rock carefully carrried him, wading through the intervening shallow waters. But in coming down the last slope of rock, he purposely stumbled, pretending it was an accident, and the poor old bird broke a wing.

Pretending to be extremely sorry, the man proceeded to set the bone, bound up the wing, and directed the old fellow to stay quiet and not to move his wings for a while, till the wounded one should have healed. He asked if the break pained very much, and on being told it did not: "Remain here," he said; "I'll soon be coming back for a visit and to bring you some food."

When the young man returned to his family, he found that the wind had all died away. There was a dead calm, so that before long, since eels were both plentiful and easily taken, there was food for all in abundance. But there can be too much even of a good thing. The calm weather continued for days, causing the sea to become covered with a sort of scum, which the Indians attribute to a sickness and vomiting among the larger fish. By this fishermen are prevented from seeing into the water, which for eel-spearing is bad. So the big bird was again visited, and when his wing, on examination, was found to have healed enough to admit of motion, he was told to keep both his wings going but with a motion gentle and steady, which produced the desired result.[130]

Making the Princess Laugh

There was once a king who owned a large farm in the neighborhood of the town where he resided. The farm was cultivated by a man who paid rent for it to the king and whose only child, a boy considered to be only about half-witted, was continually doing silly things. The man died, leaving such a sum of money that for a couple of years the rent was easily met.

268. Micmac quilled box, 4" in diameter, birchbark and porcupine quills and native dye, early nineteenth century, Maritime Provinces, Canada. Although native Northeasterners were able to render curvilinear designs by using very fine quills, the easy availability of long quills favored the development of geometric motifs with straight edges, such as those used on this exquisite box.

However, at last the inevitable day has arrived when the rent can no longer be paid.

"In a day or two," says the widow to her son, "the king will be calling for his money and we shall have nothing for him. What shall we do?"

"I don't know," replies the boy.

So the next morning she sends him off to market with one of her finest cows. And a little way along the road there is a house by the road with a man standing at the door. "Where are you going with that cow?" the man calls.

"To market," Jack calls back to him.

"Come in and rest a bit," says the man.

So Jack goes into the house, sits down, and the man says, "I want you to make me a present of that cow."

"Oh, I can't do that," says Jack. "But I'll sell her to you. We need money."

The man brings to him, on a tiny dish, a small portion of some kind of food, suggesting that he might like something to eat. Jack takes a taste of it and finding the delicacy irresistible, starts eating, unable to stop. The amount on the dish does not diminish, and he continues until his distending belly begins to hurt, when he pleads, "Take this away!"

"Give me your cow and I will," the man says; and when Jack persists in refusal, "Well then," says the man, "eat on."

The fascination of the undiminishing morsel is more than the boy can resist; but soon the increasing discomfort of his expanding midriff becomes so great, he gives up the cow and receives in return the little dish.

With no more than this in his pocket he returns to his mother, and when she asks of his trip to market and he tells her he was robbed of her cow, describing the whole adventure, she flies at him in a rage, picks up the fire-shovel, which he dodges, and is coming at him for a thrashing, when cleverly he touches to her lips a taste from the dish in his pocket and immediately she is spellbound.

"What's this?" she says. "Why it's delicious!"

He hands the dish to her and she falls to eating greedily. But sensations similar to those which had overcome her son soon begin to trouble her, and she pleads with him (as had he with the man), "Take this away!"

"Will you beat me then?" he asks.

"I certainly will!" she answers.

"Well then," says he, "eat on." Which she does, until she can stand the strain no longer, when she promises to let him go and he takes the dish away.

Next morning the old lady sends him off with another of her cows; and as he is again passing the house by the road, the man at the doorway calls out to him. The lad shouts back, "Be off with you! Yesterday you robbed me; you're not going to do it today."

Whereupon the man at the doorway draws off his belt and flings it onto the road, where it leaps up and instantly wraps itself around both the boy and the cow, binding the animal's legs to her body and lashing the boy to her side.

"Hey! Let me go!" Jack cries.

"I will when you give me that cow."

"I can't," cries Jack.

"Well then, you may lie there."

The belt begins to contract and soon both boy and cow are unable to breathe. Jack signals; he is going to give up. The man takes the cow and gives Jack the belt in return.

The old mother is beside herself. She again comes at him with the fire-shovel; but he casts down the magic belt. Instantly she is bound hand and foot, scolding at him to be let free.

"Will you beat me then?" he asks.

"I certainly will," she replies.

"Well then," says he, "you may lie there."

The belt begins to contract, and in terror the old woman relents. So next morning Jack is again on the road, and from the same doorway the same man calls to be given the cow.

"I'll give you a stone to your head!" calls Jack; and as he is stooping to pick one up, the man draws from his pocket a tiny flute and begins piping. Jack's muscles twitch. The stone drops from his hand. His legs and feet begin dancing. The cow also is dancing. Neither can stop and the jig goes on till the boy, fairly breathless, shouts, "Will you *stop* with that thing!"

"Will you give me the cow?"

"I can't!" replies Jack.

"Then dance away," says the man.

Jack jigs and turns, together with the dancing cow, until about to drop, when again he signals, forfeits the cow, and receives in return the flute.

The poor mother is fit to murder him this time entirely. But as she comes at him he takes out the flute, begins piping, and she begins to dance, soon screaming at him, "Will you stop with that thing!"

"Will you beat me then?" he asks.

"That I will!" she replies.

"Then," he says to her, "dance away."

And so she does until about to drop, and would be jigging still, but he asks again, "Will you beat me then?"

"No, no! I'm finished! You dog!"

There was another effect produced by the flute when Jack and the cow had been stopped on the road, which, namely, was of a swarm of hornets, visible only to the piper's sight, which hovers about, dancing in air, wherever the pipe is played. And yet, with all this magic and wonder, the old original difficulty remains of no money to meet the rent.

"Today is the day for the king to arrive," says the mother in great distress to her son. "What shall we do?"

"I have an idea," he replies.

Calmly going about the house, he collects earthen dishes, breaks these up, packs them into a bag, and when the bag is so full it can scarcely be tied, he seals it with a kind of gum. Presently a carriage bearing the king himself and two servants pulls up at the door, when the mother, terrified, runs and hides. But her son, confidently welcoming the visitors, bidding them to be seated, fetches what appears to be a well-filled bag of money, which when he sets it on the table, he makes rattle and chink as though loaded with coins; then producing the little magic dish, he informs the king that his father, before passing away, had given him instructions to set before his Majesty this little offering of an exquisite delicacy.

The king takes a cautious bite, looks up with appreciation, then falls to eating seriously and is joined by the two servants; while Jack, appearing to be occupied with preparing the matter of the rent-money, lifts up the bag and then, as though he had forgotten something, sets it down and departs into another room, where he remains away until his guest can be heard calling desperately. The boy lets him go on calling, delaying until he and his servants should be near to bursting, in extreme distress,

when he appears. And the trapped monarch is then readily persuaded to furnish his own ransom by yielding rent, house, farm, livestock and all.

The mother, when the company has left, comes out of hiding with nothing but love for her son, who makes over to her the entire estate and, departing to seek his fortune, takes with him no more than the enchanted dish, the magic belt, and the flute. He arrives in a town where a king resides who has promised the hand of his daughter to the first young man who can make her laugh three times, and on hearing of this, Jack strolls, one day, into the palace. Asked by the servants what his business there might be, he replies that he has heard there is a princess there, to be given in marriage to the first young man who can make her laugh three times. Whereupon, without further ado, he is conducted to an apartment where the princess waits, surrounded by a company of princely suitors, all of whom have tried but failed to make the princess laugh. They are now there to serve as judges of the next contender.

Jack brings out the little dish, of which he offers to the young lady a taste. In her delicate fingers she takes up a touch to her tongue and, having tasted, immediately reaches for more; then passes the dish to the company, when in less time than it takes to tell of it, the entire room is in a fervor of feeding, amazed not only by the irresistible flavor, but also by the undiminishing morsel on the tiny dish. Not long, however, and all are beginning to try to push the dish away while at the same time reaching for another bite, until at last, in a state of panic, they all begin shouting together at Jack to take and be off with his devilish device. Whereupon, distinctly and calmly, he declares his sole condition, which is simply: "The princess first must laugh."

She glares at him and sits stunned. Never had she imagined herself as laughing, not in pleasure, but in pain. She refuses. "Well then," says Jack "eat on."

So, inevitably the moment arrives when, not only she, but all the young men are groaning, while eating away, and beginning to murmur; then desperately urging her to give up and laugh: which, finally, she does, emitting a forced and reluctant, feeble caricature of a titter, while murmuring to herself, "He'll not make me do this again."

Jack takes back the dish, undoing the spell, and immediately all the princely suitors rush to him to expel him from the room, when presto, tossed to the floor is the magic belt and instantly, they are all bound together in a bundle, wound about from head to foot, lying helpless before him in a heap.

"Untie us!" the voice of the princess calls from the unseemly pile. "Untie us!"

"You must laugh first," Jack calls to her, stooping to listen. But no laugh is heard, and the belt begins to contract. Only when the pressure can no longer endured, does the feeble voice of a young woman in pain gives forth its second, forced and pitiful, imitation of a giggle.

The belt is released, and with one accord the young princes, struggling out of their heap, are coming at him with drawn swords, when Jack takes out the flute and begins piping and immediately they are dancing, the princess, among them, jigging along as well.

When they realize that they are to be danced to exhaustion, "Stop! Stop that piping!" they yell. "I will," calls Jack, "when the princess

laughs." And with her princely suitors, umpires, servants, and all there jigging around her, wheeling in a mazy dance with the stakes now finally herself and her father's kingdom, she is more than ever determined not to give out that fatal last laugh. Tight-lipped, she goes on and on, head beginning to wag, until, altogether out of breath, she drops to the floor, then yields to her fate, and laughs.

Now when the king, her father, is informed of this misadventure, he gives orders for the unknown victor to be brought into his presence; and when he sees the uncouth, unattractive youth, he declares the contract null and void, ordering the upstart done away with and some one or other of the princely suitors substituted in his place.

Poor Jack! He is seized and flung into a den of ferocious beasts, which immediately rush upon him. But the belt is tossed among them and instantly they are tied in a heap, while their intended victim, proceeding to a corner of the yard, sits quietly down to prepare himself for the next development.

For word has gone out to the world that a suitor at the royal palace has won the hand of the princess, and a wedding has been accordingly arranged, which is to be celebrated that very evening. This Jack has been told. And so, all goes at the wedding party merrily as a wedding bell until the hour for the bridegroom to enter the bridal chamber, when everything goes wild. For Jack has begun to pipe on his flute, summoning to his purpose an invisible swarm of hornets; so that when the counterfeit bridegroom has fully disrobed in preparation for the night of his life, through the keyhole of the wedding chamber invisible enemies come pouring who ply him with their fiery weapons mercilessly about his lower limbs. Unable to see them but fully able to feel their assault, the poor fellow begins to scream and caper about like a madman; wherupon the appalled princess, screaming as well, goes rushing from her wedding chamber for help. Domestics from all directions run to her assistance, and she declares the bridegroom is a maniac. Another is substituted, for whom the same fate is reserved; and the king concludes that he has been outgeneraled: that the young man who had won the hand of his daughter still lives and must be a personage, truly remarkable, possessed of miraculous powers. He sends for him from the animal den, where the beasts are discovered to be all tied up. A mist has filled the area and they cannot find the young man himself. They attempt to release the animals but find that this is impossible too. Then they bring their report to the king.

"Ay," says he; "just as I thought! He is a necromancer: remarkable man! Go again, seek for him, and if you find him, bring him to me."

This time they find, but hardly recognize him. He has been completely transformed. No longer an oaf, he is now a beautiful youth, of portly bearing and polished manner. The wedding is consummated with pomp, he builds for his bride a stately palace, and when the old king dies, is crowned in his stead.[131]

269. Micmac chair with porcupine quill seat, c. 3'6" high × 1'6" × 1'5", c. 1780, Nova Scotia. This chair is arguably one of the finest extant examples of Canadian Maritime quill design.

The God-Man Glooscap

The tradition respecting Glooscap is that he came to this country from the east, across the great sea; that he was a divine being, though in the form of a man; and that when he departed he went toward the west. There he is still tented, with the wigwams nearby of two important personages: Kuhkw, whose name means "Earthquake," and Coolpujot, whose name, meaning "Rolled over by Handspikes," bears reference to the round of the seasons.

Glooscap was the teacher and friend of the Micmac. All they knew of the arts he taught them: the names of the stars and constellations; how to hunt and to fish, and to cure what they took; how to cultivate the gound.

When he first arrived, he brought with him a woman whom he always addressed as Grandmother. She was not his wife, nor did he ever have a wife. He was sober, grave, and good. Indeed, all that the Indians knew of what was wise and good he taught them.

His canoe was a granite rock. On one occasion he put to sea in this craft with a young woman who proved to be a witch. This was manifested by the troubles that ensued. A storm arose and waves dashed wildly over the canoe. Accusing her of being the cause of all this through her evil deeds and determining to get rid of her, Glooscap stood in for the land, leapt ashore and setting his foot against the heavy craft, pushed it off to sea with the young witch still aboard, telling her to become whatever it was she desired to be. And she was thereupon transformed into a large, ferocious fish, called by the Indians *keeganibe*, which is said to have a huge dorsal fin, like the sail of a boat, high out of the water.

The Indians sometimes visit Glooscap in his present abode, which is in a beautiful land in the west. While among them, he had told them of such a place, instructing them to look forward to a residence there themselves, and to call it their beautiful home in the far west, where, if good, they shall go when they die.

The journey to that fair land, so distant, is long, difficult, and dangerous; the way back, however, easy and short.

Some years ago, they say, seven stout-hearted young men attempted the adventure and succeeded. Before reaching the place, they had to pass over a mountain, the ascent of which was up a perpendicular bluff, and the descent on the other side was more difficult still; for the top hung far over the base. The unbelieving and fearful could not get over that bluff at all; but the confident and good could do so with ease, as though it were a level path.

Beyond the mountain, the road passed between the heads of two huge serpents directly opposite each other, which darted out their tongues, destroying anyone they hit. But the good and the firm of heart could dart between the strokes of the tongues; after which but one more difficulty remained: a wall, as of a thick, heavy cloud, which separated the present world from the beautiful region beyond. This cloudy wall rose at intervals and fell, striking the ground with such force that anyone caught beneath it would be crushed. The good, however, could dart across when it rose and come out the other side unscathed.

In all of these adventures our seven young men succeeded; and in the land to which they came they found three wigwams: one for Glooscap, one for Kuhkw and a third for Coolpujot, three mighty personages. But Glooscap is supreme. Coolpujot has no bones. He cannot move himself, but by Glooscap's order is rolled every Spring and Fall, being turned with handspikes: hence his curious name, which means, "Rolled Over by Handspikes." In the Fall he is turned toward the West, and in the Spring toward the East, which is but an image or figure of speech denoting the revolving seasons of the year. By his mighty gaze and breath, he can sweep down whole armies and work wonders on a prodigious scale, control weathers and the elements, frost, snow, ice and the heat of the sun. Kuhkw, "Earthquake," who is also a personage of might, travels under the surface of the ground and by his power makes all things tremble.

Each of the seven visitors had a request to propose on arrival, and each received what he asked for, though not always in correspondence with the spirit of the request. For example, one, who was wonderfully enamored of a certain part of the country, asked to be given to reside there, and to live there, many years. Whereupon, at Glooscap's command, Earthquake took and stood him up there, and he became a great cedar tree, whose branches, when the wind blows, are bent and break with a great noise, scattering in every direction seeds, which have produced all the cedar-groves now to be seen in Nova Scotia and New Brunswick.

Another of the seven asked for a medicine to cure all diseases. But on failing to follow exactly the directions which had been given him, he lost it before reaching home. It had been wrapped in paper and he had been charged not to undo the packet before reaching home. But curiosity got the better of him. He could not see what difference it would make if he took just one look as he was going along. So he undid the parcel and instantly, the medicine slipped out to the ground, spread in all directions, vanishing from sight.[132]

The Evil Pitcher, Who Was Both Male and Female: How She Fell in Love with Glooscap and, on Being Scorned, Became His Enemy: Three Episodes

When Glooscap came into the world it was full of giants, monsters, sorcerers and witches, fiends and devils of all kinds. And among the witches there was one who was called *Pook-jin-skwess*, or the Pitcher, who, when Glooscap was still very young, fell in love with him. But having not yet gained the power of his later years, he fled before her; and since each, in order to make great strides, had taken the form of a giant, that was a dreadful flight and pursuit: like a storm in winter, the wind pursuing great clouds; or like a summer tempest, the lightning pursuing thunder. The snow lay deep and each wore snowshoes: his round, hers long and pointed. And when they came to the seashore, Glooscap sprang out all the way to Grand Manon Island [New Brunswick, a leap of about nine miles]. The marks of that flight and pursuit and great leap are to be seen to this day in the rocks.

*   *   *

Now the Pitcher could assume many forms, male or female, or any number at a time. And so it happened that when Glooscap arrived in his traveling at Ogumkeok, he found there a hut, and within the hut, seated by a fire, the ugliest old hag he had ever seen, dirty, ragged and loathsome in all ways, trembling in every limb, as if near death. With bleared eyes looking up at him, she begged him to fetch for her a little firewood, which he did; after which she prayed him to free her of the vermin with which she was all covered, that were maddening her with their bites. [Compare the task of the Eskimo shaman in the submarine lodge of Sedna, the Old Woman of the Sea (see I.2:183–184); also that of the Iroquois Woman Who Married a Great Serpent.]

Her vermin were all devils in disguise, spirits full of a poison that she assumed would surely kill him. but he had foreseen this adventure and had brought with him in anticipation a bag of cranberries. Bidding her bow her head therefore, he began snatching at the dangerous things, and when each, as he grabbed it, became either a porcupine or a toad, the hag would ask, "Have you found one?" "I have," he would say, and she then would tell him, "Crush it!" When he would crush, instead, a cranberry, so that on hearing the sound, she should think he had done as told, and that the poison now on his fingers would penetrate to his life. But one after another, he put the creatures under an overturned bowl before him, and this went on until the hag herself fell asleep.

When she woke, Glooscap was gone, and swarming all over the floor, having upset the bowl, were the porcupines and toads. She became furious, the more so for the intolerable insult of his having not thought it even worthwhile to kill her as she slept. And in her fury, as the rage increased, she burst into her proper form and was as beautiful as sin, wild as a devil. Gathering up her imps and putting them away, making herself the more magical by concentrating her will, she drew herself together and stepped forth to engage him again.

*   *   *

Of a day therefore, when Glooscap, having come to the top of a hill and looking out over the land, saw afar a big wigwam, he knew immediately that his enemy, the Pitcher, was there; and on arriving before it, what he found within was, an old man with two daughters. The girls came out with inviting glances to greet him, offering, with soft, sweet, very pleasant words, a string of sausages to be flung around his neck in the playful manner of maidens showing their desire to a favored youth. These were sausages made of the entrails of a bear turned inside out, washed, dried and smoked, with the fat, still clinging from the outside, now filling the interior. But in this case the offering was enchanted, so that if Glooscap had allowed it to be placed around his neck, he would have been overpowered.

His two great dogs running out before him, growled at the girls as they approached, waving charmingly their garlands, and Glooscap, letting it appear that he might be ready to be won, shouted angrily at his animals, "Stop!

270. Glooscap setting his dogs on the witches.

Stop!"—which, in the inverted way of his usual replies to questions, signified to them, "Sic 'em! Sic 'em!" So they flew at the two witches, who flashed up like fire into their own dreadful forms as female fiends, and there followed such tumult as had never in the land of the Abnaki ever before occurred. All the earth and the rocks were torn up and hurled about, and Glooscap, ever shouting at his dogs, "Stop! Those are my sisters! Stop, you dogs!" yet the more he called apparently for peace, the more fiercely did they carry the war, until in disarray the two witches fled.

Then Glooscap walked into the wigwam, where, waiting for him to arrive as food, was sitting the old sorcerer. "Are you hungry?" Glooscap asked. "Do you like sausages?" And tossing the links around the old man's neck, he slew him with a single blow.[133]

Glooscap and the Whale, or The Song of the Clams

In olden times, in the beginning of things, men were as animals and animals as men. How this happened to be, no one knows; but some say that all at first were men, and that when some gave themselves up to this and that desire, and to nothing else, they became beasts. Before that time, they could change back and forth, from one form to the other. Yet even when they were in human form, there was always something that showed what animal they were.

Now Glooscap lived on an island, and there were at first, many Indians there with the natures of animals and birds. But they all became jealous of Glooscap and made up their minds to run off, and leave him absolutely alone, thinking that, when marooned in that way, he would perish. However they had not reckoned on his power.

No one knows why he decided to remain there alone for seven years (though some say it was seven months); whether it might have been to gain magical power, or to chasten the others with suffering. But when the time had come, he went with his two dogs down to the shore, far out to sea, looked over the waves, and sang his song which the whales obey. Very soon there rose in the distance a whale, who had heard the call and was coming to Glooscap. But he was small, and when Glooscap, who was very large, put one foot on him to test his weight, the whale sank. So he sent him away.

Then Glooscap again sang his song, and there came the largest whale of all, a great and mighty female, who bore him well and easily over the sea toward land. But she was afraid of getting into shoal water, and running ashore, whereas that was just what Glooscap wanted, so as not to get his feet wet. So as she went shoreward she asked him from time to time if land were in sight, and he lied and answered, "No." And she continued rapidly on.

However, she then suddenly saw shells below, and the water had grown so shoal that in fear she called to him, "Is the land not yet in sight?" And again he lied, "We are still far away." But the water had now become so shallow, she could hear the song of the clams in the sand beneath her, singing to her to throw Glooscap off and let him drown: for those clams were his deadly enemies. Hearing but not understanding their language, Bootup the Whale asked her rider what they were saying to her—for Glooscap understood Clam—and he replied, again lying, in song:

Hurry, hurry, they tell you,
Hurry, hurry him onward,
Over the waves,
As fast as you can!

So the whale swam on like lighting and soon found herself high up on shore, when, shocked and in sorrow, she sang to him:

Alas, my grandchild,
You have been my death,
Never, never shall I leave this shore!
Nor again ever swim in the sea!

To which Glooscap sang in reply:

Fear not, Grandmother, fear not!
You have not come here ashore to suffer.
Soon again you shall swim in the sea.

With a push of his bow against her head he set her off and away, out into deep water, where, rejoicing greatly, she sang back to him:

Have you not such a thing,
My grandson,
As an old pipe,
And a bit of tobacco?

To which he answered:

Ah yes!
If it be tobacco you want,
Why, here!

And he reached out to her his short pipe, some tobacco and a light. And the great whale then happily cruised away, smoking as she passed out to sea; while Glooscap, silent on the shore, ever leaning on his maple bow, watched the lengthening cloud as it followed her road, until it vanished in the far away.

So when the Indians now see a whale blow, they say, she is smoking Glooscap's pipe.[134]

How Glooscap Overcame the Great Bull Frog

In the old days there was an Indian village far away in the mountains, little known to other men. The village was by a brook, and the people lived there very comfortably. Every day, the men hunted and the women did the work at home. And all was going very well until one day there was not a drop of water in their brook, nor anywhere round about, unless in a few rain puddles, here and there.

Then it was rumored that far away, up in a land no one had ever visited, there was another Indian village on this brook. And so they sent one of their members up along the dry bed to look into the matter. And when he had traveled for three days, he came to the place where he found that a dam had been built across the bed. No water could pass. It was all held there in a pond. So he asked the first villager he met, why this mischief had been done, and was advised to go inquire of their chief, by whose order the dam had been constructed.

When he came before that dignitary, lo! there lay in a sea of mud, lazily, a creature more monster than a man, though of human form, like a giant immense to measure: fat, bloated brutal to behold. His immense yellow eyes, like pine knots, protruded from his head. His mouth ran from ear to ear. He had broad, skinny feet with long webbed toes. He was marvelous, exceedingly.

The messenger complained to this thing, who said nothing at first, but then loudly croaked, and answered finally in a queer, hollow bellow:

Do as you choose,
Do as you choose,
Do as you choose.

What do I care?
What do I care?
What do I care?

If you want water,
If you want water,
If you want water,

Go somewhere else.

The messenger, remonstrating, described the plight of his people, dying of thirst, which seemed to please the monster, who with his great mouth broadly grinned. But he then turned over, made an immense leap toward the dam, took up an arrow and bored a hole in it. A little trickle of water came through, and then, just squatting there, the creature again bellowed:

Up and begone!
Up and begone!
Up and begone!

So the messenger departed, returning to his village, where for a couple of days there was a bit of water. But then again it stopped. And it

271. Watching the whale smoking his pipe.

was then that Glooscap—who knows all that is passing in the hearts, whether of beasts or of men—took note of the condition of the people of that village, and willed that he should be among them. For he comes as comes the wind, and no one knows either why or how.

And it had been just before his arrival that the villagers in council had resolved to send the boldest of their members to almost certain death: to go up there and cut that dam, or do something else as desperate. And to this intent, he should travel armed, and sing his death song as he went along.

Then suddenly Glooscap was among them; for he loved indeed a brave man. He appeared as an immense figure, terrible to behold. Indeed, in all the world there has never appeared anything more terrifying. For he was ten feet high, with a hundred black and red feathers in his scalplock, face painted as though with fresh blood, and around his eyes green rings. From each ear a large clam shell hung, while clinging to the back of his neck, an immense spread eagle was flapping its wings. Hearts quaked in admiration. No one could imagine what such an apparition might portend. Young and old, the squaws all declared that never in their lives had they beheld anything so lovely.

Then having been told the whole of their story, Glooscap bade them be of good cheer, and departed up the dry course of their stream. Not long, and when he had come to within sight of the upper village, he sat down upon a rock and ordered an admiring boy to bring him some water to drink. The child replied that in that village no water could be had unless given out by their chief. "Go then," said Glooscap, "to your chief and tell him to move quickly, or there is someone here who will know the reason why."

The boy was away for over an hour, while Glooscap sat quietly smoking on his pipe, until, at last returning, the youngster handed him a small cup, not half-full of dirty water. So Glooscap got up. "I'll go to your chief myself," he said, "and I think he'll soon give me something much better than this."

So having come to the sprawled out monster, he said to him, harshly, "Give me some water, and that the best, at once, you thing of mud."

With a grin, ear to ear, the monster croaked and reviled him.

Get out of here!
Get out of here!
Go find water where you can.

Glooscap's reply was to thrust his spear into the distended belly, when out there gushed a river, even all the water which, during all that time, should have been flowing along the dry bed of the village brook. For he had made it into himself. And rising tall as a giant pine, Glooscap caught up that bloated chief in his hand, crumpling him with a mighty grip, and lo! it was a bull-frog. So with contempt he hurled it into the rushing stream, where it was swept away with the current.

And ever since that time, the Bull Frog's back has had crumpled wrinkles on its lower part, where the prints remain of Glooscap's terrible squeeze.[135]

How the Lord of Men and Beasts Strove with the Mighty Wasis and Was Shamefully Defeated

Now it came to pass that when Glooscap had conquered all his enemies, all manner of ghosts, witches, devils, cannibals, and goblins, even the Great Bull Frog, he thought upon what he had done, and wondered if his work was at an end. And he mentioned this to a certain woman.

"Not so fast, Master," she replied; "for there yet remains One whom no one has ever conquered or got the better of in any way, and who will remain to the end of time unconquered."

"And who might that be?" Glooscap inquired.

"It is the mighty Wasis," she replied; "and there he sits. And I warn you, if you meddle with him, you will be in trouble."

Now this Wasis was the Baby. And he sat there on the floor, sucking a piece of maple sugar, troubling no one, greatly contented. And since the Lord of Men and Beasts had never married, he knew nothing of the manner of managing children. He was quite certain therefore, as is the wont of such people, that he would know all about it. And so, with a bewitching smile he turned to the Baby and bade it come to him.

The Baby smiled as well, but did not budge. And the Master spoke very sweetly, and made his voice like that of a summer bird; but to no avail; for Wasis sat there, sucking on his maple sugar.

Then the Master frowned and spoke terribly, and ordered Wasis to come crawling to him immediately. Whereupon the Baby burst out crying and then yelling, but did not move.

And so then, since he could do but one thing more, the Master resorted to magic. He used his most awful spells, singing his songs that raise the dead and terrify devils. And Wasis sat and looked at him admiringly and seemed to find it very interesting, but all the same, never moved an inch.

So Glooscap in despair gave up, and Wasis, sitting on the floor there in the sunshine, went goo! goo! and cackled.

And to this day when you see a babe well contented, going goo! goo! and cackling, and no one understanding why, know that it is because he remembers the time he overcame the Master who had conquered all the world. For of all beings that there have ever been since the beginning, Baby is alone the invincible one.[136]

185

How Glooscap Went to England and France and Was the First to Make America Known to the Europeans

There was an Indian woman: she was a Woodchuck. She had lost a boy, and she always thought of him. One day a strange boy came to her and called her mother. He had a whistle with which he could call all the animals. "Mother ," he said, "if you let anyone have this whistle, we shall starve."

"Where did you get it?" she asked.

"A stranger gave it to me," he said.

One day he was making a canoe. The woman took the whistle and blew it. A deer came, and a beaver. They came running; the deer first, the beaver next. The beaver had a stick in his mouth. He gave it to her, and said, "Whenever you want to kill anything, even though it's a half mile off, point this stick at it." She pointed it at the deer. It fell dead.

The boy was Glooscap. He was building a stone canoe. Every morning he went off and was gone all day. He worked a year at it, and when the canoe was finished, he took his (adopted) mother to see it. He told her he was going to make sails for it, and she asked, "Of what will you make them?"

"Of leaves," he said.

"I have something better," she said. "Let the leaves alone." She had many buffalo skins already tanned, which she had obtained by means of the whistle and magical stick. "Take as many," she said, "as you like."

He took the whistle and piped for a moose, an elk, and a bear. They came, and he pointed his stick at them. They fell dead. He dried their meat, and so provisioned his great canoe. To carry water he killed a number of seals and filled their bladders with water. And so they sailed across the sea.

This was before the white people had ever heard of America. White men did not discover this country first; Glooscap discovered England and told them there about it. He got to London, where they had never seen a canoe before. They came flocking down to look at it. They offered him a large ship for his stone canoe, and he refused it. He was afraid the ship might catch fire. They offered him servants, and he refused them. They gave him presents which almost overloaded the canoe. They gave him an anchor and an English flag.

He and his mother then went to France. The French fired cannon at him all morning and afternoon, but they could not hurt the canoe. That night he drew ashore all of their war ships and next morning the French saw this. "Who did this?" they asked. "I did," he answered. And so they took him prisoner. They stuffed him into a great cannon and fired it off. Then they looked into the cannon and there he sat, smoking his stone pipe, knocking out the ashes.

The king heard how they had treated him and told them that was wrong. Anyone who could do such things was surely a very great man. So he sent for Glooscap, who replied, "I don't want to see your king. I came to this country to have my mother baptized a Catholic." They sent boats for him; and a coach; and he was taken to the king, who put to him many questions. He wished, he said, to have his mother baptized.

This was done, and they called her Molly.

Therefore, to this day, all woodchucks are called Molly (for *Mahlinskwess*, "Miss Molly," sounds very much like *mon-in-kwes*, a "woodchuck.")

They all went down to the shore and to please the king Glooscap drew all the ships into the sea again. So the king gave him everything he asked for, and he returned home. And ever since that time, white men have been coming to America.[137]

FOUR TALES SUGGESTIVE OF
A POSSIBLE NORDIC (VIKING) INFLUENCE

How Glooscap Bound the Great Wind Bird and Made All the Waters of the World Stagnant

When Glooscap lived among men, he would frequently paddle out to sea in his canoe with bow and arrows to kill sea fowl. And there came a time when every day was so windy that he could not go out to sea at all. Then he said, "Wuchowsen, the Great Wind Bird, is doing this." And he set out to find him.

Now *Wuchowsen*, meaning Wind-blower, or Wind-blow, lives far far to the north, where he sits on a great rock at the end of the sky; and it is by the waving of his wings that he creates the wind. [Compare the Micmac tale of "The Bird Whose Wings Make the Wind."] Glooscap hunted long, therefore, before he found him, but finally, there he was, a large white bird on a high rock.

"Grandfather," said Glooscap, "have you no compassion for your grandchildren? You are creating gales and storms. It is too much. Be easier with your wings."

"I have been here," the Great Bird said, "since earliest times. Before anyone or anything was around to speak or make a sound, I first moved my wings. Mine was the first voice. And I shall ever continue to move my wings as I will."

Then Glooscap increased and rose in his might. He rose to the clouds. And he took up that giant bird as though he had been a duck, and tied together his wings, and threw him down into a chasm between sheer rocks, and left him lying.

People now could go out all day long in their canoes; for there was a dead calm. And it lasted many weeks and months. And with that all the waters became stagnant, so thick that Glooscap could not now paddle his canoe at all. Then he thought again of the Great Bird, and went to see him.

As he had left him, there he found him; for Wuchowsen is immortal. So raising him, he put him back upon his rock and set free one of his wings. And there have been no such terrific winds, since then, as there were in earliest times.[138]

"No one, who knows the Edda" states Leland, "will deny that Wuchowsen, or the Wind-blower, as he appears in the Passamaquoddy tale, is far more like the same bird of the Norsemen than the grotesque Thunder Bird of the Western tribes. He is distinctly spoken of by the Indians of Maine as a giant and a bird in one, sitting on a high cliff at the end of the sky, the wind—not thunder—coming from his pinions:

Tell me ninthly, since thou art called wise,
Whence the wind comes that over ocean passes,
Invisible to man.

Hraesvelg he is called, who at heaven's end sits,
A giant in eagle's plumage:
From his wings comes, it is said, the wind
That over all men passes.'"[139]

Glooscap and His Brother, Malsum the Wolf

Glooscap and his brother, Malsum the Wolf, were as yet unborn. They were there waiting for light to appear when Malsum, the younger, said, "Why should I wait? I'm going to enter the world and begin my life right now." To which the other responded, "That would be an evil act." So Glooscap, the elder, was born as others are, but Malsum burst from his mother's side — or as others tell, from his mother's armpit. [Compare Flint in the Iroquois Legend of the Twin Heroes. The Buddha was born from his mother's right side and there is an Armenian belief that Christ was born through the right side of the Virgin.[140]] In his wickedness Malsum rent the wall, and so the beginning of his life was his mother's death.

Who was Glooscap's mother? Glooscap's mother was the female Turtle.[141] [Compare in the Iroquois legend of The Woman Who Fell from the Sky, Big Turtle, supporter of the island Earth, who became the father of the Sky-Woman's twin grandsons, Sapling and Flint.] Glooscap and his twin grew up together, and Malsum, knowing that they both had charmed lives, asked his brother one day by what instrument he could be killed; for in this matter each had knowledge of his own secret. Glooscap answered that he could be killed only by the blow of a handful of down; but, since he knew that he would come to life again, with this reply he deceived Malsum. Glooscap then asked Malsum by what instrument he could be killed, and Malsum answered truthfully, "By the blow of a cattail or bullrush." Glooscap's name means the "Liar." [Compare the deceptive replies to all questions of Tseqabec, Glooscap's counterpart among the Montagnais. Compare, also, in the Iroquois tale, the fateful exchange of such secrets by Sapling and Flint.]

Charles G. Leland, the collector in the 1880s of these late, distorted fragments of northeastern Algonquian lore, points out that in Norse mythology, as represented in the Icelandic Eddic literature of the ninth to thirteenth centuries, the god-man Baldr is killed by an apparently harmless twig of mistletoe hurled by the blind god Hoth, whose hand is guided by Loki; and that Baldr, like Glooscap, comes to life again.[142] Commenting on this feature of the Wabanaki tale, he remarks: "In this story, as in that of Baldr and Loki, it is the very apparent harmlessness of the bane which points the incident.....In the Edda the mistletoe, the softest and apparently the least injurious of plants, kills Baldr; in the Wabanaki tale it is a ball of down or a rush."[143]

Relevant historically to the force of this observation is the fact that the period of the Icelandic Eddic literature of the ninth to thirteenth centuries was exactly that of the Viking settlements in Greenland (from A.D. 982) and the voyages of discovery to northeastern North America of Bjarni Herjulfsson (c. A.D. 1000) and Leif Eriksson (one year later). The northeasternmost North American coasts discovered and explored at that time are in the Icelandic Sagas named separately, as "Helluland," "Markland" and "Vinland,"[144] corresponding, it has been thought, to Labrador, Newfoundland and Nova Scotia—which, as we have seen, were the ancestral territories of the Nascapi and the Micmac. Noting a number of other distinctive likenesses in the two traditions, Leland even suggests that in some part or parts they must, in fact, be the same. "Either," he suggests, "the Norsemen told it to the Eskimo and the Indians, or the latter to the Norsemen. No one knows, after all, what was going on for ages in the early time, up about Jutenheim in the North Atlantic! Vessels came to Newfoundland to fish for cod since unknown antiquity, and, returning, reported that they had been to Tartary."[145]

And so it came to pass that Malsum one day collected a handful of bird down which he flung at his brother, Glooscap, who fell dead. But he recovered; and going forth, gathered bulrushes and, returning, smote Malsum with these, and he died.[146]

272.   Glooscap killing his brother the Wolf.

How Glooscap Came to this Country, Made the Elves or the Dwarfs, Then Man of an Ash Tree, and Last of All the Beasts

Some say that Glooscap first came into this country—Nova Scotia, Canada and Maine—, the land of the Abnaki, in a great stone canoe that was actually an island of granite covered over with trees, and that there were no Indians here at that time; only very far west, wild Indians. Others say, however, that he was born right here, in the land of the Abnaki tribes—the Micmac, Passamaquoddy, and the rest.

Now when he had stepped ashore from his stone canoe, which some believe was Noah's Ark, he made first the Elves and Dwarfs, the little people, dwellers in the rocks there. Then in the following way he made man. He took his bow and shot arrows into certain trees, the basket trees, the Ash; and the Indians came forth from the bark of the Ash.

Glooscap also made all the animals. He made them first very large. Then he said to the great Moose, who was as tall as the highest pines and the clouds, "What would you do if you saw an Indian coming?" "I would tear down the trees on him," Moose replied. So, realizing the Moose was too strong, Glooscap made him smaller, so that Indians should be able to kill him.

Then he said to Squirrel, who was about the size of a wolf, "What would you do if you saw an Indian coming?" "I would scratch down trees on him," Squirrel said. And so Glooscap said, "You, too, are too strong." And he made him little.

Then Glooscap asked the great White Bear what he would do if he saw an Indian coming. "I would eat him," said the Bear. So the Master told him to go live among rocks and icebergs, where no Indians would be seen.

In that way he questioned all the animals that he had made, changing their sizes, or allotting them places, according to their answers. And he chose for his dog the Loon; but the Loon was off by himself so much, that he then chose instead two wolves, one black and one white. Loons are tale-bearers and gossips.

Before Glooscap taught them how to live, people lived in darkness. In fact, it was so dark, they could not even see to kill their enemies. He taught them how to hunt, and to build huts and canoes and weirs for fish. Before he came, they did not know how to make nets or weapons. The Great Master taught them, also, the hidden virtues of plants, roots, and barks, pointing out to them such vegetables as might be used for food; also, what animals, birds and fish were to be eaten. Then, when this was done, he taught them the names of all the stars.

Glooscap loved mankind, and no matter where he might be in the wilderness, he was never far from the Indians. He dwelt in a lonely land; but wherever they looked for him they found him. Far and wide he traveled, so that there is in all the land of the Abanaki, no place where he has not left his name. Hills and rocks, rivers, lakes and islands, bear witness to his passing.[147]

How Glooscap Is Making Arrows, Preparing for a Great Battle. The Twilight of the Indian Gods

Is Glooscap living still? Yes, far away; but no one knows where. Some say that he sailed in his stone canoe toward the east, beyond the sea, and that one day, in his stone canoe, he will return. Others tell of a long and dangerous journey to a very great, long wigwam, where he is incessantly fashioning arrows. One side of the lodge is already full of them. When he has filled the whole lodge, he will come forth and make war.

And on whom is he to make war?

He is to make war on all, to kill all. And after that, there will be no more world. How soon? Don't know. Maybe long time off. And are any to be saved? Don't know. Have heard say that all some day will burn up, water all boil away. Big fire! Some good ones to be taken up to good heavens! But don't know. Just hear that. Only hear.[148]

"It was owing," states Leland, "to a mere chance question that this account of the Last Day was obtained. It was related to Mrs. W. Wallace Brown of Calais, Maine, by Mrs. Le Cool, and old Passamaquoddy Indian. It casts a great light on the myth of Glooscap, since it appears that a day is to come when, like Arthur, Barbarossa, and other heroes in retreat, he is to come forth at a new twilight of the gods, exterminate the *Iglesmani*, and establish an eternal happy hunting-ground. This preparing for a great final battle is more suggestive of Norse or Scandinavian influence than of aught else. It is certainly not of a late date or Christian, but it is very much like the Edda and Ragnarok....The Norsemen expected such a fight, when arrows would fly like hail, and Glooscap is supposed to be deliberately preparing for it.

"A very curious point remains to be noted in this narration," Leland observes. "When Indians speak of Christian, or white or civilized teachings, they say, 'I heard,' or, 'I have been told.' This they never do as regards their own ancient traditions. When Mrs. Le Cool said that she 'had heard' that some were to be taken up into *good* heavens, she declared, in her way, that this was what Christians said, but that she was not so sure of it. The Northeastern Algonquin always distinguish very accurately between their ancient lore and that derived from the whites. I have often heard French fairy tales and Aesop's fables Indianized to perfection, but the narrator always knew that they were not *N'Karnayoo*, 'of the old time.'

"Glooscap is now living in a Norse-like Asa-heim; but there is to come a day when the arrows will be ready, and he will go forth and slay all the wicked. Malsum, the Wolf, his twin brother, the typical colossal type of all Evil, will come to life, with all the giant cannibals, witches, and wild devils slain of old; but the champion will gird on his magic belt, and the arrows will fly in a rain as at Ragnarok: the hero will come sailing in his wonderful canoe, which expands to hold an army. Thus it will be on

That day of wrath, that dreadful day,
When heaven and earth shall pass away,

with all things, in blood and death and fire. Then there will come the eternal happy hunting-grounds.

"If this was derived from Christian priests, it must be admitted that it has changed wonderfully on the way. It is to me very heathen," Leland states; "grimly archaic, and with the strong stamp of an original. Its resemblance to the Norse is striking."[149]

Schoolcraft's fortunate location at Sault Ste. Marie placed him in exactly the position to investigate, as had no one before him, the "whole arcana" (as he called it) of the Northern Algonquians. Immediately to the west of him, north of Lake Superior, lay the forest primeval of the Ojibwa, and north of Lake Huron, to the east, the Ottawa. There is a native tradition which has it that the Ojibwa, Ottawa and Potawatomi arrived from the northwest originally as one tribe, which separated at what is now Mackinaw, Michigan: the Ottawa continuing on to the east, and the Potawatomi turning south into the region (now the state of Michigan) between Lakes Michigan and Huron. One may think of the Shawnee, also, as having perhaps been participants in this prehistoric migration, who continued on through Michigan into what is now Ohio, where they settled in the middle Ohio valley and there remained until in the seventeenth century they were attacked and dispersed by the Iroquois. It may well be that in the period, c. 500 B.C.–A.D. 300, the builders of the Adena and Hopewellian burial mounds (see I.2:211, Map 44, Adena Cultural sites, c. 500 B.C.–A.D. 100, and Map 45, Sites of the Hopewellian "Interaction Sphere," c. 100 B.C.–A.D. 300) were ancestral of the Shawnee.

Following the onslaught of the Iroquois, the tribe broke into three parts, which scattered out of Ohio into widely separated regions, the Cumberland Valley, remoter Southeast, and (present) Illinois. After 1725, these returned and were reunited in Ohio, where they constituted, briefly, a barrier to the advancing frontier. Tecumseh (1768–1813), the last great Indian orator and patriot to attempt to conferate the native tribes in resistance, was a Shawnee chief. Following his defeat and death in the War of 1812—as leader, in alliance with the British, of the largest Indian fighting force ever assembled—the Shawnee nation again broke into three parts and in the course of the next half-century disappeared from the historical field.

Our Shawnee folktale "The Celestial Sisters," which was recorded by Schoolcraft in the 1820s, treats of a theme (as noted above), *Ascent to stars* (Thompson A 761), that is already represented in Paleolithic cave paintings of the Middle Magdalenian era (from c. 13,000–11,500 B.C.),[150] most notably on the famous ceiling at Altamira (I.1:**136**), but also in the galleries of Lascaux (I.1:**91–93**). Schoolcraft's version of the universal theme suggests specifically, however, the Greek legend of the hunter Orion's discovery and pursuit of seven sisters who in flight ascended to the heavens, where they are to be seen as the Pleiades and he is the neighboring constellation Orion.

273. *Salmon Fishing by Torchlight*, 1845 oil painting on canvas, 1′6″ × 2′5″, by Canadian artist Paul Kane (1810–71). While spending time at a Menominee encampment on the Fox River in Wisconsin (where over 3000 Indians awaited payment for land, around Lake Winnebago, previously ceded by them to the United States government), Kane found himself enthralled by this scene of nocturnal spear-fishing and determined to record it.

For the heliacal (near-dawn) rising of the star cluster of the Pleiades (of which seven can be seen by the naked eye) occurs in spring in the Northern Hemisphere (whether in Greece or in Ohio) at the opening of the planting season, while the morning setting of the group in autumn marks the season's end, and the harvest. As the Greek legend of the origin of the seasonal constellation is specific to the interests of an agricultural order of society, so the Shawnee example should be, as well. And since the Adena and Hopewellian culture sites of Ohio and Indiana represent the earliest maize-cultivating stages of the tribal cultures of that region, c. 500 B.C.–A.D. 300, it is unlikely that Schoolcraft's story of the hunter Waupee and twelve celestial sisters should antedate that period of transition from hunting and gathering to agriculture—which brings up the irrepressible question of diffusion versus parallel development, with diffusion, however, in this case apparently ruled out.

The plot is exactly that of a standard Swan Maiden adventure. Compare, from the northwest corner of Greenland, the Smith Sound Eskimo tale of "The Goose Wife" (I.2:184–185). Compare also the Tchiakowsky ballet, "Swan Lake." Except that here the captured bride is not one of a company of wild geese or swans who descend to earth and remove their feathered garments to become beautiful young women, but one of twelve heavenly sisters who, to a sound of music, descend from the sky in a wicker basket, out of which they all leap to dance with a shining ball that is struck as a drum. The number twelve here is suspicious and suggests a possible European influence (twelve signs of the Zodiac; twelve months of the year, etc.); so also, the dance with a shining ball (possibly the moon or sun) and the sound of music accompanying the descent. Otherwise, the tale is typically Indian, and to me suggests a modified Swan Maiden

adventure turned, either by the maize-planting-and-harvesting Shawnee, or by their Adena/Hopewellian ancestors, into an origin legend in recognition of the force of the Pleiades, as measuring the passage from a hunter's way of life-by-chance to the settled, seasonally ordered way of a society established in agriculture. At some time, then, during the long season of European contacts, following the seventeenth-century shattering blow of the Iroquois, the numerical change from seven to twelve, the shining ball, and the music of the spheres, can have been added.

For the Shawnee, Potawatomi, and other members of the Central Division of the Algonquians combined in their economies the two modes, of hunting, pursued by the man, and planting, by the women. The typical seasonal routine was of family groups going off in autumn to their chosen winter hunting grounds, and in spring returning to their tribal villages or towns of bark-covered family houses grouped around a large council house and dance ground, with their cultivated fields round about. The usual ceremonies of the agricultural season were of a Spring Bread Dance at planting time, Green Corn Dance at crop ripening, and at harvest, an Autumn Bread Dance. Other important ceremonies, conducted largely in the council house, were of the initiation and ritual purification of warriors. Compare Catlin's illustrations—contemporary with Schoolcraft's researches (c. 1832)—of a Mandan (Macro-Siouan) village, council house interior, and spring festival (I.2:226-231)

North of the Great Lakes, where generally the spring-to-autumn growing season is too short for the cultivation of maize, the hunt, supplemented by wild seed- and root-gathering, continued as the unchallenged determinant, not only of the way of life, but also of the tribal rites and myths by which that way of life is interpreted in a spiritual sense and structured to accord. Hence, the Northern Algonquian trickster-hero Manabozho remains for the most part singular—like Tseqabec of the Montagnais and Glooscap of the Abnaki tribes—without a contending twin. There is no sense of a conflict of values between the wilderness way of the (male-dominated) hunt and that of the settled, agriculturally supported (female-dominated) domestic hearth. Frank G. Speck has already remarked resemblances between the folktales of the Montagnais and Ojibwa, and, as already noticed, our Nascapi tale of "How Summer was Brought North" differs only in detail from Schoolcraft's Ojibwa version, "Ojeeg Annung, the Summer-Maker," of the same adventure. The truly remarkable Ottawa tale of "The Undying Head," opens a vista backward in time to the remotest Paleolithic. There is a continuity of tradition, and that is what we are dealing with in these Algonquian tales: "Aggodahguada and his Daughter…" is related to the Buffalo story (I.2:234) and, among the selections from the trickster cycle, to that of Manabozho "In the Belly of the Great Fish."

The Undying Head

In a remote part of the north there lived a great magician, Iamo, with his young sister, who had never seen a human being. They had no need ever to venture far from home; for to procure food, he had only to go a little way from their lodge and at a particular spot stick his arrows into the ground. Next morning his sister would go there and find every arrow fixed in the heart of a deer. Thus they lived until she attained womanhood, when one day her brother said to her, "Sister, the time is near when you will become ill. Now listen carefully to my advice. If you don't, you will probably be the cause of my death. Take the fire-sticks with which we build our fires and go some distance from our lodge and build yourself a separate fire. When you need food, I shall tell you where to find it. You must cook for yourself at that time, and I shall cook for myself. During the period of your illness, do not attempt to come near to this lodge or to bring into it any of the utensils you will then be using. For the present, furthermore, since you do not know when that time will come, you must wear fastened to your belt the utensils you will then require, so that when the moment arrives, you will not have to return to our lodge to get them."

The sister promised to obey her brother in everything he had told her. But shortly after, when he was out of the lodge and she was alone there, combing her hair, she had just untied the belt to which the implements were fastened, when suddenly the event occurred to which her brother had referred. Out of the lodge she ran, but in her haste she forgot the belt and, afraid to return, stood for some time thinking. Then deciding to go in and fetch it—"For," as she thought, "my brother is not there and this will take but a moment!"—in she ran, and was coming out when the brother, returning, came in sight and immediately knew what had happened.

"Well," he said; "you have killed me. It was an accident, I know. But what can we do? What is to become of you? You have killed me."

He laid his hunting clothes and gear aside, and soon his feet began to inflame and turn black, so that he could no longer move. Then he explained to her how to set the arrows in the ground, so that she should always have a supply of food; and when the inflammation reached his first rib, he said, "My sister, my end is approaching. You must now do exactly as I say. Over there are my medicine bag and war club. In the bag are all my medicines, war feathers, and paints of all colors. When the inflammation reaches my breast, you must take the club and with its sharp edge cut my head off; place the head in the bag and, leaving the top open, hang the medicine bag back where it was. Also, pay attention to my bow and arrows. You will need one of the arrows to procure your food. The others, along with the bow, you must tie to the medicine bag. And the whole must then be arranged so that I shall be looking out toward the door. I shall speak to you now and then, but not very often."

Not long, and the inflammation reached his breast, when he said to his sister, "Now take up the war club and strike off my head." She hesitated, she was afraid. "*Strike!*" he said, and there was a smile on his face. She picked up the club and, mustering courage, delivered the blow, and when the head fell away, "Now," it said to her, "do exactly as I told you." And terrified, she obeyed.

From that time on, the head kept watch in the lodge and would advise the sister where to go and what to do to procure the kinds of food she required; until, one day, it said to her, "The time is at hand for us to be freed from this situation. I am to suffer many trials, for so the Superior Manito decrees; but shall bear them all with patience."

For indeed, there was at that time, in a certain part of the country, the village of a large warlike band, among whom there was an especially warlike family of ten brothers. It was, furthermore, the spring of the year, and the youngest of these ten had blackened his face and fasted and his dreams had been propitious. So when his fast was ended, he one night sent secretly for his brothers and to the sound of a war drum

274. Ojibwa carved wooden pipe bowl, 5″ × 2½″ × 3″, White Earth Reservation, Minnesota, late nineteenth century. Brass tacks are used for eyes and ear ornaments. A pipe stem would be inserted into the neck when the pipe was to be used.

275. Winnebago bowl carved from oak, 6¾″ in diameter, Wisconsin, mid-nineteenth century. The handle, carved in the shape of a human head, aims for general form, not naturalistic representation, and is in this respect typical of Woodlands art of the period.

they agreed to accompany him on a war excursion. Mudjikewis, third from the eldest, who was noted for his oddities, jumped up and, taking up his war club, yelled, "Yes, yes! And this is how I'll deal with those we are going to fight." With another yell, he struck the post in the center of the lodge, and the rest of them called out to him, "Slow, slow there, Mudjikewis, when you are in other people's lodges!" Then each took up the drum in turn and sang his song. The youngest then warned them not to whisper anything of their intention even to their wives; and they closed with a feast.

When the time for departure drew near, word was given to assemble on a certain night, and Mudjikewis then asked his wife to make for him a new pair of moccasins. "Why?" she asked. "You already have on a good pair." And she protested several times. "Oh well," he said to her at last, "since you *must* know, we are going on a war excursion." And so the secret was revealed.

After many such days, they came at last to a piece of high ground from which they could make out on the summit of a distant mountain the form of a mammoth bear asleep. The distance between was great, but the size of the beast was plain to be seen. "There," said the leader, "is the one to whom I've been leading you, and right there our troubles begin. He is a Manito and around his neck is an exceedingly precious wampum belt, for the gaining of which all those whose bones we have seen have lost their lives. He is as dangerous and ferocious as a female bear in a rage. Let us not be afraid, but manly. We will approach him in his sleep."

The party advanced, and when they had climbed the mountain and come close to the great bear, they paused to consider the monster. He was indeed asleep. The leader stepped forward, reached and touched the belt around his neck. "This," said he, "is it." He tried to slip it over the great head, but failed. Then each of the brothers tried, and when the last had taken hold and nearly got it over the head, the leader gave a hand, and off it came.

The old man received them. "My grandchildren," he said, "sit down and eat. Who can this great Manito be? There is none but me. But let me look."

He opened the door of the lodge and saw at no great distance the prodigious animal coming on with slow but powerful bounds. He closed the door. "Yes, indeed," he said. "A great Manito indeed. My grandchildren, you are to be the cause of my death. But you have asked my protection. I have granted it. When the bear appears, run out the other end of the lodge."

Then reaching out his hand, he took up and opened a bag, out of which he drew two small black dogs, which he set before him. "These are the ones I use when I fight," he explained, and with both hands he began stroking the sides of one of the two, when the little dog began to swell until its bulk filled lodge. It had great, strong, vicious teeth, and when it reached full size, it growled and as from instinct sprang to the door, where it immediately confronted the bear, which with another bound would have entered. A ferocious combat ensued, the skies

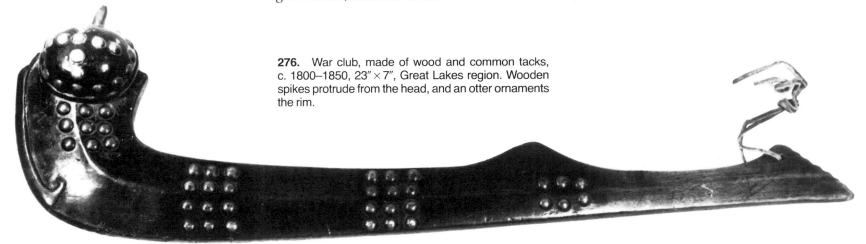

276. War club, made of wood and common tacks, c. 1800–1850, 23″ × 7″, Great Lakes region. Wooden spikes protrude from the head, and an otter ornaments the rim.

The night they started, snow was falling. They traveled all night and when daylight came, the youngest, their leader, took up a handful of snow and, tossing it into the air, said, "It was thus that in my dream I saw snow falling, so that we should not be tracked." And he warned them to hang close together, so as not to become separated. The snow kept falling so heavily all that day and the following night that they could hardly see each other. It would have been impossible to track them. And when they had traveled thus for several days, Mudjikewis, who was always in the rear, came suddenly forward, and bellowing his war cry, struck with his war club a tree, which, as though struck by lightning, broke into pieces. "Brothers," said he, "this is how I shall deal with those we are going to fight."

"Slow, slow there, Mudjikewis!" said their leader. "The one I am bringing you to is not to be thought of so lightly."

Whereupon Mudjikewis in thought fell back. "What! What! Who then can this be?" he mused. And become fearful, was silent.

Then they came to an extensive plain, along the borders of which lay human bones, bleaching in the sun. The young leader spoke. "These are of those who have gone before us. No one has ever returned to explain their fate." And again Mudjikewis, rushed suddenly ahead and with a war cry he struck with his club, a large rock, which fell to pieces. "See!" he called. "Thus shall I deal with those we fight." And again the leader cautioned, "He to whom I'm taking you is not comparable to that rock."

"Now," he whispered, "we must run."

The eldest took the great belt on his back, and when soon fatigued with its weight, passed it over to his next. And so they continued, until they had passed again the bones of all those who had gone before and were some distance beyond, when they looked back. And they saw the monster slowly rising. He stood for some time before becoming aware of the wampum missing from around his neck, when like distant thunder, they heard his howl, slowly filling the sky. Then they heard him speak. "Who can those be that have stolen my belt? The earth is not so large, but I shall discover them." And as he came down the great hill in pursuit, the earth, as if convulsed, shook with his every bound, and very soon he was drawing close.

"Brothers," called their leader as they ran, "has any one of you, when fasting, ever dreamed of some friendly spirit who might give aid to you now as a guardian?" And when only a silence followed: "Well then," said he, "in my own fast I dreamed of being in danger of death, and then saw a small lodge with smoke curling from its top, within which there was an old man who saved me. May this dream be now verified!" And dashing forward he gave a peculiar yell, a howl as though from the depths of his stomach (such a yell as is called a *checaudum*). And he came to a piece of rising ground, and behold! a small lodge with smoke curling from its top, to which they all ran. And the leader said to the old man within, "My grandfather, we come to claim your protection; for the great bear is upon us."

resounding with the rage of the two monsters, and the second dog then took to the field as the brothers fled through the opposite door.

"Run, run!" their leader cried. "The old man will soon be killed and the bear again be after us." And in fact very soon the bear came in sight, gaining upon them, when the leader again asked whether anyone but himself could do anything for their safety. And again, as they ran, there was silence.

Then dashing forward as before, their leader cried out, "In my dream I saw myself in great trouble, helped by an old man who was a Manito. We shall soon be seeing his lodge."

And indeed, as they went on, very soon there appeared before them the lodge of an old Manito, who when they entered, claiming protection, set meat before them and asked, "Who is this Manito of whom you speak? There is none but me. There is none whom I fear." He went to the door and saw the approaching bear, slowly shut the door and said, "Yes, my grandchildren, you have brought upon me great trouble."

Gathering up his medicine bag, he took out of it two small war clubs of black stone, telling the brothers to make their escape through the other side of the lodge. And as he handled the clubs they increased and became very large. The ten brothers fled, and the old man turned to face the bear just as he reached the door. He struck him with one of his clubs, which shattered, and the bear stumbled. The old man struck with the other club, which also shattered, and the bear fell senseless. But very soon he recovered from the blows. First he moved his paws. Then he rose to his feet and the second old man shared the fate of the first. The brothers heard from afar his cries as he was torn to pieces, and again the monster was in pursuit.

"Well," said their leader, as the brothers ran, "my dreams will soon be exhausted. After this one I have but one more. One time," he said, "I dreamed that, being sorely pressed, I came to a big lake, on the shore of which lay a canoe, partly out of the water and having ten paddles, all in readiness. Do not fear! We shall soon be there."

And so it was. They came to a large lake, saw the canoe with ten paddles, and immediately embarked. Scarcely had they reached the center, when they saw the bear at the shore, lifting himself on his hind legs, looking around. He waded into the water, but losing footing, turned back and commenced making a circuit of the lake, until he returned to the place from which he had started. There he began to drink up the lake, and when the brothers saw their canoe being drawn with the current to the monster's mouth, the leader said to Mudjikewis, "Now is the time for you to show what you can do. Sit at the bow, and as the canoe approaches the bear, see what effect your club will have on his skull." He agreed, and stood watching at the bow as the current drew them to the monster's mouth.

The critical moment arrived, and Mudjikewis, emitting with a yell his horrific war cry, delivered to the tremendous head a prodigious blow with his club. The animal's limbs doubled under him and he fell. But before a second blow could be dealt, the monster was disgorging violently all the water he had swallowed, and the canoe was being propelled to the opposite shore of the lake, where its occupants hastily disembarked and again were running with the bear behind them.

"This," their leader then cried, "is the last time I can apply to a guardian spirit. If we can't finish off this enemy now, our fate is sealed. Run, run," he urged, "we shall very soon arrive at his lodge." And it was then, just then, that the eyes of Iamo's undying head were by his sister seen to brighten as though with expectation. Whereupon it spoke:

"Oh my sister, in what a pitiful situation you have placed me. Very soon a party of young men will arrive and apply to me for protection. But how can I possibly give the help that I would gladly have provided? Take two of my arrows. Place them where you have been used to placing them to procure food, and have meat prepared before they arrive. When you hear them coming, calling my name, go out and say, 'Alas! It has been long since an accident befell him, of which I was the cause.' If they keep coming, ask them in and set meat before them, after which you must strictly follow my instructions.

"When the bear appears, go out to meet him. You must take with you my medicine sack, my bow and arrows, and my head; untie the sack and spread out before you my paints of all colors, my war eagle feathers, my tufts of dried hair, and everything else that the sack contains. As the bear approaches, lift these, one by one, and say to him, 'This is my deceased brother's paint,' and so on, all in order, throwing each of them as far from you as you can. The virtues contained in them will cause him to totter, and to complete his destruction, you will take my head and cast that, too, as far as you can, shout-

ing, 'See! This is my deceased brother's head!' He will then fall senseless, and by this time the brothers will have eaten. You will call them to your assistance and together cut the carcass into pieces. Yes, into *small* pieces; and scatter these to the winds—otherwise he will soon revive."

277. Potawatomi Medicine Bag, otter skin, cloth, beads, and bells, 48" long, Wisconsin, late nineteenth century. The Potawatomi and their western neighbors, unlike the Ojibwa, produced non-representational art.

The sister promised that all should be done as described, and she had had just time to prepare the meat, when the voice of the leader was heard calling on Iamo for aid. She went out and greeted them as instructed, invited them in, placed the meat before them, and while they were eating prepared to confront the approaching bear. Untying the medicine sack and taking the head, she had all in readiness when he arrived, and performed exactly as instructed. Even before the paints and feathers were expended, the bear began to totter, yet continued to approach. She flung the head as far from her as she could, and as it rolled along, blood gushed from the bear's mouth and nostrils, and with a tremendous sound the monster fell. Whereupon she cried for help, and the young men, who had regained their strength and spirits, came rushing out. Mudjikewis gave his yell and repeatedly struck the beast on the head until it was but a mass of brains. Then as quickly as possible, they cut the whole body into pieces, small pieces, which they scattered in every direction. And when then they looked around and about, where they had thrown the meat, wonderful to behold, they saw starting up and running away, to every side, small black bears, such as are seen at the present day. The country soon was overspread with these, and so it was that from this original monster the present race of bears originated.

The brothers now were triumphant but did not know what use to make of their triumph. Having spent so much time in their flight, and having traversed so vast a country, they gave up the idea of ever returning to their own people. Moreover, the game in this place was plentiful. So one day, having left the valuable wampum belt with the sister of the undying head, they moved off some distance to go hunting. They enjoyed a very successful season, and were amusing themselves, as young men do when alone, by talking and jesting with each other, when one of them suggested, "We are having all this fun to ourselves. Let us go and ask our sister to come join us and to let us bring the head here. For it also is alive and might enjoy our fellowship. Also, let us bring to our sister some food."

They went back to her and asked for the head, and she let them take it to their camp. But though they tried very hard to amuse it, very seldom did it show the least sign of enjoyment. Then one day, they were unexpectedly attacked by an unknown tribe and, though many of the enemy were slain, they were thirty to one and, in the end, left all of the brothers lying dead. One of their number discovered the head where it hung, and having eyed it for some time with amazement, finally took it down and, opening the medicine sack, was delighted by all the paints and feathers.

Fixing one of the war feathers to the head, he carried his trophy back to his friends, and they laughted at it and made sport of it. They took the paint and painted themselves, and one of them, lifting the head by the hair, said to it, "Look, you ugly thing! See how fine your paint looks on the faces of young braves!" They carried it to their village and hung it before the fire in their council house, fastening it with soaked rawhide, which by the action of the fire would shrink and tighten around it. "We then shall see," they said, "whether we cannot make it shut its eyes."

Meanwhile, for several days the sister had

191

been waiting for the brothers to bring back the head, until at last, becoming impatient, she went to recover it herself. And she found them all lying within short distances of each other, dead, and covered with wounds. A number of other bodies lay scattered among them, and she searched for the head and sack, which were nowhere to be found. She raised her voice and wept and blackened her face; then walked in various directions. And she came to the place where the head had been kept and there discovered the bow and arrows. Searching further, she found, also, some of her brother's paints and feathers. All of these she collected and bound carefully together, and having hung them on the branch of a tree for her return, she set out to find to what place her brother's head and medicine bag had been transported.

At dusk she arrived at the first lodge of a very extensive village, and employing a certain charm well known for the gaining of a kind reception, she entered and was well received by the old man and woman of the dwelling, to whom she made known her errand. The old man promised to help and told her the head was hung in the council house, where the chiefs of the village and young men kept watch over it constantly. "Come with me," he said. "I will take you there." They went, and they took seats near the door.

Now the council lodge was filled with warriors amusing themselves with games, but also keeping up a fire to smoke the head, to make, as they said, dry meat. The head moved, and not knowing what to make of it, one of the young men said, "He! Ha! It is beginning to feel the smoke!"

The sister at the door of the lodge was watching, and when her eyes met those of her brother, tears rolled down the cheeks of the head. "Well," said the chief. "I thought we would make you do something at last. Look! Look! It is shedding tears!"

They all laughed and passed jokes upon it, and the chief, on looking around, discovered the woman at the door.

"Who have you got there?" he called to the old man who had brought her. "I have never before seen that woman in our village."

"Yes you have," replied the old man. "She is a relative of mine, who stays in my lodge and seldom goes out. She asked me to bring her to this place."

In the center of the lodge there sat one of those young types who are always forward and fond of displaying themselves. "Why yes," said he. "I have seen her often and know her well. I go to their lodge every night to court her." The others laughed, going on with their games, and the young fellow never realized that he had helped her escape further notice.

She returned to the old man's lodge and immediately set out for her own country. Coming to the spot where the bodies of her adopted brothers lay, she dragged and placed them together, feet toward the east. Then taking an axe that she had, she cast it into the air, crying, "Brothers, get up from under this thing, or it will fall on you." Three times she repeated this charm, and the third time the brothers arose to their feet.

Mudjikewis commenced rubbing his eyes and stretching. "Why," said he, "I have overslept."

"No," said one of the others; "no indeed! We were all killed, and our sister, there, has brought us to life."

They took up the dead bodies of their enemies and burned them. Then their sister left to procure wives for them, and having traveled to a distant land unknown to them, came back with ten young females, whom she assigned to the ten brothers in order of age. They all then moved into a single big lodge, where the sister explained that the wives, who were all magicians, had now to take turns in going every night to her brother's head, to release it.

The eldest made the first attempt and with a rushing noise she flew through the air. Next morning she returned, and had untied but one of the knots. The others followed in turn, each likewise untying but one knot, until the youngest, finally, carried off the head, and as she came flying back, her voice could be heard, "Prepare the body of our brother!"

Immediately, they all hurried to a small lodge nearby where lay the black, headless body of Iamo, and his sister commenced cutting that part of the neck from which the head had been severed. She cut it deeply, so that it bled, while the others present, by rubbing the body and applying medicines, expelled from it the blackness. The wife who had returned with the head, by cutting its neck caused it to bleed as well. And when she had placed it close to the body, with the aid of medicines and various other charms, the company succeeded, finally, in restoring Iamo to life in all of his manliness and beauty.

All rejoiced in this fortunate termination of their trials, and when they had spent some time thus together, Iamo said to them, "Now I shall divide wampum." The brothers were told that since they had all died and been restored to life, they were no longer mortals, but spirits; and to them all were assigned different stations in the invisible world. Only Mudjikewis' place was at that time named and announced. He was to govern the West Wind and become the father of Manibozho. They were instructed to be generous to the inhabitants of the earth, giving all things with a liberal hand. And they were told, also, that of sacred things, the wampum should be held in highest regard, its shells of pale hue to be emblematic of peace, whereas those of darker hue would be of war.

Amid songs and shouts, the spirits then all took flight to their respective abodes on high, while Iamo, with his sister Iamoqua, descended to the depths below.[151]

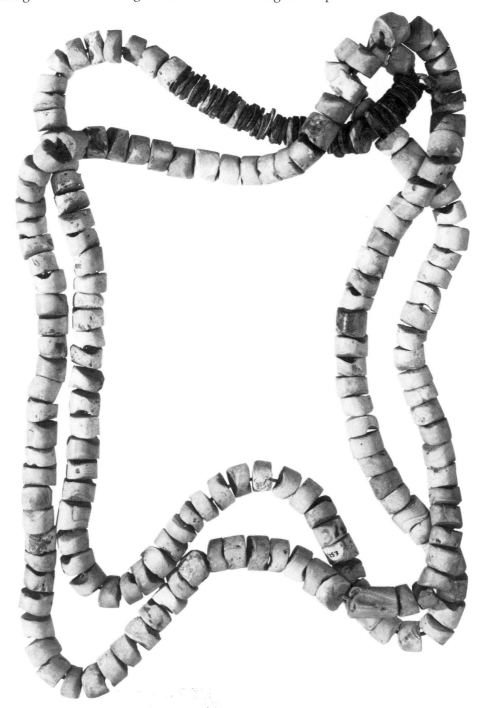

278. Wampum of whelk and disc-shaped quahog shell, Massachuset tribe, 49" in circumference, late sixteenth to early seventeenth century.

Waupee, or the White Hawk, lived in a remote part of the forest, where animals and birds abounded, and every day he returned from the hunt well rewarded. For he was one of the most skillful and celebrated hunters of his tribe. Tall and of manly form, with the fire of youth beaming from his eyes, there was no forest too dark for him to penetrate, and no track left by bird or beast that he could not follow.

One day he passed beyond any point that he had ever before visited, into an open forest through which he could see to a great distance, and continuing on, he arrived at length at the edge of a great prairie, a broad plain of flowers and grass. There was no path. But after walking for some time, he came suddenly upon a ring worn through to the soil, as though made by feet following each other in a circle; and what most excited his surprise was that there was no path leading either to or from it. Not the least trace of footsteps could be found, not even a crushed leaf or broken twig. He decided to hide in the tall grass and wait to see what the circle could possibly be.

Presently, high in the air, the faint sounds could be heard of a music. He looked up and perceived in the direction from which the music came a tiny object descending, which looked, at first, a mere speck; but it rapidly increased in size, and as it approached, its music became sweeter and louder. Rapidly it assumed the form of a basket occupied by twelve sisters of the most enchanting beauty, and the moment it touched ground, out they all leaped, to begin dancing in the magic ring, striking as they did so a shining ball, as we strike a drum.

Waupee from his place of hiding gazed upon the lovely forms, admiring them all but most taken by the youngest; until, unable longer to restrain his admiration, he leapt out and tried to catch her. Quick as birds, the moment they descried a man, the sisters fled into their basket and were again ascending to the sky, while the disappointed hunter stood gazing until they again became a spot and disappeared. "They are gone," he mused; "I shall see them no more." And he returned in sorrow to his lodge, unable to put them from his mind.

Next day he returned to the prairie and his hiding place near the ring; but in order to deceive the twelve, assumed the form of an opossum. Soon he again heard the sweet music and saw the wicker car descending. It touched ground and they commenced again their dance, now seeming to him more beautiful and more graceful even than before. He crept slowly in his opossum form toward the ring. But again they spied him and instantly were back in their car, which had risen but a short distance when one of the sisters spoke.

"Perhaps," said she, "it has come to show us how the game is played by mortals."

"Oh no!" cried the youngest. "Quick! Let us ascend!"

Whereupon they all joined in a chant and, ascending into distant sky, disappeared.

White Hawk, returning to his own form, walked sorrowfully home, reflecting on a plan to pursue the next day; and that night seemed to him very long. Next day, when he was back at the ring, he found nearby an old stump infested with mice, and thinking that a form of

that size would be unlikely to cause alarm, he gathered up the stump, set it down by the ring, and himself got into it as another mouse.

The sisters arrived and had resumed their sport, when the youngest suddenly cried, "But see! That stump wasn't here before." The others, however, just smiled and, gathering around the stump, began striking it, when out ran the mice, and Waupee among them, heading for the youngest, who was then running to the car. The rest were occupied chasing and killing the scattering mice, when White Hawk, assuming his own form, clasped his prize in his arms. The other eleven, suddenly alerted, sprang into their basket and were drawn up to the sky.

Waupee now did everything he could to console and please and entertain his captured bride and merit her affection. He wiped away her tears, described the charms of life on earth, told her of his hunting adventures, and led her gently through the forest to his solitary lodge. He felt his heart glow with joy as she entered it, and from that moment he was a happy man. A winter and a summer passed, and their happiness was increased by the birth of a beautiful boy. But his mother, after all, was the daughter of a star, and as the scenes of earth began to pall on her, she sighed to revisit her father. Recalling the charm that would carry her to the sky, she began to construct, day after day, while the child's father was away on the hunt, a wicker basket, which she carried one day to the center of the charmed ring. And having placed in it their little son, she climbed into the magic car and, lifting her voice, began to sing the celestial song. The familiar strains caught her husband's ear, who came running from the distant forest out onto the prairie, only to see his wife and child in the magic car, ascending. Desperately he called and waved, but the song continued and the basket went on up, and up. Helplessly he watched it go, diminish to a dot in the sky, and vanish. Then he bent his head to the ground and wept.

The basket, having arrived in the sky, was joyously received and welcomed, and the blissful employments of that heavenly realm soon erased from the mother's mind all memory of her spouse on earth. Not so, however, from the mind of her son. When he had grown to young boyhood, he became impatient to see again his father and to visit the land of his birth. Then his mother's heavenly father said to his daughter, "Go, my child, and take your son down to his father. Ask him to come live with us, and tell him to bring along a specimen of every kind of animal and bird he kills when he hunts."

Accordingly, she took the boy and descended, and the White Hawk, who was now held constantly to the enchanted ring, heard her voice as she came down the sky. Startled, he gazed upward and presently recognized in the descending car her form and that of his son, who were both soon clasped in his arms. In response to the wish of her father, he spent the next few nights and days collecting specimens, of which he preserved for identification only a tail, a foot, or a wing of each. And when all was ready, White Hawk and his wife and child climbed into the magic basket and, from the center of the enchanted ring, ascended.

At the celestial feast prepared for their reception a very strange confusion arose when it was announced that every person present should

279. Ojibwa rattle of polished hardwood and deer toes, c. 9¾" high, western Great Lakes region, nineteenth century. Undoubtedly created for ritual or ceremonial use, this extraordinarily beautiful rattle is an evolved example of the representational style most often associated with Woodlands sacred art. The carved bird probably represents a hawk, a figure prominent in Algonquin mythology, and most likely the guardian spirit of the rattle's owner.

choose from among the specimens brought, some foot, or wing, or tail, or claw. For according to the choices made, each was instantly transformed into the respective bird or beast and either flew or scampered away. Waupee had chosen a white hawk's feather, as had also his wife and son. They spread their wings, all three, and together descended with the other birds to earth, where that species survives to this day.[152]

Ojeeg Annung, the Summer Maker; or The Great Dipper

There lived in a wild and lonesome place on the southern shore of Lake Superior a celebrated hunter who was regarded by some as a Manito, since there was nothing he could not accomplish. He lived with a wife whom he loved, and they were blessed with a little son who had attained his thirteenth year. The man's name, Ojeeg, the Fisher, referred to a sprightly, tree-climbing little animal common to the region. And since hunting was his sole and constant occupation, his son began early to emulate him, wandering in the forest with his tiny bow and arrows, trying to kill birds and squirrels. The severe cold of the region at that time made this difficult for him, however, and he would frequently return home crying, his little fingers numb with cold. Days, months and years passed in this way, with the same everlasting depth of snow covering all the country as a white cloak.

One day, when the little fellow was returning home with a heavy heart, he saw a small red squirrel sitting on a branch, gnawing the top of a pine cone. And just as he was approaching to shoot, the squirrel sat up on its hind legs and addressed him.

"My grandson," the squirrel said, "put up your arrows and listen to what I have to tell you." The boy obeyed and the squirrel went on. "My son, I have frequently seen you pass this way with your fingers numb with cold, crying for not having killed any birds. Now, if you will strictly follow my advice, we shall correct this situation. You will then have perpetual summer, and be able to kill as many birds as you like. And I, too, shall have something to eat; for I am now on the point of starvation.

"As soon as you arrive home, you must start crying. Throw down your bow and arrows, and when your mother asks, what is the matter, do not reply; just keep on crying. In the evening, when your father returns from the hunt, he will ask your mother what is troubling you, and she will reply that you came home crying but would not tell her why. Your father will then look at you, and you will be standing, crying and sobbing, until finally he will ask: 'My son, tell me what is the matter? You know that I am a Manito and can get you whatever you want. So what is the matter? Tell me!'

"Then you must tell him that it troubles you to have the snow continually on the ground. Ask him to cause it to melt, so that you may have perpetual summer and be able to hunt, like him. Say this in a supplicating way and let him know that this is the cause of your grief.

"Your father will then say to you, 'This will be an extremely difficult thing to do. But for your sake, in my love for you, I shall do the best I can.' He will tell you that if you will only stop crying, he will bring to you summer with all its warmth and loveliness. And you must then cease crying, be quiet and content, and eat whatever is set before you."

The squirrel had finished. The boy promised to follow his advice. And when he reached home and did exactly as instructed, everything turned out as predicted. [Compare, from here on, the Nascapi tale from Labrador of "How Summer was Brought North...."]

The father, Fisher, then told his wife that before setting out on this extraordinary adventure, he wished to prepare a feast and invite certain friends to accompany and assist him. So next day they roasted a whole bear, and those who had been invited arrived punctually for a banquet. They were Beaver, Badger, Lynx, Wolverine and Otter. And when they had demolished the bear, they all agreed to meet in three days for the start of their campaign. The day arrived, and when the company began moving away, Fisher, with a premonition of how it was going to end, took leave for the last time of his beloved wife and little son.

For many days the company of seven trudged along, meeting with nothing but ordinary incidents, until on the twentieth day they arrived at the foot of a high mountain where they saw the tracks of someone who had just killed and was carrying an animal. This they knew by the blood that marked the way, and, thinking to procure something to eat, they followed the trail until they saw before them a lodge that had been hidden from view by a hollow in the mountain. Fisher then told his friends to be very sedate and on no account to laugh. For standing at the door of the lodge was a man of so deformed a shape that they could not possibly make out what sort of person he might be. His head was enormous and he had a queer set of teeth, but no arms. And they wondered how he could have killed and carried the animal whose blood they had been following. However, the secret would soon come out; for he was a very great Manito, and he invited them to come in for the night, and they all passed into his lodge.

His meat was boiled in a hollowed vessel of wood and he took it out in some way unwitnessed by his guests, giving to each a portion. But in so doing he made so many odd movements that Otter, unable to restrain himself, burst out laughing. Whereupon the Manito looked at him with a terrible look, made a great spring, and landing on top of him, would have smothered him (for that was his way of killing), when Otter, slipping deftly from under, made it to the door, through which he escaped into the freezing night.

The others remained with their host, conversing on different subjects, and the Manito told Fisher that his mission would be accomplished but would probably cost him his life. He supplied advice, describing to his guests a certain road to be sought and followed, which would lead to the place of action. And in the morning, when they had left his lodge, they found outside their friend Otter, shivering in

280. Stone pipe bowl, 2¾" high × 7⅜" long, Ojibwa, n.d. Although little is known about the provenance of this artifact, it is so similar, both in subject matter and in style of execution, to the pipe bowl depicted below (see Figure 281), that one is tempted to attribute the work to Awbonwaishkum.

the cold. But Fisher had taken care to bring along some of the meat they had been served, and when Otter had eaten this, they set off.

The indicated road was found and along it they traveled for twenty days before arriving at the place of action, of which the Manito had told them. This was the loftiest mountain any of them had ever seen. They ascended and, on arriving at its highest peak, sat down, filled their pipes and refreshed themselves. Before smoking, they performed the customary ceremony, pointing to the heavens, the four directions, the earth and the zenith, while in a loud voice addressing the Great Spirit, praying that their aim should be accomplished. But it was with astonishment and silent admiration that they all gazed up at the sky; for it seemed — since they were now resting on so high a peak — to be only a short way above their heads. Their task was for someone to break a hole in it through which the rest of them then might pass. And Otter was the first appointed by Fisher to attempt the unprecedented feat.

Consenting with a grin, he made a great leap, but fell back, stunned by the force of his fall. And the snow being moist, having landed on his back, he slid with velocity down the side of the whole mountain and, finding himself at the bottom, thinking, "This is the last time I do anything like that!" he scrambled to his feet and started for home.

Beaver was the next to try; then Lynx; then Badger; with no success. Then Fisher said to Wolverine, "Your ancestors have been celebrated for their vigor, hardihood and perseverance. We are depending on you for the success of this adventure. So you next!" And so Wolverine jumped. He failed. He jumped again, and now they could see that the sky was giving way to these repeated blows. Again mustering his strength, Wolverine for a third time jumped, going through, and the Fisher followed.

They found themselves on a beautiful plain, extending as far as the eye could see, covered with fragrant, varicolored flowers. Here and there were clusters of tall, shading trees, separated by innumerable streams, which wound their courses round and about amid the cooling shades, filling the plain with countless lakes, whose surfaces and banks were covered with waterfowl sporting and basking in the sun. The trees were alive with birds of various plumages, warbling with delight in perpetual spring.

Words cannot express the beauty and charm of that heavenly plain. Fisher and his friend saw there a number of very long lodges. They entered one of these and found it empty of inhabitants, but lined with cages of different sizes, filled with birds of differing plumage. Fisher thought of his son, and immediately began cutting open the cages, releasing the birds, who in flocks descended through the opening that Wolverine had made through the floor of the plain. The warm air of those regions also rushed through the hole, spreading its genial influence over the earth.

But when the inhabitants of that celestial realm saw that their birds had been let loose and were descending, along with their warm air, to the world below, they raised a shout like thunder, heading for the lodges; but too late! Spring and Autumn were already gone. Perpetual Summer was almost all gone, but they separated it with a blow, and only a part descended.

Wolverine, on hearing all the noise, had dashed for the opening and descended to the mounain top, but not so the Fisher. Resolved to bring happiness to his little son, he continued breaking cages until he too had to run. But the opening had now been closed and, at a loss, he started running all over the heavenly plain, and when he saw his pursuers gaining upon him, he climbed the first large tree at hand. They began shooting arrows, but without effect, since his body was invulnerable except for a space of about an inch near the tip of his tail—which, finally, one of the arrows struck; for in the chase he had assumed the shape of the animal after which he was named.

Looking down, then, from his tree, he recognized among the pursuers a number of his own ancestry, and he called down to them to desist and go home, which, on the approach of night, they did. Then he descended and tried to find somewhere a way to return to earth, but there was none, and becoming faint from the loss of blood from his wound, he laid himself down, stretching out his limbs, saying, "I have fulfilled my promise to my son, and though it has cost my life, I die satisfied in the knowledge that I have done much good, not only for him, but for my fellow beings. Hereafter, for ages to come, I shall be a sign to the inhabitants below, who will venerate my name, as having procured the varying seasons. From now on they will have eight to ten moons without snow."

Next morning, he was found dead. But they left him as they found him, with the arrow still stuck in his tail—as can be plainly seen, even today, in the northern sky.[153]

Aggodahguada and His Daughter: or The Man with His Leg Tied Up

Aggodahguada had one leg looped up to his thigh, so that he was obliged to get along by hopping. He had a beautiful daughter and his chief care was to secure her from being carried off by the king of the buffaloes. He differed from other Indians in that he lived, not in a wigwam, but in a log house; and he advised his daughter to remain indoors, and never to stroll out into the neighborhood, for fear of being carried away.

One sunshiny morning, when Aggodahguada was preparing to go fishing, before leaving he reminded his daughter of her strange and persistent lover. "My daughter," he said, "I'm going fishing, and since the day is going to be a very pleasant one, you must remember that we have an enemy nearby who is constantly lingering about. Don't expose yourself by leaving the lodge." And he started off. But when he reached the fishing group he heard a voice singing at a distance in derision of him:

> Man with the leg tied up,
> Man with the leg tied up,
> Broken hip—hip—
> Hipped.

> Man with the leg tied up,
> Man with the leg tied up,
> Broken leg—leg—
> Legged.

He saw no one, but suspecting the call to have come from his enemies the buffaloes, he hurried back to his lodge.

His daughter, meanwhile, having thought in her mind, how tiresome it was to be kept forever indoors, had climbed to the roof and there begun combing her long, black, beautiful hair, which was not only of a lovely, glossy hue, but also so very long that it hung out over the edge of the roof and to the ground.

And as she sat there, forgetful of danger, the buffalo king came galloping with his herd and, taking her between his horns, carried her away. Across the plains he cantered. Plunging into a river that bounded his own land, he carried her safely to his lodge, and there, to gain her affections, paid her every attention. But among the other females in the lodge she sat pensive and disconsolate. She scarcely ever spoke. She took no part in the domestic attentions paid by the others to his needs. Doing everything he could

think of to please and to make her happy, he told the others in the lodge to give her everything she wanted. They set before her the choicest food and gave her the seat of honor in the lodge, while he himself went hunting to procure for her the daintiest meats. And from time to time he would take up his flute and, sitting nearby, outside the lodge, dolefully woo her, repeating his piteous love song:

> My sweetheart,
> My sweetheart,
> Ah me!

> When I think of you,
> When I think of you,
> Ah me!

> How I love you,
> How I love you,
> Ah me!

> Do not hate me,
> Do not hate me,
> Ah me!

Aggodahguada, in the meantime, having arrived at his cabin only to find his daughter taken away, had made up his mind to get her back. And to this end he had immediately set out. He could easily track and follow the king until he came to the river crossing; for there had been a frosty night or two, and the water was so covered with thin ice that he could neither walk on it nor swim in it. He therefore encamped until it became solid, when he hopped across and pursued the trail.

As he went along he saw that branches had been broken off and strewed behind as signs by his daughter. And the way in which she had done this had been by means of her hair, which was all untied and, being very long, had caught on the branches as they darted by. When he arrived before the king's lodge it was evening, and he very carefully approached. He peeked in through the sides and saw his daughter sitting disconsolately. She immediately caught his eye, and knowing that it was her father come for her, she all at once appeared to relent in her heart and, asking for the dipper, said to the king, "I will go and get you a drink of water."

This apparent token, finally, of her submission delighted him, and with impatience he awaited her return. But she did not return. He went out, at last, with his followers, to recover her; but of the captive daughter nothing could be heard or seen. By the light of the moon the buffalo herd rushed out onto the plain, in search, but had not gone far when in their rear a party of hunters (headed by her father's father-in-law) was heard hooting and yelling, and a shower of arrows began pouring in upon them. Many of their number fell; but their king, being stronger and swifter than the others, broke away and disappeared toward the west, never again to appear in that part of the country.

Whereas Aggodahguada (with his leg tied up), having met his daughter when she came out the door, took her upon his shoulders and with the help of his guardian spirit hopped, hopped away, a hundred steps at a bound, till he came to the stream and with a single hop brought her back, in triumph to his lodge.[154]

281. Ojibwa steatite pipe bowl, early nineteenth century. Paul Kane collected this delightful specimen on Manitoulin Island in Lake Superior.[2]

The Great Incarnation from the North

Manabozho was living with his grandmother near the edge of a wide prairie. His birth and parentage are obscure. His grandmother, it is said, was a daughter of the moon, who had been married but a very short time when a rival (in the sky world) induced her onto a grapevine swing on the banks of a celestial lake, and with one bold thrust pitched her out into its center, from which she fell through to the earth [compare the Iroquois legend of the "Woman Who Fell from the Sky"]. Giving birth here to a daughter, the fruit of her celestial marriage, she warned the child to beware of the west wind and be careful, when stooping, never to be facing east. In an unguarded moment, however, this precaution was neglected, and a gale, invading her robes, scattered them upon its wings and at the same moment destroyed her. At the scene of the catastrophe her mother found a foetus-like mass, which she rescued and carefully nurtured until it assumed the form of the beautiful infant Manabozho.

One day, when he had grown to early manhood, Manabozho asked his grandmother to tell him whether he had any parents living, and who his relatives might be. "Yes," she answered, "you have three brothers and a father living, but your mother is dead. She was taken by your father without the consent of her parents. Your father is the West; your brothers are the North, East, and South. Being older than yourself, they have been given by your father great power over the winds, according to their names. You are the youngest of his children. I have nourished you from infancy; for your mother died in giving you birth, due to the brutal treatment of your father. I have on earth no living relative but you. Your mother was my only child and you are my only hope."

Manabozho's father, guardian of the West, was the great Manito Mudjikewis of the legend of The Undying Head, and his son, on hearing of the brutal violation of his mother, made up his mind to kill him. But he concealed this purpose from his grandmother, when, after further questioning, he told her that he was now going to seek his father [Father-quest motif, a typical feature of the young hero's life: compare, for example, Telemachus' quest for Ulysses in the Odyssey]. "It is a long distance," his grandmother said, "to the place of the West Wind." But Manabozho now was of a giant's stature and strength, and without fear.

The meeting took place on a high mountain in the west, and the father was happy to see his son, who also appeared to be pleased. They spent a number of days talking with each other, at ease, until one evening Manabozho asked, of what thing on earth his father was most afraid.

"I fear nothing," his father replied. But then, after some urging: "Yes, there is a black stone," he said. "It is found in such and such a place. If that struck me, it would do me considerable harm.—And so what of you?" the father asked, then, in return. "Of what are you most afraid?" [Compare the exchanges of Sapling and Flint, and of Glooscap and his brother Malsum.]

Manabozho, like his father, at first replied, "There is nothing I fear!" But finally pretending to be afraid even to pronounce the name, he declared, "Well yes! A bulrush root."

In the course of a later conversation, when Manabozho asked his father if he had been the cause of his mother's death and his father answered, "Yes!" Manabozho flung at him a great black rock that he had taken care to procure, and there followed a prodigious combat that went on for several days. Fragments of the black rock, which shattered when it struck, can be seen to this day scattered over the countryside. The bulrush root, on the other hand, which the father had procured, proved to be less effective than his son had led him to expect. The battle began on the summit of the western mountain with Manabozho pressing his father ever westward to the edge of the world, where the father stood and shouted, "Hold, my son! You know my power. It is impossible to kill me. Stop all this and I'll assign to you a place to match those of your brothers. The four quarters have already been assigned to them, but there is much good still to be done in the world, eliminating all the monster serpents, beasts and cannibals that are working havoc. Make it your task to take care of all these, you have now the power to do so, and your fame in the world will last forever. When you will have finished the work, I shall give you a place to sit with Kabib-boonocca, your brother in the north."[155]

Manabozho and the Flood

Manabozho had come to a sandy beach, by the lake, where he transformed himself into an oak stump, and he had not been there very long when he saw the lake become very calm. Soon hundreds of monstrous serpents came crawling out onto the beach. One of their number was beautifully white. He was their prince. The others were red and yellow.

"I have never before seen that black stump standing here," the prince said to those about him. "It may be Manabozho. He may well be somewhere about here. We had better be on our guard."

One of the largest of the serpents coiled itself around the stump to its top, pressing very hard. The greatest pressure was at Manabozho's throat, and he was just ready to cry out when the serpent let go. Eight of them in succession then did the like, but always let go, just when he was about to cry out.

"It cannot be he," they said at last. "He is too great a weak-heart to have taken that." Then they formed a circle about the prince, and after a long time they all fell asleep.

When he was sure that they were all at rest, Manabozho assumed his human form and, stepping cautiously over the serpents until he came to the prince, poised his bow and drew back the arrow to full length with the whole strength of his arm, and shot him in the left side. He then gave his victory yell and ran off at full speed.

The sound uttered by the serpents on seeing their prince mortally wounded was horrible. "Manabozho has killed our prince," they cried. "Let us catch and destroy him!"

Over hill and valley Manabozho was fleeing, running with all his strength and speed, striding a mile at a stride. But his pursuers also were spirits, and he could hear them coming behind him. He headed for the highest mountain and on its summit climbed its tallest tree, when dreadful to behold, on looking down he saw the whole lower country overflooded and the waters rising. He watched them gain the foot of his mountain, then the foot of his tree, and soon they were at his feet and climbing.

He addressed the tree. "Grandfather, stretch yourself!" And the tree did so. But the waters continued to rise. He repeated the request; and again he was obeyed. A third time; but when the tree had this time stretched a length, "That was the last," it said, "I can do no more."

The waters rose to his chin, at which point they stopped and began to abate, when hope revived in his heart. He looked about for possible aid and saw only water. It was everywhere. Then he spied a loon floating on the surface and called. "Dive down, dive deep, my brother, and fetch up some earth, so that I may fashion for us a new island."

The bird dove and was long away, but returned to the surface dead.

Manabozho spied a muskrat. "Dive!" he said. "Dive deep, and if you succeed, I shall give you a chain of beautiful little lakes in which to live surrounded with rushes, and you shall be able to live then either on land or in water."

282. Sucking Doctor, or Wabeno Medicine Man, fetish; wood with wool stroud cloth, 18" high, Ojibwa, Wisconsin, late nineteenth century. The chest cavity is filled with "medicine" and a miniature wooden figurine.

The muskrat dove, was long away, and returned to the surface senseless. Manabozho took the little body, and breathing into its nostrils, restored it to life. "Try again," he said. And a second time the muskrat dove, returning to the surface senseless. But in one of its paws it was clutching a bit of earth, from which, together with the carcass of the dead loon, Manabozho created a new earth as large as the former earth had been, and with all of its living animals, plants, and birds.[156]

In the Belly of the Great Fish

One day Manabozho's grandmother complained that since she had no oil to put on her head any more, all her hair was falling out. So he collected cedar bark for a fishline, built himself a canoe, and paddled to the middle of the lake, where he let down the line, while calling to the king of fishes, "Me-she-nah-gwai, take hold of my bait! Me-she-nah-gwai, take hold of my bait!" And he kept repeating this call until the great fish, becoming irritated and impatient and saying to himself, "That Manabozho annoys me!" turned and said to the trout, "Here, Trout, you take his line."

Trout did so, and Manabozho began hauling in his fishing line, which, however, was so heavy that the canoe stood nearly perpendicular. Nevertheless, Manabozho kept hauling until presently the trout could be seen, when he cried at him in disgust, "Why did *you* take hold of my hook, you miserable thing!" Whereupon the trout, insulted, let go.

Manabozho again dropped his line, again calling to the great king of the fish, "Me-she-nah-gwai, take hold of my bait!" And the great lord of the lake, more than ever annoyed, called to a monstrous sunfish, "You take his bait!" And the fish did so.

Manabozho with the greatest difficulty began hauling up his fishline, with his canoe turning in swift circles, and when he saw the prodigious fish coming up and realized it was not the king, he shouted at him, "You repulsive thing! Why have *you* dirtied my hook by taking it into your mouth? Let go!"

The sunfish let go, and was reporting to the king of the fish what Manabozho had said to him, when the bait came down beside them, and since the angler's voice could still be heard calling, "Me-she-nah-gwai, take hold of my bait!" in a rage the kingfish took hold of the bait himself and allowed his prodigious hulk to be drawn easily to the surface, where he opened his great mouth altogether and at one great gulp swallowed the canoe, Manabozho, and all.

And so, when Manabozho next came to himself, he was in the belly of the great fish with his canoe, and his problem now was to get out.

He searched the canoe for his war club and took it up with both hands. Above his head was the monster's heart. With a great swing, he struck it with the club and immediately felt a sudden jolt and motion, as though he were moving at a great speed. The fish was saying to his friends, "I feel sick to my stomach. It must be that filthy Manabozho that I swallowed." Then he felt another, more severe blow to his heart; and Manabozho, in there, began to think, "If I'm thrown up in the middle of the lake, I'll drown. I must prevent that." And so he drew his canoe across the fish's throat, and renewed his attack upon the heart.

At last the great fish was dead, as Manabozho first knew by the loss of motion and the beating of the great body against the shore. He waited a whole day to learn what now would occur; for he heard some sort of scratching on the outside. Presently rays of light broke through and he could see the heads of gulls who were peering in through an opening they had made. "Oho!" cried Manabozho. "My younger brothers! Make the opening bigger, and help me get out of this place."

Then they realized and told each other it was Manabozho who was in there. They pecked and scratched and worked as hard and fast as they could to release him, and when he came out, he said to them with appreciation, "In the future, for your kindness to me, you shall be called Kayoshk!" [meaning "noble grabbers or scratchers"]. The spot where the fish had been driven ashore was Manabozho's grandmother's lodge, and when he had returned to her, he told her to go and prepare for herself as much oil as she wanted.[157]

Manabozho and His Wolf Brother

There is another version of the birth of Manabozho, in which a reflection may be recognized of the Contending Twin Hero formula, as represented in the Iroquois tale of "The Woman Who Fell from the Sky."

In the beginning, we are told again, there was a lone old woman living on this island. Nobody knows where she came from, nor how she got there. She dwelt in a wigwam with her only daughter, and wild potatoes were their only food. Every day the old woman took her wooden hoe and went out to gather potatoes, which she packed home and dried in the sun. For in those days there was no such thing as fire in that part of the world.

One day her daughter begged to go with her. "No, my daughter, you stay here," she said. "Your place is at home, taking care of the lodge."

"But I don't like staying here all day alone," said the girl. "I'd much rather be with you. There is another old hoe here. I can take that along and help you."

Finally, the old woman consented, and the two went forth, armed with their hoes. They came to a damp ravine. "Here is the place," the mother said. "You can dig over there. But there is one thing I must warn you about. When digging potatoes, I want you to face south. Don't forget this. It was because I was afraid you might not be trusted to remember that I never brought you here before."

"I won't forget," said the girl. And she set to work with a will. "Oh how nice it is," she called, "to be digging potatoes." And she kept up a steady stream of talk as the two of them hoed and dug. But in time she became inattentive to her promise and had turned, no longer facing south, when a great rushing noise of wind came down on her where she stood and whirled her about. "Oh, mother!" she cried. "Help! Come quick!"

The old woman dropped everything, rushed to her aid, and seizing her with one hand, steadied herself by catching hold of some bushes. "Hold me as tightly as you can," she ordered. "Now you know why I told you to stay home."

The wind stopped and all became as calm as though nothing of the kind had occurred. The two women gathered up their burdens and hurried home, and thereafter the old woman dug potatoes alone.

Everything went well for a while, but then the daughter one day complained. "I feel very strange and different, mother. It seems there is something inside me."

The old woman scrutinized her narrowly and said nothing, and in due time she gave birth to triplets. The first born was Manabozho; the second, a little wolf named Muh'wase; and the last, a sharp flint stone that so lacerated her that she died. Her mother in a paroxysm of grief and rage hurled away the piece of flint. But Manabozho and Muh'wase she cherished and cared for until they grew to young boyhood.[158]

283. Conjurer, or Tent-Shaker Medicine Man, fetish with articulated head; wood, 17", Ojibwa, Wisconsin, late nineteenth century. Used as a puppet or ventriloquist's dummy, it has a hidden storage cavity in back.

Manabozho Plays Lacrosse

Now it happened that the beings above challenged the beings below to a mighty game of lacrosse. The goals were chosen, one at Detroit, the other at Chicago. The center of the field was at a spot called *Ke'sosasit*, "Where the sun is marked on the rocks," near Sturgeon Bay on Lake Michigan. The beings above summoned their servants to play for them: the thunderers, the eagles, the geese, the ducks, the pigeons, and all the fowls of the air. The great white underground bear called upon the fishes, the snakes, the otters, the deer, and all the beasts of the field to represent the powers below. And when everything had been arranged and the two sides were preparing for the game next day, Manabozho happened along that way and off to the side heard someone whooping at the top of his voice. Curious to see who that might be, Manabozho hastened over to the place from which all the noise was coming and there found a funny little fellow, looking like a tiny Indian, who was none other than Nakuti, the sunfish.

"And so what is the matter with you?" asked Manabozho.

"Why, haven't you heard?" asked Sunfish in astonishment. "There is to be a great ball game tomorrow. The fishes and the beasts of the field are to represent the powers below against the thunderers and the fowls of the air, on the part of the powers above."

"Oh ho!" said Manabozho. And when the little sunfish had gone his way, again whooping with delight, "Well, well!" said Manabozho to himself, "I must have a look at that game, even though I have not been invited."

The chiefs of the underworld had left their homes in the waters of the lake and climbed a high mountain from which to view the whole field. Manabozho found their tracks and, following them to that excellent viewing place, decided to remain there even in spite of the danger of discovery. Through his magic power he transformed himself into a tall pine tree, burnt on one side, and he was there standing among them at dawn when all the whooping and howling began. A tumult of voices arose on all sides, shouting "Hau! Hau! Hau!" and "Hoo! Hoo! Hoo!" when there appeared on the field the deer, the mink, the otter, all the land beings, in human form, and the fishes. Entering at their end of the field, they trotted to their places, and then all became, for a spell, silent until, suddenly, the sky grew dark and the rush of many wings made a thunderous rumbling sound above which cackling, screeching, hooting, screams and calling could be heard in one terrific babel, as there came swooping down from a darkened sky the thunderers and the golden eagles, the bald eagles and the buzzards, hawks, owls, pigeons, geese, ducks, and all manners of bird, landing and filling out their place at the other end of the field.

An expectant silence fell as the two teams moved into positions for the opening of the play. On both sides the weakest were stationed near the goals and the stronger players toward the center. Then the ball was tossed high in air and a pell mell immediately broke loose of swinging rackets, whoopings, howlings, and of players surging back and forth, one side now gaining, now the other, until one player broke loose and was suddenly racing toward the Chicago goal. Beautifully down the field he ran and

Manabozho (in his form of a tree) was straining his eyes to follow his course, when, as he was approaching the goal and the goal-keepers were all rushing to guard it, in the midst of all the brandishing clubs, legs, arms, and clouds of dust, something notable was happening which Manabozho could not see. In his excitement he forgot what he was, changed back into a man, and was now among his enemies, in plain sight.

Coming abruptly to himself, he looked around; but they were all so lost in the game that no one had yet discovered him. So he took his bow, which he had kept with him all the while, strung it and began firing at his underworld enemies, all of whom were there seated before him, lost in the play. His arrows sped true, and stunned, the company abruptly rose to its feet and in panic fled down the mountainside, to plunge into the waters of the lake, where the impact caused such waves to rise that a prodigious tide came rolling down the ball field directly to the Chicago goal. Immediately, the players and all of the viewers recognized the presence of Manabozho. No one else would ever have dared to attack the assembled powers of the underworld. A cry went up, "He is here! He is here! Manabozho is here!"

"Let's look for him!" was the next general cry.

"Let's take the waters for our guide," agreed those of the team of the powers below. Whereupon the deer, the mink, the fishes and all the beasts of the field waded into the water, which rose up and went ahead of them. It knew very well where Manabozho had gone.

For on realizing what consequences had followed from his impulsive act, Manabozho in terror had skipped away. And he was now in full flight for all he was worth, when on glancing back, he saw a tide of water following him. He increased his speed, but on it came. He ran still faster, but it gained on him. "Oh dear!" he thought. "It will get me yet!" Then he saw a high mountain, on top of which there was a lofty pine. "I guess I'll go up there," he thought. So up the mountainside he raced with the water rising behind him. "Oh my dear little brother," he said to the pine; "save me! save me!"

"How can I help?" the pine tree asked.

"You can let me climb to your top," he said. "And when the water rises to your top, you can grow and increase another length."

"But I haven't that much power," said the tree. "I can grow no more than four lengths."

"That will do," said Manabozho, with the water already lapping at his feet. "I'll take that!" And he clambered up into the branches. With all his might and main he climbed, but the water was at his feet all the way to the top.

"Oh little brother, stretch yourself," he prayed, and the pine tree shot up one length. Manabozho climbed the whole length, but the water was still at his heels. "Oh little brother, once more!" he cried, and up shot the tree, and up Manabozho climbed; but the water was still at his heels. Again at the top, and again that tree grew a length, and still the water pursued.

"Stretch only one time more, little brother, and give me just one more length," Manabozho pleaded. "Maybe that will save me. If it doesn't, I'm going to be drowned."

Up shot the tree for the fourth and last time, and Manabozho climbed to the top. The water followed, but there it stopped. Manabozho, clinging to the treetop, looked down in terror. But the water rose no more.[159]

Paradise Opened to the Indians
(Chief Pontiac's Tale)

An Indian of the Lenapee [Delaware] tribe, desiring to know the Master of Life, resolved, without mentioning his design to anyone, to undertake a journey to Paradise, which he knew to be God's residence. But to succeed in this project, he would have to find the way to the celestial regions; and not knowing anyone who had been there himself and might be able to help him find the road, he began conjuring in the hope of deriving good augury from a dream. His dream informed him that he had only to start on his journey, when by continued walking he would arrive without fail at the Master of Life's heavenly abode.

So early the next morning, he equipped himself as a hunter, taking gun and powder-horn, ammunition, and a boiler with which to cook his provisions. The first part of the journey was pretty favorable. He walked for a week without discouragement, always firm in the conviction that he was going to attain his aim. Eight days elapsed without unfavorable encounter, and on the evening of the eighth, he stopped at sunset by the side of a brook that ran along the edge of a little prairie. This, he thought, would be a favorable place for a night's encampment. And as he was setting up his lodging, he noticed that at the other end of the little prairie there were three, wide, well-beaten paths. He thought this somewhat singular, but continued in the preparation of his wigwam. He lighted a fire and, while cooking, realized that the darker the night grew, the more distinct became those three paths. This greatly surprised, even frightened him, and he hesitated in thought. Would it be best to remain here in camp, or to seek another place at some distance?

But then recalling the sense of his conjuring, or rather of his dream, he remembered that the whole aim of his journey was to visit the Master of Life, and this restored him to his senses. He thought it probable that one of those three roads might lead to the very place he was hoping to find. And so he decided to remain the night where he was, and to choose, next day, at random, one or another of those three ways.

Thus resolved, he settled down to his meal. However, his curiosity was so great that he could not wait to finish it, but got up, and leaving his encampment and fire, strode across the prairie and entered what appeared to be the widest of the paths. He followed this until the middle of the next day without seeing anything unfavorable to his purpose. But when he then paused to rest a little and take breath, he became suddenly aware of a large fire coming from under ground. This greatly excited his curiosity and he went toward it to see what it might be. It appeared to increase as he approached, and overcome with fear, he turned back. He next took the wider of the other two roads, which he followed for about as long as he had followed the first, when again he perceived a fire blazing from under ground, and his fear, which had been lulled by the prospect of the second road, revived.

Returning to the start, he took finally the third road, along which he walked for a whole day without seeing anything. But then, all at once, there burst upon his sight a mountain of marvelous whiteness. This filled him with astonishment. He took courage and advanced

284. *Pontiac in Council*, engraving by Felix Octavius Carr Darley (1822-1888). Recounting his Dantean vision, the Ottawa chief entreated his brethren to resist the encroaching tide of colonialism (see p. 172).

to explore it. Arriving at its foot, however, he found there no sign of any road or path, and in great discouragement, not knowing how to continue, he looked about, to all sides.

Then he saw seated on the mountain a female figure of dazzling beauty, and the whiteness of her garment surpassed that of fresh fallen snow. She said to him in his own language, "You appear to be surprised on finding no longer a path or way to the fulfillment of your wish. I know that you have for a long time desired to see and speak with the Master of Life, and that you have undertaken this journey to that end. The way that leads to his abode is indeed upon this mountain. To ascend it, however, you must undress yourself completely and leave all of your accoutrements and clothing here at the foot. No one will disturb them. You must then wash in the river that I am about to show you, and then ascend the mountain."

The Indian obeyed the woman's instructions without fault, but when he had done so, he was still at a loss to know how to begin to mount to the top. For the mountain was steep and as smooth as glass. He asked the woman what he should do, and she told him that if he really wished to see the Master of Life, he should use, when climbing only his left hand and left foot, which appeared to him to be impossible. But she urged him to take heart, and he commenced. And after much trouble he came finally to the top, where he was amazed to see no one at all, the woman having disappeared. He was utterly alone and without a guide.

Presently he became aware of three villages within view, constructed on a different plan from his own, much handsomer and more regular. Reflecting for a few moments, he decided to take his way toward the handsomest, and when about half way down from the summit of the mountain, recollecting that he was naked, he stopped in great confusion. But a voice told

him to go on, and to have no apprehensions, since, having already washed himself, he might with confidence now proceed. Wherefore, without further hesitation, he continued to what appeared to be the gate of the village he had chosen. There he paused for someone to come and open to him. However, as he stood there, the gate opened of itself and he saw coming toward him a handsome personage dressed all in white, who took him by the hand and told him that he was about to satisfy his greatest wish by conducting him to the presence of the Master of Life.

The Indian let himself to be led along, and they came to a place of unequaled beauty, where, lost in admiration, he saw before him the Master of Life, who took him by the hand and gave to him a hat bordered with gold, upon which to sit. Afraid of ruining the hat, the Indian hesitated, but on being told again to do so, he sat down. And God then said to him:

"I am the Master of Life, whom thou didst wish to see and to whom thou didst wish to speak. Listen to what I shall now tell thee for thyself and for all Indians. I am the Maker of Heaven and earth, the trees, lakes, rivers, men and of all that thou dost see or hast ever seen on earth or in the heavens. And because I love you, you must do my will. You must also avoid what I hate.

"I hate you to drink as you do, until you lose your reason. I want you not to fight one another, to take two wives, or to run after other people's wives. When you do that you do wrong. I hate such conduct. You should have but one wife, and keep her until death. When you go to war, you now conjure and sing the medicine song, thinking that you are speaking to me. You deceive yourselves. It is to the Manito that you then are speaking. He is a wicked spirit who induces you to evil, and for want of knowing me, you listen to him.

"The land on which you dwell, I have made for you, not for others. Why, therefore, do you suffer the whites to dwell upon your lands? Can

you not do without them? I know that those whom you call the children of your great Father [i.e., the French] supply your wants. But were you not as wicked as you are, you would not need them. You might live as you did before you knew them. Before those whom you call your brothers had arrived, did not your bow and arrow maintain you? You required neither gun, nor powder, nor anything else. The flesh of animals was your food, their skins your raiment. But when I saw you inclined to evil, I removed the animals into the depths of the forest, so that you might depend on your brothers for your necessities and for your clothing.

"Become now again good and do my will, and I shall send animals for your sustenance. I do not, however, forbid suffering among you, or among your Father's children. I love them. They know me. They pray to me. I supply their wants and give them what they bring to you. Not so, however, with those who have now come to trouble your possessions. Drive *them* away [i.e., the English]. Wage war against them, I love them not. They know me not. They are my enemies, and they are your brothers' enemies. Send them back to the lands that I made for them, and let them stay there.

"Here," then said the Master of Life to the Indian seated before him, "is a written paper which I now give to thee. Learn it by heart and teach it to all the Indians and their children."

The Indian responded that he could not read; whereupon the Master of Life told him that on returning to the earth he was to give the paper to the chief of his village, who would read it and instruct him and all the Indians in its message.

"It must be repeated," said the Master of Life, "morning and evening. Do all that I have told thee, and announce this to all the Indians as having come from the Master of Life. Let them drink but one drink a day, or two at the most. Let them have but one wife and stop running after other people's wives and daughters. Let them not fight one another. Let them not sing the medicine song; for in singing the medicine song they are speaking to an evil spirit. Drive from your land those dogs in red clothing [British soldiers, the "Red Coats"], they are only an injury to you. When you want anything, apply to me, as your brothers do, and I will give to both. Do not sell to your brothers what I have placed on the earth as food. In short, become good, and you shall want nothing. When you meet one another, bow and give to one another the hand of the heart. Above all, I command thee to repeat, morning and evening, the prayer that I have here given thee."

The Indian promised to do the Master's will and to recommend it strongly to the Indians, adding a request that the Master of Life should regard his people with satisfaction. His conductor then appeared, and on leading him back to the foot of the mountain told him to take up there his garments and return to his village.

The return greatly surprised all the inhabitants of the village, who had not known what had become of him. They asked of his journey, but since he had been warned to speak to no one until he had delivered his message to the village chief, he only motioned with his hand to show that he had returned to them from above. And having entered then the chief's wigwam, he delivered to him the prayer and the laws which had been entrusted to his care by the Master of Life.[160]

199

The Iroquois Tales

The Conversion of the Hurons

When the French came the missionaries tried to prevail on the Indians to receive their religion. They asked the Indians if they knew anything about God. The Indians replied that they did; that three or four times a year they had meetings at which the women and children were present, and then the chiefs told them what to do and warned them against evil practices. The missionaries said that this was good, but that there was a better way, which they ought to know. They ought to become Christians. But the Indians said, "We have many friends among the creatures about us. Some of us have snake friends, some eagles, some bears and the like. How can we desert our friends?" The priests replied, "There is only one God." "No," said the Indians, "there are two gods, one for the Indians, the other for the whites." The discussion lasted three days. Finally the priests said it was true, — there were two Gods, Jesus and the Holy Ghost. One of these might be the same as the Indian God. The Indians could follow all his commands, which were good, and also obey the commands of Jesus. But they would have to give up their allies among the brutes.

Some of the Hurons became Christians, but others refused to accept the new Religion.[161]

The Legend of Hiawatha

Ta-oun-ya-wat-ha, the god of rivers (compare the frequent connection of Christ with the living waters in the Bible), comes to earth and reveals his divine origin to two Onondagas by the lake [Lake Onondaga]. These become associates in his great work, and after his departure are prominent leaders in the league of peace.

Ta-oun-ya-wat-ha encounters great serpents at the outset, whose power is destroyed. Obstructions are removed from the Oswego and Seneca rivers, making their waters navigable, and at the same time Onondaga Lake is lowered by a straight cut — things done by the white man in the early part of the [nineteenth] century.

He goes about through the country procuring blessings and destroying enemies, and then lives quietly among the people as a man, taking the name of *Hi-a-wat-ha.*

When a great danger threatens his people, not yet united in one lasting brotherhood, he is summoned to meet the great council, where men have assembled from all parts of the land. Troubled in spirit and foreseeing some great trial, he does not at first respond. But when again called, he enters alone into a sacred lodge where his white canoe is kept, prays there in secret, and comes forth resigned. Freely but sorrowfully, he goes to the council, and endures the dreaded trial. When his daughter is crushed to earth and he is bereft of hope and comfort, even the great white bird [the Holy Ghost as a dove?] assumes the form of a cross, and its pure plumes assure victory to later wearers.

Overcome by affliction, he lies as one dead for three days. Roused then to life, he gives wise counsel and commands, forms the peaceful league [of the Iroquois], sets all in due order, appoints officers and, resuming his divinity, ascends in his white canoe to heaven, amid celestial music.

His counsels are followed, and the league of peace and love prospers and grows.

"Taking this as an Indian paraphrase of the life of Christ related to them two centuries ago," the recorder of this legend remarks, "we find here his birth, temptation, choice of disciples, good works, the going up to suffer before the assembled people, the solitary agony, death, and resurrection, and at last the establishment of the Church and the ascension. Even the use of the tangible means of suffering [the Cross] as a source of power and a guard against danger, so prominent in the significant French missionary teaching, is not left out."[162]

The Thunderer, Hé-no

"By *Hé-no* the earth was to be cooled and refreshed, vegetation sustained, the harvest ripened, and the fruits of the earth matured. The terror of the Thunderer was held over evil doers, but especially over witches. With power to inflict the most instantaneous and fearful punishment, he was regarded as the avenger of the deeds of evil. He is represented as having the form of a man, and as wearing the costume of a warrior. Upon his head he wore a magical feather, which rendered him invulnerable against the attacks of the Evil-minded. On his back he carried a basket filled with fragments of chert rock, which he launched at evil spirits and witches, whenever he discovered them as he rode in the clouds. In the springtime when the seeds were committed to the ground, there was always an invocation of *Hé-no*, that he would water them, and nourish their growth. At the harvest festival they returned thanks to *Hé-no* for the gift of rain. They also rendered their thanks to the Great Spirit for the harvest, and supplicated him to continue to them the watchful care of the Thunderer. There is a fanciful legend in relation to *Hé-no*, to the effect that he once made his habitation in a cave under Niagara Falls, behind the sheet, where he dwelt amid the grateful noise and din of waters. The Great Spirit had given him three assistants, who have continued nameless, to enable him to maintain a more vigilant supervision over the important interests committed to his guardianship. One of these, the legend declares, was partly of human, and partly of celestial origin.

"The legend is as follows:"

A young maiden residing at *Gä'-u-gwa*, a village above Niagara Falls, at the mouth of Cayuga creek, had been contracted to an old man of ugly manners and disagreeable person. As the marriage was hateful to her, and by the customs of the nation there was no escape, she resolved upon self-destruction. Launching a bark canoe into the Niagara, she seated herself within it, and composing her mind for the frightful descent, directed it down the current. The rapid waters soon swept them over the falls, and the canoe was seen to fall into the abyss below, but the maiden had disappeared. Before she reached the waters underneath, she had been caught in a blanket by *Hé-no* and his two assistants, and carried without injury to the home of the Thunderer, behind the fall. Her beauty attracted one of the dependents of *Hé-no*, who willingly joined them in marriage.

For several years before this event, the people of *Gä'-u-gwa* had been troubled with an annual pestilence, and the source of the scourge had baffled all conjecture. *Hé-no*, at the expiration of a year, revealed to her the cause, and out of compassion to the people sent her back to them, to make known the cause and the remedy. He told her that a monstrous serpent dwelt under the village and made his annual repast upon the bodies of the dead which were buried at his side; that to insure a bountiful feast, he went forth once a year and poisoned the waters of the Niagara, and also of the Cayuga creek, whereby the pestilence was created. The people were to be directed by her to move to the Buffalo creek. *Hé-no* also gave her careful directions touching the education of the child of which she was to become the mother. With these she departed on her mission.

After the people had removed as directed, the great serpent, disappointed of his food, put his head above the ground to discover the reason, and found that the village was deserted. Having scented their trail and discovered its course, he went forth into the lake and up the Buffalo creek, in open search of his prey. While he was thus in this narrow channel, *Hé-no* discharged upon the monster a terrific thunderbolt which inflicted a mortal wound. The Seneca yet point to a place in the creek where the banks are semicircular on either side, as the spot where the serpent, after he was struck, turning to escape into the deep waters of the lake, shoved out the banks on either side. Before he succeeded in reaching the lake, the repeated attacks of the Thunderer took effect, and the monster was slain.

The huge body of the serpent floated down the stream and lodged upon the verge of the cataract, stretching nearly across the river. A part of the body arched backwards near the northern shore in a semicircle. The raging waters thus dammed up by the body broke though the rocks behind; and thus the whole verge of the fall upon which the body rested was precipitated with it into the abyss beneath. In this manner was formed the Horse-Shoe fall.

Before the event there had been a passage behind the sheet from one shore to the other. This passage-way was not only broken up, but the home of *Hé-no* was also destroyed in the general crash. Since then his habitation has been in the west.

The child of the maiden grew up to boyhood, and was found to possess the power of darting the lightning at his will. It had been the injunction of *Hé-no* that he should be reared in retirement, and not be allowed to mingle in

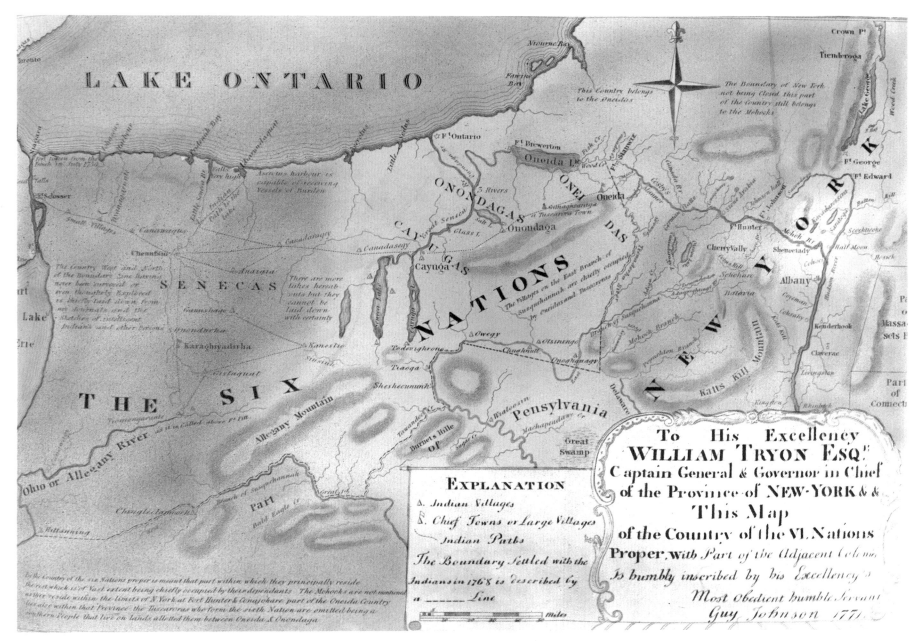

the strifes of men. On a certain occasion, having been beset by a playmate with great vehemence, he transfixed him with a thunderbolt. *Hé-no* immediately translated him to the clouds, and made him the third assistant Thunderer.[163]

A Thunderer Shot Down

There was in a certain village, in olden times, an orphan lad who had always been regarded by his friends as a very peculiar child. He was, moreover, without relatives, and completely destitute, so that he was cared for largely by the kindness of the people in general.

The boy seemed to know intuitively many things that older people did not know, and it was a custom for him to bring up and talk about many mysterious topics. Quite often when it rained he would say that he could see *Hinon* [= *Hé-no*] walking about in the clouds above their heads, and he would ask those who might be near him whether they, too, did not see *Hinon*, at the same time pointing him out to them.

At last the boy asked the people to be so good as to make for him a bow and an arrow of red willow, assuring them that he would shoot *Hinon*. So they made him a bow and an arrow of red willow, and one day while standing, during a passing storm, in the doorway of the bark lodge that he called his home, he suddenly shot at *Hinon*, the arrow winging swiftly into the clouds. Soon the people saw it come down again some distance from the orphan's lodge and, rushing to recover it, found it sticking in the earth. There was no one, nor any thing, nearby; and no matter how hard they tried, they could not draw the arrow from the ground.

Thereupon going to the orphan, they told him what they had discovered, and that they could not draw the arrow from the ground. In response, he accompanied them to the spot and, taking hold of the arrow, without trouble drew it forth. But as he did so there appeared the body of a dead human being, shot through the heart by his arrow: a small person, not more than four or five feet in height, beautifully ornamented with the finest feathers they had ever seen. The people constructed a neat little lodge of bark, which they lined with fine skins and furs, and in this they laid reverently the body of the strange personage. From time to time thereafter, they would go to view the little body, and when going to war, they would take two or three feathers from his arms in the belief that these would secure them success. All their trails would be in this manner obscured. Should they wish for rain, furthermore, they had only to dip these feathers in water and carry them about.

The people of the Tuscarora nation preserved this little body for many years, and the feathers served them during all that time. After the arrival of the whites in their original home in North Carolina, however, they were harried and driven from their territories and took refuge with the Seneca, their relatives in New York, having abandoned both the precious body and the feathers of *Hinon*.[164]

The Woman Who Married a Great Serpent

A woman and her only daughter lived together in a fine bark lodge on the outskirts of a village. The daughter was attractive in form and feature, but haughty and proud in her bearing. Many young warriors had proposed marriage, through her mother, but her customary reply was, "That man is not as handsome and fine looking as I want my husband to be." The mother had often remonstrated with her on her too haughty manner and selfish pride, but she disdained all advice.

One day the mother and daughter started off into the forest to gather wood, and when they were far from home a darkness descended upon them, so intense that the mother said, "I think we had best gather bark to make a temporary shelter, collect wood for a fire, and just stay in this place for the night." So they put together a temporary lodge and kindled a cheerful blaze, and after preparing and eating their evening meal, sat down on opposite sides of the fire to rest.

Suddenly, while the mother was dozing, a man entered and stood beside the girl. She looked up at him and was amazed and charmed by his great beauty of both face and form. He wore a wampum sash around his magnificent body and on his head a fine headdress with black eagle plumes waving over it. His entire person seemed to shine with paint and oil.

Without ceremony, he informed the young woman that he had come to marry her and would await her answer; to which she responded, "I must first tell my mother what you have said, and when I have her reply, shall again talk to you."

The stranger remained standing; and when the daughter told her mother what had been said to her, she replied, "You may do as you like. You have already refused a great many young men without good cause, as far as I know. So now it is for you to decide. You must please yourself."

Returning, the young woman repeated to the man her mother's reply, and added, "I have decided. I shall become your wife. You may follow me to my mother." Whereupon, they went to her mother together, and the girl took her seat by his side. The mother, also, thought him a very handsome youth, and so agreed to the marriage. And the two were thus husband and wife.

The husband said to his wife, "I want you to come with me to my own lodge tonight." And removing his beautiful wampum sash, he gave this to her for her mother, saying, "This shall be for your mother a sign that we are married." The woman, very much pleased with the gift, hung it up, and the young man and wife then began the journey to his lodge.

As they went their way the young woman saw in the distance a broad clearing, and when they had come into this, there was at one end a lodge which her husband pointed to, as his own. They went in, and the people inside seemed delighted that she had come. So she sat comfortably at her husband's side.

The two passed that night and the next day together, and on the second morning the young husband said, "I am going off to hunt." He left the lodge. And when he had closed the entrance flap, his young wife heard a very strange noise. She did not know what to think of it. Then all became very still. When evening came, she again heard the sound. The entrance flap was flung aside and a tremendous serpent entered the lodge. Tongue darting, it approached and placed its head in her lap, requiring her to search it for vermin. She obeyed, finding in large numbers bloodsuckers, angleworms, and other noisome things. And when she had killed all that she found, the serpent slowly withdrew from her lap and the lodge and was gone. Immediately, the young husband entered, as handsome as ever. "Were you afraid of me," he asked, "when I came in just now?" "No," she answered, "I was not afraid at all."

When again, next morning, he left the lodge and had closed the door flap, she heard again the same strange sounds that she had heard the day before. And then again, all was still. About noon, she went out to gather wood for the fire and to fetch water, and while going about, spied a huge serpent sunning itself on the rocks; then another; and presently another. And she began to feel very homesick and disheartened.

That evening her husband returned as before; and next day, when he had left her a third time to go hunting, she began seriously to think of escape from the terrible place in which she found herself. She again went out into the forest for wood, and while standing there heard a voice. Turning, she beheld a very old man, who when she looked into his face said to her, "My poor grandchild, you are most unfortunate. The seeming man to whom you are married is evil. We have tried many times to kill him, but he is crafty, very cunning, and we have not been able to destroy him. He is one of seven brothers. All of them are great sorcerers. And as happens often with such wicked beings, their hearts are not in their bodies. Their hearts are tied in a bundle of seven which is hung, hidden, under the couch of the eldest. You must get hold of that and escape with it. I and my friends shall help, all we can."

Returning to the lodge, she searched beneath the couch, and there, indeed, found in a bundle the seven hearts. Seizing this, she tucked it under her robe, and as quickly as possible fled the lodge at top speed. Right away, a voice called, "Stop! Come back!" She kept running. The voice continued: "You may think you can escape me, but you can't; no matter how you try."

All her strength seemed to leave her, but beside her, then, her grandfather was saying, "I can help you now, my grandchild." Taking hold of her garment, he pulled her out of the water; and only then did she see that she had been all that time under water.

Above them was a great black cloud. She saw the Lightning flash, and the Thunder began to shoot arrows. The Wind lashed the water to great foaming waves, and that moment, the young woman saw that her grandfather had slain the great serpent. She saw, also, standing along the shore, a number of old men resembling him, who all thanked her for the help she had given in the killing of that sorcerer and his kin. For the grandfather with his lightnings had blasted the whole bundle of hearts, and with his arrows he had shot them, and the serpent and his entire brood were now dead.

The old men along the shore drew the great length out of the water and cut it in pieces. The huge head they stuck on a pole, and it seemed to her now more fierce and ugly than before. "My grandchild," her grandfather said, "you must now come with us." And after packing suitable loads of the immense serpent's flesh, they started homeward, each with a load of the meat on his back.

In a short while they arrived at what seemed to her to be a lodge, which they all entered; and inside she saw a very old man whose hair was white as snow, and whose manner and voice were kind. To him the leader of the party said, "This woman of the human family has helped us kill the great serpent and his clan."

The old man, looking at her, said, "My granddaughter, I am indeed thankful to you." And then he said to her, "My granddaughter, come here to my side."

She went over to him, and when she stood beside him, he rubbed her body up and down with his hands fortified with his orenda, whereupon several young serpents crawled from her, which were immediately killed by those present. "You are now entirely well," the old man said. And he bade her to be seated.

For a year the young woman remained with those people. The younger members of the lodge, whenever they pleased, would go hunting; and knowing that she could not eat their food—which was in large measure the flesh of serpents—they would bring back to her maize to eat, telling her the names of those from whom they had taken it, many of which she recognized.

One day the old man said to his sons, "Perhaps it would be best for you to take our granddaughter out to hunt with you. She will in that way gain orenda." The sons agreed, saying, "That would be well." They told her then that one of their brothers was in trouble.

"Deep in the great water," they said, "there was an immense bloodsucker lying on a rock. Our missing brother shot at it, but was not quick enough to avoid its rush and was caught. He is lying down there on the rock, and we can neither kill the bloodsucker nor release him. You will come and help, will you not?" She consented, and they all started off.

On arriving at the place, they looked down into the water, far into its depths, and there could see the huge bloodsucker. They all rose, then, high into the clouds and began shooting arrows. But none of them hit the bloodsucker. Then they asked the young woman to try. She was high in the clouds, among them. Willingly, she took the bow and arrows and shot down into the water. The bloodsucker moved. She sent a second arrow, and this time there rose in the water a terrible struggle and commotion, after which all was quiet. From her place in the clouds she now could see that the great bloodsucker was dead, and that the moment he had died his captive had got loose. He was coming on up to them and when he arrived, they all rejoiced with their brother and went home.

One day the old man said, "I think it is time for our granddaughter to go back to her mother." And to her he said, "You must not do any kind of work, pounding or chopping; but for ten days keep perfectly quiet in your home."

And so they all accompanied her homeward. They walked along, it seemed to her, like ordinary people, and when they drew near to her mother's lodge, they reminded her to behave exactly as her grandfather had advised.

Then she realized that she was standing in water. A heavy shower of rain had just passed over the earth. Her mother's lodge was near at hand, and her companions bade her farewell. She walked into her mother's lodge, and the woman was delighted to see again her long-lost child.

For nine days the young woman observed the injunction of her grandfather, but on the tenth the women of her family began urging her to help them in their work. She at first refused, declaring that she had been warned not to do so. But they persisted, and so urgently that, finally, she struck with the pounder one blow, when the mortar split in two and the maize scattered over the ground. The orenda of the Thunderers had not yet entirely left her. And that was why the old man had enjoined her not to work for ten days.[165]

The Snake with Two Heads

In olden times there was a boy who was in the habit of going out to shoot birds. One day in his excursions he saw a snake, about two feet long, with a head at each end of its body. Having already killed a bird, he divided it in two parts and gave a portion to the snake in each mouth. Next day he fed it again and made up his mind to do nothing else, from now on, but hunt birds to feed the snake. Every day he went out and around, killing birds, and the snake became wonderfully large. Also, the boy became a very good shot. He killed even black squirrels and larger game to feed the increasing snake. One day he took his little sister along and pushed her toward the two-headed thing, which caught her with one of its mouths and ate her up.

The snake kept growing and eating larger and larger game. It devoured anything the boy brought it, until at last it formed a circle around the entire village of his people. The two heads came near together at the palisade gate and ate the people as they passed in and out. When there remained, finally, only one man and his sister, the two-headed monster, having swallowed all that it required, dragged itself away to the top of a mountain, where it remained.

That night the one remaining man dreamed that he should fashion a bow and arrows and take certain hairs from his sister's person, wrap them around the head of each arrow and anoint the whole head, then, with blood from her menstrual flow. This accomplished, he went up the mountain and shot the monster with one of his prepared arrows, which worked its way into its body. Every arrow that he sent did the same, until, from its two heads the great snake began vomiting everything it had eaten. Out came all the people in pieces— heads, arms, bodies, and wooden bowls: for they had thought to defend themselves with anything they had in hand. The immense snake then began to writhe and to squirm violently, when it rolled from its mountain top, down into the valley, and at last lay dead.[166]

The Serpent and the Thunderers

A long time ago in an Indian settlement were two wigwams, not far apart, and in these lived two squaws who were very good friends. They had two children of about the same age, who played together, and when they had little bows and arrows they shot together. As they grew bigger they wanted stronger bows and arrows, which their uncles made for them. They used these every day, and became skillful in killing birds and small game, and then asked for some still stronger, that they might kill larger animals. They were now young men and good hunters. One of them, being handsome and kind, was very much liked by the women, and some of the maidens would have married him, but he refused all offers. At last his friend talked with him and told him he had better marry, or something might happen for which he would be sorry. This troubled him, and he said he would soon choose a wife, but first they would go together on a long hunt.

They got ready for this, telling their mothers they were going away on a great hunt, far from the village, and might be gone many days. So their mothers took maize and roasted it, and then pounded it into meal in their wooden mortars. This was light and would keep a long time. The young men filled their sacks, took their bows, and started for their hunting ground. They walked all day, and camped in the woods. They walked all the next day and camped on the hunting ground, where they soon built a wigwam.

After this they hunted every day, and one was lucky and brought home a great deal of game, but the one whom the young squaws liked came home without any and said very little. This went on for several days, and the one who had been so happy and such a favorite seemed sorry all the time. Every morning they went off to hunt in opposite directions, and one day his friend thought he would follow him and see what he did. They went out as before, and after he had walked a little way the lucky hunter turned back into the other's path. He soon saw him running very fast through the woods, and hurried after him, calling to him to stop; but he did not. They ran till they came to a lake, and the first one plunged into the water and swam across, while his friend went around the shore. The swimmer got there first, paying no attention to his calls. They ran on to a second smaller lake, where they did the same, but this time the one on shore got ahead. The sorry young man then turned back, and his friend ran past both lakes, and was hiding in the bushes when the other came ashore. As the swimmer entered the woods the other jumped out and caught him, asking what was the matter and why he acted so strangely.

At first the young man could say nothing and seemed to know nothing, but soon came to his senses. He told his friend that he was going to be married, and so, must leave him here alone; for he could not go back to his home. If his friend wished to see him at any time, he might come to the lake, bringing fresh Indian tobacco and clean clay pipes. These things he should lay on bark fresh from the tree, and then say to the lake, "I want to see my friend."

So he went off another way and married the big serpent in the lake. When he had gone, his friend went back to the wigwam, and he, too, was now very sorry and did not wish to hunt. He built a fire and sat down alone.

It was very still for a long time, and then he heard someone coming. When he turned around a young man stood in the doorway, dressed in white and with white feathers on his head. The visitor said, "You seem to be in trouble, but for all that you are the only one that can help us. My chief has sent me to invite you to our council." Then he gave him wam-

285. *Tadodaho (1980)*, steatite sculpture by the Onondaga artist Cleveland Sandy (1949–   ), a member of the Wolf Clan. From the Six Nations Reserve, Ontario, Canada.

pum, to show that he brought him a true message. The hunter said, "Where is the council?" The young man in white answered, "You came right by our wigwam in the woods, but did not see it. Follow me, and you shall find it quite near."

So he went with him, not very far, until he saw smoke rising from the ground, and then a wigwam. Going in, he saw eight chiefs sitting quietly on the ground. All had white feathers on their heads, but the principal chief had larger feathers than the others. They gave him a place, and the hunter sat down and smoked with them. When the pipe came round to the principal chief, he rose and spoke to the young man.

"You have come to help us, and we have waited for you a long time." The young man asked, "How can I help you?" And the chief replied: "Your friend has married the big serpent in the lake, whom we must kill. He has told you how to call him when you wish to see him. We will furnish the tobacco and pipes."

The chiefs then presented the young hunter with the necessary clean pipes and fresh tobacco, and accepting these, he rose, to go to the lake.

The principal chief said: "When your friend comes, you must ask to see his wife. She will want to know if the sky is clear. When she comes, you must invite them a little way from the lake and there talk to them. The chiefs will come in the form of a cloud—on the lake, not in the sky."

So he took the fresh tobacco, and clean pipes, and fresh bark, and laid them by the shore. Then he stood by the water and called loudly to his friend, saying he was going away and wished to see him once more.

There was soon a ripple on the lake and the water began to boil, when out came his friend. He had a spot on his forehead and looked like a serpent, yet like a man. His friend talked with him, asking what he should say to his mother when he got home. Then he asked to see his wife, so that he might tell his mother what she looked like.

The serpent man replied that she might not wish to come, but that he would try. So he went to the shore and lay down, placing his lips to the water and beginning to drink. Then the hunter saw that he was going down through the water, not swimming like a man but moving like a snake. Soon the water again boiled and he came back, saying that his wife would come; but she did not. He looked around to see if the sky was clear, then returned to the shore and, drinking, again went like a snake down into the water.

Now a greater sight was seen. The lake boiled again, not in one spot, but all over, and great waves rolled up on the shore, as though there were a strong wind, but there was none. The waves grew larger, and then out of the water came the serpent man's wife. She was very beautiful and shone like silver, but the silver seemed more like scales. She had long hair falling all around her, like gold and silver glittering in the sun. And with her came her husband, through the waves and up onto the shore, where all three sat down to talk together on a log.

The hunter remembered the chief's words, and when at last he saw, a great way off, something like a cloud moving over the water, not in the sky, he asked the two to follow him into the woods, where the sun would not be so hot. They did so, and as the chiefs had advised, he said when there that he had to step aside and, turning, darted away.

At once a great cloud came over everything, with lightning and thunder where the two had been left standing, and everywhere great rain. Then all again became still.

The hunter returned to the lake, where a big and a little serpent lay dead on the ground, and the chiefs were dancing, rejoicing over their enemy. When their dance was finished, they cut up the two serpents, packing them into eight equal bundles. Each chief took one on his back, and when all were ready to go, they thanked the young man for what he had done for them and told him he would be always lucky. "Just ask us any time," they said, "for whatever you want, and you shall have it." Then they went off through the woods in Indian file, and as he watched, they seemed to step higher and higher and up into the sky, when there resounded a great thunder storm; for those chiefs had been the Thunderers.

Alone, the hunter returned to his wigwam, but it was quiet and lonesome and he was sad. He took down part of the meat of his hunting and carried it half a day's journey into the woods, where he hung it up on the trees. Then he returned for more, doing the same with all the rest until he departed home, where he told the whole story to his friend's mother, who was very sorry for the death of her son, whom she dearly loved. She then adopted in his place his friend, who now, therefore, had two mothers.

The old Oneida storyteller who had recounted this tale to a company of Onondaga friends while on a visit to their reservation in 1886 or 1887, declared on closing that it was "all a true fact" and that he had, moreover, his own opinion as to the place where the adventure might have occurred. He thought Crooked Lake, far up the valley, might have been the first across which the young man had swum, and Round Lake, then, the second. This seemed to him most likely, he said, but it was only his opinion.[167]

Two Stone-Coat Tales

Three men were camping in the woods, hunting. One of them, who was married, had his wife and child along, and while the men were off in the forest, the woman and child would remain in the lodge. The child was small and still swathed in a cradleboard.

One day when the woman returned to the lodge with water from a nearby stream, she heard talking and, on arriving at the entrance, saw a woman within, dressed in stone, who had taken up the baby and was rocking it on her knee while singing, *A'uwah, a'uwah*, "Such good eating, such good eating!" Every little while she would take a bite from the child's cheek, when the child would scream; but then spitting on her hand and rubbing the cheek, she healed it and the crying stopped. The mother, beholding all this, was appalled, and said to herself, "We are going to die." The Stone-Coat Woman looked up and, on seeing the mother, bade her come in and have no fear.

Toward night the hunters returned, and when they saw the woman dressed in stone they were terrified; but she bade them have no fear. All would be well. "I have come to help you in your hunting," she said. And so for some time they all lived there together in that lodge. The men would go hunting, day after day, and always had good luck in finding game and bringing home meat. Then one evening they said, "We have found a pond, not far away, in which there are many beavers."

"I shall go with you tomorrow," the Stone-Coat Woman said.

So next day she went with the men to the pond and, having cut a small circular hole in the ice, she called to the beavers to come out. A number came out, and these she caught and killed. Then she called again and more came out, and these too she caught and killed. And so she continued until the hunters had as many as they wanted. The men skinned the beavers and kept the furs; but the woman fell to eating the bodies raw.

One morning that woman said to the hunters, "A visitor is coming, and you must do all you can to defend yourselves. It is my husband, and he is angry. Perhaps he will kill us all. When I left him, I ran away. I came to you and he is angry. I shall fight with him when he comes, as best I can; but you must have ready a basswood stick. Sharpen it, harden it in the fire, and when he throws me to the ground, which he will do, you must spear him from behind, and that will kill him. He will be coming some time this afternoon. We must all be on the watch."

At last they saw him approaching. He walked right in and spoke to his wife. She begged him not to make trouble, declaring she would go home with him. But when he saw that there were three men in the place, he became jealous and began fighting. He knocked her down, and as he leaned over to beat her, the men rammed the basswood spear into his body, he fell dead, and the Stone-Coat Woman got to her feet. "I don't know what

will happen to us now," she said. "My husband has two brothers. They now know that he is dead, and will come to kill us. But the river is open. You have canoes. You had best escape."—And she then went off alone.

The others took to their canoes, and when they had pushed out into the river, a man came running to the shore, calling to them to come back a moment. Instead, they paddled out further, and he called, "Lucky for you, you didn't come back. I came to eat you." And so those people had a narrow escape.

*   *   *

At times men would get lost and disappear while hunting in the forest. Their friends then would suppose they had been eaten by Stone-Coats. One time, three Seneca went out on the warpath. They headed directly westward and, after a day's traveling, camped in a deep ravine at the head of a stream. When they had built their fire they saw a fine-looking man coming toward them, who, when he arrived, said to them, "I think it best that you three should do what I am about to do. I have come to let you know that there are hundreds of people on the warpath who are intending to eat people. You will be camping here tonight. They will make their camp within sight of yours. One of you three must then go to their fire and say, 'Hello! I have discovered your fire. Where are you going?' They will answer, 'We are on the warpath.' Your man must then reply, 'I too am on the warpath,' to which they will respond, 'Well then, we must fight.' Your man then must leave them and come back to your camp."

The Seneca, soon after that, saw men coming to set up camp a short distance away. Thereupon one of the three went over and said to them, "Hello! I have discovered your fire. Where are you going?" "We are on the warpath," they replied. "So am I," he answered and, looking around, saw stone clothing laid against one of the trees. The owner of the clothing was resting on the ground. The people were all Stone-Coats. And next morning the Stone-Coat army came up the ravine toward the Seneca camp. They were making a terrible noise; for the whole army was singing, "We are going to eat up the Seneca nation."

When the Stone-Coat force had come about halfway up the ravine, filling the entire space of the valley, with a great whoop they rushed forward. But at that instant great rocks began rolling down on them and great trees falling and killing them, when the Seneca saw a strange and wonderful man running along the top of the ridge and above the trees. Wherever he saw a Stone-Coat head, he would hit it, killing its owner. Only one Stone-Coat was left alive, and he, having turned and run, was never seen again. The strange man who had been hurling the rocks had been singing all the time, singing that the Seneca nation could stand against the world; and when all again was quiet, he came down to the three men and said, "I am the one whom you call *Hawenniyo*. It is I who have saved you. I did not create the Stone-Coats. Something else made them." And he said to them further, "I want you, the Seneca nation, to be the best people of all tribes in every kind of game or contest, and in hunting."[168]

*   *   *

Three False Face Adventures

A number of Seneca traveling northward from their village met a False Face with whom they had a conversation. His mouth was drawn up on one side and down on the other. "*Hawenniyo* caused me to be around," he said, "to be of help to you; but when anyone seriously mocks us, we by sorcery enchant him. We make him ill. However, if you now will go to work and fashion a mask with a face like mine, you will be able, by wearing it, to cure those whom we have afflicted. In this way you will take my place."

So the people made wooden masks, to be used as directed. And this, they say, is the origin of the Society of Maskers, or False Faces.

*   *   *

There was in Canada a man, [about a century ago, in 1884, on the Canadian side of the Niagara river, near its mouth], who had to travel a great deal among the Indian tribes and he would frequently see False Faces. One day he met one directly, who stopped and spoke to him. The man handed him a plug of tobacco to smoke and continued on his way. But when he then had accomplished his mission and was on the way back home, he again saw a False Face with his back toward him, who was standing near the same spot, and noticing that this was not the same one, he passed by without speaking. Very soon, however, he encountered the one he had met before and, saluting him, handed him again a plug of tobacco, whereupon the False Face said, "I think you should come along with me and see where it is we live." "Gladly!" the man replied, and was conducted to a rocky place where there was a cave into which they entered and where the man saw a great many False Faces. Many of them were very old, but there were many very young ones, too. His guide handed the tobacco plug to the oldest of the company, who said, "You had better give a piece of this to everyone here present." So they cut it into small pieces for distribution, and the oldest said, "Give thanks!" Whereupon they all gave thanks to the Tobacco, and all danced, and the little ones, too. They asked this man to dance, and he did so. And then, when he was going away, the oldest False Face said to him, "I want you to remember us. And when, on your travels, you are passing this way again, you must come and see us."

*   *   *

A few years previous to 1884, two young Seneca started for a False Face dance. They had their wooden masks along, in a bundle. On the way they stopped at a white woman's house and she asked, "What have you in your bundle?" "Our False Faces," they answered; "We are going to a False Face dance." "If you will put on the masks and let me see them," she said, "I will give you two quarts of cider." Going outdoors, they put on the masks and came back into the house. The woman's child, a boy of six or seven, became so frightened that he acted as though he had lost his mind; he could not talk. The mother sent to Perrysburg (N.Y.) for a doctor. He came, but he could not help the boy. The mother then went to a Seneca shaman for advice, who told her that to cure the child she should send for the False Face Society. The maskers came at her request and danced, and they rubbed the boy with ashes, also blowing some in his face; and soon he was well.

The woman, according to custom, had prepared for the False Faces a pot of pounded parched corn, boiled with pork and seasoned with maple sugar.[169]

286. *Indian New Year (Gah-noh-da-ya-onh)*, 1901 watercolor by Jesse Cornplanter (1889–1957) of a False Face dance at the Cattaraugus Reservation.

In the old days there was an Iroquois village situated in a fertile and beautiful countryside. They raised maize and beans and squash, and were for many years prosperous and contented. But there came a time when their crops began to fail. The corncobs were all bare of grain, the beanpods were empty and the squashes withered before harvest. Game had become scarce, furthermore, and the people consequently were starving.

A very old woman who was Chief and Matron of her clan was one day walking about her planted field, meditating on the misfortune of her people, when she heard a sound of weeping, as though from the middle of the planted plot. Someone, she thought, must be in distress. So she turned into the area and was surprised to find that it was the maize itself that was weeping. The beans were also weeping; and so too the squash. Overcome with a feeling of compassion, the old woman stopped by one of the little hills of maize and gently asked, "Oh, you dear Maize, why do you weep?" Between sobs the Maize replied, "You place us in the ground to grow, but do not perform your further duties. You do not cover us with sufficient earth, as you know you should. You do not hill up the earth around our feet, so that we may stand firm. You do not dig up the earth around sufficiently to give us water. Many of us have been able to live for only a day or two before going home. Very few remain, and now we too are dying because of neglect. You even let our enemies come and strangle us to death."

The old Matron listened and was stricken with pity and regret. She went to the Bean people and to the Squash people, and from each heard the same piteous complaint; so that all the way along the path back to her lodge she wept, and on arriving, sitting down on her couch, she continued to weep bitterly.

Her people, on hearing this sobbing, came to console their Matron, but on learning something of its cause, they too began to weep. Soon a considerable company had assembled, and all were in tears when the Chief arrived to find out what this was all about.

"Mother," he asked, "what caused you to weep when you were out in your garden plot?"

Composing herself, she reported as well as she could the complaint she had heard from the Maize, the Beans, and the Squash: of how she and her people had not covered them with earth enough to enable them to live and to grow, and had let their enemies [the weeds] grow up all around them.

Consulting with the others in the lodge and learning that this was the first time any of them had ever heard of this problem, the Chief summoned a council of his clan and laid before the assemblage a report of the remarkable statement of their Matron. It was then resolved by the Council that in the future anyone planting either maize or beans or squash should be careful to cover the seed with sufficient earth to provide sustenance; care for the growing plants by proper hilling, as well as by digging all around them to make the earth mellow; and lastly, by giving constant attention to the task of eliminating their enemies, pressing in to destroy them.

And so, next spring, in accordance with this

287. The Three Sisters, 1937 watercolor, 15″ × 20″, by Ernest Smith (1907–75), of a symbiotic triad that has historically been the Native American dietary staple.

resolution, the people all placed their seeds of maize, beans, and squash sufficiently deep in the ground, and the old Chief stood by the planters to see that all was properly done. Later on, when the tender sprouts had reached such growth that they required more earth to support them, the people were called together and reminded to hill up their plants and thoroughly weed away their enemies. Everything was going well and the crops maturing luxuriantly, when toward harvest time something began going wrong. There was something damaging and destroying the plants. Some sort of people, it seemed, were coming unseen and taking away the maize and beans and leaving only shells of the squash. Again the people went into mourning, imagining and confessing that they must all be guilty of some other form of negligence.

Accordingly, the following year they all took the greatest pains to obey without fault all the rules of the planting and growing season; yet again, just as the maize and beans and squash were becoming fine and fit for harvest, some nation of people unseen began stealing and taking away the whole crop.

So the Chief again called a council of his clan, to determine what might be done, and it was thereupon resolved that a number of stout and alert warriors should be stationed to watch the planted fields and learn what nation of people these were who were constantly coming to pilfer the harvest.

The watchmen took up their stations that evening and toward morning noticed a number of persons tearing off the ears of maize and gathering the bean pods. Others were picking up squash. The warriors rushed in, took the night thieves prisoner and brought them, later in the day, to the council lodge, before the Chief, who asked one of the intruders, "Where do you live?"

"A long way from here. In the forest."

"Are there many of your people?"

"We are a large nation," came the answer.

They bound the maize thieves and brought them out of the lodge, and all the chiefs and people came to see them. They did likewise with the bean thieves and the squash thieves. All were permitted to strike them with staves, and at this treatment they bitterly wept. Day after day they were subjected to such beatings, and after some time were told that if they would conduct their captors to their villages, they would be set free.

The maize thieves led a party of selected warriors into the forest a long way, and at last they came to a settlement which the warriors immediately attacked; many of its people were killed. The bean thieves and the squash thieves also led parties to their villages. It is said that the warriors had whipped the maize thieves so severely during their captivity that their faces became striped and their tails ringed from the blows that they received: and these marks have remained to this day. The maize thieves were raccoons. The squash thieves had their upper lips split, so that they should not be able again to eat squashes. Those thieves were hares, and their lips remain split to this day.[170]

The Chestnut Tree Guarded by the Seven Sisters

In a small lodge deep in a dense forest there lived a man alone with his little nephew. Every day he prepared a meal for the boy but never ate with him, and when the child one day asked his uncle to join him, the man replied, "No, I have already eaten." The boy persisting, the uncle, telling him to be quiet, said, "I have cooked that just for you."

As the little fellow grew, he began to wonder about this strange conduct of his uncle until he asked, one day, "Oh, my Uncle, I never see you eat. How is this?" Receiving no answer, he thereupon decided to spy on the old man and catch him at his secret meal. So that evening, after his supper, he said, "Oh my Uncle, I'm very tired. I feel sleepy. I'm going to go right to bed." And with that, he lay down, drew the deerskin bedcover over his head, and presently began to snore.

The wily old man waited until he felt sure that his nephew was well asleep; then, turning to his own bed, he searched carefully among the skin coverings and finally drew forth a tiny kettle and very small bundle. Placing the kettle on the bench by the fire and opening his little bundle, he took from it some sort of substance, of which he scraped a very small quantity into the kettle. Next, pouring water into the vessel, he hung it over the fire and, taking a wand from its wrappings, began gently tapping the tiny kettle, singing quietly, "Oh my kettle, I want you now to grow!" Obediently, the vessel began to increase in size, its contents growing also in bulk. Repeating the charm and continuing to tap, the old man watched his kettle grow until, deciding it was now large enough to provide all the mush he wanted, he stopped his tapping, as well as his song, replaced the wand in its wrapping, took the kettle from the fire, and sat down to his evening meal. When finished, he thoroughly washed the empty vessel and then shook it until, decreasing in size, it was again as it had been when taken from the bed; to which hiding place he finally returned it, along with the wand and tiny bundle.

Deliberately snoring, the nephew had been watching all this through an opening in his bedcovering, and having made up his mind to take breakfast with his uncle next day, he got up that morning much earlier than usual, only to find that his uncle had already eaten and was preparing something for himself. The man then went off to hunt, and the boy, in execution of the plan that he had conceived, went out to collect bark and wood for a good fire. About midday, thinking, "I'm going to be good and very helpful. My uncle when he returns will be tired, and I shall have his supper ready for him." Turning to his uncle's bed and searching among the coverings, he finally found what he was looking for, and on opening the tiny bundle discovered that all it contained was the small fragment of a chestnut.

Marveling and wondering, how it could possibly be that from this minute particle a man could make enough mush to live on, the boy proceeded to his course of action. "I must do this thing," he was saying to himself, "exactly as my uncle does. There must be in this bit of chestnut enough for just one more meal."

Very carefully scraping, he powdered into the tiny kettle every bit of his uncle's chestnut, then poured water into the vessel and set it over the flame. Drawing the wand from its skin wrapping, he watched, and when the water began to boil, tapping gently on the kettle, he sang, "Oh my little kettle, I want you now to grow." The vessel began to increase in size and the youngster was so amused by this that he kept on tapping, tapping, repeating the magical song, until the kettle had grown so large there was no room for him in the lodge. Climbing onto the roof, he continued his tapping, tapping, and song, until the kettle was the size of the lodge, and he, up there, so busy that he failed to notice his approaching uncle.

From a distance the man had seen his nephew up there, and on drawing near, heard his magical song: "Oh my kettle, grow! Oh grow, my little kettle!" Then he realized that his nephew had discovered the whole thing, and he felt extremely sad and depressed. He

called up to the lad on the roof, "My Nephew, what is this you have done?"

The boy answered in delight, "I have made enough mush for a marvelous feast." Then clambering down, he told his uncle the whole story.

The uncle asked, "Have you used up the whole chestnut?"

"Yes," he answered; "there was only a small bit left."

"You have killed me!" the poor old man exclaimed. "That is the only food I can eat. There is but one tree in the whole world on which that kind of chestnut grows, and only someone of the greatest orenda can ever come to it."

The boy just laughed. "Why the woods are full of chestnut trees. Don't worry, oh my uncle, I can get you whole bags of chestnuts."

The old man shook his head. "No, no, my Nephew, that is impossible. This is a bad thing you have done. That bit of a chestnut would have lasted me for years."

Then giving the kettle a shake to reduce its size, so that they could get into the lodge, he said, "Since I am now about to die, I may as well tell you the whole story. There is just that one tree of this kind in the world, and seven sisters own it. Great sorcerers they are, and many men have lost their lives in attempting to get to their tree, to procure even one of those chestnuts."

"I can get you one, I am sure," said the boy.

"No," said the old man, "you can't. You are still only a boy. You would lose your life. Those sisters keep a great eagle perched on the top of their tree, to guard it, and the tree is very tall. He watches night and day. Even the cleverest man, attempting to approach, would be seen, and the eagle then would screech, when out would come the seven sisters and club the intruder to death. Men have taken on the forms of birds and beasts, supposing they could deceive them; but all, so far, have failed. Those seven sisters have beaten to death every living thing that has ever tried to approach their marvelous tree."

Unimpressed, the youth next morning said to his uncle, "I am going to try to get to that tree. You must tell me now where it stands."

And the uncle, realizing that his nephew's mind was not to be changed, replied, "Go toward the rising sun. When you have traversed the forests, you will come to a big open space. In the middle of that clearing you will see a very tall tree. And beside the tree you will see a lodge. On the top of the tree sits the eagle, watching with his sharp eyes all directions. And in the lodge the seven sisters dwell."

"So now, cheer up, oh my uncle," the young man said, as he turned to walk to the sunrise. "Before you will have finished eating all the mush that is in that kettle, I shall bring you a bag full of chestnuts." And he started away on his walk.

Traveling for some time through a forest, he presently spied and killed a deer, which he cut up. The venison filled his bag. Then he came to a place from which he could see through the forest an opening, and he realized that from this point on he would have to exercise caution. His fetish was the mole; and so he called, "My Friend, I want you now to come to me. Oh come to me, you Mole!"

In a very short time the leaves at his feet began to rustle and a mother mole appeared.

"What is it you want of me?" she asked.

"I have done a great mischief to my uncle," he answered, "by scraping away all of his chestnut. I want you to help me now get more for him. Let me enter into your body, and you then carry me underground to that tall tree out there, on which there is a big eagle sitting. When you are right beneath the tree poke out your nose a little, so that I may see.—But I shall have to bring along my bag. Do you think you can carry us both?"

"Oh yes, " said the mother mole. "I can carry you both."

The youth magically reduced his size, and when he had entered the body of the mole, it directly made its way to the tree, where, upon arrival, it thrust its nose out of the ground and said, "The eagle is watching."

In a flash, the youth, stepping with his bag out of the body of the mole, began scattering venison right and left, and the eagle, flying immediately down, began eating it up voraciously. There were chestnuts lying all over the ground, and while the bird was thus preoccupied, the young man so speedily filled his bag that by the time the watchbird had finished his meal, the mole was already bearing him with his loaded bag back to the forest. The eagle then uttered its screech of alarm, and the seven sisters, running out with their clubs, perceiving that the nuts were already gone, with no one anywhere in sight, fell upon and clubbed their eagle nearly to death.

The mole with her cargo having arrived in the forest, the youth said to her, "Let me now hide my chestnuts here and return with you to the lodge of the seven sisters. I want to hear what they are going to say, to learn if they are planning to follow us to try to recover these chestnuts."

The mole took him back into her little body, and he told her to go again underground until she came to the lodge by the tree. She did exactly as he asked, and when she arrived at the lodge, thrust her nose and mouth above ground. The youth then stuck his ear out of the mole's mouth and listened to what was being said.

"It must be," said one of the sisters, "a young man just grown. No one, since his uncle, has succeeded in stealing our chestnuts. Perhaps he now has a nephew as crafty as he himself used to be; and it may be that he, too, is now going to live on our chestnuts."

"Well, they are stolen," then said another voice. "We may as well let them go."

Upon hearing this last, the youth asked his mole to carry him back at once to the forest, and on arriving there, he dismissed his mole with thanks for its aid; then hurried home.

When he arrived, he found his old uncle sitting by the fire, singing his death song. "I must now die of hunger," the old man sang, "for my nephew will never return."

Whereupon the nephew rushed into the lodge with a cry. "Oh, my Uncle, I have brought you here those chestnuts in a full bag." And the old man, amazed, gave to their guardian spirits thanks, while welcoming his nephew with joy. He is still making chestnut puddings. The nephew became a great hunter. Anything he desired, he obtained; for he had the mole as guardian spirit and aid.[171]

*   *   *

Grandmother Porcupine, Mother Bear,
and the Lost Boy

A long time ago, several Onondaga families went off to camp together by the wildwood streams, where fish, deer, bear, otter, beaver, and other game could be caught for winter use. They traveled for several days, and the hunting ground where they finally pitched camp was a beautiful place, with its little hills and river with high banks.

In the party were five little boys, who had their own little bows and arrows. Imitating their fathers and uncles, they went about in the woods together, hunting. But there was one among them, much smaller than the others, who was greatly teased by the older four. Sometimes they would run off and hide, leaving him crying in the woods; then show themselves and have a great laugh. Sometimes they would run as though heading for the camp, shouting that a wolf or bear was pursuing them, leaving the little one far behind, crying with all his might. Often he returned alone to the camp, when the others had left him.

One day these five little fellows found lying on the ground a great hollow log, and one of them suggested, "Perhaps there's a rabbit or red squirrel in there. Let's shoot inside and see." All agreed, and taking the little boy's arrows, they shot these instead of their own; then said to him, "You go in there now and get your arrows back." "No, no," he replied, and began crying. "I'm scared something might catch me." The others coaxed, and when one of them said he would get his uncle to make for him a new bow and new arrows, persuaded, he stopped crying, got down on hands and knees, and crawled in.

When he had gone a little way, he found one of his arrows and handed it out. This gave him courage to go farther, and when he was some distance in, one of the four outside suggested, "Let's stop this thing up and trap him in there." The others agreed, and fetching rotten wood and old dead limbs, they stopped the opening, and when the mischief was done, returned to camp, saying nothing to anybody about the little boy trapped in the log.

It was two days before the mother and father realized that their boy was missing. They had thought he might have been staying the night with the family of one of his friends. When a search was begun, the four were asked what they knew, but all replied that they knew nothing; that on their last expedition the little boy had not been along. The whole camp than turned out for the search, and finally gave up, supposing the little fellow must have been killed and eaten by a wolf or bear.

Within the log, meanwhile, when first shut up, the little fellow had tried to get out. He had kicked and pushed, but the chunks of rotten wood were too large and too tightly wedged to be moved. Then he began screaming for help, but nobody came. For three days and nights he screamed and cried, now and then falling asleep, and on the fourth night, finally, thought that he heard somebody coming. He listened. Then he was sure. An approaching, slow tramping of human feet

and a crying, as though of an old woman, seemed to be coming his way. The tramping and crying came very close. Then he heard another sound, as though someone had sat down on the log. The old voice was crying in earnest. Every now and then the old person would say aloud, "Oh how tired I am, and I may have come too late! He may be dead! He may be dead! I do not hear my grandchild crying." Then there was a rap on the log and the old voice called his name: "*Ha-yah-noo! Ha-yah-noo*, are you still alive?"

Ha-yah-noo (or "Footprints under the Water," for this was the little boy's name) cried out that, yes! he was still here and alive. The old woman said, "Oh how glad I am! How glad, to find my grandchild still here and alive!" Then she asked, could he not get out? And he answered, no! that he had tried. "I'll get you out," she said, and he heard pulling at the chunks of old wood. But then again, she began crying. She was too old, she said; too tired and too old.

Now this old woman was *O-ne-ha-tah*, Grandmother Porcupine. She lived in an old hemlock tree, not far from the spot where the boy had been trapped. For three days and nights she had heard him crying. But she was so very feeble and old, it had taken her all this time to come down to help her grandchild in his trouble. Unable to help, she had however three children, all of whom (she said) were very strong. She must get them to help.

It was almost daylight when they arrived and *Ha-yah-noo* heard them pulling at the chunks. At last the old woman's voice called to him, "Come out now! My children have pulled the chunks away!" And when the little boy came crawling out of the log, there he saw four wild animals standing, Grandmother *O-ne-ha-tah* and her three children, as she called them: *Oo-kwa-e*, the Bear; *Sken-o-doh*, the Deer; and *Tah-you-ne*, the Wolf. "Now," she said to them, "I want one of you to take care of this little boy, and love him as your own child. You all know that I have become very old. If I were younger I would take care of the boy myself."

Tah-you-ne, the Wolf, was the first to speak. She declared she could take care of the boy, since she lived on the same kind of meat he ate. "No!" said the Grandmother Porcupine; "you are too greedy. You would eat the boy up as soon as he was left alone with you." The Wolf then became angry, showed her teeth and snapped them at the boy, who was frightened and wanted no such mother.

Next to speak was *Sken-no-doh*, the Deer. She said that she and her husband could take care of the boy very well. They lived on maize and other things that she knew the little boy would like. Moreover, her husband would carry him on his back, wherever the family went. But then, "No!" said the Grandmother Porcupine; "you are always traveling about. You can't take the boy. You never stay in one place. You run extremely fast and make very long journeys. The boy cannot go about like that. You would have no home for him in the winter. Little boys like to have homes." Whereupon the Deer ran away, very happy, as though glad to be rid of the boy.

Oo-kwa-e, the Bear, who was the last to speak, was sure, she said, that she could take care of the little boy; for she lived in a big stone house and had plenty to eat. She ate fish and meats, all kinds of berries and nuts, and even

wild honey, all of which she was sure the boy would enjoy. She had a good warm bed, furthermore, for him to sleep on through the winter, and was a loving mother to her children. She would rather die than see any of them harmed or abused.

On hearing all of this, Grandmother Porcupine agreed. "You are just the right one," she said to the Mother Bear. "Take the boy with you to your home."

And so it was *Oo-kwa-e*, the Bear, who took the boy and brought him, like a loving mother, to her den. When they arrived, she said to her two children, "Don't play roughly with him, and he will be your good and kind little brother." She gave him berries to eat, and they all lived together happily and well.

Her stone dwelling was a cave in the rocks, but to the little boy it seemed a great house with rooms. The little bears never teased, but lived with him in the most friendly way, and were to him as human children. It was now quite late in the fall, however; the days had become short and dark. One day the Mother Bear said, "It is now late and dark; we had all better go to bed." The nights were cold, but the bed was warm. And they slept that way until spring.

One evening it thundered. The Bears do not wake up until in the springtime thunder is heard. Thundering, it made so much noise they thought the ceiling was coming down. Then said the Mother Bear, "Why, it's getting light! We had better get up." She was gentle and kind. And they lived that way a long time together happily, she going out to and fro in the woods, wandering for food, while her children amused themselves at home. Every now and then, through the summer, Bear people would arrive and say, "In such and such a place are plenty of berries." These would be strawberries, raspberries, or others, according to the season. Later they told of chestnuts and nuts of other kinds, of which the Bear people are fond. "Let us go," the Mother Bear then would say; "let us go and gather some." Then she and her little bears would go, taking the boy along too; for they always expected a good time.

But the other bears knew nothing of the little boy and when, on coming near, they would see him, "There is a human being!" they would cry, "Let us run! Let us run!" And, scampering as fast away as bears could run, they would drop and leave behind their heaps of berries or nuts—which the old Mother Bear, she and her children, then would gather up and take home; which was an easy way to get lots of food. And so her little boy had become very useful to the Mother Bear.

The boy had lived with them for about three years, in the same way every year, when the Mother Bear one day said, "There is someone coming to kill us." They looked out and saw a man approaching through the woods with his bow and an arrow in hand. There was a dog at his side, running all around, searching for game. Said the Mother Bear, "I must see what I can do." And, taking up a forked stick, she pointed the open fork toward the hunter. It was seen by him as a line of thick brush, through which he decided not to go. So he turned aside and went another way, and for that time they were safe.

Another day, and the Mother Bear said, "There is again someone coming. This time we may all be killed." And she again held up the forked stick. But the man paid no attention. He came right on toward her stone dwelling. The stick itself split and there was nothing in his way. Then she took a bag of feathers and tossed these outside where they flew around and around, up and down, and seemed a flock of partridges. The dog chased after them, through the bushes and the trees; and so the second man went away.

The days went by, and a third time the Mother Bear saw an approaching hunter. This time she said, "We are now certainly all to be killed." And turning to the boy, she said, "Your father is now coming. He is too good a hunter to be fooled. There is his dog with his four eyes [two eyes, with a light spot above each, an especially auspicious sign]. He too is of the best of hunters."

As the man approached, she tried the forked stick, but it split, and still the hunter and his dog came on. She scattered out the feathers and they flew about as before. But the hunter and his dog paid no attention. The two continued to approach. At last the dog arrived at the entrance to her dwelling and barked. The man notched his arrow and drew his bow, to shoot anything that came out. And the Mother Bear said, "Now, my children, we must all take up our bundles and go."

So each of the little Bears took up a little bundle and laid it on his back, but there was no bundle for the boy. When all were ready, the Mother Bear said, "I'll go first, whatever may happen." She went out the door, and the moment she went out, the hunter shot and she was killed.

Then the elder of the two children said, "I'll go next." And the moment he left the cave, he too was killed.

The other little Bear was afraid, and said to the boy, "You go first." But he, also, was afraid, and said, "No, you go. I have no bundle." For the Bears try to get their bundles between themselves and the hunter. So the little Bear and boy went out, at last, together, the Bear trying to keep behind the boy, but the man shot and he was killed. Then, as the hunter prepared to shoot again, the boy called out, "Don't shoot me! I'm not a bear!"

The father let fall his arrow. He knew at once his little boy's voice, and said, "Why didn't you call out before? I wouldn't then have killed the Mother Bear and her Cubs. Those Bears, it appears, have been good to you. I greatly regret what I have done."

But the boy replied, "You did not really kill the Bears, although you thought you did. You shot only the bundles. I saw these being thrown down and the spirits of the Bears running off behind them."

Even so, the father was very sorry. He now wished that he had been kind to the Bears, as they had been kind to his boy. And he began to look at the boy more closely, to see how he had grown and changed; then noticed that between his fingers there were long hairs growing; for, having lived so long among them, he had begun to turn into a Bear.

Extremely happy, the good father took the boy with him back home, where his friends and relatives and the whole town rejoiced. All day they had a great feast, and all night they danced—and they were still dancing when I came away.[172]

Origin Legend of the Bear Songs and Dances

This is how it happened [according to a Seneca shaman] that the Bear Songs and Dances became manifest on their human side, in relation to human beings in their quest for happiness. It is the legend of a boy about two years of age kidnapped from the temporary camp of a party of hunters, the child's mother having been left with him alone in the camp, to keep the fire and to have dinner cooked when the hunters returned in the evening. While she was thus occupied, the little fellow would be playing outside the lodge.

One day the little boy was surprised to see a strange man coming toward him. "My child," the man said, "I have come for you. My children want you to play with them. You should have friends. You are alone here. You will be happy playing with my children." He took the boy's hand and away they started, into and through the forest.

On arriving at the strange man's lodge, they found there two little fellows of about the same age as the kidnapped boy, and their father said to them, "See! I have brought to you the boy you have been wanting for your friend. You must now be kind to him; never hurt, vex, or annoy him. For the time that he is with us on this visit, let everything be pleasant, and whatever happens, be kind to him."

As the family then moved about from place to place in the forest, the children played together happily, and when in the lodge the visiting boy observed carefully everything that he saw there. He saw that these people were accustomed to eating well. They lived on various kinds of nuts, on honey, and on huckleberries, mulberries, and other berries of many kinds. He saw, also, that they had plenty of maize to eat; and he learned that, of all, they

liked the chestnut best, and after the chestnut, honey, and after these, huckleberries and mulberries. It was their custom to work independently when gathering these articles of food and to collect as much as possible, in season.

When the boy had been with these people a good number of days, the head man of the lodge, who had brought him to that place, said to him, "I am going now to tell you something which you must tell to your own people when you have returned to your home. You must let them know that we want very much to find a way to give aid to them when they are afflicted by any of those sicknesses that commonly trouble mankind. We have observed that disease travels about from place to place among you, and that when it has selected its victim, that person at once realizes that he has pains in a certain part of his body. We want your people to know and to remember that we have the power, if they will call on us, to cause the evil thing to turn aside and pass on one side or other of a person, in such a way that he will not become seriously ill and will soon recover his health.

"Now look carefully at this thing that we have, and which it is our custom to use. We use it when it so happens that a hunter is approaching. The object is held up before us, and the hunter is turned away from us."

The boy, examining the object, saw in the man's hands a forked wooden rod. "This is the way I use this thing," said the man, holding the forked rod out before him and continuing: "The forks must point toward the hunter, and as he follows their direction he is bound to pass to either one side or the other of the place in which we stand. As he passes I move the rod around past my side toward the rear

288. *The Boy Cub*, 1939 water color wash, 15" × 20", by Ernest Smith. Bears are ubiquitous in mythological lore (see pp. 213-215).

209

of my position. That is how we ward away the hunter and prevent him from finding and hurting us.

"It is this thing that we shall use in giving aid to mankind in their necessities, if only they will appeal to us. And this is how this should be done. First, when the people desire to make their appeal, let them prepare a drink composed of huckleberries and mulberries, into which they are then to put maple sugar. When this has been made ready, they shall take native tobacco and, while casting it upon the fire, say, 'Oh you Bears! Do you now partake of this native tobacco, which our Creator has provided for us, and with which He intended that mankind should support their prayers to Him, no matter to what object of his creation they might wish to direct their appeals. So now, you Bears, who move from place to place in the forest, and all those with whom you are united in bonds of mutual aid, we ask you to assist us in bringing about such conditions that we may think in peace, and that those who are being called away by death may recover health and contentment of mind. The drink of berry juices, which you Bears so highly prize, has been prepared and sweetened with maple sugar, and now, some of the family of mankind are about to assume your bodily forms. In this way they will reach to you in making their appeals.'

"One then shall cast upon the fire native tobacco, while saying, 'Now be it known that the ceremony is about to begin, which is of you Bears.' The people at the ceremony shall then be exsufflated by the masters, and each shall take of the berry drink while saying, 'Oh you Bears, unto you severally I give thanks.'

"That is all that will have to be done. The duty then will devolve upon us to do all that we can to give aid to mankind.

"But when we are engaged in giving this aid, we shall not be visible to mankind. Moreover, there is something more to be told. You must take back with you the songs that we are accustomed to sing when enjoying ourselves in our dances."

The man began thereupon to sing the songs, which the boy was to learn and bring back with him. The words of the songs were such as these:

"No matter what this human being's desire may be,
by this act shall it be accomplished."
"Of those things which grow as plants of the earth,
I know all the virtues."

Such were the words of the songs which the boy heard that strange man sing.

Far back in the hunting lodge, meanwhile, of the boy's bereaved family, when the mother became aware of the fact that her child had disappeared, she hunted for him everywhere, and when the men returned that evening, they too joined in the search. They sought for him even to the banks of a river that flowed some distance from their hunting ground, even looking for tracks of the boy on both of its banks. Then, boarding canoes, they paddled up and down stream, to learn whether he had drowned. And finally, they searched the whole neighboring forest. Then the father of the child went off to hunt, and when he returned, he said to his wife, "It is perhaps proper, now, that we should prepare a 'reunion' feast; for it

289. *Thanking the Spirit of the Bear*, 1938 watercolor, 40" × 30", by Ernest Smith.

seems our child has perished." Thereupon, the mother began preparing the food, and when it was ready, placed it on the ground in the customary place for eating, and they two sat down to eat. Taking a portion of the food and setting it aside, the mother said, "As respects this food, my child does now become its owner and disposer." And with that they finished their feast of "reunion of the living."

After the lapse of some time the mother said to her husband, "Perhaps we two should now leave for our home, going back to our own people. I am not at peace in my mind here, because of what has happened." The husband consenting, they packed their small belongings and, boarding their canoe, started for home, where the news of what had happened to them quickly spread among their people. The following year, as the anniversary approached of the disappearance of their child, the mother suggested, "Is it not perhaps a good thing, that we should go back to the place where our dear child was lost, so that we again may prepare food there, as we did when he was with us?" And again the father replied, "Let it be done as you desire. I am willing to go."

And so they again started for the hunting grounds, going most of the way by canoe, and at last, on reaching the place where they had formerly encamped, they built their fire where it had been before and the father, as usual, went off to hunt. One day the mother said, "The day has come that is the anniversary of our loss. We two shall now have again a feast of the 'reunion of the living.' We shall set aside a portion for our lost child, and it shall come to pass just as if he were present with us." She set the food on the ground in the usual place, when it was ready, and the two sat down to eat. She took a portion of the food and, setting it aside, said, "This food which I have set aside, I give to my child." And when they had finished the meal they gave thanks for life and for the food that nature had supplied them.

Then the mother said, "There is nothing now to do but to return home." Her husband, in agreement, replied, "I see no reason why that, too, may not be done. My thoughts, like yours, are not pleasant in this place. Let us not remain here longer."

They prepared to leave the hunting camp and again boarded their canoe, the woman sitting in the bow and the husband in the stern, paddling. Wistfully, the woman gazed along the banks as they rapidly moved along, and when they had gone some distance her eyes were passing along the slope of a mountain rising from the riverside, covered with a dense growth of underbrush and shrubs, suddenly she started. There walking along at the edge of the dense undergrowth was her child. She stood up in the canoe, exclaiming in excitement, "There is my child! Again I see my child! Oh look! There he is, walking!"

The father also recognized the boy and, quickly turning, paddled rapidly for shore to the place where he had just been seen. As soon as the canoe touched land, both alighted and the father, running toward the child, who apparently was awaiting them, was followed by the mother at his heels. But as they approached, the boy fled into the shrubbery with his parents in pursuit. The father had some difficulty overtaking him, and when he had been caught, the mother came and, excitedly, they began asking questions. He made no reply and seemed too frightened to understand what was taking place. So the father lifted him in his arms and took him back to the canoe, where they saw that although his face, hands, and feet were still natural in appearance, the other parts of his body were covered with a fine fur, like that of a bear.

In the greatest agitation they paddled homeward, and when they had brought their little boy into their lodge, the neighbors came to visit them and their children sought to play with the boy. At first it was impossible for him either to play with them or to converse with them; indeed, it took him a long time to begin to be able to talk at all. However, gradually his speech returned, and in time he voluntarily recounted to his parents the circumstances of his disappearance. He told of the strange man who had carried him away to his home, and of all the strange things he had seen as he traveled around with those people. He told them of the food those people ate, and of how the strange man who had taken him away had instructed him in a message which was to be carried back and related in detail, by which mankind would be enabled to perform the ceremony of the Bears.

Then he taught the people all the songs of the Bears which he had learned, and the correct use of the forked rod of wood for the turning away disease, the same which the Bears themselves made use of in turning hunters away from their dens. And it was in this manner that boy made known to the Seneca the Bear ceremony and how to perform it.

Such is the legend of the origin of our Bear songs and dances.[173]

290. Seneca clown mask, pine, c. 10¼" high, c. 1850. Iroquois ceremonies were punctuated by clowns wearing unpainted masks, contrasting with the sacred False Face masks that were usually painted red and black.

As we pass, in reading the last two of these tales, from a storyteller's to a shaman's version of the adventure of a boy adopted by a family of bears, the radical contrast is immediately evident of fictional and mythic narrative. The question has been argued as to which will have been original. Did myths develop from folktales or are folktales developed from myths? Franz Boas (1858–1942), who was the leading, unquestioned authority in North American anthropological circles during the first four decades of this century, in 1916 published an article, "The Development of Folk-Tales and Myths," in which, on the basis of his own substantial studies of Native American (mainly Northwest Coast) materials, he argued "that the contents of folk-tales and myths are largely the same, that the data show a continual flow of material from mythology to folk-tale and *vice-versa*, and that neither group can claim priority.

"The formulas of myths and folk-tales," he continued, "if we disregard the particular incidents that form the substance with which the framework is filled in, are almost exclusively events that reflect the occurrences of human life, particularly those that stir the emotions of the people. If we once recognize that mythology has no claim to authority over novelistic folklore, then there is no reason why we should not be satisfied with explaining the origin of these tales as due to the play of imagination with the events of life.

"It is somewhat different with the incidents of tales and myths, with the substance that gives to the tales and myths their highly imaginative character. It is true enough that these are not directly taken from every-day experience; that they are rather contradictory to it. Revival of the dead, disappearance of wounds, magical treasures, and plentiful food obtained without labor, are not every-day occurrences, but they are every-day wishes; and is it not one of the main characteristics of the imagination that it gives reality to wishes? Others are exaggerations of our experiences; as the power of speech given to animals, the enormous size of giants, or the diminutive stature of dwarfs. Or they are materializations of the objects of fear; as the imaginative difficulties and dangers of war and the hunt, or the monsters besetting the steps of the unwary traveler. Still other elements of folk-lore represent ideas contrary to daily experience; such as the numerous stories that deal with the absence of certain features of daily life, as fire, water, etc., or those in which birth or death are brought about by unusual means. Practically all the supernatural occurrences of mythology may be interpreted by these exaggerations of imagination."[174]

Let us consider: (1) "the play of imagination with the events of human life….exaggerations of our experience": This approach to an explanation of the "supernatural occurrences of mythology" is known as *Euhemerism*, after Euhemerus, a Greek mythographer of the fourth century B.C. who, on recognizing that already some thirty years after the death of Alexander the Great this magnificent youth had become deified, concluded that the mythological gods are but deified human beings, and mythological happenings, imaginative transformations of historical events.

(2) "Imaginative occurrences giving reality to every-day wishes….or materializations of the objects of fear": Such a reductive psychological interpretation of those "highly imaginative" features of mythology which "are not directly taken from every-day experience, but are rather contradictory to it," is itself directly taken from Sigmund Freud's *The Interpretation of Dreams* (1900, English translation 1913).[175] The inadequacy of Euhemerus and Freud, however, to an interpretation of the full range of the figurations of myth is today generally recognized by serious students of this subject, in the light largely of what is now known of the phenomenology of yoga and shamanic practice. For the shaman's visionary journeys and encounters are in no sense imaginative inventions giving reality to every-day wishes and fears. They are experiences of ranges of psychological (i.e., spiritual) reality, altogether beyond knowledge of the every-day mind and imagination. Moreover, it is from those vehement experiences, not the invention of the storytellers of folktales, that knowledge of the gods derives, the torments of hell, transformative passages of purgatories, beatitude in heaven, and whatever is beyond.

It was in the early 1950s that R. Gordon Wasson's investigations of the Mexican pre-Columbian mushroom cult (in collaboration with Albert Hofmann, the Swiss chemist renowned for his discovery in 1943 of LSD) established the prominence of hallucinogens in the religious exercises of the whole Maya-Aztec culture field.[176] Aldous Huxley's *The Doors of Perception* (1954),[177] describing his own visionary experiences under the influence of mescalin, then opened the way to a popular appreciation of the ability of hallucinogens to render perceptions of a quasi, or even truly mystical profundity. In the *American Anthropologist*, 1967, J. Silverman published an inter-disciplinary article on "Shamans and Acute Schizophrenia."[178] And for the past three decades Stanislav Grof has been engaged in a master project of comparative psychedelic researches through which an exact coordination has been established and described, relating mythological, psychological, and parapsychological ranges of experience and symbolization. Mircea Eliade's masterwork on shamanism, meanwhile, *Le Chamanisme et les techniques archaïques de l'extase* (Paris, 1951; English, 1964),[179] had in one definitive volume presented an overview of the literature and world-range of the subject.

As Grof points out in his recent publication, *Beyond the Brain: Birth, Death and Transcendence in Psychotherapy*: "Most researchers studying the effects of psychedelics have come to the conclusion that these drugs can best be viewed as amplifiers or catalysts of mental processes. Instead of inducing drug-specific states, they seem to activate pre-existing matrices or potentials of the human mind. The individual who ingests them does not experience a 'toxic psychosis' essentially unrelated to how the psyche functions under normal circumstances; instead, he or she takes a fantastic inner journey into the unconscious and superconscious mind. These drugs thus reveal, and make available for direct observation, a wide range of otherwise hidden phenomena that represent intrinsic capacities of the human mind and play an important part in normal mental dynamics."[180]

"Those individuals who successfully integrate their inner journeys," Grof declares further, "become familiar with the territories of the psyche. Such individuals are also capable of transmitting this knowledge to others and of guiding them along their path. In many cultures of Asia, Australia, Polynesia, Europe, and South and North America, this has been the traditional function of the shamans (Eliade 1964). The dramatic initiation experiences of shamans that involve powerful death-rebirth sequences are interpreted by Western psychiatrists and anthropologists as indicative of mental disease. Usually referred to as 'shamanic disease,' they are discussed in relation to schizophrenia, hysteria, or epilepsy.

"This reflects the typical bias of Western mechanistic science and is clearly a culture-bound value judgment, rather than an objective scientific opinion. Cultures that acknowledge and venerate shamans do not apply the title of shaman to just any individual with bizarre and incomprehensible behavior, as Western scholars would like to believe. They distinguish very clearly between shamans and individuals who are sick or insane. Genuine shamans have had powerful, unusual experiences and have managed to integrate them in a creative and productive way. They have to be able to handle everyday reality as well as, or even better than, their fellow tribesmen. In addition, they have experiential access to other levels and realms of reality and can facilitate nonordinary states of consciousness in others for healing and transformative purposes. They thus show superior functioning and 'higher sanity,' rather than maladjustment and insanity. It is simply not true that every bizarre and incomprehensible behavior would pass for sacred among uneducated aboriginal people."[181]

In Volume I a sufficient review appears of shamanic instances to make further discussion and illustration here superfluous. Of especial interest are the instances of the Oglala Sioux Holy Man and Keeper of the Sacred Pipe, Black Elk (I.2:224–225), the three Eskimo shamans, Autdaruta, Igjugarjuk and Najagneq (I.2:166–169), and the important observations by E. Lucas Bridges and Father Martin Gusinda of two shamans of Tierra del Fuego, respectively, Houshken, shaman of the Ona, and Tenenesk, of the Yahgan (I.2:160–164, **283, 284, 438**). Other instructive accounts are Radcliffe-Brown's of the *oko-jumu*, or "Dreamers," of the Andamanese (I.1:119–121), and Spencer and Gillen's of an Australian ritual of shamanic initiation (I.2:169–170). The most extensive autobiographical accounts by shamans of their visionary journeys and transformative initiations are from Siberia (I.2:171–179). Add to these the extraordinary account of the vision experienced at the age of nine by the Oglala Holy Man, Black Elk—as rendered in John G. Neihardt's *Black Elk Speaks*[182]—and the case is made, beyond question, for a fundamental distinction between the symbolic levels of the folktale and shamanic vision.

It is notable that in the shaman's tale of the boy adopted by a family of Bears there is no mention of any mother Bear; nor are the Bears described as of animal form. A "strange man" appears, summons the boy, conducts him to his wilderness lodge, instructs him there in a sacrament of magical songs and dances, and grants him leave to return with these to the benefit of his people. The scenario corresponds, in the main, to that of Black Elk's visionary journey and shamanic revelation, which occurred, like that of the boy of the legend, when he was nine years old. The Onondaga tale is given as a legend of the origin of their Bear songs and dances. It is a tale of mythological force and, accordingly, there is attention paid throughout to religious forms and details: as related, not only to the Bear ceremonial itself, but also to the little family ritual of "reunion of the living," twice enacted in memory of their lost child by the boy's parents.

In contrast, the Seneca folktale of the lost little boy trapped in a log is a testimonial to the mothering power of Nature as represented especially in the familiar wilderness figure of a mother bear at large with her two cubs, gathering berries. The long history of mankind's veneration of this endearing yet dangerous beast is discussed and illustrated in Volume I (I.1:54–56, **94**; also I.2:147–155, **290**). Origins of the cult date demonstrably from, at latest,

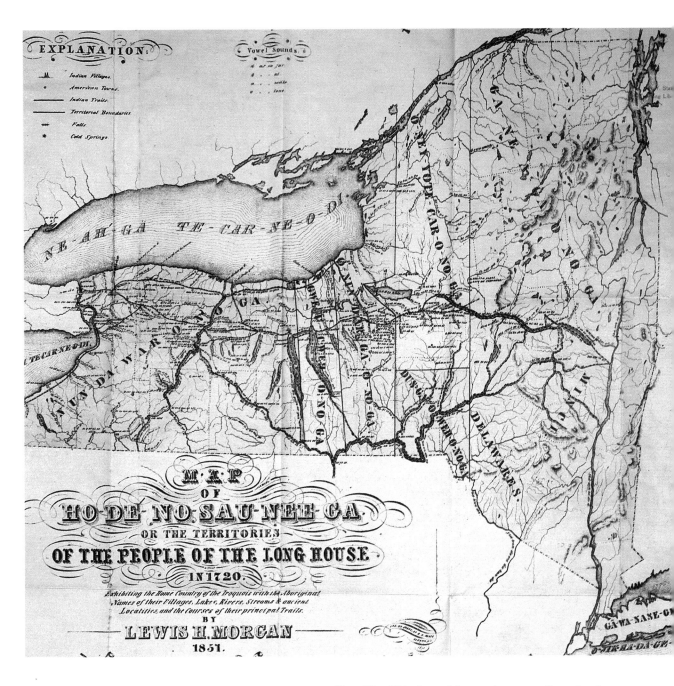

Map 20. This turn-of-the-century map (from Lewis Morgan's *The League of the Ho-de-no-sau-nee, or Iroquois*, published 1901) pictures the territorial extent of the Iroquois confederacy in 1720, before large-scale settlement by European colonists began to encroach on the League's domain.

the end of the last interglacial age (the Riss-Würm), circa possibly 200,000 years ago.

Whereas, however, the evidence discussed in Volume I demonstrates a relationship of the Bear cult only to male hunting lore and shamanic initiation rites, the associations in this Iroquois folktale are with a primeval domestic context: not as accounting for a dance ceremonial that might have been practiced already in the Paleolithic temple caves (I.1:58–66, 73–79), but as representing an order of anxieties and concerns that must have been constant to family life in the contemporary dwelling sites (I.1:66–73).

There is little in this folktale that cannot be comfortably interpreted in Euhemerist-Freudian terms, as an imaginative exaggeration of every-day wilderness experience, materializing objects of fear and giving reality to wishes. The little fellow's sojourn in the hollow log suggests a classic nightmare-image of return to the womb. The detail of three days in the log suggests an intended mythic association (compare Christ's three days and two nights in the tomb); however, the level of interest of the narrative is not mythic. The tale is not, like the shaman's version of the adventure, explained as an account of the

sense and origin of a religious ceremonial. Its function, as simply a folktale, is entertainment. The abrupt "nonsense ending"—"and they were still dancing when I came away"—is a typical, storyteller's terminal device, such as in the Brothers Grimm collection abounds, by which a tale is relieved of weight and set apart, as it were, in a frame: "And so they lived happily ever after."

The myth and the folktale, that is to say, are of two distinct literary categories, which are not to be confused; and although, as Franz Boas points out, "the data [may] show a continual flow of material from mythology to folk-tale and *vice-versa*," the levels of experience and concern of the two are distinct.

Of serious concern, therefore, must be the category and relevant authenticity of the "data" from which the anthropologist is to arrive at his judgment. And as anyone familiar with the bibliography of this field of scholarship cannot but realize, the available data are, for the most part, the so-called "myths and tales" orally col-

213

lected from available, paid or friendly "informants" by ethnologists usually ungrounded in the local language. And as noted already (I.2:262), it makes a considerable difference whether a shaman or an uninitiated but knowledgeable storyteller be the informant.

Waldemar Jochelson (1855–1937), who together with Franz Boas was a member of the Jessup North Pacific Expedition of the American Museum of Natural History in 1900–1901, reported that among the Koryak and Yukhagir of northeasternmost Siberia among whom he worked while Boas was collecting from the Kwakiutl of the Canadian Northwest Coast, the original, master guardians of the local mythologies were no more. All that could be recorded were the recollections of individuals already acculturated and, as a consequence, the gathered ethnological "data" were not of the properly "mythological" category, but "folkloristic."

"The fragmentary and disjointed character of the Koryak tales here presented," Jochelson declares in comment on his own collection, "cannot be expained [alone] by the fact that the tales about Big Raven have absorbed all other kinds of tales, but also by the fact....that the Koryak myths are in a period of decline. At present there are no more story-tellers who are ready to present the current episodes in interesting combinations, and who weld the mythological stories into long tales. The best proof of this is the fact that the art of story-telling has now passed over entirely to the women, while, until recently, the men were the best story-tellers....It may be said that the primitive form of the folklore, in which all forms of tales relate to deities and spirits, is disappearing as a consequence of contact with a higher civilization. It disappears without being transformed into folk-lore pure and simple, independent of religion, such as epic hero-tales, fables, and allegories.... Koryak folk-lore is passing away...."[183]

It was on the basis of very much the same sort of uncontrolled, secondary material, gathered from the Indian towns along the British Columbian Northwest Coast, that Jochelson's contemporary, Franz Boas, thought to argue, "that the contents of folktales and myths are largely the same, that the data show a continual flow of material from mythology to folktale and *vice versa*, and that neither group can claim priority." For in such retelling, the two originally distinct literary categories have become to such a degree undifferentiated that, unless the researcher is ready and willing to distinguish current popular from traditional esoteric lore, local fictional from archetypal mythological imagery and experience, the whole oral heritage may be classified, "scientifically," as of the same source and value, and a theory of the origins, development, and functions of mythology established

291. Bear Comb of bone, found on the now-uninhabited village of Totiactor on Dann's Farm, near the town of Lima, Livingston County, New York, and acquired by the American Museum of Natural History in 1897.

wherein the spiritual sources and implications remain unnoticed and ignored.

A broader, comparative method and interest, such as Jochelson's science represented (see, for example, his nineteen-page "List of Episodes of Koryak Tales Compared with Similar or Identical Elements of Other Mythologies"),[184] immediately discloses and distinguishes the archetypal features of a tradition. For example, in relation to the matched pair of North American versions of the adventure of a lost and recovered Bear-boy, Marija Gimbutas, in her comprehensive

survey and appraisal of the symbolic themes and motifs of the earliest known Old World Neolithic sites, refers to the prominence of the bear as a mother-figure in European traditions dating from no later than the seventh millennium B.C.

"The holiness of the bear," she writes, "an animal of great strength and majesty, the glory of the forest, is universal in the northern hemisphere. As a vegetation spirit, the male bear was sacrificed once a year to assure the renewal of life in the spring. Upper Paleolithic portrayals of bears with bleeding mouth, nose, ears, and dart marks [I.1:**133**] may be associated with the annual sacrifice of that animal. The other aspect of the bear's holiness, specifically related to the female, is her association with motherhood. Folk memories tell us that the bear was an ancestress, a mother life-giver, as were the deer and the elk-doe. [Compare in the Iroquois tale, the Deer, along with the Bear, as a candidate for foster-parent.]

"'Bear Madonnas' in the form of a woman wearing a bear mask and holding a cub are known from Vinča art of the fifth millennium B.C. Another series of terracotta figurines, protraying women with an animal mask and a pouch on their backs, may represent a mythical Bear Nurse. An articulate example is a figurine from Čuprija, central Yugoslavia, of the mid-Vinča period. Hundreds of 'hunchback' figurines have been discovered in Karanovo mounds (so far unpublished, probably because of their 'ugly' appearance). The earliest such nurses date to the seventh millennium B.C. Several figurines with pouches or shoulder straps have been discovered at Achilleion...from the end of the seventh millennium B.C."[185]

Between these Early Neolithic, Southeast European, Bear-goddess rites and mythic themes and the details of our two North American tales of the Bear-boy adventure, so many essential coincidences appear that a shared background cannot but be suspected; and indeed, in the vast extension of a Paleolithic, circumpolar Bear-cult across the northern ecumene, from Finland eastward to Greenland (I.2:147–155), such a prehistoric background is provided. In both domains—though at opposite terms of the vast Eurasian-North American culture-field—a significant shift of accent from the heroic male to the mothering female aspect of the venerated species appears with the development of agriculture and the transformation, thereby, of the spiritual environment from that of the Way of the Animal Powers to that of the Seeded Earth. The terracotta figurine from Yugoslavia, fifth millennium B.C., mentioned by Gimbutas, of a "Bear Madonna"[186] might be taken as an appropriate illustration to the Native American folktale of the Mother Bear of the Lost Boy; and in that association the full possibility of the mythological context out of which the two Iroquois variants of the tale can have been derived becomes apparent—in confirmation, namely, of the reference to the Bear-boy's three days and two nights in the log.

This is a motif that dates back to an ageless mythological archetype associated with the apparent death and resurrection of the moon. The annual hibernation of the bear, who is thought to be nourishing himself at that time on a juice drawn from his paws (I.2:147), has given him the character of an incarnation of the Year-god. By a conflation of lunar and solar death-and-resurrection motifs (such as in the Christian legend is represented in the identification of the Good Friday/Easter weekend with that of the first full moon following the vernal equinox) the lunar theme of three days and two nights dark has been applied in the Seneca tale to the ordeal of the cruelly sacrificed little boy. Also, in both of these so widely separated Neolithic traditions there is an essential association of the Bear with the giving of health.

Jochelson has described religion as pursuing two ends: "on the one hand it strives to account for the origin and organization of the world; on the other, it tends to adjust human life to the universal order. The first end is attained by the intellect, while the second is essentially based on emotions, that is on the sense of dependence of human welfare on certain powers which are at liberty to grant the necessaries of life or to withhold them, to cause evil or disease among men or to abstain from hostile acts towards him. On this feeling is based applied religion or cult. A cult presupposes a conception of powers, and...how to coerce these powers.

"In the religious conceptions of the peoples I have studied," Jochelson continues, "these powers comprise certain classes of supernatural beings. To facilitate the understanding of these powers I apply to them the terminology adopted in recent times by English anthropologists, although these terms do not always perfectly correspond to the character of one or another of the supernatural beings. The supernatural powers are:

anthropomorphic deities;
spirits in the sense of the animistic theory, that is souls or spirits which animate objects or dwell in them but may also live an independent existence;
the phenomena of animatism, that is, conceptions of inanimate objects as living beings;
spirits hostile to man.

Finally I must include in this classification," he concludes, "inanimate objects designated as fetishes. Supernatural powers can be controlled by means of incantations..., sacrifices and prayers."[187]

In manifest contrast to all this, the psychological level of the folktale as a narrative composed and orally delivered for instructive entertainment, or for simply entertainment (or specifically for publication by a visiting anthropologist), is of an order of experience and concern inherently removed from the *tremendum* of any genuine instant of religion. The contrast recognized by Lorna Marshall among the Bushmen of Botswana, between their comical, outrageously disrespectful treatment of their principal divinity as a folktale figure, Mantis, and their utter inability even to pronounce aloud the god's occult name (I.1:91–92), gives testimony to this irrefragable distinction. The properly religious dimension of their lives relates to the level of interest, not of their folktales, but of the "out of body" experiences of their trance dancing (I.1:94–99), which, as an intensively practiced "archaic technique of ecstasy" (to use Eliade's felicitous term), is a generative source of experiences demonstrably of the order of those of shamanism and yoga.

Stanislav Grof, through his years of practice of LSD-assisted therapy and research, has found it useful, as he states the case, to distinguish four major types of psychedelic experience:

1. The abstract or aesthetic experiences:
These are the most superficial, in the sense of easy availability for an average person. They have no specific symbolic content related to the personality of the subject and can be explained in terms of the anatomy and physiology of the sensory organs.

"With the eyes closed, most LSD subjects have incredibly colorful and dynamic visions of geometric designs, architectural forms, kaleidoscopic displays, magic fountains, or fantastic fireworks. Sometimes, this can take the more complex form of interiors of gigantic temples, naves of Gothic cathedrals, cupolas of monumental mosques, or decoration in Moorish palaces ('arabesques'). Colors are unusually bright and explosive, color contrasts much stronger than usual, and the world can be perceived in a way characterized by various movements in modern art, such as impressionism, cubism, surrealism, or superrealism. Sometimes inanimate objects are described as coming to life; at other times the entire world can appear geometrized and ornamentalized. Probably the most interesting perceptual phenomena in this group are optical illusions. Various ordinary elements of the environment may be seen transformed into fantastic animals, grotesque faces, or exotic sceneries. Although the changes of perception are most striking in the optical field, they can also involve hearing, touch, smell, or taste. Characteristic occurrences at this stage are synaesthesias, where external stimuli produce responses in inappropriate sensory organs; thus LSD subjects can report such extraordinary phenomena as seeing music, hearing pain, or tasting colors. The above experiences, although fascinating from the aesthetic and artistic point of view, seem to have very little relevance from the point of view of therapy, self-exploration, and personal growth."[188]

2. The psychodynamic, biographical, recollective experience:
"The next type or level of the psychedelic experience...involves complex reliving of emotionally relevant memories from various periods of the individual's life and symbolic experiences that can be deciphered as variations on, or recombinations of, biographical elements in a way quite familiar to dream images as described by psychoanalysis. The Freudian theoretical framework is extremely useful for dealing with the phenomena on this level; most of these experiences leave the Newtonian-Cartesian model [of the universe and the psyche] unchanged. This is not very surprising since Freud himself used the principles of Newtonian mechanics quite explicitly and consciously when he was formulating the conceptual framework of psychoanalysis.

"It might come as somewhat of a surprise that, on occasion, memories from the first days or weeks of life can be relived with photographic accuracy of detail. Also, memories of serious physical traumas, such as episodes of near drowning, injuries, accidents, operations, and diseases, appear to be of greater importance than those of psychological traumas emphasized by contemporary psychology and psychiatry. Such memories of physical traumas seem to be of direct relevance for the development of various emotional and psychosomatic disorders. This is true even for memories of experiences associated with operations that were conducted under general anesthesia. However, as new as some of these findings may be for medicine and psychiatry, they have little significance as indicators of the need for a major paradigm shift."[189]

3. The perinatal type of experience:
"More serious conceptual problems are associated with the third type of psychedelic experience, which I term," states Grof, "*perinatal.* Clinical observations from LSD therapy suggest that the human unconscious contains repositories or matrices, the activation of which leads to the reliving of biological birth and a profound confrontation with death. The resulting process of death and rebirth is typically associated with an opening of intrinsic spiritual areas in the human mind that are independent of the individual's racial, cultural, and educational background. This type of psychedelic experience presents important theoretical problems....

"....The symbolism that accompanies the experiences of dying and being born can be drawn from many different cultures, even if the corresponding mythological themes had not previously been known to the subject. On occasion, this involves not only the well-known symbolism for the death-rebirth process that exists in the Judaeo-Christian tradition—the humiliation and torture of Christ, death on the cross, and resurrection—but details of the Isis and Osiris legend, the myths of Dionysus, Adonis, Attis, Orpheus, Mithra, or the Nordic god Baldr, and their very little known counterparts from pre-Columbian cultures. The wealth of information involved in this process in some of the LSD subjects is truly remarkable.''[190]

4. The transpersonal experience:

"The most critical and serious challenge for the Newtonian-Cartesian model of the universe," Grof goes on then to report, "comes from the last category of psychedelic phenomena, an entire spectrum of experiences for which I have coined the term *transpersonal*. The common denominator of this rich and ramified group of unusual experiences is the individual's feeling that his or her consciousness has expanded beyond the ego boundaries and has transcended the limitations of time and space.

"Many experiences belonging to this category can be interpreted as regression in historical time and exploration of [one's] biological, cultural, or spiritual past ....vivid sequences on the cellular level of consciousness that seem to reflect existence in a previous incarnation.

"Some other transpersonal phenomena involve transcendence of spatial rather than temporal barriers. Here belong the experiences of consciousness of another person, group of persons, or all of humanity. One can even transcend the limits of a specifically human experience and tune into what appears to be the consciousness of animals, plants, or inanimate objects. In the extreme, it is possible to experience the consciousness of all creation, of the entire planet, or of the entire material universe.

"Individuals who encounter transpersonal experiences of this kind in their psychedelic sessions frequently gain access to detailed and esoteric information about the corresponding aspects of the material universe that by far exceeds their educational background and their specific knowledge of the area in question....

"Another important group of transpersonal experiences involves telepathy, psychic diagnosis, clairvoyance, clairaudience, precognition, psychometry, out-of-the-body experiences, and other paranormal phenomena....

"In many instances, transpersonal experiences in psychedelic sessions seem to be inextricably interwoven with the fabric of events in the material world. Such *dynamic interconnections between inner experiences and the phenomenal world* suggest that somehow the network involved in

the psychedelic process transcends the physical boundaries of the individual....When certain transpersonal themes emerge from the subject's unconscious during the psychedelic process, this is often associated with a highly improbable incidence of certain external events that appear to be related in a very specific and meaningful way to the inner theme. The life of such a person shows at this time a striking accumulation of most unusual coincidences; he or she might live temporarily in a world governed by synchronicity, in Carl Gustav Jung's terms, rather than simple linear causality. It has happened...that various dangerous events and circumstances started to accumulate in the lives of subjects who in their LSD sessions were approaching the experience of ego death. And, conversely, they cleared up in an almost magical way when this process was completed....

"Similarly, when a Jungian archetype is emerging into the consciousness of an LSD subject during psychedelic therapy, its basic theme can become manifest and be enacted in the individual's life. Thus at a time when the problems related to the Animus, Anima, or Terrible Mother are being confronted in the sessions, ideal representatives of these archetypal images tend to appear in the subject's everyday life. When elements of the collective, or racial, unconscious or mythological themes related to a specific culture dominate a person's LSD sessions, this can be accompanied in everyday life by a striking influx of elements related to this particular geographic or cultural area; appearance of the members of that particular ethnic group in the subject's life, unexpected letters from, or invitations to visit, the country involved, gifts of books or accumulation of the themes in question in movies or television programs shown at the time.

"Another interesting observation of this kind was made in connection with past incarnation experiences in psychedelic sessions. Some LSD subjects occasionally experience vivid and complex sequences from other cultures and other historical periods that have all the qualities of memories and are usually interpreted by the individuals themselves as a reliving of episodes from previous lifetimes. As these experiences are unfolding, LSD subjects usually identify certain persons in their present lifetime as being important protagonists in these karmic situations....

"It can be demonstrated without much effort," states Grof in evaluation of these observations, "that most of the material from LSD psychotherapy, although quite puzzling and incomprehensible from the point of view of mechanistic science, presents far less difficulty when approached in the spirit of quantum-relativistic physics, information and systems theory, cybernetics, or recent discoveries in neuro-

physiology and biology. Modern consciousness research has produced much evidence supporting the world views of the great mystical traditions. At the same time, revolutionary developments in other scientific disciplines have seriously undermined and discredited the mechanistic world view, narrowing the gap between science and mysticism that in the past seemed absolute and unbridgeable.''[191]

Whatever the relevance of these observed psychedelic experiences to the findings of modern science may be, their conformity to reports from every quarter of the globe of yogic, shamanic, and other types of mystical passage beyond the bounds of conventional sanity is remarkable. "Many LSD subjects have independently reported their insights," states Grof, "that consciousness is not a product of the central nervous system and, as such, limited to humans and higher vertebrates. They saw it as a primary characteristic of existence that cannot be further reduced to, or derived from, anything else....As LSD subjects enter the perinatal realm and confront the twin experiences of birth and death, they typically realize that the distortion and inauthenticity of their lives does not limit itself to partial segments or areas. They suddenly see their entire picture of reality and general strategy of existence as false and inauthentic. Many previous attitudes and behaviors that used to appear natural and were accepted without questioning are now perceived as irrational and absurd. It becomes clear that they are derivatives of a fear of death and remnants of the unresolved trauma of birth. In this context, a driven and hectic life pattern, haunting ambitions, competitive drives, a need to prove oneself, and the inability to enjoy are seen as unnecessary nightmares from which one can awaken. Those who complete the death-rebirth process connect with intrinsic spiritual sources and realize that a mechanistic and materialistic world view is rooted in fear of birth and death....

"The most profound and basic changes in understanding the nature of reality occur in connection with various types of transindividual experiences....Matter tends to disintegrate not only into playful energy patterns but into cosmic vacuum. Form and emptiness become relative and, ultimately, interchangeable concepts....Although for the practical purposes of daily life one still thinks in terms of solid matter, three-dimensional space, unidirectional time, and inner causality, the philosophical understanding of existence becomes much more complex and sophisticated; it approaches that found in the great mystical traditions of the world. The universe is seen as an infinite web of adventures in consciousness, and the dichotomies between the experiencer and the experienced, form and emptiness, time and timelessness, determinism and free will, or existence and nonexistence have been transcended."[192]

This indeed is the *māyā* veil: the very manner of envisioning the mystery of Being that has been approached, since time out of mind, by way of those "archaic techniques of ecstasy" of which Eliade has given us the account. It can be approached, as well, through participation in the rituals of birth-death and rebirth of any of the great or lesser religious traditions of mankind. Moreover, it is the fundament of mythology—and not to be explained away, as due to the "play of imagination with the events of human life."

* * *

In contrast, the folktale is presented typically as an individual adventure, commencing in a context of every-day experiences, but then passing into realms of mythological beings and forces, in relation to which the adventure is achieved. The folktale told for entertainment is of a kind quite apart from myth, more lightly conceived and loosely composed, so that its elements, separating, may ride away on any passing breeze, pleasantly floating from place to place, to be recomposed wherever they may fall; whereas mythologies are culture bound. Indeed, they are the structuring, enspiriting supports of the cultures to which they appertain. They do not travel unless carried intact, either in support of an expanding culture field, or as the burden of a deliberate mission. However, on losing credibility or function, or on being supplanted by another, a mythology may disintegrate, when its elements, separating out, may be taken into folktales or reshaped as literary epics and romances. The knights and ladies of Arthurian romance had been the gods and goddesses of a late Celtic, Irish and Welsh mythology;[193] and the Jinn, likewise, of the story world of Islam had been divinities of the pagan Arabs.

Folktales of an altogether different category are those narrated, not for entertainment simply, but either for instruction, especially of the young, or (like those already noticed, told of Mantis by the Bushmen) as mischievous burlesques in mockery of powers that in the local rituals and cult are held in awe. Such tales, like the mythologies out of which they are developed and to which they remain attached, are of course culture-bound. The narrative patterns and motifs, however, of which they are composed, may be readily matched from the universal treasury—even when, as in the Onondaga legend of the origin of their Bear songs and dances, the tale will have been turned to the validation of some local ceremonial or cult.

The originally Finnish, but now internationally practiced geographic-historical method of gaining control of as much as can be known of this ocean of story, having originated in Julius Krohn's method in tracing back from the *Kalevala* the diverse ways along which its constituent elements arrived in Finland, has been developed by way, largely, of the researching Monograph. The technique for the preparation of a document of this kind, has been described as follows:

"1) The scholar undertaking to write a monograph on any folk narrative (folk tale, saga, legend, anecdote), must know all the extant versions ('variants') of this narrative, whether printed or unprinted, and no matter what the language in which they appear.

"2) He must compare all these versions, carefully, trait by trait, and without any previously formed opinion.

"3) During the investigation, he must always keep in mind *the place and time of the rendering of each of the variants.*"[194]

Italics mine: for such attention to the precise location and date of each of the recordings under consideration is the systematic first principle of the Finnish geographic-historical method of folktale collection, comparison, and interpretation. By mapping the distribution of the known variants of any given tale or motif and distinguishing, then, the earlier from the later, it becomes possible (if enough versions are available) to trace the folktale or element back to its source. "The homeland of any given folk tale," states Friedrich von der Leyen in discussion of this procedure, "can generally be judged to be the region in which the richest harvest of variants appears; furthermore, where the structure of the tale is most consistent, and where customs and beliefs may serve to illuminate the meaning of the tale. The farther a folk tale wanders from its home, the greater the damage to its configurations."[195]

Another labor undertaken by associates of the Finnish school was the classification of tales according to type, where the pivotal publication is Antti Aarne's *Verzeichnis der Märchentypen*[196] as revised, translated, and brought up to date as of 1961, in *The Types of the Folktale* by the American folklorist Stith Thompson.[197]

A related publication, covering by intention the whole field of modern folktale research, collection and classification, is Stith Thompson's own, six-volume, *Motif-Index of Folk-Literature.*[198] "Outside of Europe," Thompson declares, "Aarne's index is of little use. In the remoter parts of the world, whither any adequate study must lead us, the European tale-types are applicable to very few stories. Yet there is much common matter in the folk-literature of the world. The similarities consist not so often in complete tales as in single motifs. Accordingly, if an attempt is made to reduce the traditional narrative material of the whole earth to order (as, for example, the scientists have done with the world-wide phenomena of biology) it must be by means of a classification of single motifs—those details out of which full fledged narratives are composed. It is these simple elements which can form a common basis for a systematic arrangement of the whole body of traditional literature. Only after such cataloguing will it be possible to make adequate use of the collections now existing in print and in manuscript."[199]

Viewing the Iroquois tales of the present series in terms of Aarne's European Folktale Types, we find that every one of the Native American adventures would there be classifiable, one way or another, as of *Tales of Magic.*

A number of scholars have remarked in these tales from the North American Woodland a cluster of motifs suggestive especially of Celtic themes. In the Tuscarora adventure of "A Thunderer Shot Down," for example, the arrow stuck in the ground that can be withdrawn only by its owner suggests the Arthurian sword in the stone that can be withdrawn only by King Arthur,[200] while the life-sustaining nuts from the "Chestnut Tree Guarded by Seven Sisters" suggest the Hazel Tree of the Nuts of Wisdom in the Irish legend of Finn MacCool.[201] Significantly, the food-supplying vessel of the Indian tale is neither of birchbark nor of wood, but is a (European) kettle, a variant evidently of the magical "cauldron of plenty" of the Irish sea-god Manannan mac Lir,[202] from which in his palace in the "Land under Waves," Tir fa Tonn,[203] Manannan dispenses to his guests an immortal ale.[204]

To Tir fa Tonn, the "Land under Waves," there is an immediately evident relationship to be recognized in the Seneca tale, "The Woman Who Married a Great Serpent," where it is finally revealed that the whole adventure of the marriage has taken place under water. The Irish Celtic Elysium can be represented, not only as a Land under Waves, but also as revealing itself on the earth's surface, to be entered through a mist, exactly as in this Indian tale the adventure is entered through a sudden, enveloping darkness; whereafter, on leaving, escorted by a company of Thunderers, the woman comes sloshing through the water of a recent rain. Yet another characteristically Celtic theme represented in this tale is of the animal transformation of a supernatural spouse.[205]

And so, how are we now to explain the appearance of such a cluster of Celtic motifs in a cycle of North American folktales? Might they have arisen here independently? Or shall we notice that these tales were collected in the nineteenth century, when there had already been for some three hundred years a European presence in the neighborhood, both of French and of English, Irish also, as well as Scots and Germans? Or might there have been even an earlier European presence, say from the period of the Vikings, eleventh to c. fourteenth centuries A.D.?

George Catlin, living and painting as a guest, in 1832, in a Mandan village on the Middle Missouri (near what is now Fort Clark, above Bismarck, North Dakota), was concerned to explain the shades of complexion and colors of hair of the people whose portraits he was daily committing to canvas. "There are a great many of these people," he wrote, "whose complexions appear as light as half-breeds; and amongst the women particularly, there are many whose skins are almost white, with the most pleasing symmetry and proportion of features; with hazel, with grey, and with blue eyes....The diversity in the colour of hair is also equally as great as that in the complexion; for in a numerous group of these people (and especially amongst the females, who never take pains to change its natural colour, as the men often do), there may be seen every shade and colour of hair that can be seen in our own country, with the

exception of red or auburn, which is not to be found.

"....Their traditions, so far as I have yet learned them, afford no information of their having had any knowledge of white men before the visit of Lewis and Clark, made to their village thirty-three years ago. Since that time there have been but very few visits from white men to this place, surely not enough to have changed the complexions and customs of a nation. And I recollect perfectly well that Governor Clark told me, before I started for this place, that I would find the Mandans a strange people and half white.[206]

"The Mandan canoes, which are altogether different from those of all other tribes, are exactly the Welsh *coracle*, made of *raw hides*, the skins of buffaloes, stretched underneath a frame made of willow or other boughs, and shaped nearly round, like a tub; which the woman carries on her head from her wigwam to the water's edge, and having stepped into it, stands in front, and propels it by dipping

her paddle *forward*, and *drawing it to her*, instead of paddling by the side.[207]

These observations of a competent painter's eye can be neither dismissed nor readily explained; for surely, neither "parallel development" nor "convergence" will account for the blue eyes and fair hair of a people of North American Indian race; whereas the coincidence of their knowledge and use (unique, apparently, in the New World) of a craft very like the Celtic, Welsh and Irish coracle only compounds the enigma. Catlin's own considered guess was based on reports (as he declares) "according to numerous and accredited authors," of a party of ten ships which in the fourteenth century departed from North Wales under direction of a certain Prince Madoc or Madawc, and never returned, but "according to the history and poetry of their own country, settled somewhere in the interior of North America, where they are yet remaining, intermixed with some of the savage tribes."[208]

The fourteenth century here suggested was the last of that season of Viking voyages to the New World which followed upon the discovery and settlement of Greenland in 982 and Bjarni Herjulfsson's subsequent sighting of the North American coast, when, blown off course on the way from Iceland to Greenland, he returned to tell of an unknown shore, which, in the year 1001, Leif Eriksson, together with some thirty others, set out to explore and possess—some think as far south as to Virginia.

That Iceland itself had been settled in the tenth century by Celtic Christians from the Hebrides as well as by the pagan Norse is a fact now well established.[209] So that, whatever the actual fate of the fourteenth century Madawc adventure may have been, the possibility of a Celtic contribution from an early date to the motif index of the North American Woodland folktale (as well as, perhaps, to certain local racial strains) cannot be categorically dismissed. The Mandan tribe was virtually annihilated by a smallpox epidemic five years after Catlin's visit; and since fair skin, blue eyes and blond hair leave no remains for the archaeologist, there has been no discussion in the literature of Catlin's very interesting query.

Another detail in the adventure of "The Woman Who Married a Great Serpent" giving evidence of a remote connection is that of the startling first appearance of the sorcerer-husband in his serpent form, when, sliding along the floor of the lodge, he placed his head in the woman's lap and required her to search it for vermin. I know of only one other occurrence of this type of trial (which I do not find named, by the

292. *Mint, a Pretty Girl*, 1832 portrait, 29" × 24", by George Catlin, who remarked on his amazement at this twelve-year-old's curious grey hair.

way, in the Thompson index). It appears, namely, in Eskimo mythology, as an essential shamanic feature associated with their "Old Woman," Sedna of the Sea (I.2:183–184). This old "Food Dish," as she is sometimes called, sits in her dwelling, alone beneath the earth, before a burning lamp under which there is a vessel to receive the oil continually flowing from it. And either it is from this vessel, or it is from somewhere else in the interior of her lodge, that the animals of the hunt go forth. When angry, however, she withholds them and the people starve.

The Greenland Eskimo ascribe the Old Woman's anger to a plague of filthy parasites that fasten themselves to her head and are called by a name that means "abortions" or "dead-born children." As these accumulate, she becomes resentful and withholds her herds, at which time it becomes the task of the *angakok*, the shaman, to go down to her and relieve her of her pain. It is a very difficult and perilous way to the Old Woman of the Sea: first, a passage through a region of the happy dead; then the crossing of an abyss on the flat of an ever-turning, slippery wheel; next, a boiling kettle full of ferocious seals and, on approaching the entrance to the Old Woman's place, the terrifying dogs and seals by which it is guarded. Beyond these there is the crossing of a second abyss, by way of a bridge as narrow as the edge of a knife. Other dangers are a large burning lamp, two rocks that strike together, and a pelvis bone to be passed. The task of the angakok on arrival, finally, is to free the Old Woman's head of the parasites that infest it and are the whole occasion of her anger.

It is only in the mythology of this Eskimo shamanic adventure that the rationale of the Iroquois folktale is revealed, which is, namely, that the young woman's perverse "refusal of suitors,"[210] which had removed her from service to the fundamental biological end of continuation of the race, had been no less contrary to the order of life than the practice of abortion. Only through her endurance of a shamanic type of ordeal could her offense to Nature be expiated, whereby indeed, having suffered the abyss, she sustained such a transformation of consciousness that, as a veritable shaman, she participated in the orenda even of thunder.

The motif that I have just called *Refusal of suitors* appears frequently at the opening of an American Indian tale as introductory to a supernatural adventure. By this removal of herself from the customary order of life, the young woman has forfeited the protection of the socially established rites and tasks by which adolescents normally are assisted through the dangerous pass from childhood and dependency to an assumption of the responsibilities of adult participation in the lifeways of their tribe. The ascription

of such refusal to a male, as in the Oneida tale, "The Serpent and the Thunderers," is exceptional. The resultant dangers, however, are equivalent, and the spiritual crises, the same: which follow, namely, from a release of the mind to experiences from beyond the pale of village knowledge and control. These are represented as supernatural and, in conformity to the initial refusal of a natural marriage, appear as marriage to a supernatural—which, according to the character and preparation of the young idealist, may be either to a demon, clown, or trickster, or to a god. In the analogous case of the Virgin Mary, it was to a god. In the case of the Woman Who Married a Great Serpent, to a demon—as a trial, however, in the way of initiation to an expansion of consciousness proportionate to that of the shaman.

The supernatural adventure is represented in terms of the mythology which we have already recognized as from India and Central Asia, of the unrelenting antagonism of the Sunbird (or Thunderbird) and the Serpents, Garuda and the Nagas. The folktale commences in a sphere of ordinary village life. A refusal to participate forebodes, however, a perilous adventure, whereby the life-dream is to be opened from commitment to the conditions of a local social existence to experiences initiatory to an empowering comprehension of the informing spiritual powers of the universe. The adventure proceeds in two stages. The first is of the dark and overpowering primal urges of the will in nature as typified in reptilian consciousness; and the second, when the murk of this abyssal ground will have been fathomed to the depth, an awakening beyond, to a resolution and harmonization of darkness and light, genic demiurgic bondage and spiritual flight, in the realization of a life fulfilled.

In the Seneca tale, "The Snake with Two Heads," it is a minimized folktale apparition of the mythological demiurge itself that has engaged the youngster's imagination, under a classic form known to both Chinese and American mythologies (I.2:**320, 321**). The same is represented in Mayan art in the iconographic "ceremonial bar." In the arts of Shang and Chou China, between the envisioned monster's opposed heads there appears in mid-body the mask of the "Glutton," *t'ao t'ieh*, symbolic of the generative force to which sacrifices are made; and along the Northwest American Coast the same dread visage appears between the serpent heads of the Kwakiutl demiurge Sisiutl. An account is given (I.2:199–200) of the Bella Coola (Northwest Coast) five-layered universe (two layers below the earth, two layers above), where, on the topmost level, on a windswept, treeless plain, Qamaits, the world-generating goddess dwells alone, save for a double-headed horned serpent in the saltwater pond, behind her house.

The chance discovery by a child and feeding of a little serpent that grows into a swallowing monster and eats up the whole village is a folktale motif termed by Leo Frobenius, *Schlangengrossziehen*, "Snake-nurturing," of which he has cited an example from the Melanesian island, Aurora, in the New Hebrides, along with the Seneca tale here reviewed.[211]

Of especial interest in the Seneca tale is the magic by which the monster was finally undone; namely, by arrows annointed with menstrual blood, around which had been wrapped "certain hairs from the woman's person." A fundamental mythic theme known from many parts of the world is of the lethal power of the male, solar force, when untempered by the lunar, female. In the Bella Coola cosmic image of the World-mother Qamaits, bathing in a salt-water pond inhabited by a double-headed horned serpent equivalent to the Kwakiutl demiurge Sisiutl, the water in the pond and the salt in the water correspond to Qamaits herself, respectively, and her demiurgic consort.

A consistent metaphysical thesis can be recognized as stated and restated over the whole consistent range of the mythological revelation here represented; so that wherever such a bizarre folktale told for entertainment occurs as that from New York State just reviewed, or its counterpart from Melanesia, there can be no reasonable argument as to priority, whether of the myth, or of the folktale. No mythology of which we have record can be understood as of purely local invention: local reinterpretation, yes! but not local origination. We have no knowledge, and can have none, of the ultimate beginnings of such a majestic metaphorical revelation of the structuring forms and forces of whatever is experienced as existence, as consistently appears throughout these only recently documented complexes of mythic imagery and ritual practice. A few clues are afforded, which then can be interpreted according to whatever scholarship may be in fashion at the time.

Today, for example, when the evidence of shamanic practice revealed in the Paleolithic painted caves of southern France and northern Spain, c. 14,000 B.C. (I.1:73–79), is viewed in relation to the evidences of a broad geographical dispersal of this visionary tradition, West-to-East, across Asia into America and south to Tierra del Fuego (I.2:131–133), and considered, further, in relation to the experiences of contemporary shamans and trance-dancers (I.1:90–99; also I.2:156–179, 190–191, and 224–233) as comparable to the visionary transformations of consciousness to be achieved through yoga—which have been studied in some depth, as well, through ingestion of the same hallucinogens as those used by practicing shamans (see Grof's discussion above, pages 215–217): the conclusion would seem to be warrantable, of a profound psychological break-through, from the bounds of our every-day horizon of empirical experience and judgement, to a boundless revelation of raptures transcendent of measured speech, communicable only by connotation through metaphors, which then are misread by the every-day mind as denotations of bizarre facts. And it then is these that furnish storytellers with their most fascinating folktale motifs.

In contrast, in the sixteenth and seventeenth centuries, the Jesuit missionaries to New France apparently interpreted the mythologies of their intended converts to heaven in terms of an established thirteenth-century Scholastic formulation. In Thomas Aquinas's *Summa contra gentiles,* for example, in Book I, Chapter 3, which is entitled, "In what way is it possible to make known the Divine Truth," we find the following:

"Now in those things which we hold about God there is truth in two ways. For certain things that are true about God wholly surpass the capability of human reason, for instance that God is three and one; while there are certain things to which natural reason can attain, for instance that God is, that God is one, and others like these, which even the philosophers proved demonstratively of God, being guided by the light of natural reason."

Whereafter, in Chapter 4, entitled, "That the truth about divine things which is attainable by reason is fittingly proposed to man as an object of belief," it is declared: "Accordingly, the divine clemency has made this salutary commandment, that even some things which reason is able to investigate must be held by faith: so that all may share in the knowledge of God easily, and without doubt or error. Hence it is written....[Isaiah 54:13] 'All thy children shall be taught of the Lord.'"[212]

Undoubtedly, it was a consideration of this kind that enabled the priests converting the Hurons (as related to Horatio Hale in the 1880s by Chief Mandarong and his French wife) to recognize in the native knowledge of God a revelation delivered of the Holy Spirit by the light of reason, while at the same time urging upon them in addition, the suprarational knowledge of God as a Trinity, made manifest in the historical cult of Jesus, which they had come to preach.

It may be remarked in this regard, that in contrast to this Scholastic recognition of a degree of divine inspiration in native mythologies and ceremonial, Puritan Missions know nothing of any such provision for Christian clemency, and as a consequence, whereas south of the Rio Grande, and even in the formerly Roman Catholic Southwest, Native Americans still dwell in ancestral pueblos and dance to their Kachinas, throughout the Anglo-Saxon region of the nineteenth-century

will to conquest known as "manifest destiny," not only the native gods, but the natives themselves, are now all but extinct.

To appreciate the quality of the spiritual connotations implicit in the metaphorical figures developed from this Late Paleolithic, shamanic inheritance, one has but to regard thoughtfully such a magnificent form, for example, as that of the great Shiva Maheshvara, "Shiva the Great Lord," (I.1:**5**) where the metaphorical triune form of the North Pacific Coast Sisiutl (as of two opposed horned-serpent heads with a mask between, corresponding to the Chinese *t'ao-t'ieh*, or "Glutton") is in its majestic aspect revealed as symbolic of the immanent ground of all being and becoming. As there stated in the caption: "The profile at the beholder's left is male, that at the right, female; the presence in the center is the mask of Eternity, the ever-creating *mysterium*, out of which all pairs of opposites proceed: female and male, love and war, creation and annihilation. Though beheld externally, this mystery is to be known internally as the indwelling Source and End of all that has been or is ever to be."

As Alpha and Omega, Shiva, Sisiutl, Dionysos, or whomever, may be contemplated either as creating or as consuming, either as the Uncreated Creating (to use Scotus Erigena's Neoplatonic term), or as the Uncreated Uncreating, in which latter mode the god becomes exactly the all-consuming *t-ao-t'ieh*, or "Glutton," to whom sacrifices are made, and whose threatening mask appears, appropriately, on many early Chinese sacrificial bronzes. In the Tsimshian folktale, "Raven becomes Voracious" (I.2:186), the popular North Pacific Coast Trickster, himself, becomes transformed into an uncontrollable embodiment of this mythic figment; and in the same way, in our Seneca folktale of a boy sacrificing his sister to a ravenous "snake with two heads," it is again a metaphysical symbol that has been put to use in the way of a folktale motif.

The depths of insight signified in the native mythologies of the Americas are of two degrees and two origins. The elder, which is psychologically the profounder, is of the Paleolithic, shamanic heritage, originating from the transpersonal experiences of an extraordinary class of individuals. The second is of the popular mind: and here we may recognize, with Euhemerus, Freud, and Franz Boas, the dreamwork of the every-day imagination.

Broadly viewed, the shamanic themes belong, as it were, to the world. Stemming from ranges beyond what Grof has termed, "the psychodynamic, biographical, recollective experience," opening, through the "perinatal type," fully into "the transpersonal experience," they duplicate "not only the well-known symbolism for the death-rebirth process that exists in the Judeo-Christian tradition—

the humiliation and torture of Christ, death on the cross, the resurrection—but details of the Isis and Osiris legend, the myths of Dionysus, Adonis, Attis, Orpheus, Mithra, or the Nordic god Baldr, and their very little known counterparts from pre-Columbian cultures."[213] Moreover, beyond this liminal range, in full knowledge, possession and occupation of the "transpersonal" sphere," "The most profound and basic changes in understanding the nature of reality occur. ...Matter tends to disintegrate.... into cosmic vacuum. Form and emptiness become relative and, ultimately, interchangeable concepts....the philosophical understanding of existence approaches that found in the great mystical traditions of the world."[214]

In contrast, mythic themes and motifs stemming from the popular mind are usually of a distinctly local geographical definition, though imaginatively developed according to psychological patterns described by Grof as of the "psychodynamic, biographical, recollective experience." Here, as he declares, "The Freudian theoretical framework is extremely useful." And so it is that here, and here alone, that part or aspect of mythology (as distinguished from the folktale) is to be found to which Boas's interpretation can be applied, of "imaginative occurrences giving reality to every-day wishes....or materializations of the objects of fear." Examples from the series here in discussion are to be seen in the village tale of "The Weeping of the Maize...."; "Three Stone-Coat Tales" and "Three False Face Adventures," as well as in idea of such a personified natural phenomenon as the "Thunderer, He-no." Likewise of this popular vein are the details of the family life and magic of the Bears: for example, their invention of that really marvelous forked stick by which approaching hunters could be caused to turn astray.

The remarkable ease with which a native legend of shamanic type can be turned to reflect a homologous import is well represented in the Onondaga version here presented of the legend of Hiawatha. Mythologies of the down-coming and return to heaven of an Avatar appear in practically every developed tradition of the world; and in just this way motifs derived from any one of the legends may be taken over by another.

293. Cayuga whirlwind mask, painted wood, Grand River Reservation, Ontario. Such a mask was hung in a tree facing an approaching storm, or thrown at it, to divert the tempest.

THE SOUTHEAST

From the journals of the French Huguenot Jean Ribant, upon landfall on the coast of Florida, at the mouth of the St. Johns River, April 30, 1562:

A good number of the Indians…without any token of fear or doubt [were] all naked and of a goodly stature, mighty, fair and as well shaped and proportioned of body as any in people in all the world, very gentle, courteous and of a good nature.

[The land is] the fairest, fruitfulest and pleasantest of all the world, abounding in honey, venison, wild fowl, forests, woods of all sorts, palm trees, cypress, cedars, bays, the highest, greatest and fairest vines in all the world with grapes accordingly, which naturally and without man's help and trimming grow to the top of oaks and other trees that be of a wonderful greatness and height. Fair meadows [there are]…full of sundry wild beasts, as we perceived well, both then by their passing there and also, afterward, in other places, by their cries and braying which we heard in the night-time. To be short, it is a thing unspeakable, the commodities to be seen there and shall be found [sic] more and more in this incomparable land, never as yet broken with plough-irons, bringing forth everything according to its first nature, whereof the eternal God endued [sic] it. [An] abundance of fish, as is incredible…havens, rivers and islands of such fruitfulness as cannot with tongue be expressed, and where, in short time, great and precious commodities might be found…gold, silver, pearls, turquoise…[the land] lacketh nothing.

294.

297.

298.

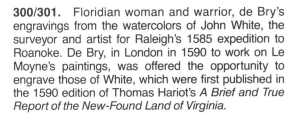

299.

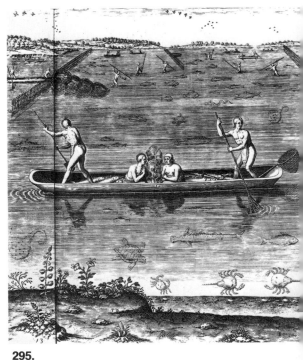

295.

294–299. From Theodore de Bry's *America* (1590), these engravings—based upon watercolors (now lost) by Jacques Le Moyne, who accompanied Jean Ribant on his first voyage to Florida—provided Europeans with their first views of the native population's daily life: how they cultivated their fields (**294**), fished (**295**), hunted deer (**296**), broiled fish (**297**), harvested crops (**298**), and transported bounty to storehouses (**299**).

300/301. Floridian woman and warrior, de Bry's engravings from the watercolors of John White, the surveyor and artist for Raleigh's 1585 expedition to Roanoke. De Bry, in London in 1590 to work on Le Moyne's paintings, was offered the opportunity to engrave those of White, which were first published in the 1590 edition of Thomas Hariot's *A Brief and True Report of the New-Found Land of Virginia.*

301.

296.

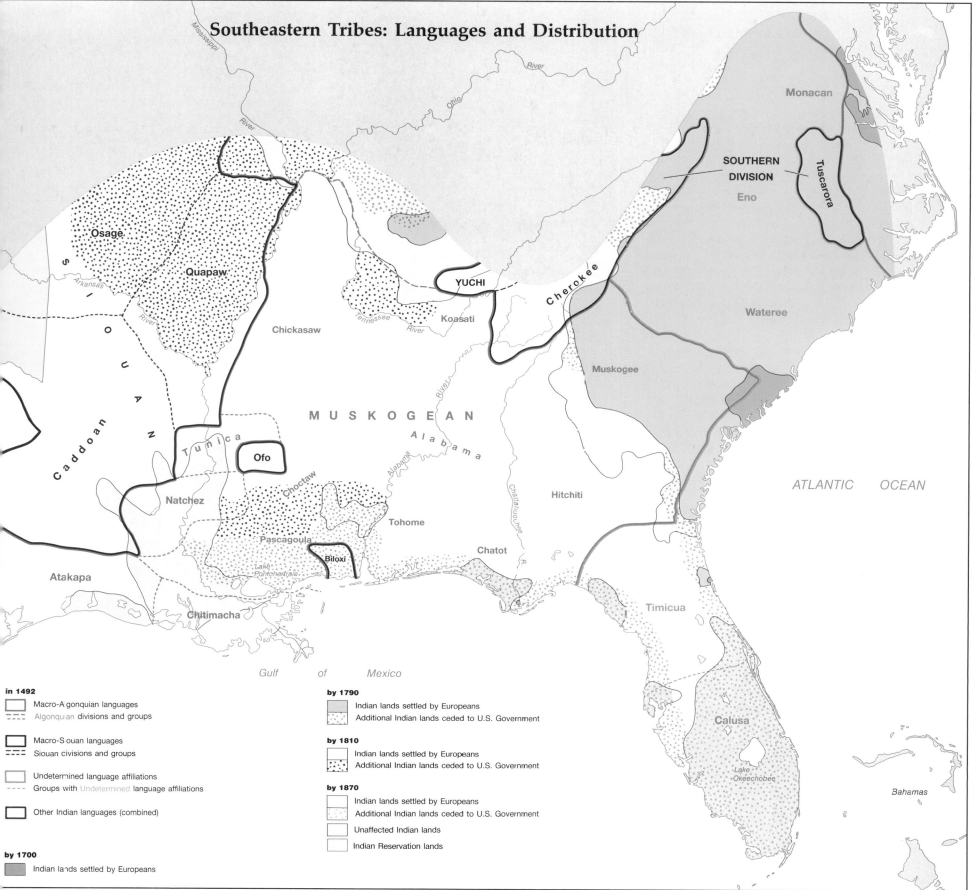

Southeastern Tribes: Languages and Distribution

Mississippi River

Ohio River

Monacan

SOUTHERN DIVISION

Eno

Tuscarora

Osage

Quapaw

YUCHI

Cherokee

Koasati

Wateree

Chickasaw

Tennessee River

S I O U A N

Arkansas River

Muskogee

C a d d o a n

Tunica

Ofo

M U S K O G E A N

Alabama

Natchez

Choctaw

Alabama River

Hitchiti

Chattahoochee River

Tohome

ATLANTIC OCEAN

Pascagoula

Chatot

Atakapa

Biloxi

Lake Pontchartrain

Chitimacha

Timicua

Gulf of Mexico

Calusa

Lake Okeechobee

Bahamas

in 1492
- ☐ Macro-Algonquian languages
- --- Algonquian divisions and groups
- ☐ Macro-Siouan languages
- --- Siouan divisions and groups
- ☐ Undetermined language affiliations
- --- Groups with Undetermined language affiliations
- ☐ Other Indian languages (combined)

by 1700
- ☐ Indian lands settled by Europeans

by 1790
- ☐ Indian lands settled by Europeans
- ☐ Additional Indian lands ceded to U.S. Government

by 1810
- ☐ Indian lands settled by Europeans
- ☐ Additional Indian lands ceded to U.S. Government

by 1870
- ☐ Indian lands settled by Europeans
- ☐ Additional Indian lands ceded to U.S. Government
- ☐ Unaffected Indian lands
- ☐ Indian Reservation lands

21.

The People of the Trail of Tears

The Removal of the Cherokee

As recounted by Private John G. Burnett, Captain Abraham McClellan's Company, 2nd Regiment, 2nd Brigade, Mounted Infantry, Cherokee Indian Removal 1838-39:

This is my birthday, December the 11th 1890. I am eighty years old today. I was born at King's Iron Works in Sullivan County, Tennessee, December the 11th, 1810. I grew into manhood fishing in Beaver Creek and roaming through the forest hunting the Deer, the wild Boar and the timber Wolf. Often spending weeks at a time in the solitary wilderness with no companions but my rifle, hunting knife, and a small hatchet that I carried in my belt in all of my wilderness wanderings.

On these long hunting trips I met and became acquainted with many of the Cherokee Indians, hunting with them by day and sleeping around their camp fires by night. I learned to speak their language, and they taught me the arts of trailing and building traps and snares. On one of my long hunts in the fall of 1829 I found a young Cherokee who had been shot by a roving band of hunters [compare I.2:**427**] and who had eluded his pursuers and concealed himself under a shelving rock. Weak from loss of blood the poor creature was unable to walk and almost famished for water. I carried him to a spring, bathed and bandaged the bullet wound, built a shelter out of bark peeled from a dead chestnut tree. Nursed and protected him, feeding him on chestnuts and roasted deer meat. When he was able to travel I accompanied him to the home of his people and remained so long that I was given up for lost. By this time I had become an expert rifleman and fairly good archer and a good trapper and spent most of my time in the forest in quest of game.

The removal of the Cherokee Indians from their life long homes in the year of 1838 found me a young man in the prime of life and a Private soldier in the American Army. Being acquainted with many of the Indians and able to fluently speak their language, I was sent as interpreter into the Smoky Mountain Country in May, 1838, and witnessed the execution of the most brutal order in the History of American Warfare. I saw the helpless Cherokees arrested and dragged from their homes, and driven at the bayonet point into the stockades. And in the chill of a drizzling rain on an October morning I saw them loaded like cattle or sheep into six hundred and forty-five wagons and started toward the west.

One can never forget the sadness and solemnity of that morning. Chief John Ross led in prayer and when the bugle sounded and the wagons started rolling many of the children rose to their feet and waved their little hands good-by to their mountain homes, knowing they were leaving them forever. Many of these helpless people did not have blankets and many of them had been driven from home barefooted.

On the morning of November the 17th we encountered a terrific sleet and snow storm with freezing temperatures and from that day until we reached the end of the fateful journey on March 26th 1839, the sufferings of the Cherokees were awful. The trail of the exiles was a trail of death. They had to sleep in the wagons and on the ground without fire. And I have known as many as twenty-two of them to die in one night of pneumonia due to ill-treatment, cold, and exposure. Among this number was the beautiful Christian wife of Chief John Ross. This noble hearted woman died a martyr to childhood, giving her only blanket for the protection of a sick child. She rode thinly clad through a blinding sleet and snow storm, developed pneumonia and died in the still hours of a bleak winter night, with her head on Lieutenant Greggs' saddle blanket.

I made the long journey to the west with the Cherokees and did all that a Private soldier could do to alleviate their sufferings. When on guard duty at night I have many times walked my beat in my blouse in order that some sick child might have my overcoat.

I was on guard duty the night Mrs. Ross died. When relieved at midnight I did not retire, but remained around the wagon out of sympathy for Chief Ross, and at daylight was detailed by Captain McClellan to assist in the burial like the other unfortunates who died on the way. Her uncoffined body was buried in a shallow grave by the roadside far from her native mountain home, and the sorrowing Cavalcade moved on.

Being a young man I mingled freely with the young women and girls. I have spent many pleasant hours with them when I was supposed to be under my blanket, and they have many times sung their mountain songs to me, this being all that they could do to repay my kindness. And with all my association with Indian girls from October 1829 to March 26th 1839, I did not meet one who was a moral prostitute. They are kind and tender-hearted and many of them are beautiful.

The only trouble that I had with anybody on the entire journey to the west was a brutal teamster by the name of Ben McDonal, who was using his whip on an old feeble Cherokee to hasten him into the wagon. The sight of that old and nearly blind creature quivering under the lashes of a bull whip was too much for me. I attempted to stop McDonal and it ended in a personal encounter. He lashed me across the face, the wire tip on his whip cutting a bad gash in my cheek. The little hatchet that I carried in my hunting days was in my belt, and McDonal was carried unconscious from the scene.

I was placed under guard, but Ensign Henry Bullock and Private Elkanah Millard had both witnessed the encounter. They gave Captain McClellan the facts and I was never brought to trial. Years later I met 2nd Lieutenant Riley and Ensign Bullock at Bristol at John Robertson's show, and Bullock jokingly reminded me that there was a case still pending against me before a court martial and wanted to know how much longer I was going to have the trial put off.

McDonal finally recovered, and in the year 1851 was running on a boat out of Memphis.

The long painful journey to the west ended March 26th, 1839, with four thousand silent graves reaching from the foothills of the Smoky Mountains to what is known as Indian territory in the West. And covetousness on the part of the white race was the cause of all that the Cherokees had to suffer.

Ever since Ferdinand De Soto made his journey through the Indian country in the year of 1540, there had been a tradition of a rich Gold mine somewhere in the Smoky Mountain Country, and I think the tradition was true. At a festival at Echata on Christmas night 1829, I danced and played with Indian girls who were wearing ornaments around their necks that looked like Gold.

In the year of 1829, a little Indian boy living on Ward creek had sold a Gold nugget to a white trader, and that nugget sealed the doom of the Cherokees. In a short time the country was over run with armed brigands claiming to be Government Agents, who paid no attention to the rights of the Indians who were the

302. *The Trail of Tears*, 1942 oil on canvas, 5'4" × 3'6", by Robert Lindneux (1871-1970), depicts a moment in the massive and tragic displacement.

legal possessors of the country. Crimes were committed that were a disgrace to civilization. Men were shot in cold blood, lands were confiscated. Homes were burned and the inhabitants driven out by these brigands.

Chief Junaluska was personally acquainted with President Andrew Jackson. Junaluska had taken five hundred of the flower of his Cherokee scouts and helped Jackson to win the battle of the Horse Shoe leaving thirty-three of them dead on the field. And in that battle Junaluska had driven his Tomahawk through the skull of a Creek warrior, when the Creek had Jackson at mercy.

Chief John Ross sent Junaluska as an envoy to plead with President Jackson for protection

for this, but Jackson's manner was cold and indifferent toward the rugged son of the forest who had saved his life. He met Junaluska, heard his plea, but curtly said "Sir your audience is ended, there is nothing I can do for you." The doom of the Cherokee was sealed, Washington D.C. had decreed that they must be driven West, and their lands given to the white man, and in May 1838 an Army of four thousand regulars, and three thousand volunteer soldiers under command of General Winfield Scott, marched into the Indian country and wrote the blackest chapter on the pages of American History.

Men working in the fields were arrested and driven to the stockades. Women were dragged

from their homes by soldiers whose language they could not understand. Children were often separated from their parents and driven into the stockades with the sky for a blanket and the earth for a pillow. And often the old and infirm were prodded with bayonets to hasten them to the stockades.

In one home death had come during the night, a little sad faced child had died and was lying on a bear skin couch and some women were preparing the little body for burial. All were arrested and driven out leaving the child in the cabin. I don't know who buried him.

In another home was a frail Mother, apparently a widow and three small children, one just a baby. When told that she must go the Mother gathered the children at her feet, prayed a humble prayer in their native tongue, patted the old family dog on the head, told the faithful creature good-bye, with a baby strapped on her back and leading a child with each hand started on her exile. But the task was too great for that frail Mother. A stroke of heart failure relieved her sufferings. She sunk and died with her baby on her back, and her other two children clinging to her hands.

Chief Junaluska who had saved President Jackson's life at the battle of Horse Shoe witnessed this scene, the tears gushing down his cheeks and lifting his cap he turned his face toward the Heavens and said "Oh my God if I had known at the battle of the Horse Shoe what I know now American History would have been differently written."

At this time, 1890, we are too near the removal of the Cherokees for our young people to fully understand the enormity of the crime that was committed against a helpless race, truth is the facts are being concealed from the young people of today. School children of today do not know that we are living on lands that were taken from a helpless race at the bayonet point to satisfy the white man's greed for gold.

Map 22.

Future generations will read and condemn the act and I do hope posterity will remember that private soldiers like myself, and like the four Cherokees who were forced by General Scott to shoot an Indian Chief and his children had to execute the orders of our superiors. We had no choice in the matter.

Twenty-five years after the removal it was my privilege to meet a large company of Cherokees in uniform of the Confederate Army under command of Colonel Thomas, they were encamped at Zollicoffer. I went to see them. Most of them were just boys at the time of the removal but they instantly recognized me as "the soldier that was good to us." Being able to talk to them in their native language I had an enjoyable day with them. From them I learned that Chief John Ross was still ruler of the nation in 1863. And I wonder if he is still living. He was a noble hearted fellow and suffered a lot for his race.

At one time he was arrested and thrown into a dirty jail in an effort to break his spirit, but he remained true to his people and led them in prayer when they started on their exile. And his Christian wife sacrificed her life for a little girl who had pneumonia. The Anglo-Saxon race should build a towering monument to perpetuate her noble act in giving her only blanket for comfort of a sick child. Incidentally the child recovered, but Mrs. Ross is sleeping in an unmarked grave far from her Smoky Mountain home.

When Scott invaded the Indian country

some of the Cherokees fled to caves and dens in the mountains and were never captured and they are there today. I have long intended going there and trying to find them but I have put off going from year to year and now I am too feeble to ride that far. The fleeting years have come and gone and old age has overtaken me, I can say that neither my rifle, nor my knife are stained with Cherokee blood.

I can truthfully say that I did my best for them when they certainly did need a friend. Twenty-five years after the removal I still lived in their Memory as "the soldier who was good to us."

However murder is murder whether committed by the villain skulking in the dark or by uniformed men stepping to the strains of martial music.

Murder is murder and somebody must answer, somebody must explain the streams of blood that flowed in the Indian country in the summer of 1838. Somebody must explain the four thousand silent graves that mark the trail of the Cherokees to their exile. I wish I could forget it all, but the picture of six hundred and forty-five wagons lumbering over the frozen ground with their Cargo of suffering humanity still lingers in my memory.

Let the Historian of a future day tell the sad story with its sighs and tears and dying groans. Let the great Judge of all the earth weigh our actions and reward us according to our work.

Thus ends my birthday story, this December 11th 1890.[215]

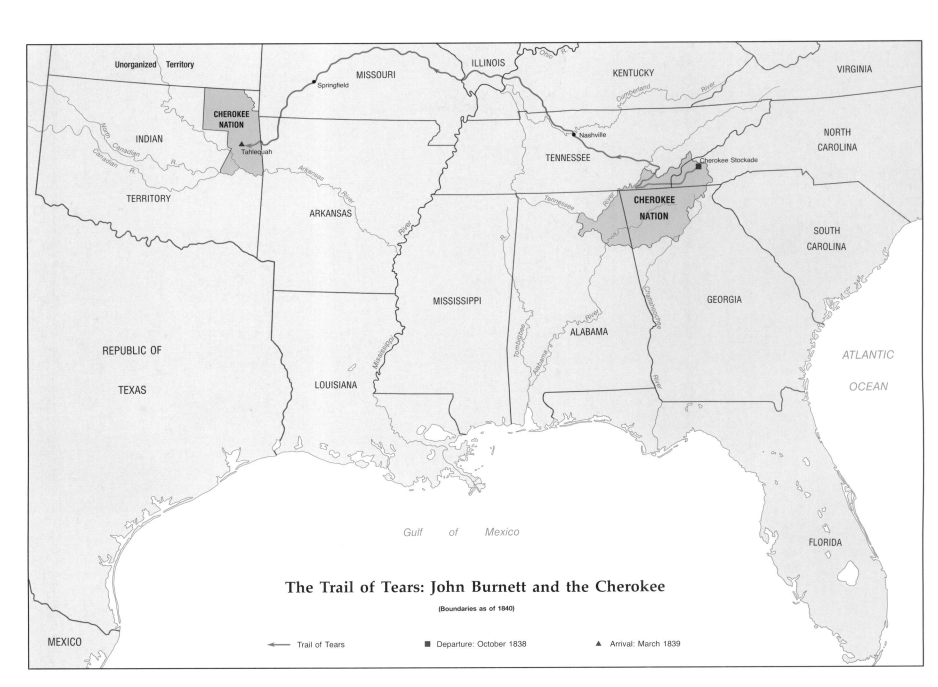

The Trail of Tears: John Burnett and the Cherokee

(Boundaries as of 1840)

← Trail of Tears   ■ Departure: October 1838   ▲ Arrival: March 1839

The Heritage of Ham

The British in 1763, following their victory in the French and Indian War (1754-1763) and acquisition thereby of hegemony over both Canada and a great part of what is now the United States, proclaimed a program for the creation of an apartheid, two-nation state, which remained in principle a model for the new nation that was brought into being two decades later. The British "Proclamation Line" was to have extended along the Appalachian divide, allowing whites to preempt whatever lay to the east, and reserving as Indian territory all that lay to the west. In the course of the following century, however, the British Line became known as the American Frontier and by something called Manifest Destiny was translated, first, to the Ohio, then, to the Mississippi, next, to the Missouri, and finally, when homesteaders, ranchers, gold-miners and the railway had broken across the Great Plains (the buffalo methodically slaughtered and all resident Native Americans reduced to reservations), on April 22nd, 1889, at noon, the last pretext to an inviolable Indian Territory was jettisoned

304. Manuscript illumination from a mid-eighteenth-century transcript of Friar Pablo Beaumont's *Cronica de Mechoacan*, showing the conversion, penances, instruction, and baptism of the Indians by the friars.

when 2,000,000 acres of protected land were thrown open by Congressional decree to the first Oklahoma "land run." Eighteen years later, and what in my first schoolboy geography had been labeled "Indian Territory" was, in 1907, admitted as the 46th state of the union. Whereupon, of course, the Promised Land of the Cherokee, Chickasaw, Choctaw, Creek, Seminole and other affected tribes of the Indian Removal Act of 1830—which by treaty was to have endured "as long as grass grows or water runs"—was simply no more. The whole cruel deception of an apartheid American continent had disappeared as by a magician's sleight of hand. Oklahoma: from the Choctaw, *okla*, "people," *humma*, "red."

The Spanish and Portuguese programs for their America, in contrast, had been of a mixed native and European population governed by European, but not exclusively European, elites. The Mediterranean races are not as averse as the Anglo-Saxon to mixed marriages. Moreover, members of their middle and working classes had failed to respond like the English to the allure of the New World, and there was consequently no pressure of land-hungry homesteaders claiming living-space and justice for themselves. Towns were mainly trading and supply centers and the colonists chiefly soldier-usurpers, adventurous traders, administrators, and the privileged recipients of royal land grants to be worked by native serfs. An important humanizing force missing in the English Puritan colo-

303. Bartolomé de Las Casas (c. 1474–1566) in his study. Both in his pastoral work and in his seminal writings (see p. 228), he worked tirelessly to end Spanish enslavement of Native Americans.

nies, furthermore, was of propertyless, unmarried priests, economically disinterested, concerned only for the spiritual welfare of the natives they had come to save — whereof the career of Bartolomé de las Casas (c. 1474–1566) provides an example.

Having in 1502 arrived in Hispaniola, ten years after Columbus, Las Casas first served as a *doctrinero* (lay teacher of the catechism), and was given an *encomienda* (an allotment of land along with its inhabiting natives).

227

305. *Fr. Bartolomé de Las Casas, Protector de Los Indios*, from "Illustracion Espanola y Americana" (1892).

Ten years later he was ordained a priest (the first ordained in the New World), and after participating, as such, in the conquest of Cuba, where again he was given an *encomienda*, in 1514 he announced in a sensational sermon his return of his serfs to the governor, and the following year sailed back to Spain to inaugurate there his lifelong campaign for the Indians and a "reformation of the *Indies*." Support for his radical *Plan para la Reformación de las Indias* having been gained from the highly influential Archbishop of Toledo (Francisco Jiménez de Cisneros, future co-regent of Spain), he was named priest-protector of the Indies, and on his second return to Spain, in 1517, with plans for the founding of "towns of free Indians" (a project that in practice failed), he was invited to plead his cause before Parliament, with the Emperor Charles V in attendance.

Las Casas joined the Dominican order in 1523, and four years later, as prior of the convent of Puerto de la Plata in northern San Domingo, began the writing of his uncompromising *Historia de las Indias*, as an exposure, eye-witnessed and detailed, of the "sins" of domination, injustice and oppression of the Spanish Conquest of America, prophetic of a punishment inevitably to fall upon Spain as a consequence of God's judgment.

In a tract, *De único modo*, composed in 1537, "Concerning the Only Way of Drawing All Peoples to the True Religion," Las Casas offered a program for the peaceful evangelization of the Indian,

306. Early engraving depicting African slaves working the fields under the watchful eye of an overseer.

which, the following year, he demonstrated by actually opening to the *padres* the formerly unconquered (and thought to be unconquerable) region of Tuzutlan, near the Golfo Dulce of southernmost present-day Costa Rica. Having composed in the native tongue a number of ballads celebrating the life and passion of the Savior, he sent native minstrels singing these through the villages and towns, until the people, of themselves, asked voluntarily for teachers and further news of this spiritual master.

In 1539, Las Casas left America on his third visit to Spain, where he was received in audience by the Emperor, who approved subsequently, and in 1542 signed, *Las Leyas Nuevas*, "The New Laws," whereby *encomiendas* were to be no longer hereditary, but the peons set free after one generation.

Ordained a bishop in 1544, Las Casas set sail from Spain with forty-four Dominicans for his see in Chiapas, Guatemala, where, instantly on arrival, he issued his *Avisos y reglas para confesores de españoles*, "Admonitions and Regulations for the Confessors of Spaniards," wherein he forbade absolution to be given to anyone holding Indians in *encomienda*. Opposition was so strong and general, however, that in 1547, at the age of seventy-three, he returned to Spain for the last time, where in his remaining years he continued and concluded the writing of his formidable *Historia de las Indias*, "so that," as he defined his aim, "if God determines to destroy Spain, it may be evident that His just reason for it is the destruction that we have wrought in the Indies." At the age of ninety-two, on July 17th, 1566, in the Dominican convent of Nuestra Señora de Atocha de Madrid, Las Casas died.[216]

He has been blamed for having recommended in his "Plan for the Reformation of the Indies" that instead of the native Indians, who throughout the Caribbean were being wiped out both by disease and by the unaccustomed toil, physically stronger and more accustomed Africans should be employed. And it was indeed in 1517, the year of his second return to Spain, that Spanish noblemen were granted the right to import to Hispaniola African slaves—which is why, today, the population of the Caribbean is not of Caribs and Arawak, but principally of Bantu.

Hardly, however, can the unspeakable horrors of the transatlantic slave trade, as it developed through the sixteenth, seventeenth, eighteenth, and early nineteenth centuries, be put upon Las Casas. Slavery in the African native states was an institution of long standing; as it was also in the Arab world. There was already in Seville an important slave market dating from the Muslim period, 711–1248, and from as early as the mid-fifteenth century, the Portuguese had been trading in black slaves imported from the Guinea coast. The principal transporters of slaves across the Atlantic, furthermore, were the English, with the French, the Dutch, and others participating, and the Portuguese reserving to themselves the monopoly to Brazil. British bottoms out of Liverpool, bearing rum, firearms, cotton goods and trinkets to the African slave-trade ports, to be bartered there for manacled human beings, carried these then to the Indies (with a calculated loss on the way of some twenty percent of the lives), to be there exchanged for molasses, which would in England be converted to rum for continuation of the trade.[217]

The first shipload of black slaves to reach

228

the colony in Virginia was brought in a Dutch ship in 1619, and within a century there were at work on American rice and tobacco plantations no less than 59,000 Africans. The invention in 1793 of the cotton gin made for such a multiplication of plantations that by the outbreak of the Civil War in 1861, when the total population of the 11 Confederate states was hardly more than 9,000,000, no less than 3,500,000 of this number were black slaves.[218]

The biblical justification for a Puritan-Christian toleration of this trade in human lives and misery was the oft-cited episode in Genesis 9:18–27, of Noah's nakedness discovered and mocked by his youngest son Ham, but then decently covered by Shem and Japheth. Whereupon the old man (who, as announced in Genesis 7:6, was at that time six hundred years old), when he "awoke from his wine and knew what his youngest son had done to him, he said, 'Cursed be Canaan; a slave of slaves shall he be to his brothers.' He also said, 'Blessed by the Lord my God be Shem [ancestor of the Semites] and let Canaan be his slave. God enlarge Japheth [ancestor of the Gentile nations] and let him dwell in the tents of Shem [i.e., accept the Semitic word of God], and let Canaan be his slave."[219]

And in the same spirit of Old Testament piety the Puritan tide rolled from the East in good conscience over the Western Indian plains, as had Joshua over Canaan, singing psalms of thanksgiving and praise to the God of Abraham, Isaac, and Jacob, even while hallowing the land with biblical names reflective of God's justification of their mission: New Canaan, Connecticut; Goshen, Connecticut; Goshen, Virginia; Goshen, New York; Goshen, Massachusetts; Goshen, New Hampshire; Goshen, Maryland; Goshen, Kentucky; Goshen, Alabama; Goshen, Ohio; Goshen, Indiana, Utah, California, and Oregon; Sharon, Connecticut; Sharon, Vermont; Sharon, Massachusetts; Sharon, Pennsylvania; Sharon, Georgia; Sharon, Tennessee; Sharon, South Carolina; Sharon, Wisconsin; Sharon, North Dakota; Sharon; Kansas; Sharon, Oklahoma; Bethel, Oklahoma; Bethel, Vermont; Bethel, Kentucky; Bethel, Maine; Bethel, North Carolina; Bethel, Ohio; Jericho, New York; Jericho, Vermont; and so on, over the whole beautiful face of America, bearing testimony to the exotic mythological foundation of our destiny.

307. *Emigrants at Kanesville, on the Missouri River,* 1937 watercolor, c. 11″ × 15″, by William Henry Jackson (1843–1942), depicting colonial settlers moving westward along the Oregon Trail in 1865.

Ponce de León, de Soto, La Salle, and John Smith

The dispossessed Indian populations of the whole territory of the Confederacy had been the inheritors, and in part direct descendants, of the Mound Builders of the Mississippian culture of c. A.D. 700–1200. Remains of the great ceremonial capital of this northern reflex of the Mesoamerican, pre-Toltec civilization of Teotihuacán ("City of the Gods," or "Where Men Become Gods") lie across the Mississippi from St. Louis. Known as Cahokia and preserved in Cahokia Mounds State Park, Illinois, its geometrical arrangement of more than one hundred pyramidal and flat-topped mounds (one of which is the largest prehistoric earthen construction in the world) covers an area of some six square miles. Comparable mounds, along with other evidences of the influence of this nuclear center, extend from Oklahoma, east to the Carolinas, Georgia and northern Florida (see I. 2:214–218, and Map 46), the grade of civilization represented being about comparable to that of the Late Neolithic and Chalcolithic Ages of Europe and the Near East, c. 7000–3500 B.C.

Among the first Europeans to enter and explore the prosperous towns and territories of this Native American culture

308. Juan Ponce de León (1460–1521).

fighting much of the way, at Mobile he and his army turned north and, on entering Tennessee, came to the Father of Waters, the broad tide of which they contrived to cross, south of Memphis, during May 1540.

Continuing on across Arkansas, in Oklahoma de Soto and his army turned back, and again coming to the Mississippi, near present Ferriday, Louisiana, taken with a fever, de Soto died, May 21st, 1542. Whereupon his men, to protect (they said) his body from the Indians, consigned it to the waters of the river. Ponce de León, in 1521, was slain near Charlotte Harbor, Florida, by an arrow.

The participation of France in this royal European chess game of claiming Asian, African, North and South American territories, and inhabitants, simply by sending an armed Christian to occupy an unchallenged square, was accomplished for the Mississippi basin by the passage down

309. Robert Cavelier de La Salle (1643–87).

310. Hernando de Soto, painting by Charles Hardman.

the length of the river in 1682 of Robert Cavelier, sieur de La Salle (1643–1687). Having received in 1666 a grant of land in "New France" (which is to say, in Canada), on the isle of Montreal, at the place now called La Salle, this imaginative young fur-trader had there set up a trading outpost which in 1669 he sold, to found an empire for his king. And indeed, on a visit to France in 1677–78, he received permission from Louis XIV to explore "the western parts of New France." A project long in his mind had been to achieve a juncture of this northerly "New France" with the rich littoral of the Gulf by way of the Mississippi, and with this work now accomplished, his next historic idea was to fortify the Delta and from there invade and appropriate as much as possible of Spanish Mexico: for which enterprise he was provided by his king with money, ships, and men. However, the expedition foundered. Shipwrecks, piracy and disease on the way from France, with quarrels carried on between La Salle and his naval commander, brought the fleet finally to port at the mouth, not of the Mississippi, but of the Brazos River in Texas, where La Salle was murdered by a mutineer, March 19th, 1687.

British claims to the region were being based, meanwhile, on the expanding interests of their colony in Virginia, which, following the mysterious disappearance of Sir Walter Raleigh's settlement in Roanoke, 1584–1590 (see I.2:220–221), had been in 1607 successfully restored in Jamestown by John Smith, of whom the famous story is told of his rescue from execution by Powhatan's own thirteen-year-old daughter Pocahontas.

And so the great stage was set for a battle-royal of three piratical European states over the American lands of tribes engaged in territorial battles of their own.

province, claiming its lands and populations for their king, were two Spaniards: the first, Juan Ponce de León (1460–1521), who, seeking the mythological Fountain of Youth, put to shore at Easter time, 1513, on the Florida coast, near the site of modern St. Augustine, naming the land of his discovery *Pascua Florida*, in honor of Christ's Resurrection; and the second then, a quarter of a century later, was Hernando de Soto (c. 1496 or 1500–1542), fresh from the conquest (with Pizarro) of the Inca empire of Peru. With an army of one thousand men, this battle-seasoned conquistador set forth May 30th, 1539, from a Florida landing south of Tampa Bay, and marching north to a native town at the site of present-day Tallahassee, settled there with his army for the winter. In the spring, continuing along the Gulf, with hard

The Natchez Solar Dynasty and Extinction

The French, controlling the Mississippian heartland and with coastal settlements at New Orleans (Louisiana), Biloxi (Mississippi), and Mobile (Alabama), early gained the confidence of their powerful Choctaw neighbors of south and middle Mississippi, by whom they were then supported in their wars, not only with the English, but also against neighboring native tribes, the first of whom to feel the weight in this way of "New France" were the Natchez.

These were a people of Muskogean linguistic stock, as were also the Choctaw and many of the other Southeastern tribes of the Mississippian heritage. At the time of their virtual extinction by the French in a brief series of three wars, 1716, 1723, and 1729, the Natchez had been an agricultural community of about 6000 (able to put between 1000 and 1200 warriors in the field), inhabiting nine villages between the Yazoo and Pearl rivers, east and south of present-day Natchez, Mississippi. From accounts of contemporary fur-traders and explorers it appears that they raised earthen mounds upon which to build their large village temples of wattles and sun-baked clay, within each of which a symbolic fire was kept burning, which once a

year, on the eve of their important midsummer festival, was let die, to be rekindled immediately at dawn—when all the village fires, which had also been allowed to go out, were relighted from this source.

A supreme chief, called the Great Sun, maintaining a household of several wives (possibly a symbolic number), was served by a voluntary retinue of hunters and other attendants who, at the time of his death, would be sacrificed along with the wives and any others who might wish to follow. Parents might also offer their children.

The little nation was stratified of four castes: (1) Suns, (2) Nobles, (3) Honored People, and (4) Commoners. Members of the upper three castes were required to marry Commoners, whereby children of women of the upper three retained the rank of their mothers, while those whose mothers were commoners fell one grade

below their fathers. Descent from the Sun was thus, by way of matrilineage, attributed to all members of the aristocratic upper stations, whereas the Commoner caste included (and may have originated with) members of alien blood who had been captured and adopted, or received as refugees from neighboring tribes.

Like the other native peoples of the Southeastern culture province, the Natchez were advanced agriculturalists, raising principally maize, beans, and squash, the classic North American triad. They were also one of a number of southeastern tribes that practiced head-flattening (which may have been regarded as an aristocratic sign of rank). Their rectangular dwellings, of sun-baked clay and wattles with arched cane roofs, stood in rows around a central ceremonial plaza. They fashioned pottery and, from the inner bark of the mulberry tree, a cloth that is described as "woven," but probably was a tapa, of which their garments were made.

The last of their calamitous wars with the French, fought in 1729, was caused by an attempt on the part of the French governor, Chopart, to appropriate the site of their principal village for a plantation. The Natchez responded with a massacre at Fort Rosalie, where the French, since the year of their first Natchez war, in 1716, had maintained a redoubt. To which the French reply, with the formidable aid of their Choctaw allies, was an onslaught of such

ferocity that the Natchez, as a nation, were annihilated. Abandoning all nine of their villages, they separated into five bodies. One small group remained as derelicts haunting the neighborhood of their proper home. A second body escaped to Sicily Island, Louisiana, where, two years later, they were attacked by the French, many of them killed, and about 450, men, women and children, captured and sold into slavery in the Indies. A third, rather large party fled as far as to South Carolina, whence they later migrated north, to settle with the Cherokee, while a fourth company came to rest in Alabama, on an affluent of the Coosa river. The largest number fled directly north and were accepted by the Chickasaw, who were another people of Muskogean speech, so closely related to their enemies, the Choctaw, that they must once have been the same tribe.[220]

311. Suicide ritual of the Natchez from Joseph Lafitau's *Moeurs des Sauvages Amériquains* (1724).

312. Mississippian mummy of a child, showing the traditional flattened forehead. Intentional deformation of the forehead was known in North America primarily among the Indians west of the Cascades, and among the Natchez and other inheritors of the Mississippian culture. This limited distribution suggests a late introduction from the south. Although there is no evidence that head-flattening affects either health or mental capacity, by the turn of the century it had fallen into disuse.

313. Full-body tattooing was also widespread among the native southeastern population, as evidenced by this detail from a de Bry engraving.

From a letter of the Jesuit Father Le Petit to Father d'Avaugour, Procurator of the Missions in North America.

New Orleans
July 12th, 1730

My Reverend Father:

The peace of Our Lord.

You cannot be ignorant of the sad event that has desolated that part of the French Colony established at *Natchez*, on the right bank of the Mississippi river, at the distance of a hundred and twenty leagues from its mouth. Two of our Missionaries who were engaged in the conversion of the Savages have been included in the almost general massacre that the barbarous Nation made of the French, at a time too when they had not the least reason to suspect their perfidy. A loss so great as this infant mission has sustained will continue for a long time to excite our deepest regrets.

This Nation of Savages inhabits one of the most beautiful and fertile countries in the world, and is the only one on this continent that appears to have any regular worship. Their Religion in certain points is very like that of the ancient Romans. They have a temple filled with Idols, which are various figures of men and animals, and for which they have a most profound veneration. Their Temple in shape resembles an earthen oven a hundred feet in circumference. They enter it by a little door about four feet high and not more than three in breadth. No window is to be seen there. The arched roof of the edifice is covered with three rows of mats, placed one upon the other, to prevent the rain from injuring the masonry. Raised above the roof are three figures of eagles made of wood and painted red, yellow, and white. Before the door is a kind of shed with folding doors, where the Guardian of the Temple is lodged. All around it runs a circle of palisades on which are seen exposed skulls of all the heads that their Warriors have brought back from their battles with the enemies of the Nation.

Inside the Temple are shelves arranged at a certain distance from each other, on which are placed cane baskets of an oval shape, and in these are enclosed the bones of their ancient Chiefs, while by their side are those of their victims, who, to follow their masters into the other world, allowed themselves to be strangled. Another separate shelf supports many flat baskets very gorgeously painted, in which they preserve their Idols. These are figures of men and women made of stone or baked clay, the heads and the tails of extraordinary serpents, some stuffed owls, some pieces of crystal, and some jaw-bones of large fish. In the year 1699 they had there a bottle and the bottom of a glass, which they regarded as very precious.

In this Temple they maintain a perpetual fire, and they are especially careful to prevent

its ever blazing. They do not use anything for it but dry wood of the walnut or oak, the old men being obliged to carry, each in his turn, a large log into the enclosure of the palisade. The number of Guardians of the Temple is fixed, and they serve by the quarter. The one on duty lives in the shed, watching to see that the fire does not go out. He keeps it fed with two or three large logs, which are not to burn except at the ends, and which they never place one upon the other, for fear of their breaking into a blaze.

Of the women, the sisters of the great Chief alone are permitted to enter the temple. Entry is forbidden to all others, as well as to the common people, even when they are bringing something for the feast in memory of their relatives whose bones repose in the Temple. This ceremony lasts for one moon. They present the dishes to the Guardian, who places them beside the basket in which the bones of the dead are preserved. Afterward, the dishes are set on the palisade surrounding the Temple and abandoned there to the fallow-deer.

The Sun is the principal object of veneration of these people. Since they cannot conceive of anything that might be beyond this heavenly body, nothing seems to them more worthy of their homage. For the same reason, their high Chief, who knows nothing on earth of greater dignity than himself, holds the title of Brother of the Sun, and the credulity of the people maintains him in the despotic authority that he claims. To enable him to converse the better with the Sun, they raise an artificial mound of earth on which to build his cabin, which is of the same construction as the Temple. The door fronts the East, and every morning the great Chief honors by his presence the rising of his elder brother, saluting him with many howlings as soon as he appears above the horizon. Then he gives orders to light his calumet and makes to him an offering of the first three puffs; afterward raising his hand above his head and, turning from the East to the West,

Sauvage en habit d'hiver.

314. *Sauvage en Habit d'Hiver,* watercolor by Alexandre de Batz, an obscure French artist, who from 1732–35 created a series of drawings of the Indians of Louisiana. This Attacapa male wears a fur cap and a robe made of buffalo-skin (complete with tail). The inside of the robe is decorated with a painted pattern. Note the mouse tucked in the man's belt.

315. De Batz watercolor of an Acolapissa temple.

316. Watercolor by De Batz of Indians brought to Louisiana by the French as allies against the Nachez: four Illinois braves (one dancing, crouched) with a woman and child, together with a seated Fox ("Renard") woman captive, a Negro boy, and a local Attacapa warrior, again wearing a mouse tucked into his belt.

232

shows him the direction which he must take that day in his course.

There are a number of beds in his cabin, at the left hand on entering; but on the right there is only the one bed of the great Chief himself, ornamented with various painted figures. This bed consists of nothing but a mattress of canes and reeds, very hard, with a square log of wood for a pillow. In the center of the cabin is to be seen a small stone, and no one may approach the bed until he has made a circuit of this stone. Those entering salute with a howl, and pass all the way to the back of the room before looking to the right, where the great Chief is sitting. Then they render another salute by raising their arms above their heads and howling thrice. If it is someone whom the Chief holds in consideration, he responds by a slight sigh, making a sign to him to be seated; who thanks him for his graciousness by emitting another howl. At every question the Chief puts to him, he howls once before answering, and on taking leave, gives forth a single howl that is prolonged till he is out of the presence.

When a great Chief dies, they demolish his cabin and raise a new mound on which to build the cabin of the one who is to replace him in this dignity; for a great Chief never lodges in the dwelling of a predecessor. The old men prescribe the Laws for the rest of the people, and one of their principles is to have a sovereign respect for the supreme Chief, as being the Brother of the Sun and Master of the Temple. They believe in the immortality of the soul, and when they leave this world they go, they say, to live in another, there to be recompensed or punished. The rewards to which they look forward consist principally in feasting, and their punishments in privations of every pleasure. Thus they think that those who have been faithful observers of their laws will be conducted into a region of delights, where all kinds of exquisite viands will be furnished them in such abundance that their delightful days will flow on in the midst of festivals, dances, and women. In short, they expect to revel in all imaginable pleasures; whereas, on the contrary, violators of their laws will be cast upon lands unfruitful and covered entirely with water, where they will have no corn of any kind, but be exposed entirely naked to the sharp bites of mosquitoes. All Nations will make war upon them, and they will never eat meat, having for nourishment only the flesh of crocodiles, rotten fish and shell-fish.

These people obey blindly the least wish of their great Chief, looking upon him as absolute master, not only of their property, but also of their lives; and not one of them would dare to refuse him his head, should he demand it. For whatever labors he demands of them, they are forbidden to exact wages. The French, who are frequently in need of hunters, or of rowers for their long voyages, never apply to anyone but the great Chief, who furnishes them with all the men they wish and receives payment without passing any part of it on to those unfortunates who are not permitted even to complain. One of the principal articles of their Religion, particularly for servants of the great Chief, is that of honoring his funeral rites by dying with him, so that they may serve him in the other world. In their blindness they submit willingly to this law in the foolish belief that in the train of their Chief they will experience the greatest happiness.

That you may have an idea of this bloody ceremony, you must know that as soon as an heir presumptive has been born to the great Chief, every family having an infant at the breast is required to pay him homage. They choose from among these infants a certain number to be destined for the service of the young Prince, and as soon as these are of a competent age, they furnish him with employments suited to their talents. Some pass their lives in hunting or in fishing, to supply his table; some in agriculture; others constitute his retinue. If he happens to die, all of these servants [who are of the same age] sacrifice themselves with joy to follow their dear master. They first put on their finery and repair to the place before the Temple, where all the people will have assembled. After having danced and sung sufficiently, they pass around their own necks a cord of buffalo hair with a running knot, and instantly the Ministers appointed for such executions come forward and strangle them, advising them to rejoin their master and render him in the other world even more honorable services than those to which they were assigned in this.

When the principal servants of the deceased great Chief have been dispatched in this way, they strip the flesh from their bones, especially those of their arms and thighs, and leave them for two months in a kind of tomb to dry, after which they are stowed in the Temple, by the side of those of their master. As for the other victims, their relatives carry the bodies home with them, and bury them.

In like manner, on the death of the brothers and sisters of a great Chief, this ceremony is observed. The attendant women are strangled unless they have infants at the breast, in which case they continue to live for the purpose of nourishing them. And we often see many who endeavor to find nurses, or who themselves strangle their infants, so as not to lose the right of sacrificing themselves in the public place, according to the usual ceremonies, as the law prescribes.

The Government is hereditary. It is not the son of the reigning Chief who succeeds his father, however, but the son of the Chief's sister, or first Princess of the blood. This policy is founded on the knowledge they have of the licentiousness of their women. They are not sure, they say, that the children of the Chief's wife may be of the blood Royal, whereas the son of the sister of the Chief must be, at least on the side of the mother. The Princesses of the blood never marry any but men of obscure family, and they have but one husband. However, they have the right of dismissing him whenever it pleases them, and of choosing another. If the husband is ever guilty of infidelity, the Princess may have his head cut off in an instant. But she is not subject to the same law; for she may have as many Lovers as she pleases, without the husband having any power to complain. In the presence of his wife he acts with the most profound respect, never eats with her, and salutes her with howls; as is done, also, by her servants. The only satisfaction he has is, that he is freed from the necessity of laboring, and has entire authority over those serving his Princess.

In former times the Nation of the *Natchez* was very large. It counted sixty Villages and eight hundred Suns or Princes. Now it is reduced to six little Villages and eleven Suns. In each Village there is a Temple where a perpetual fire is kept burning, as in that of the great Chief, whom all the Village Chiefs obey.

The great Chief nominates the most important officers of the State, which are, namely: two War Chiefs; two Masters of Ceremony, to conduct the worship of the Temple; two Officers to preside over the ceremonies observed when foreigners arrive to treat of peace; another, as Inspector of Public Works; four more, charged with arrangement of the festivals of public entertainment and to receive such Strangers as may come to visit. All of these Ministers, executing the will of the great Chief, are treated with the same respect and obedience that he himself would have received had he given the orders.

Every year the people assemble to plant a single vast field with Indian corn, beans, pumpkins, and melons; in the same way then again assembling for the harvest; there being a large cabin situated on a beautiful prairie set apart to receive and store the fruits. Every summer, toward the end of July, the people gather by order of the great Chief for a splendid feast that he provides, which lasts for three days and three nights, and to which each contributes what he can. Some bring game, others fish, and so forth. There is almost constant dancing. The great Chief and his sisters are seated in an elevated lodge covered with boughs, from which they regard the joy of their subjects, while the Princes, Princesses, and others of distinguished rank, are seated very near the Chief, to whom they show their respect and submission by no end of courteous considerations.

The great Chief and his sister enter the place of assembly on a litter borne by eight of the principal men. The Chief holds in his hand a great scepter ornamented with painted plumes, and all the people dance and sing about him in testimony of their joy. The last day of the festival he summons all together and delivers a long sermon, exhorting them to observe faithfully their duties to Religion, venerate above all things the spirits residing in the Temple, and instruct thoroughly their children. Should anyone by some act of zeal have distinguished himself, he would at that time receive public recognition and praise. Such a case occurred in the year 1702, when the Temple having been struck by lightning and reduced to ashes, seven or eight women cast their infants into the flames to appease the wrath of Heaven. These women the great Chief called heroines, extolling them for their courage in sacrificing that which they held most dear. And he concluded this panegyric by exhorting other women to imitate, under similar circumstances, so noble an example.

The family fathers bring without fail to the Temple their first fruits of corn and vegetables; and all gifts to the Nation are first offered, likewise, at the Temple Gate, whence the guardian, after having displayed and presented them to the spirits, carries them to the dwelling of the great Chief, who distributes them as he judges best, without anyone showing the least dissatisfaction.

They never plant their fields without first

le transport du Grand Soleil

Plan du Fort.

Prisonier au Cadre.

the day hunting to furnish food for those at work on the building.

The *Natchez* are permitted by their laws to have as many wives as they choose. The common people, nevertheless, have generally but one or two, which is not the case with the Chiefs. For, having the right to compel people to cultivate their fields without pay, the number of their wives is no expense to them.

Chiefs' marriages are made with little ceremony. They simply send to fetch the father of the girl they wish to espouse, and tell him that they will bestow on her the rank of their wives. They do not fail, however, as soon as the marriage is consummated, to make a present to the father and mother. Although they have many wives, they keep but one or two in their own cabins; the rest remain at the houses of their parents, where their husbands go to see them when they wish.

At certain periods of the moon these savages live separately from their wives. Jealousy has so little part in their hearts that they find no difficulty in lending their wives to their friends. This indifference to the conjugal union results from the liberty they have in changing it when it seems good to them, provided that their wives have never borne children to them, for if any have been born of the marriage, nothing but death can separate the two.

When this nation sends off a war party, its Chief sets up two sorts of pole painted red from top to bottom and ornamented with red feathers; also with arrows and tomahawks, which are likewise painted red. The poles point in the direction to which the war is to be carried. Those hoping to join the party, after ornamenting and daubing themselves with various colors, come to harangue the War

317. The Natchez leader, the Great Sun, wearing his crown of swan feathers with scarlet tassels, being carried on a litter to the new corn harvest festival.

318. A male war captive, after singing and dancing before the temple, was scalped, lashed naked to a wooden frame, and then tortured and burned. The victim was expected to continue singing his death song for as long as he lived.

presenting the seed, with accustomed ceremonies, in the Temple. On approaching a Temple, they raise their arms in respect and utter three howls, after which they deeply bow, placing their hands on the earth, and again stand erect, three times, with as many reiterated howls. On passing before a Temple, they only pause to salute it merely with downcast eyes and raised arms; but should a father or mother see a son neglect this slight ceremony, they would immediately punish him with a repeated cudgeling.

Such are the ceremonies of the *Natchez* Savages with respect to their Religion. Those of marriage are very simple. When a young man thinks of marrying, he has only to address himself to the father of the girl, or if she have none, her eldest brother, and they agree on a price, which he pays in skins and merchandise. If the girl has lived a licentious life, they make no difficulty in accepting her if there be the least idea that she would change her conduct when married. Nor do they trouble themselves as to the reputation of her family, provided that she pleases them; the only care of the girl's relatives being to inform themselves whether the youth is an able hunter, valiant warrior, and competent workman. These qualities diminish the price they have a right to ask for the marriage.

When the parties have agreed, the future husband goes off hunting with his friends, and when he has enough either of game or of fish to feast both families, they assemble at the girl's parents' house, where the newly married pair eat from the same dish and are attentively served. After eating, the bridegroom puffs the calumet, first towards his wife's parents, then toward his own; after which the guests retire. The following day, the newly married youth conducts his wife to the cabin of her father-in-law, where they live until his family has built for him a cabin of his own; during which season he passes the whole of

Marche du Calumet de Paix.

319. In ceremonial procession, warriors follow behind the bearer of the calumet of peace.

234

Chief. Their speeches, following one after another, go on for nearly half an hour each and consist of a thousand protestations of service, assuring the leader that they ask for nothing more than to die with him, are eager to learn from so great a warrior the art of taking scalps, and fear neither hunger nor the fatigues to which they are going to be exposed.

When a sufficient number of braves have presented themselves to the War Chief in this way, he has brewed for them in his cabin a beverage called the "war medicine," which is an emetic made from a root that they boil in immense kettles of water. Seated around the kettle, the warriors, sometimes as many as three hundred, are served, each with two pots of the drink; the ceremony being to swallow the two at a single draft and immediately throw up with such violent straining as to be heard at a great distance.

Following this ceremony, the War Chief appoints the day of departure, allowing time for each to prepare his own provisions for the campaign. During this period, the warriors repair morning and evening to the area before the Temple, where after dancing and relating in detail the brilliant deeds in which their bravery has already been manifest, they chant their death songs.

When on the war-path, they march in single file. Four or five of the best walkers lead the way, keeping in advance of the rest a quarter of a league, to watch out and give immediate alarm. Every evening, an hour before sunset, they encamp, lying around a large fire, each with his arms nearby. They take precaution before retiring to send out twenty warriors to a distance of half a league around the camp to assure against surprise. They do not post sentinels during the night, but as soon as they have supped, extinguish all fires.

As the War Chiefs always take with them their idols (or what they call their spirits), well secured in skin pouches, at night they suspend these from a small pole, painted red, which they erect slanting toward the enemy, and the warriors, before going to sleep, pass one after another, war club in hand, in a dance before these pretended spirits, uttering at the same time, in the enemy's direction, the fiercest threats.

The *Natchez*, like all the other Nations of Louisiana, distinguish by appropriate names those who have killed a greater or lesser number of the enemy, and the old War Chiefs bestow these titles according to merit. To deserve the name of a great man-slayer, it is necessary, either to have taken ten slaves, or to have carried off twenty scalps. Anyone understanding their language can tell from the name alone the extent of a warrior's exploits. Those who have taken a scalp for the first time or for the first time have made a captive, on their return do not sleep with their wives, or eat meat. They are to eat nothing but fish and a kind of pap. This condition lasts six months, and if they fail in its observation, they imagine that the soul of the one they have killed will by sorcery cause their own death, that they will never again overcome an enemy, and that their slightest wound will be fatal.

They take extreme care that the great Chief should not in any way expose his life when he goes to war. If, carried away by his valor, he should happen to be killed, the Chiefs and other principal warriors of the party would be put to death on their return. But executions of this kind are almost without example, for all the precautions taken to preserve him.

When one of these Savages dies, his relatives come to mourn his death for an entire day. They then array him in his finest clothes, paint his face and hair and decorate him with feathers, after which they carry him to a prepared grave, placing by his side his arms, a kettle, and provisions. For a month his relatives come at dawn of day and at the beginning of night, to weep for half an hour at his grave, his nearest relatives continuing in this observance for three months.

When a foreign Nation comes to treat of peace with the *Natchez* Savages, they send ahead couriers to give notice of the day and hour they are to arrive, and the great Chief then orders his Masters of Ceremony to prepare for the grand occasion. They commence by naming those who are to furnish food each day for the Strangers, such expense falling never on the Chief, but always on his subjects. Then they clear the roads, sweep the cabins, and arrange the seats in a large hall which is on the mound of the great Chief by the side of his cabin. His throne, which is there on a raised platform, is painted and ornamented, and the earth-floor of the hall is covered with beautiful mats.

The day the Ambassadors are to make their appearance, all the Nation assembles. The Masters of Ceremony conduct the Princes, Chiefs of the Villages, and Old Chiefs of quality, to special seats near that of the great Chief. And when the Ambassadors arrive, they stop and chant the song of peace. The ambassage consists ordinarily of thirty men, followed by six women. Six of the handsomest men, with the finest voices, march in front, followed by the rest, all chanting and marking time with the *sicicouet* [which is an Algonquian word, denoting the rattle or small drum commonly used by shamans for their incantations].

When the great Chief invites this party to approach and they advance, those bearing the calumets come chanting and dancing with marvelous agility, now circling about each other, now presenting themselves frontwise, and always with the most violent movements and extraordinary contortions. When they have entered the great Chief's circle, dancing about the chair on which he is seated, they stroke him with their calumets, from his feet even to his head, and then retire, returning to the others of their company, where they fill with tobacco one of their calumets and with one of their number holding in hand a flame, advance all together before the Chief, and, upon lighting the pipe, direct the first puff toward the Heavens, the second toward the Earth, and the rest around the horizon, after which, without further ceremony, they offer the pipe to the Prince and the other Chiefs.

This ceremony concluded, the Ambassadors in token of the alliance rub their hands over the Chief's belly and then all over their own bodies, after which they set their calumets on a small forked stick before his throne, while the one especially charged with the representation of his Nation delivers an address that lasts for about an hour. This finished, a sign is made to the visitors to be seated on benches near the great Chief, who responds

320. Before horses were introduced into the Americas by Europeans, Indians frequently captured wild game by surrounding it, as illustrated in this Du Pratz drawing.

with a discourse of about equal length; after which the Master of Ceremonies lights the great calumet of peace and offers this to the visitors. Puffing, they all swallow their smoke, and the great Chief then inquires whether all have arrived safely (which is to say, whether all are in good health), whereupon those who are seated near the Visitors, one after another, perform the same courteous office; after which they are conducted to the cabin prepared for them, where they are feasted.

At sunset the same evening, the Ambassadors, calumets in hand, go about singing, seeking the great Chief, and lifting him from his cabin to their shoulders, they carry him to their own cabin, where they spread on the ground a large skin upon which they invite him to be seated. One of them, then standing behind him, placing his hands on his shoulders, agitates his whole body, while the others, seated in a circle on the ground, chant the histories of their own most distinguished deeds.

After this ceremony, which is repeated, night and morning, for four days, the great Chief returns to his cabin, and when then he pays his last visit to the Ambassadors, these set a stake before his feet about which they seat themselves, and the Warriors of the Nation, dressed in all their finery, dance around this, each striking it in turn while recounting his exploits. There follows then a presentation of such gifts to the Ambassadors as kettles, hatchets, guns, powder, and shot.

Next day the Ambassadors are permitted to walk through the whole Village, which before had not been allowed them. And for a number of evenings they are entertained by the men and women of the Nation, dressed in their most beautiful clothes, dancing in the public plaza far into the night.

When the Visitors are ready to return home, the great Chief's Masters of Ceremony supply them with provisions for the journey.[221]

The "Five Civilized Tribes"

As the Choctaw were allied with the French, so the Chickasaw with the English. Their territories, north of the Choctaw, spread from the Mississippi eastward, through Tennessee, northern Mississippi, northern Alabama and Georgia. Their chief landing place on the river was at Chickasaw Bluffs (now Memphis), about where de Soto crossed with his army. From here a trail of more than 160 miles led to their villages, which were not, like those of their relatives, clustered, but lay scattered for miles along streams and rivers; for the Chickasaw were seminomadic, less committed to agriculture than the more sedentary Choctaw. Turbulent, restless and warlike, with a spectacular record of victories over every tribe they confronted, they were dedicated enemies of the Choctaw, as now also of their French allies, and so, would serve the English well as a buffer to the west.

An equivalent buffer to the south, against the warriors and missions of Spain, was supplied by the confederacy of the Creeks, who again were a people of Muskogean speech. Since the Creek territories included most of southern Alabama and Georgia, they had been the first north of Florida to be affected by the passage of a Spanish army. A visitor to the area in 1559, Tristan de Luna, commenting in his journal, remarked the "deplorable condition" to which the natives had been reduced in the regions penetrated by de Soto. A little over a century later, following the founding in 1670 of Charleston, South Carolina (originally Charles Towne, after Charles

323. Chickasaw Indian, 1720 copper engraving in Bernard Romans' *Concise Natural History of East & West Florida.*

II), English slavers and merchants probing southward began noticing Spanish missionaries probing northward. Military excursions followed, and before the end of the century the Spaniards had burned to the ground four considerable Creek towns, whereby the colonists acquired a confirmed ally in their slaving raids for Indian labor to supplement the Africans on their multiplying plantations.

In northern Florida and along the Georgia coast the Spanish had been founding missions similar to those in California. Their Indians, Christianized, pacified and disarmed were of the local tribes, chiefly

the once warlike Timucua (see I.2:217–220) and the Apalachee, a neighboring Muskogean people, both of whom are now extinct.

For in the year 1704 a full scale destruction of the whole Spanish mission complex was accomplished by an army of some 50 English and 1000 Creeks, whereby 6000 head of livestock were butchered, 6000 to 7000 defenseless mission Indians captured, and three Franciscan missionaries burned at the stake.

The vacated, devastated areas became only gradually repopulated during the next half century by immigrant Creeks, vestigial Apalachee, Timucua, and various other fragmented tribes, as well as by runaway slaves, both black and red, from the Carolina plantations. Principally of Creek-Muskogean linguistic stocks, these people had become known by the end of the century as Seminoles, from the Creek *Sim-a-no'-le* or *Isti-simanole*, meaning "runaway," or "separatist." (The few still inhabiting the region prefer to call themselves Ikaniuksalgi, or "Peninsula People.") And so it was, that at the time of the brutal enforcement of the removal act of 1830, by which the whole region of the future Confederacy was to be "cleared of [unenslaved] Indians," the tribes affected were chiefly five: the Seminole, Creek, Chickasaw, Choctaw, and Cherokee. With the exception of the last, the Cherokee, who were a people of Iroquoian linguistic stock, these were tribes of Muskogean speech and shared, in the main, a system of ceremonials related to that of the Natchez, derived from, and continuing into the so-called historic period, the precolumbian Mississippian heritage represented in the monuments of Cahokia.

321. *Drinks the Juice of the Stone, in Ball-Player's Dress,* 1834 painting of a Choctaw by George Catlin.

322. *Ball Play of the Choctaw—Ball Up,* 1834–35 painting by George Catlin. Similar games, with local variations, were ubiquitous in the Americas.

The Creeks, who first appeared on the world-historical stage as allies of the English in their Florida campaign of 1703–1708—which in 1704 had culminated in the extinction, not only of the Franciscan Florida missions, but also of their Apalachee and Timucua communicants—were a composite of related tribes inhabiting the greater part of Alabama and Georgia. United in a confederacy comprising the largest division of Muskogean speaking peoples in the Southeast, they were given by the Colonists the name by which they are known because of the numerous streams (creeks) in their fertile and thus desirable land. Geographically, during the colonial period, their fifty or more leading towns were grouped as Upper Creek (on the Coosa and Tallapoosa rivers in Alabama) and Lower Creek (along the middle and lower Chattahoochee, on the Alabama-Georgia border). At an early date they had sold to Great Britain their territories between the Savannah and Ogeechee rivers, all the coast to the St. John's river, and all the islands up to tidewater, reserving for themselves St. Catherine, Sapelo, and Ossabaw islands and from Pipemakers Bluff to the Savannah. Following the founding of the colony of Georgia by James Oglethorpe in 1733, expressions of friendship were ceremoniously confirmed when a company of their leaders were brought to London for an audience with King George II and Queen Caroline. And with that, of course, their doom was sealed. Settlers and traders, inspired by Oglethorpe's successful advertisement of his project, swarmed into the colony, and the inevitable retreat of the natives began, which but a century later culminated in the Removal Act of 1830.

Six distinct American languages were spoken by the members of the Creek Confederation: Muskogee (spoken by about half the tribes), Hitchiti, Koasati, Natchez, Yuchi and Shawnee. Shawnee is an Algonkian tongue; Yuchi is unclassified; and Natchez, though now recognized as Muskogean, is to such a degree idiosyncratic that in John Wesley Powell's early classification of American Indian languages it is listed as of a separate, "Natchesan" family, all its own.[222] Speakers of Hitchiti and Koasati were by the dominant Muskogee designated by a term signifying "Stinkards," and one may see in this something comparable to the Natchez designation of a "Commoner" caste, though there seems to have been no such requirement among the Creeks as that of the Nobility-Commoner marriage ruling of the Natchez. The Hitchiti, dwelling along the lower Chattahoochee river (between Georgia and Alabama, through

western Florida, to the Gulf), appear to have been the remnant of an earlier people of southeastern Georgia and themselves claimed to be of more ancient occupancy than the Muskogee, while the Koasati seem to have included members of an earlier tribe of central Alabama, the Alabimu. The designation specifically of the Hitchiti and Koasati as "Stinkards," whereas the Natchez, Yuchi, and Shawnee were not included in this judgment, may be explained by the history of a conquest, subjugation, and perhaps even enslavement of the antecedent Alabimu and Hitchiti populations of the area, while the Natchez, Yuchi, and Shawnee had been only later accepted into the fellowship, as in a sense adopted.

Like the temples of the Natchez and of the vast capital at Cahokia, those of the Creeks were set upon earthen mounds upon which stairways led to the temple door (see Figure 326). Their towns were of rectangular dwellings built of poles, wattle and mud, having pitched roofs covered with bark or thatch, and with smoke holes open at the gables. Capital towns,

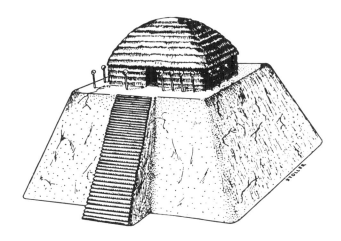

326. Lower Mississippi Valley Temple, considered to be of the Coles Creek culture, a probable archaeological antecedent to the historical Natchez and Creek.

324/325. Portraits of the two Creeks who traveled to New York in 1790 to discuss land cessions with George Washington. The sketches were made surreptitiously by John Trumbull (1750–1831), who observed that they had "a dignity of manner...worthy of a Roman senator."[3]

with large, ceremonial central squares, were of two orders: "red towns," dedicated to the cults, leadership, and ceremonies of war, and "white towns," to those of peace. Like most of the peoples of the Southeast, from the Mississippi to Florida, the Natchez to the Timucua, the Creeks, male and female, were tattooed; the members of their noble classes, over the whole body (see II.1:**45**). Such indelible decorations were insignia of social rank. The various chiefly grades were based, on the other hand, not on heredity, but on demonstrated merit, whether in war leadership, or in the acquisition of tribal wisdom and personal spiritual power.

Like all the other tribes of the Mississippian heritage, the Creeks were agriculturalists, dependent on the classic American Thanksgiving harvest of maize, beans and squash. And like agriculturalists everywhere, they ordered their lives and ceremonial calendar according to the ineluctable laws of nature, as made manifest most evidently in the order of the rhythm of the seasons.

Their principal annual event was a New Year festival known as the Busk, or "Fast" (Creek *puskita*, "a fast"), which in the lesser towns lasted four days, but in the more important centers, eight. Like the annual festival of the Iroquois, already noticed (see pages 133–138), the Busk was an occasion of general amnesty and forgiveness, no less than of harvest and thanksgiving, a season of change of mind, absolution of crime, of injury and of hatred, signalized in symbolic dances, solemn purgative and renewal rites, days and nights of fast and prayer, feasting and joy.

327. A ceremonial preparation of the "black drink," as pictured in an engraving by Theodore de Bry, after a watercolor by Jacques le Moyne.

328. *Mico Chlucco: The Long Warrior*, a Seminole in ceremonial dress, engraving by William Bartram (1739-1823), from a sculpture by J. Trenchard (b. 1747).

A description of the festival, day by day, as it was celebrated in the "white" or peace town of Kasihta, in 1789–99, is given in Benjamin Hawkins' "Sketch of the Creek country in 1798 and 99," of which the following is an abstract and discussion.

The day of the beginning of the celebration was determined by the chief, or *miko*, and his council, and the opening ceremonies took place in the great town square.

First day: In the morning the whole square was swept clean and sprinkled with white sand while the "black drink" was being prepared. So named by English traders for its color, this drink was a decoction made by boiling in water leaves of the *Ilex casseine* (the Creek name was *assi-luputski*, "small leaves"), the effects of which are described as "purgative, vomitive, and diuretic," but also, as of a "powerful agent for the production of the nervous state and disordered imagination necessary to 'spiritual' power."[223] Known also as "Carolina Tea," the caffeine-laden drink was employed by tribes of the Gulf states and adjacent regions generally as "medicine" for ceremonial purification. The leaves and shoots were gathered, dried, roasted, and stored in baskets until needed. Potions could be prepared of differing strengths for different uses, which the Indians, before drinking, agitated to make frothy. The plant was held in great esteem, and the leaves formed an article of trade.

When the town square had been put in order, a fire-maker, specially appointed, kindled by friction the New Fire, its four logs arranged symbolically crosswise to the cardinal points; after which the women of the Turkey clan performed their Turkey dance, while a very strong emetic known as *passa* was being prepared. This was drunk from about noon to the middle of the afternoon. Then came the Tadpole dance by four men and four women known as Tadpoles, after which, from evening, all night until dawn, the men performed a dance known as *hinika*. The "old men's tobacco" was also prepared this first day.

Second day: At about 10 A.M. the women performed the Gun Dance, so called for the men's firing of guns throughout its course. At noon, then, the men approached the New Fire, rubbed some of its ashes on their chins, necks, and bellies, and plunged headlong into the river. New Maize, meanwhile, was being prepared by the women for the feast, to which the men returned from the river. As they arrived in the square, before the feast began, they rubbed some of the maize between their hands, and then on the face and chest.

Third day: The men sat in the square.

Fourth day: The women, rising early, proceeded to the New Fire, from which each received a flame to kindle a similarly constructed set of logs on her own hearth, which she had previously cleaned and sprinkled with sand. A ceremony of ash-rubbing and plunging into the water was then performed by the women, after which they all tasted salt and performed the Long Dance.

Fifth day: The four logs of the original fire having lasted only four days, another four were similarly arranged and the Fire kindled as before, after which the men drank the black drink.

Sixth and seventh days: The men sat in the town square.

Eighth day: In the square and outside of it the most solemn ceremonies were conducted. A concoction supposed to have virtue as a physic, made by beating and stirring into water fourteen kinds of plant, was drunk by the men and rubbed over their joints, after priests conducting the ceremony had blown into it through small reeds. Another mixture composed of the ashes of pine boughs and old corn cobs stirred in water was prepared in a pot by four little girls, after which two large pans of a mixture of water and clay were prepared by the men. The chief and the warriors all rubbed themselves with portions from each of these mixtures, after which two men, especially appointed, brought to the chief's house flowers of the old men's tobacco, of which everybody present received a share. The chief and his counselors then walked four times around the burning logs, throwing into the fire, each time they were at the east, portions of the old men's tobacco, and each time they were at the west, pausing, facing west, before going on. After all of which, the following, concluding ceremony was performed:

At the chief's house there had been displayed for some time a cane with two white feathers at its tip. At the moment of sunset, a man of the Fish clan took this down and, followed by all present, began walking toward the river. At halfway, he uttered a death whoop, which he repeated three times more before arriving at the water's edge, where he stood while the company following congregated along the bank. Everyone present placed a grain of tobacco on his own head and into each ear, and at a signal four times pronounced, threw tobacco into the river. At a like signal, announced again four times, every man dove into the river to fetch from the bottom four stones, with which they crossed themselves on their breasts four times, throwing one stone back into the water with each crossing, uttering at each the death whoop. They all then washed themselves and, with the cane with its two feathers held aloft, returned to the square, where it was planted. Then everybody walked through the town visiting, and after nightfall came the mad dance with which the celebration ended.[224]

An appreciative comment on the Busk by the naturalist and explorer, Benjamin Franklin's friend John Bartram (1699–1777), published by his son William, illuminates the spiritual aspect of the annual fast, which in its psychological sense might be likened to an eight-day compression of Ash Wednesday, Lent, Good Friday, and then Easter. "When a town celebrates the busk," Bartram wrote, "having previously provided themselves with new clothes, new pots, pans, and other household utensils and furniture, they collect all their worn-out clothes and other despicable things, sweep and

cleanse their houses, squares, and the whole town, of their filth, which with all the remaining grain and other old provisions, they cast together into one common heap and consume it with fire. After having taken medicine, and fasted for three days, all the fire in the town is extinguished. During this fast they abstain from the gratification of every appetite and passion whatever. A general amnesty is proclaimed, all malefactors may return to their town, and they are absolved from their crimes, which are now forgotten, and they are restored to favor."[225]

As another observer, Albert Gatschet, remarks, it appears that the Busk is not a solstitial celebration, but a rejoicing over the first fruits of year. "The new year begins with the busk, which is celebrated in August or late in July. Every town celebrated its busk at a period independent from that of the other towns, whenever their crops had come to maturity. In connection with the busk the women broke to pieces all the household utensils of the previous year and replaced them with new ones, the men refitted all their property so as to look new. Indeed the new fire meant

the new life, physical and moral, which had to begin with the new year. Everything had to be new or renewed—even the garments hitherto worn. Taken altogether, the busk was one of the most remarkable ceremonial institutions of the American Indians."[226]

Known also as the "Green Corn Ceremony," the Busk, or Fast, was celebrated by the Chickasaw and Choctaw as well as by the Creek. The festival is clearly a counterpart, furthermore, of the Natchez New Fire ceremony of social and universal renewal, celebrated also in midsummer at the time of the ripening of crops. Thus shared by the entire Muskogean community of Southeastern North America and over the whole extent of the territory of the Mississippian mound builders, the festival was almost certainly an essential expression in ritualistic terms of the mythology to which the mounds of Cahokia were dedicated.

329. On the first day of the Green Corn Ceremonial (also called the Busk), a specially-appointed fire-maker lights the New Fire, its four logs having been arranged to align with the cardinal directions. Section of a diorama at the Ocmulgee site, near Macon, Georgia.

The Tuscarora and the Cherokee

The Cherokee—who were a detached tribe of the Iroquoian family inhabiting the Alleghenies from Virginia and West Virginia south, through the Carolinas and eastern Tennessee into Georgia and Alabama—also celebrated the Busk, and a question still under examination and debate is of the antiquity of their participation in this Muskogean, Mississippian tradition. The Tuscarora, who were likewise of an Iroquoian lineage, may or may not have practiced the full Fast; for what little is known of their ceremonials is fragmentary and superficial, since they had the misfortune to inhabit, not the Carolina mountains, but the fertile and desirable flatlands between the mountains and the sea. No sooner had English colonists, under a grant from Charles II issued in 1663, begun indulging their insatiable British requirement for slaves and empire than a history of depredations began which by 1710 had become intolerable.

Map 23.

Not only were village territories being turned into plantations, but men, women and, more especially their children, were being kidnapped and sold into slavery. "Blackbirding," the custom is called as it was then being practiced upon Ireland and elsewhere in the Empire, notably in Australia and the South Seas.

On June 8, 1710, a formal embassy of the Tuscarora presented to the people and government of Pennsylvania a petition for sanctuary, that they might move their whole tribe out of the infected native area and live somewhere else in peace. Two commissioners were designated by the Governor and Provincial Council of the Colony of Pennsylvania to meet this embassy in Lancaster county, at Conestoga, the ancestral town of another beaten-down Iroquoian nation. There were five Conestoga chiefs and the Shawnee high chief in attendance, along with the two commissioners, when the ambassadors of the Tuscarora delivered their proposals, which were attested by eight wampum belts that had been sent, as they declared, as an overture to ask for a cessation of hostilities until spring, when their chiefs and headmen would come in person to

sue for the peace they so much desired.

"By the first belt, the elder women and mothers besought the friendship of the Christian people, the Indians and the government of Pennsylvania, that they might fetch wood and water without risk of danger.

"By the second, the children born and those about to be born, implored for room to sport and play without the fear of death or slavery.

"By the third, the young men asked for the privilege to leave their towns without the fear of death or slavery to hunt for meat for their mothers, their children, and the aged ones.

"By the fourth, the old men, the elders and the people, asked for the consummation of a lasting peace, so that the forest (the paths to other tribes) might be as safe for them as their palisaded towns.

"By the fifth, the entire tribe asked for a firm peace.

"By the sixth, the chiefs asked for the establishment of a lasting peace with the government, people, and Indians of Pennsylvania, whereby they would be relieved of 'these fearful apprehensions that they have felt these several years.'

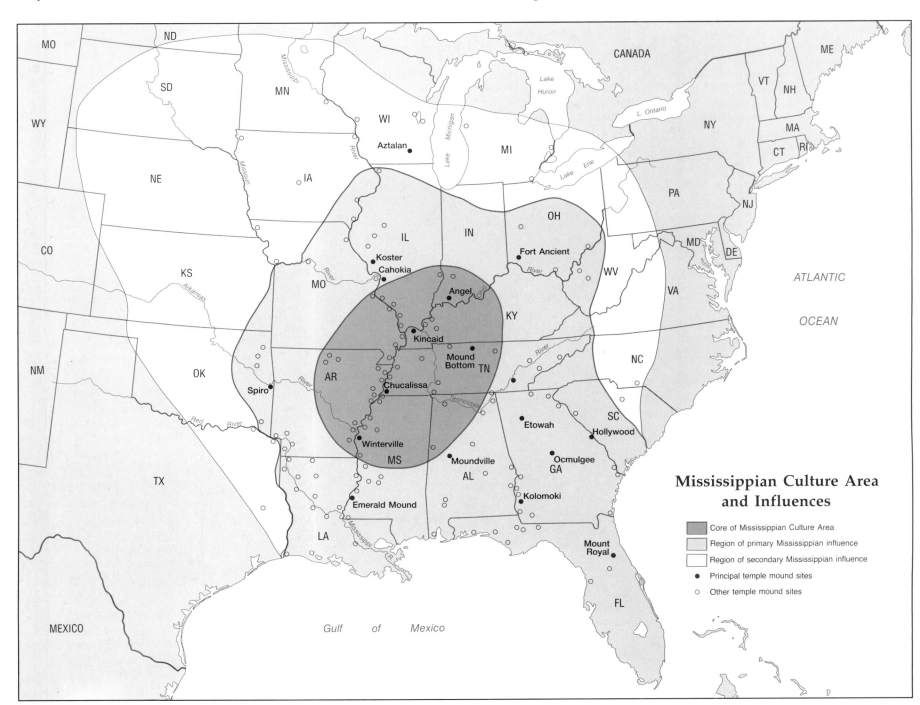

Mississippian Culture Area and Influences

- ▨ Core of Mississippian Culture Area
- ▨ Region of primary Mississippian influence
- □ Region of secondary Mississippian influence
- ● Principal temple mound sites
- ○ Other temple mound sites

"By the seventh, the Tuscarora begged for a 'cessation from murdering and taking them,' so that thereafter, they should not fear 'a mouse, or anything that ruffles the leaves.'

"By the eighth, the tribe, being strangers to the people and government of Pennsylvania, asked for an official path or communication between them."[227]

As remarked by J. N. B. Hewitt of the American Bureau of Ethnology, in comment upon this proposal of despair:

"Stripped of metaphor and the language of diplomacy, the purport of this message is plain; it was the statement of a tribe at bay, that in view of the large numbers of their people who were being kidnapped to be sold into slavery or who were being killed while seeking to defend their offspring and their friends and kindred, they desired to remove to a more just and friendly government than that whence they came. At this time there was no war between them and the white people; there had as yet been no massacre by the Tuscarora, no threat of hostility on the part of the Indians, yet to maintain peace and to avoid the impending shedding of blood, they were even then willing to forsake their homes."[228]

The commissioners of Pennsylvania informed the delegates that "to confirm the sincerity of their past carriage toward the English, and to raise in us a good opinion of them, it would be very necessary to procure a certificate from the government they leave, to this, of their good behaviour, and then they might be assured of a favorable reception." And so that was that.

The Conestoga chiefs stated, on the other hand and in contrast, that by the advice of their council it had been determined to send these belts, brought by the Tuscarora, to the council of the Five Nations; and it was the reception of these belts with their messages which, four years later, moved the leaders of the People of the Longhouse to receive and give harbor to the Tuscarora as the Sixth Nation of their League.

For meanwhile, on September 22nd, 1711, the inevitable had occurred, namely, along the Pamlico and Trent rivers, where formerly there had stood Tuscarora towns, a party of Tuscarora massacred some 130 of the colonists. A Colonel Barnwell was immediately sent from South Carolina to aid the hard pressed North Carolinians and there had followed an extremely ugly three-year war, which had involved, among other obscenities, an episode of rank cannibalism enacted, not by Tuscaroras, but the allies of the South Carolinian Colonel. The year of the termination of this brutal affair, in 1713, there appeared in the *Boston News Letter* an advertisement offering for purchase Indians captured by Colonel Barnwell in the war's execution. By that time refugees of the tribe were appearing in the Iroquois areas of New

The Three Cherokees, came over from the head of the River Savanna to London 1762. (*Their Interpreter that was Poisoned.*)

York, and on September 10th, 1713, a chief of the Onondaga tribe, in conference with commissioners of Governor Hunter of the colony, is reported to have pleaded in the following terms for this tribe's permission to receive and give harbor to these people:

"Brother Corlaer tells us the Queen's subjects toward the South are now at war with the Tuscarora Indians. These Indians went out heretofore from us, and have settled themselves there; now they have got into war and are dispersed....They have abandoned their castles and are scattered hither and thither; let that suffice; and we request our brother Corlaer to act as mediator between the English of Carolina and the Tuskaroras, that they may no longer be hunted down, and we assure that we will oblige them not to do the English any more harm, for they are no longer a Nation with a name, being once dispersed."[229]

In their own day, when first encountered by Europeans, the Tuscarora had been dwelling mainly along the Roanoke, Neuse, Taw and Pamlico rivers of North Carolina, inhabiting some fifteen to twenty-four large towns, and able to field (as variously estimated) some 1200 to 6000 warriors. Three tribes had constituted the nation. Their name, from the Iroquoian *skaru'ren*, "hemp gatherers," referred to their gathering and use of Indian hemp (*Apocynum cannabinum*), both for fiber and for "medicine." They were competent agriculturalists, raising maize, beans, and squash, and their festivals—when several towns or villages united to celebrate some event, or when two or more tribes assem-

330. British-Cherokee relations having been strained by Indian reprisals against lawless frontiersmen, these three Cherckee chiefs, accompanied by an interpreter, visited London in 1792 as goodwill ambassadors.

bled to negotiate a peace—were celebrated with dances and with feasts prepared under direction of the women chiefs. According to an early observer, Jno. Lawson, Surveyor-General of North Carolina (who in 1711, at the outbreak of the war, was captured by the Tuscarora and painfully executed), each dance had its peculiar song "made new for every feast; nor is one and the same song sung at two several festivals. Some one of the nation, which has the best gift of expressing their designs," he explained, "is appointed by their king and war captains to make these songs." To these festivals, he declared further, people come from the towns within fifty or sixty miles, "where they buy and sell several commodities."[230]

Another observer, De Graffenried (who was captured with Lawson and tried, but by the tribal council acquitted) has left an account of their trial.

In the open area of the town square a large fire had been kindled. An old "shaman or high priest" was designing on the ground two white rings of sand or flour. In front of himself and Lawson a wolf skin was laid on the ground, and a short way beyond that a warrior stood in threatening posture, holding in one hand a knife and in the other a tomahawk. He was apparently the executioner, and did not move from the spot.

On the farther side of the fire a circle of men, women, and children danced with

241

grotesque and frightful attitudes and contortions, while in the center of their circle two singers sat, intoning a dismal song, "rather more fit," De Graffenried thought, "to provoke tears and anger than joy." Within the circle of the dance the shaman was uttering threats and adjurations against the enemies of his people, performing his exorcisms against their "medicine" (orenda); when at times there would come in the dancing a pause, and then, suddenly, with shouts and howls, the dancers scattered into the neighboring forest, returning shortly with their faces painted black, white, and red in bands, hair loose and flying, bodies oiled and sprinkled with down from the cattail flag and with small white feathers. Some were arrayed in all kinds of furs. And the dance was immediately resumed.

Behind the two prisoners a double line of armed warriors stood, who held their posts until all was over; and back of them, seated on the ground, was the council of war, in a circle, deliberating gravely the fate of their two noted captives; the decision, finally disclosed, being that De Graffenried should be released, but that Lawson, who had engaged in a bitter argument with one of the high chiefs, should be dealt with as that chieftain wished.

The manner of Lawson's execution, as learned from Indian sources, appears in a letter from a certain Major Christopher Gale wherein it is reported that his captors stuck the unfortunate man "full of fine small splinters of torchwood, like hog's bristles, and so set them gradually on fire"[231] — which was an execution of the same sacrificial tradition, apparently, as that observed in the year 1637 by three Jesuit Fathers among the Hurons of Canadian Quebec (II.1:39–43).

A judgment of the character of the Tuscaroras in comparison with that of the North Carolinian Christians, appears in the words of unfortunate Surveyor-General Lawson himself. In his view, they possessed many amiable qualities; in fact, they were "really better to us than we to them, as they always freely give to us of their victuals at their quarters, while we let them walk by our doors hungry, and do not often relieve them. We look upon them with disdain and scorn, and think them little better than beasts in human form; while with all our religion and education, we possess more moral deformities and vices than these people do."[232]

* * *

A people of the same racial lineage, but very much more fortunately situated than the brutalized Tuscarora, were the Cherokee in their mountain region, which no one wanted for plantations or for anything but hunting, until gold was discovered in the early 1830s and serious agitation immediately began to "clear the Indians out." Their name, from the Choctaw, chiluk-ki, "cave people," is a reference to the great and numerous caves in their country. How long they had resided there, no one has yet determined. Indeed, inasmuch as they are of Iroquoian stock, no one, as yet, even knows from what part of the continent their ancestors derived. There have been theories placing the origin of the Iroquois in the north, in the south, from the distant west, and now, most recently, in New York state itself, or as they say, in situ, which, in spite of the very distinguished names associated with this suggestion, can be reasonably regarded only as an elaborate way of saying, we don't know; since there is demonstrably no group of people anywhere on earth that can be said to have originated in situ, whereas all have indeed acquired in situ their locally adapted habits and characteristics, even to some extent their physical forms (see II.1:19).

In the words of William A. Ritchie, a leading protagonist of this sophisticated argument: "as a mechanism to account for the northeastern position of the Iroquois people and their culture, migration fails in demonstrating any route north, south, or west, over which archeology can convincingly trace a prior or developmental movement."[233] Accordingly, the Iroquois cultures would have derived, in his view, from "already recognized archeological assemblages within the Northeast."[234] Which may be all very well as regards the material culture; but what of the people?

Gordon R. Willey, from another perspective, has suggested that "the burial mound tradition was brought into the East, from the South, by peoples of Hokan-Siouan affiliation, possibly the Iroquoians."[235] In which statement there is a vast correlation implied of North American cultural connections, based not on the evidences of archeology (which, as Ritchie has conceded, tell us nothing to this point), but on linguistic affiliation; specifically, between languages of the Hokan phylum (of California, Baja California, Northwest Mexico, Arizona, Nevada and Colorado), and those of the Macro-Siouan families, both of which are of Plains tribes, the Iroquoian of the Northeast, Catawba of the Carolinas, and Yuchi of the southern Appalachian mountains (see Map 18).

During the years just preceding the American Revolution, Benjamin Franklin's friend, the botanist John Bartram (whose comments on the Muskogean Busk are quoted on page 239), riding horseback on a research adventure in the Appalachian hills about the headwaters of the Savannah and Little Tennessee rivers, observed and commented on the remains of the early Cherokee towns that he had gone up there to investigate. What he found—as summarized by Joffre L. Coe in a paper published in 1961 on "Cherokee Archeology"—was an "association of town houses and mound substructures in nearly every town."[236] For example, at the headwaters of the Savannah river, where an old native settlement known as Keowee once had stood, what Bartram found, as he wrote of them, were "the feeble remains of the once potent and renowned Cherokees: the vestiges of the ancient Indian dwellings yet visible on the feet of the hills bordering and fronting the vale, such as posts or pillars of their habitations. There are several Indian mounts or tumuli, and terraces."[237] Farther on, he came upon the ruins of the "ancient famous town of Sticoe. Here was a vast Indian mount or tumulus and great terrace, on which stood the council-house, with banks encompassing their circus; here were also Peach and Plum orchards; some of the trees appeared yet thriving and fruitful."[238] Still farther along, at Whatoga, he found "the council-house, which was a very large dome or rotunda, situated on the top of an ancient artificial mount."[239] And at what had once been the "capital town of Cowe," there was the town house standing "on the top of an ancient artificial mount of earth, of about twenty feet perpendicular."[240]

Bartram's considered conclusion, based in part on his finding that the "Cherokees themselves are as ignorant as we are, by what people or for what purpose these artificial hills were raised," was that the Cherokee had "found them in much the same condition as they now appear, when their forefathers arrived from the West."[241] Which statement may well have been the source of the popular belief (which I recall having shared in my boyhood) that the mound-builders were of an earlier time and race than the Indians. Coe points out that in scholarship, Bartram's statement has been taken as prima facie evidence for the facts that: (1) Cherokees did not build temple mounds, and (2) Cherokees only recently settled in the area; both of which propositions, he holds, are "untenable in light of present knowledge."[242]

William Webb, in 1938, had concluded that the circular town houses built on earthmounds which he examined in eastern Tennessee had been built by earlier Creeks.[243] Likewise, T. M. N. Lewis and Madeline Kneberg, at sites in Tennessee on the Hiwassee and Tennessee rivers, identified the mound-building period with the Creeks and concluded that the Cherokee had arrived in that area only long after white contact.[244] Willey's determination on linguistic grounds suggests, on the contrary, that the Iroquoian peoples originally shared with the Muskogean the heritage of the Mississippian civilization, and that they must have arrived in their historical territories as carriers of its legacy: which was of advanced maize, beans, and squash agriculture; palisaded villages and towns, the latter with large central plazas for the enactment of ceremonials;

artificial mounds upon which to erect temples, council houses, and chiefly or priestly residences; also festivals regulated to the seasons, principally in association with the agricultural year. Moreover, since languages do not migrate of themselves, but are of one piece with the people who speak them, it surely follows that the original carriers of any Hokan-Siouan-Iroquoian dialect cannot possibly have originated from the north, where those languages do not exist.

It would seem, therefore, that the language (at least) of the Iroquois did, indeed, derive from the south—in fact, ultimately from the Southwest—and that a people speaking this dialect of the Hokan-Siouan language complex must have brought it with them into what now is New York State. In the course of this northward passage or migration, the Cherokee and Tuscarora, Yuchi and a few others, lingered as "detached" tribes in the South, while the rest, who were to constitute the "Five Nations" continued along with the Huron and others into the long established Algonkian, Northeast Woodland region, where as conquerors they flourished, while assimilating to their own purposes, not only such local hardware as archaeologists find and classify (pottery styles, for example), but also mythological software (such as descent from the sky and the dog sacrifice: see pages 132–136).

The circumstances, meanwhile, of Siouan tribes residing in the West, along the northern Mississippi, Missouri, and out onto the Plains have already been briefly discussed (I.2:222–223). For there, too, a branch of the linguistic Siouan phy-

lum had moved (that is to say, had been carried by a people) north, along the riverway into Algonkian territory, where a single exceptional tribe, the Sioux, Dakota, or Lakota, carved out for itself an immense domain, extending from Minnesota to the Rockies and from the Yellowstone River to the Platte. There is an immense linguistic continuum that has thus been recognized in North America as having prevailed from northwest Mexico and the North American Southwest (Hokan phylum), eastward to the Mississippi, up the length of which it extended (Siouan branches), and on to the East Coast, up which again there is an extension (the Yuchi, the Catawba, and the Iroquoian family of the Cherokee and Six Nations).

In the Southwest, two important phyla from the north cut across the continuity of this broad Hokan-Siouan domain. The earlier, the Aztec-Tanoan, stemming from the region around Utah, drove deeply into Mexico, where (as the name proclaims) it produced the language (Nahuatl) of the Aztec civilization. The second, Na-Dené, or Athabascan, sent a remote spur all the way from northwestern Canada and Alaska into Arizona and New Mexico, where the Navaho and Apache gave up whatever Alaskan traits they may have brought with them and took on, adapting to their own special aims, the mythologies of the Southwest.

Similarly, in the Southeast, the Hokan-Siouan continuity was broken into by an extension, again from the north, of languages of the Macro-Algonkian phylum, of which the principal representatives throughout the Mississippian mound-

331. Detail from *Panorama of the Monumental Grandeur of the Mississippi Valley 1850*, by John J. Egan.

building territories of the Southeast were the Chickasaw, Choctaw, Creek, Natchez, and (then later) Seminole tongues.

In this perspective the Cherokee would appear to have been, not later mound-builders than the Creek, but probably earlier: that is to say, if the Macro-Algonkian penetration south represents—like the Aztec-Tanoan and Na-Dené, in the West—developments later than that of the Hokan-Siouan dispersal. The rapidity with which an intrusive tribe can assimilate the culture of the region in which it has settled is evident, for example, in the character of the Algonkian towns and villages of the Powhatan confederacy of Virginia, which were of a classic Southeastern form (see I.2:**390,391**).

A common mythological heritage of Mississippian origin or affinity was shared, therefore, by the Hokan, Macro-Siouan, and Muskogean speaking tribes, of which the Mandan (Siouan) Okipa festival, pictured and described in 1832 by George Catlin (I.2:226–231) was an outstanding manifestation. The Muskogean Busk was another. So too was its counterpart, the Green Corn Festival, or *Ah-dake'-wa-o*, of the Iroquois (see page 132). In the fragmented myths and folk memories of the Southeastern people of the Trail of Tears, the "Five Civilized Tribes," Iroquoian Cherokee and Muskogean Choctaw, Chickasaw, Creeks, and Seminoles, vestigial traces appear throughout of the informing ideas of these rites.

243

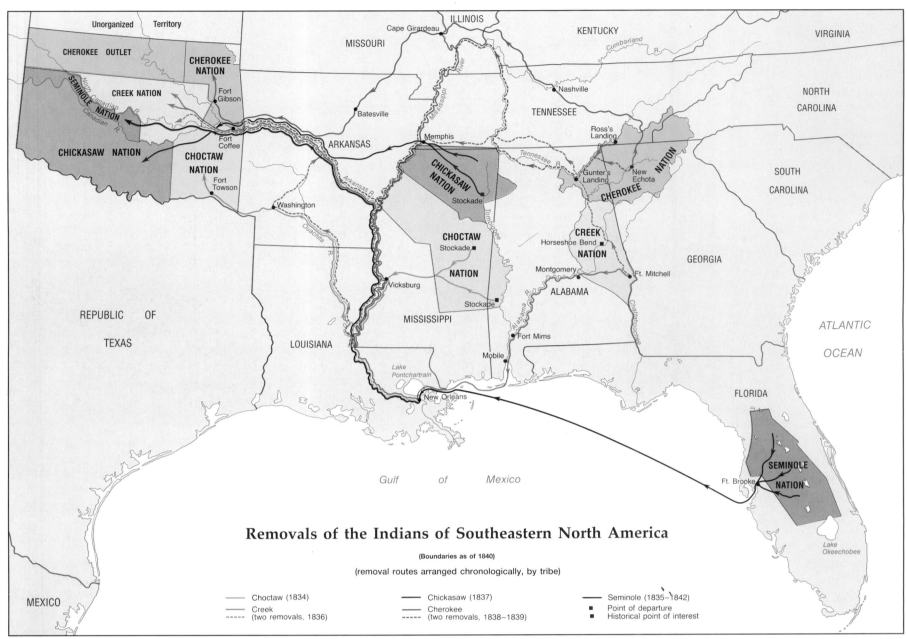

Removals of the Indians of Southeastern North America

(Boundaries as of 1840)

(removal routes arranged chronologically, by tribe)

—— Choctaw (1834)	—— Chickasaw (1837)	—— Seminole (1835–1842)
—— Creek	—— Cherokee	■ Point of departure
---- (two removals, 1836)	---- (two removals, 1838–1839)	■ Historical point of interest

Map 24.

The Removals

Cherokee life and culture were of the general Southeastern model and closely resembled the Creek. When first encountered in the mid-sixteenth century by de Soto and his followers, their palisaded towns in the southern Alleghenies, north of those of the Creeks, were distinguished, like the Creek, as red and as white, red devoted to the leadership and ceremonies of war and white to those of peace. Like all the Southeastern tribes, the Cherokee were advanced agriculturalists, not only raising the classic crops of maize, beans, and squash, but also, as Bartram found, planting orchards of peach and of plum (see page 242). Their temples or council houses (within which burned the sacred fire) were, like those of the Creeks, elevated upon flat-topped pyramidal mounds of earth, which, according to Bartram's observation, might be as high as twenty feet. Their simple dwellings are described as windowless log cabins roofed with bark, and with one door and a smoke hole. Thirty to sixty or more of such would constitute a town. In their ritual prayers, seven clans are mentioned, pertaining apparently to their

"Seven Mother Towns," each of which had its chief by matrilineal descent. An annual First Fruits, or Green Harvest Festival, corresponding to the Creek Busk, included as a prominent feature the New Fire rite.

Relations with the Carolina colonists began about 1690, at which period estimates of the Cherokee population varied from twelve to twenty-three thousand inhabiting some sixty towns and villages in the southern Appalachian mountains. Rum was introduced to them around 1708, chiefly by the Tuscaroras, who were selling it (according to Lawson) at "so many mouthfuls for a buckskin, they never using any other measure." The buyer always choosing a man having the largest mouth possible to accompany him to market, the mouthful then was scrupulously emptied into a bowl carried for the purpose.[245] In 1736 the first mission among them was founded by a Father Priber. Three years later a smallpox epidemic seriously reduced their number, and in 1750 wars began with the whites.

In the main, however, the Cherokee fared rather well and even prospered in the course of the eighteenth century, as did also a number of the other relatively unmolested tribes of the Southeast. Live-

stock was acquired and farming methods were improved. Horse-breeding was developed as a profitable trade, the Chickasaw horse and the Choctaw pony becoming appreciated breeds. Many Indians took to European clothes and European houses. Many Europeans, including people of wealth, married into Indian tribes. Indeed, such a fundamental transformation of the native life and culture was occurring that differences between the local Mississippian and colonial European manners of life were disappearing. In the Indian communities such native festivals continued to be celebrated as the Busk, and the wild ball game, Chunky (the "Younger Brother of War": see Figure 322), continued to be played. Otherwise, an unprejudiced eye would have found little to mark as critically separate or different between the darker- and lighter-skinned communities of the South. Hence the popular designation, the "Five Civilized Tribes."[246]

The Cherokee in the Revolution were allies of the English, and continued the struggle without interval until 1794. White pressure and encroachment on their lands during this period caused some to move down the Tennessee river and form new settlements at Chickamauga and other points about the Tennessee-Alabama line, which may account for the finding by Lewis and Kneberg that the Cherokee at Hiwassee Island arrived late (see page 242). Another large party moved altogether to the West and settled in Arkansas.

Shortly after 1800, missionary and educational work began among the Cherokee, and a period of rapid adaptation to the American way of life followed, which continued through the next quarter century. Roads were built along with schools and churches. In 1820, under Chief Junaluska—who during the Creek War of 1813–14, at the battle of Horseshoe Bend, had saved, according to his own report General Andrew Jackson's life (see page 225)—a Cherokee government was formed modeled on that of the United States; and in 1820 or 1822, a Cherokee of mixed blood named Sikwayi or Sequoya devised a system of writing (a syllabary) suitable to the Cherokee language which immediately caught on; so that within a few months the Cherokee were a literate nation. Parts of the Bible were printed in Cherokee in 1824, and in 1828 a weekly newspaper, *The Cherokee Phoenix*, in Cherokee and English, began publication.[247]

With the outbreak of the War of 1812, the Creek nation split into two parties, one anti-English, the other anti-American, the latter inspired largely by the ideals and genius of the Shawnee leader Tecumseh (1768-1813), who in Ohio, as a boy of six—where at that time the whole scenario of murder, massacre, and invasion of native lands in reenactment of the promise of Canaan was once again in production—had seen his father murdered by whites. His mother was a Creek, who instilled in him a spirit of hatred and revenge. In the Revolution he joined the Indian forces serving with the British and during the years intervening between wars—in the spirit of a revelation which one of his brothers, Tenskwatawa, had received from the "Master of Life"—he gave himself with all his heart to the task of uniting the Indian tribes in a single defensive movement, abjuring intertribal wars, throwing off white customs and the consolation of whiskey, and joining in a common front against the invasion. Traveling the continent as spokesman of this cause (in his time he was compared in his eloquence with the Kentuckian, Henry Clay), he gained in the Southeast, among the "Civilized Tribes," the support and approval only of a section of his mother's people, the Creeks. The Chickasaw, Choctaw, and Cherokee rebuffed him; and the field was set for a disaster.

The War of 1812, in its origin, had had very little to do with the Indians. The British in their contest with Napoleon had established, in their classic style, a naval blockade of the Continent, which in that instance the young American Republic, still knowledgeable of Albion, had refused to respect, and as a consequence, their ships were attacked, boarded, searched, and numbers of their seamen removed and impressed into the Royal Navy (blackbirding on the high seas). Along the Canadian border, however, there had been, indeed, for some time in practice, a covert British campaign of support to Indian tribes resisting American advances into the West, and it had been in relation to this campaign that Tecumseh and his cause had been receiving British arms and encouragement.

In 1811, the Governor of the Indiana Territory, William Henry Harrison (who in 1840 was to be elected ninth president of the United States, partly on the merit of the following adventure), marched with his army up the Wabash River and camped at Tippecanoe, near the settlement of Tecumseh's brother, Tenskwatawa, the prophet, who imprudently attacked the camp and in the ensuing battle was so decisively defeated that, with his reputation and following broken, he fled to Canada.

In 1812, Tecumseh, with what has been described as "perhaps the most formidable force ever commanded by a North American Indian,"[248] joined the British on the Canadian side of the Detroit River, at Ft. Malden, whence an attack was launched to the capture of Detroit and some 2500 United States soldiers.

In 1813, Tecumseh and his force, together with the British General Henry A. Procter, descended into Ohio and there laid siege to Harrison at Ft. Meigs, on the Maumee River, when Admiral Perry's victory over the British fleet on Lake Erie, September 10th 1813, exposed their rear,

332. Sequoia, inventor of the Cherokee alphabet. 1828 portrait by Charles Bird King.

and Harrison, pursuing their flight to the Thames River, Ontario, there put to rout both the Indians and the British. Tecumseh was slain, and Indian resistance in the Middle West was forever undone.

Also in 1813, inspired by Tecumseh's victories, a party of Alabama Creeks fell upon a company of frontiersmen at Ft. Mims, Georgia, on the lower Alabama River, where they massacred 553; in response to which, General Andrew Jackson, of the Tennessee militia, with 5000 of his militiamen, wiped out (the term massacre is not used to describe a civilized military operation) Tallasahatchia and Talladega, two Creek towns.

333. *The Battle of the Thames*, colored engraving by Ralph Rawden. Colonel Johnson's mounted men are depicted charging a party of British artillerists and Indians. In a subsequent counterattack, the famed Tecumseh was slain.

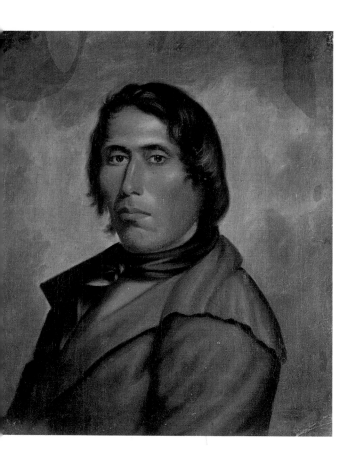

334. Portrait believed to be of Tecumseh (in white man's clothing), obtained in 1894 from a relative of explorer William Clark, who fought him. Artist unknown.

In 1814, in March, a large number of the terrified anti-American Creek population of Alabama and Georgia having taken refuge in what was thought to be an impregnable fortress on a bend—Horseshoe Bend—of the Tallapoosa River, Jackson with his army of 3000 militiamen—supported by an auxiliary force of five hundred Cherokee under the leadership of Chief Junaluska (of whom we have already heard), as well as by a company of pro-American Creeks—brought up two cannon, demolished the Creek defenses, and the power of the Indian tribes of the old Mississippian civilization was ended. Eight hundred warriors were slaughtered (not to mention women and children), five hundred women and children were imprisoned (we are not told to what end), and on August 9th, by the terms of a treaty signed at Ft. Jackson, the Creeks ceded to the United States 23,000,000 acres (about half) of Georgia and Alabama. Whereas in 1790, when the United States had been young and vulnerable, and the Creeks necessary for defense of the southern border against Spain, a treaty had been negotiated according to which the Indians ceded certain lands above the 31st parallel on a guarantee of the remaining boundaries of their tribe, ensuring thus a Creek territory of some 84,000 square miles.

In January, 1815, when a British invasion force was approaching the city of New Orleans from the Gulf of Mexico, General Jackson with his army of frontiersmen knocked them out. A treaty of peace had already been signed, December 24th, the year before. But this did not diminish the political value of this victory.

In 1817, under a pretext of pursuing

runaway slaves into their hideouts, General Jackson, with a force exceeding 3000, entered Florida, the same areas which in 1704 had by Carolina colonials and their Creek allies been purged of the Christianized Apalachee and Timucua, together with their Franciscan pastors. Thus began what is known as the First Seminole War, of 1817-18, which eventuated in Spain's ceding Florida to the United States in the year 1819.

In 1819, the state of Alabama was created from Cherokee and Creek territories. In violation of earlier treaties, tribal governments were outlawed.

In 1820, the Choctaw ceded 5,000,000 acres of land in west central Mississippi to the United States.

In 1823, the Seminoles ceded all of their lands except a central reservation, north of Lake Okeechobee, which by the terms of the Treaty of Ft. Moultrie was guaranteed to them.

In 1828, General Jackson was elected seventh president of the United States; at about which time gold was discovered near present Dahlonega, Georgia, and agitation began, to "clear the Indians out."

In 1830, the Indian Removal Act was signed into law by the former Indian fighter, Andrew Jackson, authorizing the president to exchange for desirable Indian territories within state borders prairie lands in the West. All former treaties were by this decree, in fact, annulled.

In 1831, November, the first stage of the Choctaw removal began with a company of 4000 starting on a trek of five hundred miles through the iced landscapes of an exceptionally cold Midwestern winter. The entire operation, accomplished by way of migrating bands of this kind, required three years for completion, through the winter of 1834.

In 1832, the Creeks acceded to and signed a removal treaty, according to which no Indians should be forced to move against their will, but "shall be free to go or stay as they please."

Also in 1832, the Seminoles, who had but nine years before been guaranteed their Florida reservation, were required, by the terms of a treaty negotiated by a number of their chiefs at Paynes Landing, to remove beyond the Mississippi within three years. The wildcat treaty was by many repudiated, and eventuated, from 1835–42, in one of the bloodiest, costliest, and longest Indian wars in American history. Led by Osceola (c. 1804–1838)—who, in 1835, with a group of braves murdered both General Wiley Thompson, the United States Indian Agent at Ft. King who was supervising the removal, and Charley Emathla, one of the chiefs who had signed the betrayal and was about to emigrate with his people—the Seminoles hid their families and fought to defend their homes, at a cost to the United States of 2000 soldiers killed and $40,000,000 to $60,000,000,

at a time when a dollar was a dollar and a filet mignon dinner cost ten cents.

In 1835, on December 20, by the treaty of New Echota, which, in spite of a long and hopeless struggle under leadership of their great chief, John Ross (see page 224), they were compelled to sign, the Cherokee sold their entire remaining territory and agreed to remove beyond the Mississippi to a country set apart for them.

In 1836, the Creeks of the treaty of 1832 were driven from their lands and 15,000 set on the road. The military escort was to accomplish the removal as an "operation of war...to subdue them and remove them to the West." Their "hostiles" were manacled; some chained together. The action was found by the Supreme Court unconstitutional, but the President had his will. On arrival in the promised land, 3500 died of disease and exposure.

In 1837, the Chickasaw removal was accomplished.

Also in 1837, Osceola, under a flag of truce, along with several other of the Seminole chiefs, went to St. Augustine for a parley with Gen. T. S. Jesup; by whose special order the Indians were seized on arrival and imprisoned. Osceola, removed to a jail in Charleston, died there the following year, and the Second Seminole War dragged on to 1842.

In 1838, Martin van Buren, successor to Andrew Jackson, ordered General Winfield Scott to enforce the provisions of the treaty of New Echota. 18,000 began the trek that is remembered today as the Trail of Tears. A few hundred escaped to the mountains. 4000 perished along the way. In a steamboat accident on the Mississippi, 311 drowned.

335. Osceola, the Black Drink, a Warrior of Great Distinction, 1838 painting by George Catlin.

246

Bright Eyes, Standing Bear, and Judge Dundy's Decision, April 18, 1879

To conclude this grim chronicle I present here two entries from the Bureau of American Ethnology's 1910 *Handbook of American Indians North of Mexico:*

"Bright Eyes. True name, Susette La Flesche. The eldest child of Eshtamaza, or Joseph La Flesche, a former head chief of the Omaha. She was born in Nebraska about 1850 and attended the Presbyterian mission school on the Omaha reservation. Through the interest of one of her teachers, Susette was sent to a private school in Elizabeth, N.J., where she made rapid progress in her studies. After her return home she taught in a Government day school on the Omaha reservation and exercised a stimulating influence on the young people of the tribe. In 1877–78 the Ponca were forcibly removed to Indian Territory from their home on Niobrara river, South Dakota. Not long afterward Susette accompanied her father to Indian Territory, where he went to render such help as he could to his sick and dying relatives among the Ponca. The heroic determination of the Ponca chief, Standing Bear, to lead his band back to their northern home; their sufferings during their march of more than six hundred miles; his arrest and imprisonment; and, after a sharp legal struggle, his release by *habeas corpus,* in accordance with Judge Dundy's decision that 'an Indian is a person,'[249] led to steps being taken by a committee of citizens to bring the matter of Indian removals before the public.

"Arrangements were made to have Standing Bear, accompanied by Susette La Flesche and her brother, visit the principal cities of the United States under the direction of Mr. T. H. Tibbles, and tell the story of the Ponca removal. The name 'Bright Eyes' was given Susette, and under that cognomen she entered upon her public work. Her clear exposition of the case, her eloquent appeals for humanity, her grace and dignity of diction and bearing aroused the interest of the thousands who listened to her. As a result, a request was urged on the Government that there be no more removals of tribes, and this request has been respected where practicable. In 1881 Bright Eyes married Mr. T. H. Tibbles. Later she and her husband visited England and Scotland, where she made a number of addresses. After her return to this country she lived in Lincoln, Neb., and maintained activity with her pen until her death in 1902."[250]

*   *   *

"Standing Bear (*Mon-chu-non-zhin*). A Ponca chief of whom little was known

336. Bright Eyes (Susette La Flesche).

until the removal of his people from N. Nebraska to Indian Territory because the reservation confirmed to them by treaty had been included in the land granted to the Sioux. When the order for removal was given, January 15, 1877, Standing Bear strongly opposed it, but in February he and nine other chiefs were taken south to choose a reservation. They followed the official, but would not select a place. Their wearisome journey brought them to Arkansas City, Kansas, whence they asked to be taken home; being refused, they started back afoot, with a few dollars among them and a blanket each. In forty days they had walked five hundred miles, reaching home April 2, to find the official there unwilling to listen to protests and determined to remove the people. He called the military, and the tribe, losing hope, abandoned their homes in May. Standing Bear could get no response to

337. Standing Bear (*Mon-chu-non-zhin*).

his demand to know why he and his people were arrested and treated as criminals when they had done no wrong.

"The change of climate brought great suffering to the Ponca; within the year a third of the tribe had died and most of the survivors were ill or disabled. A son of Standing Bear died. Craving to bury the lad at his old home, the chief determined to defy restraint. He took the bones of his son and with his immediate following turned northward in January 1879, and in March arrived destitute at the Omaha reservation. Asking to borrow land and seed, his request was granted, and the Ponca were about to put in a crop when soldiers appeared with orders to arrest Standing Bear and his party and return them to Indian Territory. On their way they camped near Omaha, where Standing Bear was interviewed by T. H. Tibbles, a newspaper correspondent, and accounts of their grievances appearing in the Omaha newspapers, the citizens became actively interested and opened a church where to a crowded house the chief repeated his story. Messrs. Poppleton and Webster proffered legal services to the prisoners and in their behalf sued out a writ of *habeas corpus.* The United States denied the prisoners right to a writ on the ground that they were 'not persons within the meaning of the law.' On April 18 Judge Dundy decided that 'an Indian is a person within the meaning of the law of the United States,' and had a right to the writ when restrained in violation of law; that 'no rightful authority exists for removing by force any of the prisoners to Indian Territory,' and therefore, 'the prisoners must be discharged from custody.'

"Standing Bear and his band returned to Nebraska. In the winter of 1879–80, accompanied by Susette La Flesche ('Bright Eyes,') and Francis La Flesche, as interpreters, with T. H. Tibbles, Standing Bear visited the cities of the East, where, by relating his story of the wrongs suffered, he won attention and sympathy. Many people wrote to the President and to other executive officials of the Government, and to members of Congress, protesting against unjust treatment of the Indians. In the spring of 1880 the Senate appointed a committee to investigate the Ponca removal, the report of which confirmed the story of Standing Bear, and a satisfactory adjustment was effected. Better lands were given those Ponca who chose to remain in Indian Territory; payment was made to all who had lost property, and a home was provided for Standing Bear and his followers at their old reservation. Here, in Sept. 1908, after having been instrumental in bringing about a change of Governmental policy toward all Indians and their homes, the chief died at the age of seventy-nine and was buried among the hills overlooking the village site of his ancestors."[251]

The Origin of Maize and Game

When I was a boy, this is what the old men told me they had heard when they were boys.

Long ages ago, soon after the world was made, a hunter and his wife lived with their only child, a little boy, at Looking-glass Mountain [in North Carolina, Transylvania County, near Brevard]. The father's name was Kanati, "The Lucky Hunter"; his wife's name was Selu, meaning "Maize." Whenever Kanati entered the woods, without fail he returned bearing a load of game which his wife butchered and prepared, washing the blood from the meat in the river that ran by their house.

Their little boy used to play every day down by that river, and one morning his parents overheard what they thought was laughing and talking, as though two boys were down there in the bushes. So when their child came home that evening, they asked who had been playing with him all day.

"He comes out of the water," the boy replied, "and calls himself my elder brother. He tells me his mother was cruel to him and threw him into the river."

Then they knew that the other boy had sprung from the blood that Selu had been washing from the meat, at the water's edge.

Every day after that, when their little boy went off to play, the other would join him; but since he always went back into the water, the old people never had a chance to see him. So finally, one evening, Kanati said to his son. "Tomorrow, when the other boy comes to play, get him to wrestle with you, and when you have your arms around him, call out for us."

Promising to do so, the next day when his friend appeared, the boy challenged him to a wrestling match and the other at once agreed. But as soon as they had their arms around each other, Kanati's son began calling for his father, and both parents immediately came running. Seeing them, the wild boy struggled to break free, screaming, "Let me go! You threw me away!" But his brother held on until his parents had arrived, when they seized the wild boy and took him home with them. There they kept him until they had tamed him. But he was always wild and artful in his disposition, leading his brother into every mischief. Then the old people realized that he was one of those people who are endowed with *adawehi*, "magic power," and they called him *Inagi Itasuhi*, "The One who grew up Wild."

Noticing that whenever Kanati went into the mountains, he returned either with a fat buck or a doe, or maybe a couple of turkeys, the wild boy one day said to his brother, "I wonder where our Father gets all that game. Let's follow him next time, and find out." And so, a few days later, when Kanati picked up his bow and a few feathers and started off, the boys waited a little, then followed, keeping out of sight until they saw that their father was about to enter a swamp where there were reeds of the sort that hunters now use to make arrow shafts; whereupon the wild boy changed himself into a tuft of bird's down, which the wind took up and carried to alight on Kanati's shoulder.

Not realizing what had happened, the man began cutting reeds and fitting feathers to them, making arrows, while the wild boy thought, in his altered shape, "I wonder what those things are for." Kanati finished his work and came out of the swamp, continuing on his way, when the wind blew the down from his shoulder into the woods, and the wild boy, resuming his shape, went back and told his brother what he had seen.

Keeping out of sight, the two followed their father up the mountain until he stopped at a certain place and lifted up a large stone. At once a buck came running out, which Kanati shot with one of the arrows he had made, and, lifting the animal onto his back, started home.

"Oho!" said the boys. "He keeps all the deer shut up in that hole and, whenever he wants venison, just lets one of them out and kills it with those things that he makes in the swamp." They hurried and arrived home before their father, who, with that heavy deer to carry, did not know they had followed him.

A few days later, the boys themselves went to the swamp, cut some of the reeds, made seven arrows, and then started up the mountain to the place where their father kept all the game. There they lifted up the rock, and out came running a deer. As they were drawing back to shoot it, another came out, another and another, until the boys, becoming confused, forgot what they were about. Deers' tails, in those days, hung down like the tails of other animals, but as one of the bucks ran past, the wild boy's arrow struck its tail and it stood straight out behind. This pleased the pair, and when the next ran by, the other brother struck its tail and it pointed upward. This, they decided, was great fun. So when the next ran by and the wild boy's arrow struck its tail and it stood straight up, his brother's struck the next so hard that the animal's tail curled over his back, and the boys thought this very pretty. So ever since that time, the deer has carried his tail curled over his back.

Deer continued to pass until the last had come out of the hole and scattered into the forest. Then followed droves of raccoons, rabbits, and all the other four-footed animals. Last, great flocks emerged of turkeys, partridges, and pigeons, darkening the air like a vast cloud, and with their wings they made such a great noise that Kanati, who was sitting at home, heard the sound, like thunder on the mountains, and he thought, "those two bad boys have got into trouble. I must go see what they have done."

So Kanati climbed the mountain, and when he came to the place where he kept the game, he found only the two boys standing by the rock; all the animals and birds were gone. He was furious, but not saying a word, he went down into the cave and kicked the covers from four jars that were standing in one of the corners; when out swarmed bed-bugs, fleas, gnats and lice, which, pouring out of the cave, enveloped the two boys, who, yelling with pain and terror, tried to beat the insects off. There were thousands, crawling all over them, biting and stinging, until they both dropped to the ground, nearly dead.

Kanati stood, looking on, until he thought they had had enough; when he simply shooed the vermin away and gave the pair a lecture. "Now, you two," he said, "you have always had plenty to eat and have never had to work for it. Whenever you were hungry, all I had to do was to come up here and get a deer or turkey and bring it home to your mother to cook. But now you have let all the animals out, so that, after this when you want a deer to eat, you will have to hunt through all the woods for it and may then not even find one. Go home now to your mother, while I see if I can find something for our supper."

When the boys reached home they were tired and hungry and asked their mother for something to eat. "There is no meat," she said; "but wait here and I will get you something."

Taking up a basket, she went out to the provision house, which had been built up high from the ground, on poles, out of the reach of animals. There was a ladder to climb up by, and one door, but no other opening. And so every day, from that day on, when getting ready to cook dinner, Selu would take up her basket, go out to the provision house, and return with the basket full of beans and maize.

The boys had never been inside the provision house, and very soon they began to wonder where all the maize and beans could be coming from. For the house was not very large. And so, one evening when their mother had left with her basket, the wild boy said to his brother, "Let's go see what she does there."

They climbed up two of the poles at the back of the provision house and, pulling out chunks of clay from between the logs, peered in. What they saw was their mother standing in the middle of the room with her basket on the floor in front of her. Leaning over, she rubbed her stomach—*so*—and the basket was half full of maize. Then she rubbed under her armpits—*so*—and the basket was full of beans.

The brothers looked at each other.

"Our mother is a witch," they said. "If we eat any of that, it will poison us. This will never do. We must kill her."

They returned to the house and when their mother came in, before they spoke she knew their thoughts.

"So you are going to kill me," she said.

"Yes," they said; "you are a witch."

"Well then," she said, "when you have killed me, clear a large piece of ground out in front of the house and drag my body around it in a circle, seven times. Then drag me over the ground inside the circle seven times, and stay up all night and watch. In the morning you will have plenty of maize."

They killed her with their clubs, cut off her head and set it up on the roof, warning it to watch, there, for Kanati. Then they set to work to clear the ground. But instead of clearing the whole area in front of the house, they cleared only seven small plots; which is why maize now grows in only a few parts of the world.

Next they dragged their mother's body around each of the seven small plots, and wherever her blood fell to the earth there sprang up maize. However, instead of dragging the body seven times across the whole piece of ground, they dragged it only twice; which is why the Indians still work their crops only twice. The brothers sat up all night and watched their maize, and in the morning it was grown, fully ripe.

Kanati then came home. And he looked around. But he could not find his wife. So he asked the boys where their mother was. "We killed her," they said. "She was a witch. Her head is up there on the roof."

Kanati went out and when he saw his wife's head on the roof he was appalled; and he said

248

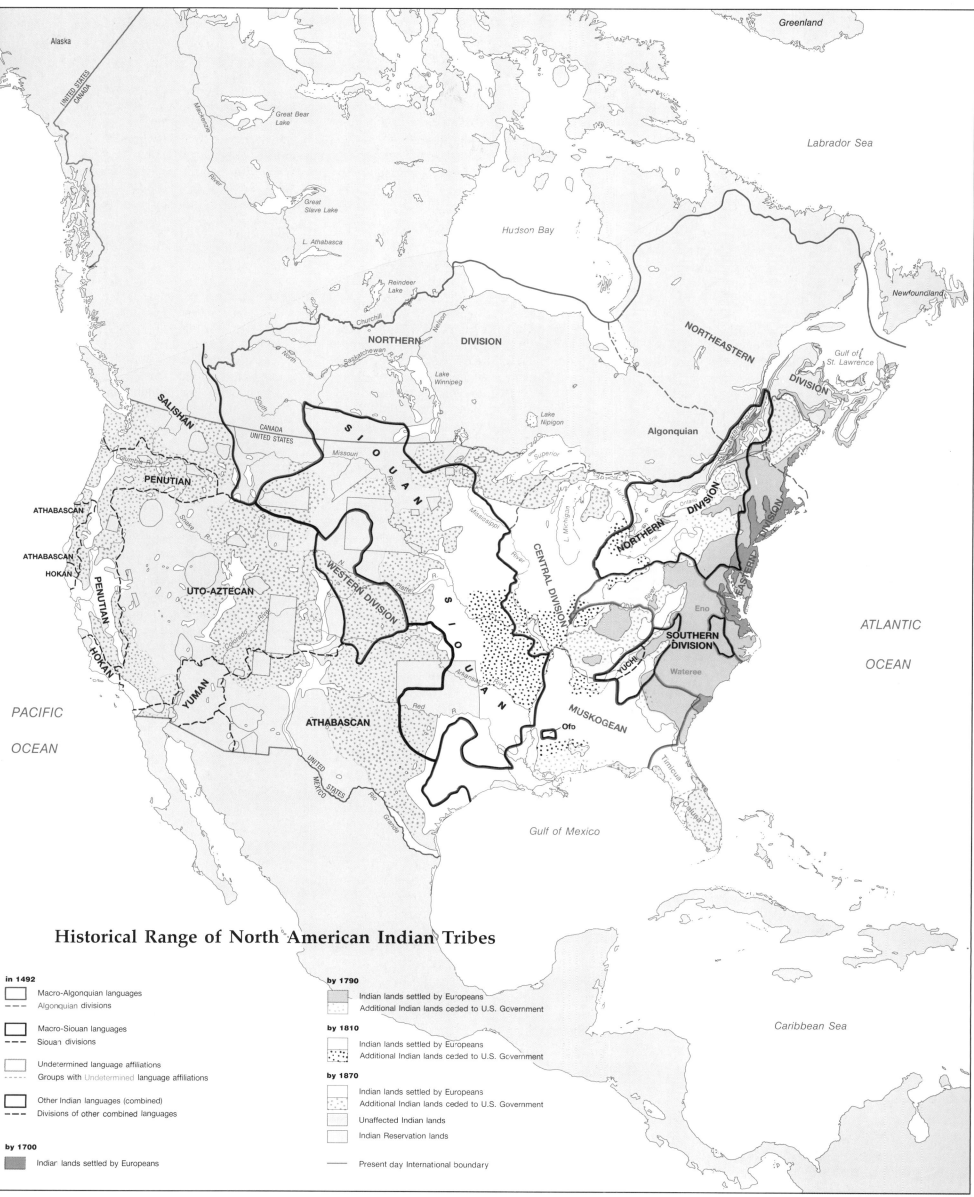

Historical Range of North American Indian Tribes

in 1492

☐ Macro-Algonquian languages
--- Algonquian divisions

☐ Macro-Siouan languages
--- Siouan divisions

☐ Undetermined language affiliations
···· Groups with Undetermined language affiliations

☐ Other Indian languages (combined)
--- Divisions of other combined languages

by 1700

■ Indian lands settled by Europeans

by 1790

▨ Indian lands settled by Europeans
▧ Additional Indian lands ceded to U.S. Government

by 1810

☐ Indian lands settled by Europeans
▦ Additional Indian lands ceded to U.S. Government

by 1870

☐ Indian lands settled by Europeans
▨ Additional Indian lands ceded to U.S. Government

☐ Unaffected Indian lands

☐ Indian Reservation lands

— Present day International boundary

Map 25.

249

to the boys, "I am through with you two. I am going to live with the Wolf people." And he turned and walked away. But before he had gone very far, the wild boy changed into a tuft of down, which a wind carried to Kanati's shoulder.

The Wolf people were in council in their townhouse when Kanati arrived in their settlement. With the tuft of down still on his shoulder, he entered the council chamber and sat down. The Wolf chief asked his business, and he answered, "I have two very bad boys at home, and want you to go, seven days from now, and play with them."

It was as though he meant for them to go play a game of ball; but the Wolf people knew that what he really meant was that the wolves should go and kill the two of them. They promised to do so, and the tuft of down immediately blew from Kanati's shoulder, going up with the smoke through the hole in the roof and coming down on the ground outside the council house, where the wild boy took his right shape again and scurried home to tell his brother everything he had heard.

When the boys began getting things ready, the wild boy—the magician—advised his brother on what should be done. They raced around the house in a wide circle, to make a trail around it, except on the side from which the wolves were expected to appear. Then they put together four bundles of arrows, which they set down at four points outside the circle. After that they went into the woods to hide, and there they awaited the wolves.

On the appointed day a great army of wolves arrived and they surrounded the house, not noticing that they were already inside an enclosing circle. For they had come in through the opening. And when they were all entirely within, the surrounding trail turned into a high, enclosing fence, and the boys, outside, began shooting arrows. The trapped wolves, unable to jump the fence, were all killed except a few, who through the opening had escaped into a nearby swamp, around which the boys now began running. A circle of fire sprang up in their tracks, consuming all except two or three of the wolves, who got away. And these, then, were all the wolves that at that time were left in the world.

The two boys were now living alone.

Presently some strangers arrived, who had heard that they had a wonderful grain from which bread could be made; for only Selu and her family had up to that time known about maize. The brothers willingly gave the strangers seven kernels, with instruction to plant them on the way home, next night, sitting up all night to watch the maize grow, which in the morning would have seven ripe ears. These then were to be planted the following night and watched in the same way; and so again, the next night and the next, until the company reached home, when they would have maize enough for their people.

The strangers lived seven days journey away. The took the gift and started home. And that night, having planted the seven kernels, they watched with care until dawn; when there were seven tall green stalks to be seen, and on each a ripened ear. These they gathered gladly and, continuing on their way, the next night they planted all the corn they had, which again they watched until daybreak, when they gathered an abundant harvest.

But their way was long, and the sun was hot, and the people were growing tired. And so, on the last night, having planted their grain, they fell asleep, and in the morning the maize had not even sprouted. What remained they carried home with them and, planting it with extreme care, they were able to celebrate a harvest. But ever since that time, maize, which before would have riped in a night, has had to be watched with care through half a year.

Now since Kanati had never returned home to his boys, but continued on his way, the two brothers at last decided that they had to go to find their father. The wild boy had a wheel, which he rolled toward the quarter where it is always night (the West). In a little while the wheel came rolling back, and the boys knew that their father was not there. Then the wild boy rolled the wheel to the South, and again the wheel came back; to the North, and again the wheel returned, and they knew that their father was not there. Then he rolled it toward the Sun Land (the East), from which it did not return. "Our father is there," said the wild boy. "Let us go find him."

So the two brothers set off toward the East, and after traveling a long time, they caught up with Kanati, who was walking along with a little dog trotting by his side.

"You bad boys!" their father said to them. "So you have found me here!"

"Yes," the brothers said. "We always accomplish whatever we set out to do. We are men."

"This little dog," Kanati said, "overtook me four days ago."

The boys knew that the dog was the wheel that they had sent out to find their father.

"Well, since you have found me," Kanati said, "we may as well travel together. But I shall lead."

Soon they came to a swamp, and Kanati warned the brothers that there was something in there that was dangerous, and to keep away from it. When he had walked on ahead and was out of sight, however, the wild boy said, "Let's see what that thing is."

So the two went in together, and in the middle of the swamp discovered a large panther asleep. The wild boy took out an arrow and shot the panther in the side of the head. It turned its head and the other boy then shot him on that side. It turned its head away again, and the two brothers shot together—*tust, tust, tust!* But the panther was unhurt and paid no more attention to the pair.

They left the swamp and soon overtook Kanati, who was waiting for them. "Did you find it?" he asked.

"Yes," they said, "but it did us no harm. We are men."

Kanati was surprised, but said nothing, and they went on, coming presently to a place where Kanati turned and warned the boys to be very careful. "We are coming," he said, "to a tribe called 'The Cookers.' If they catch you they will put you in a pot, cook, and eat you." Then he walked on ahead.

The boys came to a tree that had been struck by lightning, and the wild boy told his brother to gather up some of the splinters. After that they were passing the settlement of the cannibals, who, as soon as they saw the boys, came running, yelling, "Great! Great! Here are two fat ones for a feast!"

They caught the two and dragged them into their townhouse, sending out word to all, to come and enjoy a feast. And having kindled a great fire, they filled a large pot with water, set it to boil and, seizing the wild boy, flung him in and put on the lid.

His brother, who was not the least afraid, made no attempt to escape, but kneeling quietly down, began putting splinters into the fire, as though to make it blaze the more; until at last, when the cannibals thought the meat about done and lifted the lid, a blinding light filled the townhouse, lightning darting about from one side to the other, beating down all the cannibals, till not a single one was left alive. Then it flashed up through the smoke hole and, next moment, there were the two boys standing outside the townhouse, as though nothing had happened.

The boys walked on and soon caught up with Kanati, who seemed much surprised to see them. "What!" he said, "Are you two here again?"

"Oh yes," they said, "we never give up. We are great men."

"So what did the cannibals do to you?"

"They brought us to their townhouse; but they couldn't even hurt us," the two replied.

They walked along, and soon Kanati was out of sight again. But the boys kept on until they came to the edge of the world. (For the earth is a flat plane, and the sky a dome of solid rock, continually rising and falling; so that the space at their coming together is forever opening and closing.) When the two boys came to the edge of the world the sky was just coming down. So they waited until it went up again, then passed through and began climbing the outside. They climbed to the top, and there they found Kanati, sitting together with Selu, who, when they saw the two brothers arriving, received them kindly and told them they might stay a while, but would then have to leave, to go live where the sun goes down.

The brothers remained with their parents seven days, then left and began walking toward the sunset land, where they now live.[252]

338. Iroquois warriors set forth to confront the arriving explorers. Detail from Thomas Hart Benton's *Jacques Cartier's Discovery of the St. Lawrence Valley* (1957), a mural installed in 1959 at the St. Lawrence-Franklin D. Roosevelt Power Project, Massena, New York.

251

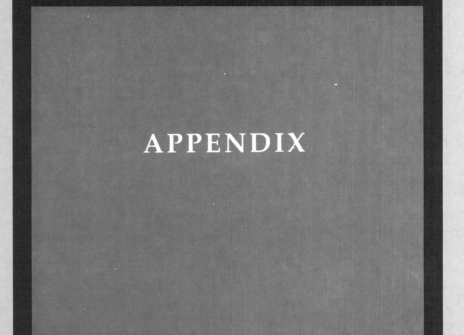

APPENDIX

ENDNOTES

[1]Carl O. Sauer, *Agricultural Origins and Dispersals* (New York: The American Geographical Society, 1952), p. 40. Re-edited and published with additional chapters under the title *Seeds, Spades, Hearths, and Herds* (Cambridge: M.I.T. Press, 1969).

[2]Ibid., p. 25.

[3]Ibid., pp. 45–46.

[4]Ibid., pp. 46–47.

[5]Ibid., pp. 47–48.

[6]Ibid., pp. 48–49.

[7]Julian H. Steward, ed., *Handbook of South American Indians*, Smithsonian Institution, Bureau of American Ethnology Bulletin 143, 7 vols. (Washington D.C., 1944–1957), vol. 6, pp. 487–543.

[8]The information in parentheses in this paragraph is not from Sauer, but from Carroll L. Riley et al., eds., *Man across the Sea* (Austin: University of Texas Press, 1971), taken from, respectively, pp. 320–327, 309–19, 328, 25, 24, 26, and 376–400.

[9]Claude Lévi-Strauss, "The Use of Wild Plants in Tropical South America," in Steward, ed., op. cit., vol. 6, pp. 465–486.

[10]Sauer, op. cit., pp. 42–43.

[11]I am following, in the paragraphs to come, the superb article by Michael D. Coe, "History of Meso-American Civilization," *The New Encyclopaedia Britannica*, 15th ed., where a chaos of information from literally hundreds of specialist monographs has been reduced to order. See also in Robert Wauchope, ed., *Handbook of Middle American Indians*, 13 vols. (Austin: University of Texas Press, 1964–73), Richard S. MacNeish, "Archeological Synthesis of the Sierra," vol. 11, pp. 573–581; and James B. Griffin, "Mesoamerica and the Eastern United States in Prehistoric Times," vol. 4, pp. 111–117.

[12]Richard I. Ford, "'Artifacts' That Grew: Their Roots in Mexico," *Early Man*, vol. 2, no. 3 (Autumn 1980), p. 19.

[13]Charles C. Di Peso, "Macaws...Crotals... and Trumpet Shells," in *Early Man*, vol. 2, no. 3 (Autumn 1980), p. 4.

[14]MacNeish, "Archeological Synthesis of the Sierra," in Wauchope, op. cit., vol. 11, pp. 573–581.

[15]Betty J. Meggers, Clifford Evans, and Emilio Estrada, *Early Formative Period of Coastal Ecuador* (Washington, D.C.: Smithsonian Institution Press, 1965), pp. 157–178.

[16]James A. Ford, *A Comparison of Formative Cultures in the Americas* (Washington, D.C.: Smithsonian Institution Press, 1969), p. 12 and Table 3, p. 28

[17]Ibid., pp. 12 –13 and Table 4, p. 29.

[18]Ibid., p. 13 and Table 5, p. 29.

[19]Richard I. Ford, op. cit., p. 21.

[20]Mentor L. Williams, ed., *Schoolcraft's Indian Legends* (East Lansing: Michigan State University Press, 1956), pp. 58–60.

[21]Lewis H. Morgan, *League of the Ho-dé-no-sau-nee, or Iroquois*, 2 vols., (New York: Dodd, Mead and Company, 1901 and 1904), vol. 1, p. 5.

[22]Herbert M. Lloyd, ed., in Morgan, op. cit., vol. 2, "Notes," pp. 190–191, citing Joseph François Lafitau, *Moeurs des Sauvages Amériquains comparées aux Moeurs des Premiers Temps*, 4 vols. (Paris, 1724), vol. 3, p. 84.

[23]Ibid., p. 251.

[24]Ibid., p. 301.

[25]Morgan, op. cit., vol. 2, pp. 175–176.

[26]Waldemar Jochelson, *The Koryak*, Memoirs of the American Museum of Natural History (New York, 1910–1926), vol. X, part 1, pp. 90–91.

[27]Lloyd, in Morgan, op. cit., p. 264, citing Reuben Gold Thwaites, ed., *The Jesuit Relations and Allied Documents, Travels and Explorations of the Jesuit Missionaries in New France*, 73 vols. (Cleveland: Burrow Brothers, 1896–1901), vol. 60, p. 218.

[28]Ibid., citing *Jesuit Relations*, vol. 60, p. 240.

[29]Ibid., p. 265, citing *Lieutenant-Colonel Hubley's Journal*, Sept. 10, 1799.

[30]Ibid., citing Francis Parkman, *The Jesuits in North America in the Seventeenth Century*, p. lxxxv.

[31]Jochelson, *The Koryak*, p. 92.

[32]Ibid., pp. 92, 98.

[33]Morgan, op. cit., vol. 1, p. 70.

[34]See ibid., vol. 2, p. 225, note 58.

[35]Ibid., vol. 1, pp. 195–196, abridged and recast.

[36]Ibid., pp. 199–213.

[37]Ibid., vol. 2, p. 165.

[38]Ibid., vol. 1, pp. 215–216.

[39]Lloyd, in ibid., vol. 2, citing Thwaites, *Jesuit Relations*, vol. 42, p. 154, cited in notes, Appendix B, pp. 255–260, abridged and recast.

[40]Morgan, op. cit., vol. 1, p. 216.

[41]*The Gospel According to Thomas*, Coptic text established and translated by A. Guillaumont, H.-Ch. Puech, G. Quispel, W. Till, and Yassah 'abd Al Masih (New York: Harper and Brothers, 1959), pp. 43 and 57.

[42]W. P. Clark, *The Indian Sign Language* (Philadelphia, 1885).

[43]Morgan, op. cit., vol. 2, pp. 233–235.

[44]Ibid., vol. 1, p. 320, note 1.

[45]Ibid., pp. 318–319.

[46]Ibid., p. 220.

[47]Ibid., p. 224.

[48]Ibid., p. 237.

[49]Ibid., pp. 239–241.

[50]Lloyd, in ibid., vol. 2, p. 265, citing Father Pierron in the *Jesuit Relation of 1669–1670*.

[51]See Gilbert Murray's "Critical Appendix on the Orphic Tablets," in Jane Ellen Harrison, *Prolegomena to the Study of Greek Religion*, 3rd ed. (Cambridge: Cambridge University Press, 1922), pp. 659 ff.

[52]Morgan, op. cit., vol. 1, pp. 224–248, abridged and recast.

[53]J.N.B. Hewitt, "Iroquois Cosmology," *Twenty-first Annual Report of the Bureau of American Ethnology* (Washington, D.C., 1899–1900), p. 255, note b.

[54]Ibid., p. 312, note a.

[55]Ibid., p. 311, note b.

[56]Ibid., p. 309, note a.

[57]Ibid., p. 255–339, abridged and recast.

[58]Carl Kerenyi, in "Kore," C. G. Jung and Carl Kerenyi, *Essays on a Science of Mythology*, Bollingen Series XXII (New York: Pantheon Books, 1949), p. 101, quoting Leo Frobenius, *Der Kopf als Schicksal* (Munich, 1924).

[59]Alexander Marshack, *The Roots of Civilization* (New York: McGraw-Hill, 1972), p. 335 and note 17.

[60]Marija Gimbutas, *The Goddesses and Gods of Old Europe, 7000–3500 B.C., Myths, Legends, and Cult Images* (Berkeley: University of California Press, 1974).

[61]Ibid., p. 196.

[62]Oswald Spengler, *Der Untergang des Abendlandes* (Munich: C. H. Beck'sche Verlagsbuchhandlung, 1930), vol. 2, p. 3, translated by Joseph Campbell.

[63]Ibid., translated by Joseph Campbell.

[64]Joseph Campbell, *The Hero with a Thousand Faces*, Bollingen Series XVII (New York: Pantheon Books, 1942), p. 30; citing James Joyce, *Finnegans Wake* (New York: Viking Press, 1939), p. 581.

[65]Arnold van Gennep, *Les Rites de Passage* (Paris, 1909), translated by Monika B. Vizedom and Gabrielle L. Caffee as *The Rites of Passage* (Chicago: University of Chicago Press, 1960).

[66]T. S. Eliot, *Four Quartets* (New York: Harcourt, Brace and Co., 1943), "Burnt Norton" II, lines 16 and 19.

[67]Henry Adams Bellows, *Poetic Edda* (New York: The American-Scandinavian Foundation, Oxford University Press, 1923), Hovamol 139–143.

[68]Gimbutas, *Goddesses and Gods of Old Europe*, pp. 169–171.

[69]Sigmund Freud, *The Interpretation of Dreams*, Part IV, "The Psychology of the Dream Process," in A. A. Brill, trans. and ed., *The Basic Writings of Sigmund Freud* (New York: Random House, 1938), p. 480.

[70]Stephen Chapman Simms, *Traditions of the Crows*, Field Museum Anthropological Series II, no. 19 (Chicago, 1903), p. 303, abridged and recast.

[71]Jeremiah Curtin, *Seneca Indian Myths* (New York: E. P. Dutton, 1923), pp. 192–194.

[72]*Enuma elish*, Tablets I to IV. See Joseph Campbell, *The Masks of God*, 4 vols. (New York: The Viking Press, 1964), vol. 3, "Occidental Mythology," pp. 78–83.

[73]Bellows, op. cit., Vafthrusnismol 21.

[74]Ananda Coomaraswamy, "On the One and Only Transmigrant," in Roger Lipsey, ed., *Coomaraswamy*, Bollingen Series LXXXIX, 2 vols. (Princeton: Princeton University Press, 1977), vol. 2, citing *Satapatha Brahmana* X.5.2.13,16, p. 67.

[75]Ibid., citing *Brihadaranyaka Upanishad* III.7.23, III.8.11.

[76]Ibid., citing *Rig Veda* I.115.1.

[77]Ibid., citing *Brihadaranyaka Upanishad* I.4.7.

[78]Ibid., citing *Bhagavad Gita* III.15.

[79]Ibid., citing *Maitri Upanishad* VI.7.

[80]Ad. E. Jensen, *Hainuwele: Volkerzählungen von der Molukken-Insel Ceram* (Frankfurt-am-Main: V. Klostermann, 1939), pp. 39–40. Translation, abridged and recast, by Joseph Campbell.

[81]*Ashtavakra-samhita* 182, translation by Joseph Campbell.

[82]*Buddha-carita* II.18., translation by Joseph Campbell.

[83]See Heinrich Zimmer, Joseph Campbell, ed., *Philosophies of India*, Bollingen Series XXVI (New York: Pantheon Books, 1951), Part III, "The Philosophies of Eternity," pp. 181–279.

[84]Genesis 3:8.

[85]James Joyce, *Finnegans Wake* (New York: Viking Press, 1939), p. 255.

[86]Bellows, op. cit., Voluspo 32–33.

[87]Following Heinrich Zimmer, *The Art of Indian Asia: Its Mythology and Transformations*, 2 vols., completed and edited by Joseph Campbell (New York: Pantheon Books, 1955), vol. 1, pp. 52–53.

[88]Kwang-chih Chang, *Shang Civilization* (New Haven: Yale University Press, 1980), pp. 153–156; and for the dating of Anyang, pp. 322–329.

[89]Jochelson, *The Koryak*, p. 355. See also I.2:179.

[90]Frederick Webb Hodge, ed., *Handbook of American Indians North of Mexico*, Smithsonian Institution, Bureau of American Ethnology Bulletin 30 (Washington, D.C., 1907), vol. 1, p. 38, s.v. "Algonkin," citing J.N.B. Hewitt.

[91]Ibid., p. 39.

[92]*The New Encyclopaedia Britannica*, 15th ed., s.v. "North American Indian Languages."

[93]Gordon R. Willey, *An Introduction to American Archaeology*, 2 vols. (Englewood Cliffs, N.J.: Prentice-Hall Inc., 1966), vol. 1, p. 419.

[94]Hodge, op. cit., vol. 1, s.v. "Apalachee."

[95]Ibid., s.v. "Algonquian Family."

[96]C. G. Jung, "The Complications of American Psychology," in *The Collected Works of C. G. Jung*, Bollingen Series XX, 2nd ed., 18 vols. (Princeton: Princeton University Press, 1964), in vol. 10, "Civilization in Transition," p. 510.

[97]Ibid., pp. 509–510.

[98]Ibid., p. 511.

[99]Ibid., p. 508.

[100]*The New Encyclopaedia Britannica*, 15th ed., vol. 13, s.v. "American Indians."

[101]Ibid.

[102]George Catlin, *The North American Indians, Being Letters and Notes on Their Manners, Customs, and Conditions, Written during Eight Years' Travel amongst the Wildest Tribes of Indians in North America, 1832–1839*, 2 vols. (Philadelphia: Leary, Stuart and Company, 1913).

[103]Williams, op. cit., p. xxii, note 9, citing Schoolcraft, *Personal Memoirs of a Residence of Thirty Years* (Philadelphia, 1851), p. 693.

[104]Ibid., citing Schoolcraft, *Algic Researches* (New York, 1839).

[105]Helen Hunt Jackson, *A Century of Dishonor* (Boston: Roberts Brothers, 1885).

[106]Theodor Benfey, *Pantschatantra: Fünf Bücher Indischer Fablen, Märchen, und Erzählungen. Aus den Sanskrit übersetzt mit Einleitung und Anmerkungen* (Leipzig, 1859), p. xxvi.

[107]The tales of the Grimm collection, classified according to type, as suggested by Antti Aarne (Antti Aarne, *Verzeichnis der Märchentypen*, Folklore Fellows Communications, vol. 1, no. 3, Helsinki, 1911. See also Johannes Bolte and Georg Polivka, *Anmerkung zu den Hausmärchen der Brüder Grimm*, 5 vols. [Leipzig, 1911–1912], vol. 4, pp. 467–470), are as follows:

- I. Animal Tales (wild and domestic), 26 examples.
- II. Ordinary Folktales.
  - A. Tales of Magic: (1) Supernatural Adversaries, 30 examples; (2) Supernatural or Enchanted Husband, Wife, or Other Relative, 22 examples; (3) Supernatural Tasks, 3 examples; (4) Supernatural Helpers, 16 examples; (5) Magic Objects, 12 examples; (6) Supernatural Power or Knowledge, 9 examples; (7) Other Tales of the Supernatural, 7 examples.
  - B. Religious Tales, 12 examples.
  - C. Novella (Romantic Tales), 12 examples.
  - D. Tales of the Stupid Ogre, 3 examples.
- III. Jokes and Anecdotes (Numbskull Stories, Stories about Married Couples, Stories about a Woman or Girl, Stories about a Man or Boy, Clever Man, Stupid Man, Lucky Accidents, Tales of Lying), 29 examples.

I have published the full, numbered listing in my Folkloristic Commentary to the Pantheon Books (now Random House) edition of 1944.

The classification of the Grimms' tales according to the historic periods of their invention or adoption, by Friedrich von der Leyen (Jakob Grimm, *Kinder- und Hausmärchen Gesammelt durch die Brüder Grimm*, 2 vols. Friedrich von der Leyen, ed. [Jena: Diedrichs, 1919], vol. 1, pp. vii–xxvii) as follows:

(1) Tales of Primitive Belief, 9 examples; (2) Hero Sagas from the Period of the Germanic Migrations, 5 examples; (3) Minstrel Work of the Tenth Century, 18 examples; (4) Chivalrous Work of the Middle Ages, 53 examples; (5) Tales Showing Oriental Influence, 22 examples; (6) Animal Stories, 18 examples; (7) Work of the Townsmen of the Fourteenth to Sixteenth Centuries, 47 examples; (8) Tales from the Seventeenth and Eighteenth Centuries, 25 examples; (9) Jokes and Anecdotes, 17 examples.

Again, the numbered, complete listing is to be found in my Folkloristic Commentary to the only complete edition of Grimm's fairy tales now available in English: *The Complete Grimm's Fairy Tales* (New York: Pantheon Books, 1944; Random House, 1972), pp. 844–845.

[108]Francis Parkman, *The Conspiracy of Pontiac*, 2 vols. (Boston: Little, Brown & Co., 1877), vol. 2, Appendix C, p. 328.

[109]Stith Thompson, *Motif-Index of Folk-Literature*, 6 vols. (Bloomington: Indiana University Studies, 1932–1936). The example of this Type, "Animals go a-journeying," in the Grimm collection is Märchen Number 27, "The Bremen Town Musicians." Antti Aarne has devoted a Folklore Fellows Monograph (*Die Tiere auf der Wanderschaft*, FFC XI) to a full-scale discussion of the Type (his Type Number 210), listing a range of variants comprising Finnish-Swedish, Estonian, Livonian, Latvian, Lithuanian, Swedish, Danish, Irish, French, Dutch, Walloon, German, Hungarian, Slovenian, Serbocroatian, Russian, Turkish, Indian, Indonesian, Chinese, Franco-American, West Indian (Negro), and Spanish-American examples.

Bolte and Polivka, in their twenty-two-page commentary on "The Bremen Town Musicians" (Bolte and Polivka, *Anmerkung zu den Hausmärchen der Brüder Grimm*, vol. 1, pp. 237–259), discuss in detail, besides numerous European examples, others from Sumatra, the Near East, and Algiers.

Stith Thompson (*Tales of the North American Indians* [Cambridge: Harvard University Press, 1929], p. 302, note 108) recognizes as a Native American example of the Type, the Skidi Pawnee account of "Big Turtle's War Party" (see I.2:239), citing a numerous list besides, of other Indian variants of the adventure, from the Plains tribes (Osage, Arapaho, Pawnee, Ponca, Cheyenne, Blackfoot, and Oglala), those of the Central Woodland (Ojibwa, Kickapoo, Menomini, and Peoria), of the Eastern Woodland (Iroquois), and of the Southeast (Cherokee).

[110]Thompson, *Tales of the North American Indians*, pp. 291–292. Thompson lists examples among the Eskimo (of both Greenland and Alaska); on the North Pacific Coast (Tlingit, Tahltan, and Kathlamet); the Plateau area (Chilcotin, Thompson River tribes, and Coeur d'Alene); California (Shasta, Modoc, Yuki, Yokuts, Cahuilla, Paviotso, and Luiseno); among the Plains tribes (Crow, Arapaho, Ute, Wichita, Cheyenne, Pawnee, Ponca, Blackfoot, Dakota, Canadian Dakota, Sarcee, Gros Ventre, and Assiniboin); the Northeast Woodland (Micmac, and to which our Nascapi tale should be added); Woodland Iroquois (Seneca, Onondaga, and Wyandot); the Southeast (Cherokee and Caddo); and the Southwest (Hopi).

[111]The registered examples of the Type being variously, with local adaptations, Finnish, Finnish-Swedish, Livonian, Estonian, Lithuanian, Swedish, Danish, English, Flemish, Walloon, French, German, Hungarian, Slovenian, Russian, African (Nigeria, Zanzibar, and Zimbabwe), Indian, Indonesian, Polynesian (Society Islands), Spanish-American, Missouri French, Louisiana Creole, West Indian (Negro), American Negro (Georgia, as in Joel Chandler Harris's *Uncle Remus*), and American Indian—to which last, the fol-

lowing distribution is indicated in Stith Thompson's list (*Tales of the North American Indians*, pp. 302–303): North Pacific Coast (Tlingit); Plateau (Okanagon); Plains (Osage, Arapaho, Skidi, Pawnee, Ponca, Cheyenne, Blackfoot, Oglala, Wichita, Dakota, and Plains Ojibwa); Central Woodland (Ojibwa, Kickapoo, Menomini, and Peoria); Woodland Iroquois (Seneca); Northeast Woodland (Malacite, Micmac, and Passamaquoddy); Southeast (Cherokee, Natchez, and Biloxi); and Southwest (Hopi and Laguna). In addition, Thompson points to examples recorded from Angola, Sri Lanka, Burma, China, the Celebes, and the Philippines.

[112]Thompson, *Motif-Index of Folk-Literature.* The relevant headings from Thompson's *Index* are as follows:

A 511	Supernatural birth of a culture hero
A 511.1	Culture hero snatched from mother's side
A 511.2.1	Twin culture heros quarrel before birth
A 511.3	Culture hero incarnated through birth from a virgin
A 512	Culture hero creator's son
A 521	Culture hero as a dupe or trickster
A 522	Animal as culture hero
A 525	Good and bad culture heroes
A 525.1	Culture hero fights with his elder brother
A 530	Culture hero establishes law and order
A 531	Culture hero (demigod) overcomes monsters
A 531.1	Culture hero spares certain evil spirits
A 531.2	Culture hero banishes snakes
A 535	Culture hero swallowed and recovered from animal
A 541	Culture hero teaches arts and crafts
A 560	Culture hero's (demigod's) departure
A 561	Divinity's departure for west
A 562	Divinity's departure for east
A 570	Culture hero still lives
A 580	Culture hero's (divinity's) expected return.

[113]Paul Radin, "The Basic Myth of North American Indians," in Olga Frobe-Kapteyn, ed., *Eranos-Jahrbuch 1949* (Zurich: Rhein-Verlag, 1950), p. 359.

[114]Williams, op. cit., pp. 304–306, from Schoolcraft, *The Red Race of America* (New York, 1847), pp. 203–206.

[115]Mircea Eliade, *Shamanism: Archaic Techniques of Ecstasy*, Willard R. Trask, trans., Bollingen Series LXXVI (New York: Pantheon Books, 1964), p. xvii.

[116]*The New Encyclopaedia Britannica*, 15th ed., s.v. "Montagnais and Nascapi."

[117]Frank G. Speck, "Montagnais and Nascapi Tales from the Labrador Peninsula," *Journal of American Folklore*, vol. 38, no. 7 (March–February, 1925), pp. 1–2.

[118]Ibid., pp. 27–28, abridged and recast.

[119]Ibid., pp. 28–31, abridged and recast.

[120]Ibid., pp. 22–23, abridged and recast.

[121]Ibid., p. 12, abridged and recast.

[122]Ibid., pp. 18–19, abridged and recast.

[123]Ibid., p. 15, abridged and recast.

[124]Ibid., pp. 13–15, abridged and recast.

[125]Ibid., pp. 1–3, abridged and recast.

[126]Ibid., p. 12–13, abridged and recast.

[127]*The New Encyclopaedia Britannica*, 15th ed., s.v. "Abnaki," "Micmac," "Passamaquoddy," and "Penobscot."

[128]Elsie Clews Parsons, "Micmac Folklore," in *Journal of American Folklore*, vol. 38, no. 147 (January–March, 1925), pp. 90–91. As related to Elsie Clews Parsons by Isabelle Googoo Morris in the summer of 1923, at Laquille, a small Indian settlement on the outskirts of Annapolis Royal, Nova Scotia; abridged and recast.

[129]Ibid., p. 90, as related to Parsons by Isabelle Googoo Morris; abridged and recast.

[130]Silas Tertius Rand, *Legends of the Micmacs* (New York: Wellesley College Philological Publications, 1894), Legend no. 68, p. 360; abridged and recast.

[131]Ibid., pp. 34ff., abridged and recast.

[132]Ibid., p. 232, abridged and recast.

[133]Charles Godfrey Leland, *The Algonquin Legends of New England* (Boston: Houghton, Mifflin and Co., 1898), pp. 36–41, abridged and recast.

[134]Ibid., pp. 31–35, abridged and recast.

[135]Ibid., pp. 114–119, abridged and recast.

[136]Ibid., pp. 120–122, abridged and recast.

[137]Ibid., pp. 127–130, abridged and recast.

[138]Ibid., pp. 111–112, abridged and recast.

[139]Ibid., p. 113, quoting *Poetic Edda*, Vafthruthnismol 36–37.

[140]Ibid., p. 15, note 1.

[141]Ibid., p. 107.

[142]Bellows, op. cit., Voluspo 33 and 61–62, Lokasena 28, Baldrs Draumar 8–9, and Gylfaginning 49.

[143]Leland, op. cit., pp. 109–110.

[144]As deduced from the Icelandic *Groenlendinga saga* of *Flateyjarbok* ("Tale of the Greenlanders" in the "Songbook") and *Eiriks saga* ("Saga of Erik"). These are thirteenth-century accounts. See A. M. Reeves, ed., *The Finding of Wineland the Good* (London, 1895), pp. 145–148 *Groenlendinga saga*) and 122–139 (*Eiriks saga*).

[145]Leland, op. cit., p. 133.

[146]Ibid., pp. 15–16 and 106, abridged and recast.

[147]Ibid., pp. 18–19 and 28–30, abridged and recast.

[148]Ibid., pp. 130–131.

[149]Ibid., pp. 131–132.

[150]André Leroi-Gourhan, *Treasures of Prehistoric Art* (New York: Harry N. Abrams, Inc., no date), pp. 329–330 and 493.

[151]Henry Rowe Schoolcraft, *Algic Researches*, 2 vols. (New York: Harper & Bros., 1839), vol. 1, pp. 96–121, abridged and recast.

[152]Ibid., pp. 67–73, abridged and recast.

[153]Ibid., pp. 57–66, abridged and recast.

[154]Ibid., vol. 2, pp. 34–39, abridged and recast.

[155]Ibid., vol. 1, pp. 138–143, abridged and recast.

[156]Ibid., pp. 165–167, abridged and recast.

[157]Ibid., pp. 144–145, abridged and recast.

[158]Alanson Skinner and John V. Satterlee, *Tales of the Menomini*, Anthropological Papers of the American Museum of Natural History (New York, 1913), vol. 13, p. 239, abridged and recast.

[159]Ibid., p. 255, abridged and recast.

[160]Parkman, op. cit., vol. 1, pp. 204–207, abridged and recast.

[161]As related by Chief Mandarong (Joseph White) and his French wife to Horatio Hale, *Journal of American Folklore*, vol. 2 (1889), pp. 249–250, abridged and recast.

[162]W. M. Beauchamp, "Onondaga Customs," *Journal of American Folklore*, vol. 1, (1888), pp. 201–202. Summarized, with comments by Beauchamp, from an account recorded in 1845; abridged and recast.

[163]Morgan, op. cit., vol. 2, pp. 149–151, abridged and recast.

[164]Jeremiah Curtin and J. N. B. Hewitt, "Seneca Fiction, Legends, and Myths," *32nd Annual Report of the Bureau of American Ethnology* (Washington, D.C., 1918), pp. 456–457, abridged and recast.

[165]Ibid., pp. 86–90, abridged and recast.

[166]Ibid., p. 106, abridged and recast.

[167]W. M. Beauchamp, "Onondaga Tales," *Journal of American Folklore*, vol. 1 (1888), pp. 44–47, abridged and recast.

[168]Curtin and Hewitt, op. cit., pp. 437–441, abridged and recast.

[169]Ibid., p. 365 and pp. 457–458, abridged and recast.

[170]Ibid., pp. 701–704, abridged and recast.

[171]Ibid., pp. 149–151, abridged and recast.

[172]Beauchamp, "Onondaga Tales," pp. 173–179, abridged and recast.

[173]Curtin and Hewitt, op. cit., pp 658–663, abridged and recast.

[174]Franz Boas, *Race, Language, and Culture* (New York: The Macmillan Company, 1940), p. 405. Article reprinted from *The Scientific Monthly*, vol. 3 (1916), pp. 335–343, "The Development of Folk-Tales and Myths."

[175]Sigmund Freud, *The Interpretation of Dreams*, 1900. Authorized English translation of 3rd German edition by A. A. Brill, *The Basic Writings of Sigmund Freud* (New York: The Modern Library, published by Random House, 1938).

[176]For a thorough treatment of the subject, see R. Gordon Wasson, *The Wondrous Mushroom: Mycolatry in Mesoamerica*, Ethnomycological Studies no. 7 (New York: McGraw-Hill Book Co., 1980); see also R. Gordon Wasson, "The Hallucinogenic Mushrooms of Mexico: An Adventure in Ethnomycological Exploration," *Transactions of The New York Academy of Sciences*, Series II, vol. 21, no. 4 (February 1957), pp. 325–339; and R. Gordon Wasson and Roger Heim, *Les Champignons Hallucinogènes du Mexique: Études Ethnologiques, Taxonomiques, Biologiques, Physiologiques, et Chimiques* (Paris: Editions du Muséum National d'Histoire Naturelle, 1958).

[177]Aldous Huxley, *Doors of Perception* (New York: Harper & Bros., 1954).

[178]Julian Silverman, "Shamans and Acute Schizophrenia," *American Anthropologist*, vol. 69 (Feb. 1967), pp. 21–31.

[179]Mircea Eliade, Willard R. Trask, trans., *Shamanism, Archaic Techniques of Ecstasy*, Bollingen Series LXXVI (New York: Pantheon Books, 1964).

[180]Stanislav Grof, *Beyond the Brain: Birth, Death, and Transcendence in Psychotherapy* (Albany: State University of New York Press, 1985), pp. 29–30.

[181]Ibid., pp. 299–300.

[182]John G. Neihardt, *Black Elk Speaks* (Lincoln: University of Nebraska Press, 1961), pp. 21–47.

[183]Jochelson, *The Koryak*, pp. 343–344.

[184]Ibid., pp. 363–382.

[185]Marija Gimbutas, *The Language of the Goddess* (San Francisco: Harper & Row, in press), part I, chapter 13.

[186]Gimbutas, *The Goddesses and Gods of Old Europe*, p. 293.

[187]Waldemar Jochelson, *The Yukaghir and the Yukaghirized Tungus*, Memoirs of the American Museum of Natural History (New York, 1910–1926), vol. 13, part 2, p. 136.

[188]Stanislav Grof, *LSD Therapy* (Pomona, Calif.: Hunter House, 1980), pp. 203–204.

[189]Grof, *Beyond the Brain*, pp. 37–38.

[190]Ibid., pp. 38–41.

[191]Ibid., pp. 41–51.

[192]Ibid., pp. 44, 49, and 50–51.

[193]Roger Sherman Loomis, *Celtic Myth and Arthurian Romance* (New York: Columbia University Press, 1927); also *The Grail: from Celtic Myth to Christian Symbol* (New York: Columbia University Press, 1963).

[194]Walter Anderson, "Geographisch-historische Methode," in Lutz Mackensen, *Handwörterbuch des deutschen Märchen* (Berlin and Leipzig, 1934 ff.), vol. II. For an example of such a monograph, see Archer Taylor, *The Black Ox*, FFC vol. XXIII, no. 70 (Helsinki: Suomalainen Tiedeakatemia/Academia Scientarum Fennica, 1927).

[195]Friedrich von der Leyen, *Das Märchen: ein Versuch*, 3rd ed. (Leipzig: Quelle & Mayer, 1925), p. 36.

[196]Antti Aarne, *Verzeichnis der Märchentypen*, FFC, vol. 1, no. 3 (Helsinki: Suomalainen Tiedeakatemia/Academia Scientarum Fennica, 1910).

[197]Antti Aarne, *The Types of the Folktale: A Classification and Bibliography*, Stith Thompson, trans. and ed., second revision, FFC no. 184. (Helsinki: Suomalainen Tiedeakatemia/Academia Scientarum Fennica, 1964).

[198]Stith Thompson, *Motif-Index of Folk-Literature* FFC nos. 106–109, 116–117 (Helsinki: Suomalainen Tiedeakatemia/Academia Scientarum Fennica, 1932–1936); also issued as Indiana University Studies, vols. XIX, nos. 96, 97; XX, nos. 100, 101; XXI, nos. 105, 106; and XXII, nos. 108–110 (Bloomington, Ind.: Indiana University Press, 1932–1936).

[199]Ibid., FFC vol. 1, no. 106, pp. 2–3.

[200]Stith Thompson motif D1654.4, *Immovable Weapon.*

[201]Motifs D950.1, *Magic Hazel Tree*, and D1346.4, *Tree of Immortality.*

[202]Motifs D1171, *Magic Vessel*, and D1472.1.12, *Magic Kettle Supplies Food.*

[203]Motif F133, *Submarine Otherworld.*

[204]Motifs A153.2, *Magic food gives immortality to gods*, and D1346.3, *Food of immortality.*

[205]Motifs B650, *Marriage to animal in human form*; B652, *Marriage to reptile in human form*; and D621.1, *Animal by day, man by night.*

[206]Catlin, op. cit., vol. 1, pp. 93–94.

[207]Ibid., vol. 2, p. 297.

[208]Ibid., vol. 2, p. 295.

[209]*The New Encyclopaedia Britannica*, 15th ed., s.v. "Iceland."

[210]Stith Thompson motif T311, *Woman averse to marriage.*

[211]Leo Frobenius, *Das Zeitalter des Sonnengottes* (Berlin: Georg Reimer, 1904), pp. 68–70 and 100–101.

[212]*The Summa contra Gentiles of Saint Thomas Aquinas*, literally translated by the English Dominican Fathers from the latest Leonine Edition (New York, Cincinnati, Chicago: Benziger Brothers, 1924), vol. 1, pp. 4–5 and 7–9.

[213]Grof, *Beyond the Brain*, pp. 38–41.

[214]Ibid., pp. 44, 49, and 50–51.

[215]This account of the Cherokee removal was dictated by Burnett shortly before his death, to his son or grandson, who recorded it for the grandchildren. It is here reprinted with the kind permission of the Board of Directors of the Museum of the Cherokee Indian, Cherokee, North Carolina, from their booklet, *Cherokee Legends and the Trail of Tears* (Knoxville, Tenn.: S. B. Newman Printing Company, 1956), pp. 20–27.

[216]My review of the Life follows mainly the article by Enrique Dussel in *The New Encyclopaedia Britannica*, 15th ed., 1982, Macropaedia, vol. 10, pp. 684–686, with additional information from Manuel Gonzalez Calzada, *Las Casas, el Procurador de los Indios* (Mexico: Talleres Gráficos, 1948).

[217]*The New Encyclopaedia Britannica*, 15th ed., s.v. "Slavery in the New World."

[218]Ibid., s.v. "Civil War, U.S."

[219]Genesis 7:6.

[220]I have been following chiefly the article "Natchez," in Hodge, op. cit., vol. 2, pp. 35–36.

[221]Reuben Gold Thwaites, ed., *The Jesuit Relations and Allied Documents* (in 73 volumes), selected and edited (in one volume) by Edna Kenson (New York: Albert and Charles Boni, 1925), pp. 406–420; citing lxviii, Doc. cciii., translation modified for ease of reading.

[222]John Wesley Powell, *7th Annual Report of the American Bureau of Ethnology* (Washington, D.C., 1891).

[223]Hodge, op. cit., vol. 1, p. 150.

[224]Benjamin Hawkins, *A Sketch of the Creek Country, in 1798 and 99* (Savannah: Georgia Historical Society Collection, vol. III, 1848), sketch 75. From the summary by Alexander Chamberlain, in Hodge, op. cit., vol. 1, pp. 176–177, abridged and recast.

[225]Hodge, op. cit., vol. 1, p. 177, quoting William Bartram, *Travels through North and South Carolina, Georgia, East and West Florida, the Cherokee country, the extensive territories of the Muscogulges or Creek Confederacy, and the country of the Chactaws* (Philadelphia, 1791; London, 1792).

[226]The quotation is from Alexander F. Chamberlain, in Hodge, op. cit., vol. 1, pp. 177–178, in comment on Albert S. Gatschet, *A Migration Legend of the Creek Indians*, vol. 1 (Philadelphia, 1884), p. 182.

[227]J. N. B. Hewitt, "Tuscarora," in Hodge, op. cit., vol. 2, pp. 843–844.

[228]Ibid., p. 844.

[229]Ibid., p. 845, citing *Documents relating to the colonial history of New York*, 15 vols. (Albany, 1853–87), vol. 5 (1855), p. 376.

[230]Ibid., p. 851, citing Jno. Lawson, *A new voyage to Carolina; containing the exact description and natural history of that country; together with the present state thereof, and a journal of a thousand miles' travel thro' several nations of Indians* (London, 1700).

[231]Ibid., p. 850.

[232]Ibid., p. 843, citing Lawson, *A new voyage to Carolina.*

[233]William A. Ritchie, "Iroquois Archeology and Settlement Patterns," in William N. Fenton and John Gulick, eds., *Symposium on Cherokee and Iroquois Culture*, Smithsonian Institution, Bureau of American Ethnology Bulletin 130 (Washington, D.C., 1961), pp. 29–30.

[234]Ibid.

[235]Ibid., p. 29, note 3, citing Gordon R. Willey, "Archaeological Perspective on Algonkian-Gulf Linguistic Relationships," *Southwestern Journal of Anthropology*, vol. 14, p. 269. Cited without comment.

[236]Joffre L. Coe, "Cherokee Archeology," in Fenton and Gulick, op. cit., p. 53.

[237]Ibid., citing Mark Van Doren, ed., *The Travels of William Bartram* (New York: Dover Publications, 1928, reprinted 1955), p. 270.

[238]Ibid., citing Van Doren, op. cit., p. 280.

[239]Ibid., citing Van Doren, op. cit., p. 284.

[240]Ibid., citing Van Doren, op. cit., p. 296.

[241]Ibid., citing Van Doren, op. cit., p. 296.

[242]Ibid., pp. 52–54.

[243]Ibid., pp. 55–57, reviewing William S. Webb, *An Archaeological Survey of the Norris Basin in Eastern Tennessee*, Smithsonian Institution, Bureau of American Ethnology Bulletin 118 (Washington, D.C., 1938).

[244]Ibid., reviewing T. M. Lewis and Madeline Kneberg, *Hiwasee Island: An Archaeological Account of Four Tennessee Indian Peoples* (Knoxville: University of Tennessee Press, 1946).

[245]J. N. B. Hewitt, "Tuscarora," in Hodge, op. cit., p. 851.

[246]I have here compressed the account of this transformation in Alvin M. Josephy, Jr., ed., *The American Heritage Book of Indians* (New York: American Heritage Publishing Company, Inc., 1961), pp. 218–219.

[247]Sequoia, after whom the big redwoods of California are named. He was known also by the name of his German father, as George Gist or Guest. Born about 1760 in the Cherokee town of Taskigi, Tennessee, he died in San Fernando, near Tamaulipas, Mexico, in August 1843, while in search of a lost band of Cherokee that, according to tradition, had crossed the Mississippi before the Revolution, and had wandered to some mountains in the West.

[248]Glenn Tucker, author of *Tecumseh: Vision of Glory* (1956), in his article in *The New Encyclopaedia Britannica*, 15th ed., s.v. "Tecumseh."

[249]U.S. *v.* Crook, 5 Dillon, 453.

[250]Alice C. Fletcher, "Bright Eyes," in Hodge, op. cit., vol. 1, pp. 165–166.

[251]Livingston Farrand, "Standing Bear," in ibid., vol. 2, p. 633.

[252]James Mooney, "Myths of the Cherokee," *Journal of American Folklore*, vol. 1 (1888), pp. 98–106, translation modified for ease of reading.

CAPTION ENDNOTES

[1]*G. Peter Jemison: Mid-Career Retrospective, Works from 1971–1986.* Brochure from the exhibition, April 6 to May 8, 1981, at the Museum of the Plains Indian and Craft Center, Browning, Montana.

[2]Paul Kane noted that the pipe had been carved "…by Awbonwaishkum out of dark colored stone, his only tools being an old knife and broken file." From *Sacred Circles: Two Thousand Years of North American Indian Art*, catalogue from the exhibition of the same name at the Nelson Gallery of Art–Atkins Museum of Fine Arts, 1976, p. 100.

[3]Alvin M. Josephy, Jr., ed., *The American Heritage Book of Indians* (New York: American Heritage Publishing Company, Inc., 1961), p. 231.

A NOTE ON THE INDEXES

References to pages, captions, maps, and map captions.

In the Place Name Index and the Subject Index, references to pages are page numbers, e.g.,

Rip Van Winkle, 161

which means that a reference to Rip Van Winkle is to be found on page 161. In both indexes, commas, rather than dashes, are used to indicate separate mentions of a topic on adjacent pages, e.g.,

132, 133

References to captions consist of a boldface caption number (or range of caption numbers), followed by a hyphen and a page number, e.g.,

240-146

249–299-222

References to maps consist of a boldface capital "M" and a map number followed by a hyphen and a page number, e.g.,

M18-165

INDEX OF PLACE NAMES

CREDITS AND ACKNOWLEDGEMENTS

PICTURES

Key:
AMNH = American Museum of Natural History, New York; **BECHS** = Buffalo & Erie County Historical Society; **CGL** = Charles Godfrey Leland, *The Algonquin Legends of New England* (Boston: Houghton, Mifflin, and Company, 1898); **DAM** = Denver Art Museum; **MAI** = Museum of the American Indian, New York; **MH** = Thomas McKenney and James Hall, *Portrait Gallery of American Indians;* **MHS** = Minnesota Historical Society, St. Paul; **MPM** = Milwaukee Public Museum; **NMAA** = National Museum of American Art, Washington D.C.; **NYHS** = New York Historical Society; **NYPL** = New York Public Library; **PMA** = Philbrook Museum of Art, Tulsa; **PMAE** = Peabody Museum of Archaeology and Ethnology, Cambridge, Mass.; **PMS** = Peabody Museum, Salem, Mass.; **RMSC** = Rochester Museum and Science Center; **ROM** = Royal Ontario Museum, Toronto; **SI/NAA** = Smithsonian Institution, National Anthropological Archives, Washington, D.C.; **SMAI** = Schoharie (NY) Museum of the American Indian.

COVER: DAM
Frontispiece: Musée Guimet, Paris

226 Cayuga Museum of History and Art, Auburn, New York; 227 MAI; 228 James A. Tuck, St. Johns, Newfoundland; 229 Museum of the Plains Indians, Browning, Montana; 230 National Park Service, Appomatox, Virginia; 231 National Gallery of Canada, Ottawa; 232 MAI; 233 NYPL; 234 RMSC; 235 MH; 236 BECHS; 237 MH; 238–239 RMSC; 240 PMA; 241 SMAI; 242 MPM; 243 MAI; 244 SMAI; 245 NMAA; 246 NYHS; 247 New Orleans Museum of Art; 248–249 SMAI; 250 Columbia University Libraries; 251 SMAI; 252 AMNH; 253 SI/NAA; 254 NYPL; 255 Library of Congress; 256 DAM; 257 AMNH; 258 NYPL; 259 CGL; 260 NYPL; 261 Museum für Völkerkunde, Munich; 262 PMA; 263 SI/NAA; 264 PMS; 265 CGL; 266 PMS; 267–268 DAM; 269 Private Collection, Montana; 270–272 CGL; 273 ROM; 274 MHS; 275 DAM; 276 Mr. and Mrs. Rex Arrowsmith; 277 DAM; 278 PMS; 279 DAM; 280–281 ROM; 282–283 MPM; 284 NYPL; 285 SMAI; 286 New York State Museum, Albany; 287–289 RMSC; 290 DAM; 291 AMNH; 292 NMAA; 293 MAI; 294–301 NYPL; 302 Woolaroc Museum, Bartlesville, Oklahoma; 303–306 NYPL; 307 National Park Service, Scotts Bluff, Nebraska; 308 NYPL; 309 National Archives, Washington, D.C.; 310–311 NYPL; 312 Tennessee State Museum, Nashville; 313 NYPL; 314–316 PMAE; 317–320 SI/NAA; 321–322 NMAA; 323 NYPL; 324–325 SI/NAA; 326 Ruth Underhill, *Red Man's America* (Chicago, 1953); 327 SI/NAA; 328 NYHS; 329 National Park Service, Ocmulgee, Macon, Georgia; 330 Colonial Williamsburg Foundation; 331 St. Louis Art Museum; 332 MH; 333 Brown University, Ann Brown Military Collection, Providence; 334 Field Museum of Natural History; 335 Gilcrease Institute of American Art, Tulsa; 336–337 SI/NAA; 338 New York Power Authority, Massena, New York.

EXTRACTS

From Stanislav Grof, *Beyond the Brain: Birth, Death, and Transcendence in Psychotherapy* (Albany: State University of New York Press, 1985), used with permission.

From Stanislav Grof, *LSD Therapy* (Pomona, Calif.: Hunter House, 1980), used with permission.

From *Cherokee Legends and the Trail of Tears* (Knoxville, Tenn.: S.B. Newman Printing Company, 1956), used with the permission of the Board of Directors of the Museum of the Cherokee Indian, Cherokee, North Carolina.

MAPS AND CHARTS

Map 1. Based in part on information adapted from Carl O. Sauer, *Seeds, Spades, Hearths & Herds: The Domestication of Animals and Foodstuffs,* 2nd ed. (Cambridge: M.I.T. Press, 1969), used with permission of the American Geographical Society; Carl O. Sauer, *Agricultural Origins and Dispersals* (New York: American Geographical Society, 1952); D. B. Grigg, *The Agricultural Systems of the World* (New York: Cambridge University Press, 1974); A. Sheratt, ed., *The Cambridge Encyclopaedia of Archaeology* (New York: Crown Publishers/Cambridge University Press, 1980), used with permission of Scepter Books, Inc.; R. van Chi-Bonnardel, *The Atlas of Africa* (New York: The Free Press/Macmillan Publishing Co., Inc., 1973), used with permission of Editions Jeune Afrique; J. F. Ajayi et al., *Historical Atlas of Africa* (New York: Cambridge University Press, 1985); Stuart Struever, ed., *Prehistoric Agriculture* (Garden City, N.Y.: American Museum of Natural History, 1971); P. Vidal-Nacquet, ed., *The Harper Atlas of World History* (New York: Harper & Row, 1987); Geoffrey Barraclough, ed., *The Times Atlas of World History* (London: Times Books Ltd., 1978); *Cultivated Plants and Their Wild Relatives* by P. M. Zukovski. 1962, CAB International, Wallingford, Oxfordshire, U.K.; and

F. E. Zeuner, *A History of Domesticated Animals* (New York: Harper & Row, 1963).

"Two Agricultural Systems" Chart. Based in part on research conducted by Lothian Lynas, of the New York Botanical Garden, researcher; in part on information adapted from Carl O. Sauer, *Seeds, Spades, Hearths & Herds: The Domestication of Animals and Foodstuffs,* 2nd ed. (Cambridge: M.I.T. Press, 1969); from A. Sheratt, ed., *The Cambridge Encyclopaedia of Archaeology* (New York: Crown Publishers/Cambridge University Press, 1980), pp. 365–374, 375–381; and from Stewart Struever, ed., *Prehistoric Agriculture* (Garden City, N.Y.: American Museum of Natural History, 1971), p. 526; and in part on art from a variety of sources as redrawn by Enid Kotchnik.

Map 15. Based in part on information adapted from Carl O. Sauer, *Seeds, Spades, Hearths & Herds: The Domestication of Animals and Foodstuffs,* 2nd ed. (Cambridge: M.I.T. Press, 1969), used with permission of the American Geographical Society; Carl O. Sauer, *Agricultural Origins and Dispersals* (New York: American Geographical Society, 1952); D. B. Grigg, *The Agricultural Systems of the World* (New York: Cambridge University Press, 1974); A. Sheratt, ed., *The Cambridge Encyclopaedia of Archaeology* (New York: Crown Publishers/Cambridge University Press, 1980), used with permission of Scepter Books, Inc.; R. van Chi-Bonnardel, *The Atlas of Africa* (New York: The Free Press/Macmillan Publishing Co., Inc., 1973), used with permission of Editions Jeune Afrique; J. F. Ajayi et al., *Historical Atlas of Africa* (New York: Cambridge University Press, 1985); Stuart Struever, ed., *Prehistoric Agriculture* (Garden City, N.Y.: American Museum of Natural History, 1971); P. Vidal-Nacquet, ed., *The Harper Atlas of World History* (New York: Harper & Row, 1987); Geoffrey Barraclough, ed., *The Times Atlas of World History* (London: Times Books, Ltd., 1978); *Cultivated Plants and Their Wild Relatives* by P. M. Zukovski. 1962, CAB International, Wallingford, Oxfordshire, U.K.; F. E. Zeuner, *A History of Domesticated Animals* (New York: Harper & Row, 1963); Charles C. DiPeso, "Macaws... Crotals...and Trumpet Shells," *Early Man,* vol. 2, no. 3 (Autumn 1980); and W. H. Sears, "Seaborne Contacts between Early Cultures in the Lower Southeastern United States and Middle through South America," in Elizabeth P. Benson, ed., *The Sea in the Pre-Columbian World,* Dumbarton Oaks Research Library and Collections (Washington, D.C.: Trustees for Harvard University, 1977).

"From Nomadism to Seed Gardening" Chart. Based in part on information adapted from James A. Ford, *A Comparison of Formative Cultures in the Americas* (Washington, D.C.: Smithsonian Institution Press, 1969); and based in part on art from the following sources, as redrawn by Sally Black: from Gordon R. Willey, *An Introduction to American Archaeology,* (Englewood Cliffs, N.J.: Prentice-Hall, 1966), vol. 1, *North and Middle America,* p. 42; from D. G. Trigger, ed., *Handbook of North American Indians,* vol. 15 (Washington, D.C.: Smithsonian Institution Press, 1978), p. 18, fig. 2; p. 19, fig. 2; from *Past Worlds: The Times Atlas of Archaeology* (London: Times Books Ltd., 1988), pp. 12–20; p. 206, fig. 3, item F; p. 206, fig. 3, item G; p. 210, fig. 2; p. 212, fig. 2; p. 216, fig. 2; p. 219, fig. 2; from Michael Coe et al., *Atlas of Ancient America* (New York: Facts on File Publications, 1986), pp. 8–9, 106, 110–111, 112–113, 122–123, 129, 136, 200–201, 202–203; from Michael Wood, ed., *World Atlas of Archaeology* (Boston: G. K. Hall & Co., 1985), pp. 349, 365; from James A. Ford, *A Comparison of Formative Cultures in the Americas* (Washington, D.C.: Smithsonian Institution Press, 1969), chart 2, items 1–2, 7–9, 12, 15–20, 22; chart 5, items 1, 10, 12–14, 20, 25–26, 33, 44–45, 53, 66–67, 69–70, 73, 81, 84, 86, 90, 92–93; chart 10, items 20–21, 27, 31–32, 34–36, 39–40, 42–43; from A. Sheratt, ed., *The Cambridge Encyclopaedia of Archaeology* (New York: Crown Publishers/Cambridge University Press, 1980), p. 436; from B. M. Fagan, *People of the Earth* (Boston: Little, Brown, and Co., 1980), p. 356; and from *Peoples and Places of the Past: The National Geographic Illustrated Cultural Atlas of the Ancient World* (Washington, D.C.: The National Geographic Society, 1983), pp. 380–402, 404–407.

Map 16. Based in part on information adapted from *Past Worlds: The Times Atlas of Archaeology* (London: Times Books Ltd., 1988); Michael Coe et al., *Atlas of Ancient America* (New York: Facts on File Publications, 1986); Michael Wood, ed., *World Atlas of Archaeology* (Boston: G. K. Hall & Co., 1985); and Charles C. DiPeso, "Macaws...Crotals...and Trumpet Shells," *Early Man,* vol. 2, no. 3 (Autumn 1980).

Map 17. Based in part on information adapted from C. Waldman, *Atlas of the North American Indian* (New York: Facts on File Publications, 1985); Michael Coe et al., *Atlas of Ancient America* (New York: Facts on File Publications, 1986); P. C. Harris and G. J. Mathews, *Historical Atlas of Canada,* vol. 1, *From the Beginning to 1800* (Toronto: University of Toronto Press, 1987); G. J. Mathews and R. Morrow, *Canada and the World, an Atlas Resource* (Scarborough, Ont.: Prentice-Hall Canada, Inc., 1986); and *Atlas of Alberta* (Edmonton: University of Alberta Press/Toronto: University of Toronto Press, 1969).

Map 18. Based in part on information adapted from C. Waldman, *Atlas of the North American Indian* (New York: Facts on File Publications, 1985); and Michael Coe et al., *Atlas of Ancient America* (New York: Facts on File Publications, 1986).

Map ... Waldman, *Atlas of th...* on Fi... *Ancie...*

Map 2... Fleisch... Watts, ... *States H...* Inc., 19... *Atlas of C...* 1965); and ... N.C.: Chero...

Map 23. Based ... man, *Atlas of th...* File Publications, ... *America* (New York: ...

Map 24. Based in pa... Fleischmann, *The Cheroke...* Watts, Inc., 1971); *The Ameri...* *States History* (New York: Ame... Inc., 1966); J. W. Morris and E... *Atlas of Oklahoma* (Norman: Univer... 1965); C. Waldman, *Atlas of the Nort...* York: Facts on File Publications, 1985); ... *Tragedy* (New York: The Macmillan Compa... Prucha, *A Guide to the Military Posts of the Unit...* 1895 (Madison, Wis.: The State Historical Society ... sin, 1964).

Map 25. Based in part on information adapted from C. Waldman, *Atlas of the North American Indian* (New York: Facts on File Publications, 1985); Michael Coe et al., *Atlas of Ancient America* (New York: Facts on File Publications, 1986); P. C. Harris and G. J. Mathews, *Historical Atlas of Canada,* vol. 1, *From the Beginning to 1800* (Toronto: University of Toronto Press, 1987); G. J. Mathews and R. Morrow, *Canada and the World, an Atlas Resource* (Scarborough, Ont.: Prentice-Hall Canada, Inc., 1986); and *Atlas of Alberta* (Edmonton: University of Alberta Press/Toronto: University of Toronto Press, 1969).

HISTORICAL ATLAS OF WORLD MYTHOLOGY

Developed and first published in part by Van der Marck Editions, New York.

Editorial Director: *Robert Walter*

Designer: *Jos. Trautwein/Bentwood Studio*

Art Editor: *Rosemary O'Connell*

Associate Editor: *Antony Van Couvering*

Indexer: *Maro Riofrancos*

Research Assistant: *Hugh Haggerty*

Maps and Charts: *Cartographic Services Center of R.R. Donnelley & Sons Company*

Map Design: *Sidney P. Marland III*

Map Research, Compilation, and Project Coordination: *Luis Freile*

Map Drafting and Production: *Robert Hoover*

Design Consultant for Agricultural and Artifacts Charts: *Jeannine Schonta*

Type Composition: *Typographic Art, Inc.*

Printing and Binding: *Royal Smeets Offset, B.V., The Netherlands*

Grateful acknowledgement is made to the following for their noted contributions to this volume: Peter Kvietok, American Museum of Natural History, New York, for clarifying the vagaries of South American archaeology; and Chris Johansen, Museum of the American Indian, Schoharie, New York, for her assistance and support.